Hockey Facts & Stats

2012–13

Hockey Facts & Stats

2012–13

Andrew Podnieks

Collins

Hockey Facts & Stats, 2012–13
Copyright © 2012 by Andrew Podnieks.
All rights reserved.

First edition

Published by Collins, an imprint of HarperCollins Publishers Ltd

No part of this book may be used or reproduced in any manner whatsoever without the prior written permission of the publisher, except in the case of brief quotations embodied in reviews.

HarperCollins books may be purchased for educational, business, or sales promotional use through our Special Markets Department.

HarperCollins Publishers Ltd
2 Bloor Street East, 20th Floor
Toronto, Ontario, Canada
M4W 1A8

www.harpercollins.ca

ISBN: 978-1-44341-778-5

Library and Archives Canada Cataloguing in Publication data is available upon request.

Printed and bound in Canada
9 8 7 6 5 4 3 2 1

CONTENTS

INTRODUCTION

There were so many stories in 2011–12, spanning such a vast range, that it's challenging to put the entire season into a succinct summary. From the Los Angeles Kings to Sidney Crosby, from Phoenix to discipline to Ryan Nugent-Hopkins and the continuing woeful state of the Toronto Maple Leafs, there was a little bit of everything. Or, make that a lot of everything.

The biggest story, though, must surely be the rise of the Kings, who took a mediocre regular season and turned it into an historic one. They made a coaching change just before Christmas, bringing in Darryl Sutter, but still managed only to sneak into the playoffs by finishing in eighth place with 95 points, five more than Calgary.

But in the playoffs, an impressive roster of contributors made an enormous impact. As a team, the Kings became the first ever to go up 3–0 in all four playoff series. This despite never having home-ice advantage. Of course, part and parcel with this record was a record 10 straight road wins. The best players played as the team's best players, and the role players performed with meticulous efficiency.

Goalie Jonathan Quick was an easy choice for Conn Smythe Trophy honours, but if he hadn't been selected, there were several teammates just as worthy: defenceman Drew Doughty, who started the year with a concussion but was sensational in the postseason; captain Justin Brown, who was especially effective in shorthanded situations in the first two rounds; the former Philadelphia duo of Mike Richards and Jeff Carter; and the incredible Anze Kopitar, who came from a non-traditional hockey country, Slovenia, and developed into a world-class star.

But this Cup win, 45 years in the making, was only one storyline in 2011–12. The ongoing saga of the Phoenix Coyotes was surely another that captivated fans in Canada hoping Quebec City might once again have a team. The club's financial distress continued, but a potential new owner came forward hoping to keep the team in Scottsdale, Arizona. Still, the prospects of this were dimmed by the discovery that he didn't have the cash needed to buy the team—and the saga continued.

Of course, the greatest on-ice difficulty continued to be head shots. Crosby returned after a 10-month absence, but after only eight games he suffered another concussion and missed most of the rest of the season. Many of the game's best players joined him on the sidelines for short periods of time, while at least one, Chris Pronger, may well have had his career ended by a head injury.

The game's new players were particularly impressive this year, notably the top choice, Edmonton's Ryan Nugent-Hopkins, and the second choice, Colorado's Gabriel Landeskog of Sweden, who came to Canada to develop in the Ontario Hockey League. Both players finished with 52 points, the most by rookies, but the Swede won the Calder Trophy. But, while one standout Swede arrived, another departed. Nicklas Lidstrom, arguably one of the greatest blueliners of all time, called it quits at age 41, leaving a sizeable gap in the Detroit defence in the process.

As for the Leafs, the laughingstock of the league, they missed the playoffs for a franchise-worst seventh year in a row and were now the only team not to have appeared in even one playoff round since the end of the lockout in 2005. Other Canadian teams faced their own adversity as the Canucks were ousted from the playoffs early (by the Kings), while both Alberta teams also failed to qualify. Montreal had a weak season, and while Ottawa performed above expectations, the Sens, too, failed to get past the first round of playoffs.

And so the NHL heads into a 2012–13 season fraught with uncertainty as the collective bargaining agreement expired on September 15. Would there be an early resolution? Would there be another lockout? Could NHL commissioner Gary Bettman and NHLPA executive director Donald Fehr work through a new CBA for the next generation of players? The league had created some momentum since the previous lockout in terms of revenues and U.S. TV audiences, and the outdoor game in Michigan between the Leafs and Red Wings promised to be record-setting—but would it, too, be undone by, as they say, labour unrest?

The game was in many ways healthy, and in just as many ways unhealthy, but the new year, just like the previous one, promised to be, if nothing else, eventful.

Andrew Podnieks
August 2012

GLOSSARY OF ABBREVIATIONS

NHL TEAMS

ANA=Anaheim Ducks, BOS=Boston Bruins, BUF=Buffalo Sabres, CAL=Calgary Flames, CAR=Carolina Hurricanes, CHI=Chicago Blackhawks, COL=Colorado Avalanche, CBJ=Columbus Blue Jackets, DAL=Dallas Stars, DET=Detroit Red Wings, EDM=Edmonton Oilers, FLO=Florida Panthers, LA=Los Angeles Kings, MIN=Minnesota Wild, MON=Montreal Canadiens, NAS=Nashville Predators, NJ=New Jersey Devils, NYI=New York Islanders, NYR=New York Rangers, OTT=Ottawa Senators, PHI=Philadelphia Flyers, PHO=Phoenix Coyotes, PIT=Pittsburgh Penguins, STL=St. Louis Blues, SJ=San Jose Sharks, TB=Tampa Bay Lightning, TOR=Toronto Maple Leafs, VAN=Vancouver Canucks, WAS=Washington Capitals, WIN=Winnipeg Jets.

International

BLR	Belarus
CAN	Canada
CZE	Czech Republic
DEN	Denmark
FIN	Finland
GBR	Great Britain
GER	Germany
ITA	Italy
LAT	Latvia
NGR	Nigeria
RUS	Russia
SLO	Slovenia
SUI	Switzerland
SVK	Slovakia
SWE	Sweden
USA	United States

Leagues

AHL	American Hockey League
DEL	Deutsche Eishockey Liga (Germany)
KHL	Kontinental Hockey League
SEL	Elitserien (Sweden)

NHL 2011–12

2012 STANLEY CUP FINALS GAME STORIES

GAME 1   MAY 30   LOS ANGELES 2 AT NEW JERSEY 1 (OT)

The Kings defeated New Jersey 2–1 in overtime to go up 1–0 in the Stanley Cup finals. It was the Kings' ninth straight road win in the 2012 playoffs and third straight victory in OT. A simple move inside the L.A. blue line created the play that won the game. Marek Zidlicky pinched in at the Kings' line and was caught up ice. Justin Williams got the puck at centre, but as two Devils came to him he made a great backhand pass to open ice in the middle, where Anze Kopitar collected the puck and went in on a breakaway. He then deked Martin Brodeur badly and stuffed the puck in the open side at 8:13 of the fourth period. Colin Fraser got the only goal of the first period when he snapped home a nice pass from Jordan Nolan behind the net. Anton Volchenkov was given credit for the tying goal when he snapped a quick shot from the point, but the puck went in off the shoulder of Slava Voynov in front of Jonathan Quick, who faced only 17 shots.

GAME 2   JUNE 2   LOS ANGELES 2 AT NEW JERSEY 1 (OT)

The Devils got better goaltending, had more quality scoring chances, played on home ice—but still lost. The hero for Los Angeles on this night was Jeff Carter, who scored at 13:42 of overtime to give the Kings a commanding 2–0 series lead heading home for the next two games. Carter carried the puck inside the New Jersey end and fired a shot at Brodeur, but the goalie kicked the puck away. Carter got the rebound, circled the net and came out front, and fired again, his shot to the short side finding its way through traffic to the back of the net. Drew Doughty gave L.A. a 1–0 lead 7:49 into the game when he made a fine solo dash almost from one end of the ice to the other. New Jersey didn't tie the score until 2:59 into the third period when Zidlicky's point shot was deflected in front by Ryan Carter, beating Quick to the far side.

GAME 3   JUNE 4   NEW JERSEY 0 AT LOS ANGELES 4

The Kings won for the third time in as many games against the Devils, becoming the first team ever to go up 3–0 in all four rounds of one playoff year. Tonight, they did it with one expected weapon—goalie Jonathan Quick—and one unexpected one: special teams. Quick blocked all 22 shots for his third shutout of the playoffs. More surprisingly, the Kings scored twice on the power play, the only weak link in their game, and shut down the Devils during six shorthanded situations through two periods, including a lengthy five-on-three in the opening period. Alec Martinez got the first goal of the game early in the second when he banged in a loose puck from the side of Brodeur's goal. The Kings made it 2–0 at 15:07 on a gorgeous three-way passing play. Justin Williams took the puck down the right side and made a back pass off the boards to Dustin Brown, who fired a perfect pass across to Anze Kopitar, who had beaten his man, Zach Parise, and was roaring towards the goal. No sooner was the puck on Kopitar's stick than he drilled a one-timer over the sliding Brodeur. Jeff Carter and Justin Williams scored man-advantage goals two and a half minutes apart early in the third period to make it 4–0.

GAME 4   JUNE 6   NEW JERSEY 3 AT LOS ANGELES 1

For the third time in their four playoff series, the Kings failed to close out an opponent on home ice. Tonight, the visiting Devils skated to an impressive 3–1 victory. The Kings had a sensational chance to get the first goal early in the third period when Simon Gagne intercepted a lax pass from Bryce Salvador at the L.A. blue line. He couldn't speed away for the breakaway, but made a great pass to Trevor Lewis, who went in alone but couldn't beat Brodeur with a deke. It was the Devils who struck first: Salvador pinched to keep the puck in the Los Angeles end, and Dainius Zubrus did some fine spadework down in the corner. He got the puck back to the point, and Quick made a save on Salvador's shot, only to have Patrik Elias backhand the rebound into the open side at 7:56. The Kings responded almost immediately. Drew Doughty's low point shot just a minute later on a power play went through several bodies and between Brodeur's pads. The Devils got the go-ahead goal with less than five minutes to go, thanks to a turnover at centre ice. David Clarkson brought the puck in, found Adam Henrique on the far side, and Henrique buried a quick shot past the blocker of Quick. Ilya Kovalchuk got an empty-netter to close out the scoring.

GAME 5   JUNE 9   LOS ANGELES 1 AT NEW JERSEY 2

The Kings lost on the road for the first time in these 2012 playoffs, and the Devils made the series a lot more interesting after their 2–1 win to send the finals back to California for game six. The difference this night was timely goaltending and capitalizing on scoring chances, the Devils besting L.A. in both critical categories. The Devils got the only goal of the first period on a lucky bounce during a power play. Goalie Jonathan Quick played the puck behind his own goal, but the angle of his clearing attempt wasn't accurate and Zach Parise swooped in and wrapped the puck in before Quick could get back to his crease at 12:45. Justin Williams tied the game in the second period. Taking the puck down the right side, he cut to the middle once inside the New Jersey end and continued unobstructed. He waited for traffic to clog the middle, and then drilled a great shot past Brodeur to the stick side at 3:26. The Devils went ahead midway through the period when a gentle point shot from Salvador bounced off Slava Voynov and into the net.

GAME 6   JUNE 11   NEW JERSEY 1 AT LOS ANGELES 6

Los Angeles reeled off three quick power-play goals in the first period to squash any historic comeback bid by New Jersey, winning its first Stanley Cup in franchise history in the process. Midway through the period, Steve Bernier hammered Rob Scuderi into the boards from behind and drew a five-minute major and a game misconduct. On the ensuing power play, the Kings scored three times, claimed a huge 3–0 lead, and were on their way to victory. Dustin Brown, Jeff Carter and Trevor Lewis got the goals. Carter made it 4–0 early in the second period when he drilled a shot in the slot past Brodeur. New Jersey got its lone goal late in the second when Petr Sykora's shot was stopped by Quick, but Henrique netted the rebound at 18:47. The Kings finished the night off in style. As the Devils pressed for a goal, Brodeur came to the bench with more than four minutes left, but on a delayed penalty Lewis got his second of the night with an empty-netter. Just 15 seconds later, Brodeur back in, Matt Greene made it 6–1. The celebrations began, and when the buzzer sounded the Kings had gone from eighth place in the Western Conference to Stanley Cup champions in a matter of two months.

2012 AWARD WINNERS—BIOGRAPHIES

EVGENI MALKIN—ART ROSS TROPHY, HART TROPHY & TED LINDSAY AWARD

Even though he missed seven games during the regular season, Pittsburgh centre Evgeni Malkin still won the regular-season scoring race by 12 points. He was the only NHLer to reach the 100-point mark, finishing with 109. And Malkin did all this without the help of teammate Sidney Crosby, who missed much of the season with concussion problems. Malkin led the Penguins to an impressive 108 points in the standings, fourth-best in the league, and he was a dominant presence every time he was on the ice. As a result, he not only won the Art Ross Trophy, but was also named MVP of the league both by the players (Ted Lindsay Award) and the media (Hart Trophy).

STEVE STAMKOS—ROCKET RICHARD TROPHY

Only 22 years old, Stamkos won his second goal-scoring title but his first outright, having tied with Crosby two years earlier. He hit 60 goals, bettering Malkin's 50, and proved far and away the most consistent scorer of the last four years since he first entered the league. Stamkos is most like Mike Bossy, a pure scorer with a dynamite shot—in his case, a one-timer from the off wing being his greatest weapon.

BRIAN CAMPBELL—LADY BYNG TROPHY

Not since Red Kelly in 1954 had a defenceman won the title of "most gentlemanly player," a feat so remarkable because, by definition, a blueliner is supposed to be physical and hard-nosed. Campbell is that, but he managed to be so while accruing a mere three minor penalties all season (and for the second straight season to boot). As well, Campbell averaged some 25 minutes of ice time per game with Florida, so respected is his value to the team.

JONATHAN QUICK—CONN SMYTHE TROPHY

From seemingly out of nowhere, Quick emerged this season as arguably the top goalie in the league. Although he has been the number-one goalie for Los Angeles for the last three years, his performance in the playoffs was beyond measure. Quick had 10 shutouts in the regular season and posted an incredible 1.95 goals-against average, but in the postseason he led the Kings to a 16–4 record in which they became the first team ever to lead all four playoff series 3–0. No doubt about it: without his play, the team wouldn't have won the Stanley Cup.

HENRIK LUNDQVIST—VEZINA TROPHY

Having just completed his seventh NHL season, all with the Rangers, Lundqvist finally was acknowledged as the top goalie during the regular season. He had a 1.97 GAA, won 39 games and posted eight shutouts, all totals that ranked among the leaders. As well, on a team with few superstars, he took the Rangers to the Eastern Conference finals, where they lost to New Jersey. At 30 years of age, Lundqvist is in his prime and may well have won his first of several editions of the Vezina Trophy.

GABRIEL LANDESKOG—CALDER MEMORIAL TROPHY

Swedes do not typically play major junior hockey in Canada as a route to the NHL, but Landeskog is not your average Swede. In 2009, he started his OHL career with Kitchener, and despite being an outsider, so to speak, his play on ice was as impressive as his comportment off, allowing the team to make him captain for his second season. He was drafted second overall by Colorado in 2011, made the Avs at training camp, and never looked back. His 52 points tied him with Ryan Nugent-Hopkins for the lead among rookies.

ERIK KARLSSON—JAMES NORRIS TROPHY

Just 22 years old and playing in his third NHL season, Karlsson emerged unexpectedly to not only play a huge role with Ottawa, but to become one of the game's dominant defencemen. He is by no means the biggest, strongest or toughest blueliner, but he plays the game with incredible finesse and reliability, cut more from the Nicklas Lidstrom cloth than, say, that of Chris Pronger. He had 78 points and was a +16 on a mediocre team, providing the Senators with a reliable performance every night. Such was the impression he made around the league that he beat out two highly respected veterans in Shea Weber and Zdeno Chara to claim his first Norris Trophy.

MAX PACIORETTY—BILL MASTERTON TROPHY

The stats show that Pacioretty played only 37 games in 2010–11, a low number because of an injury suffered in March 2011. Coming down the left wing, Pacioretty was hammered by Zdeno Chara into the boards just where the glass started at the end of the players' benches. Pacioretty's head hit the end of the glass, and he fell to the ice unconscious. His recovery took months, but by training camp he had returned to full health. He then went out and had a career year, playing in more games (79), scoring more goals (33) and assists (32), and recording more points (65) than in any previous season.

PATRICE BERGERON—FRANK J. SELKE TROPHY

Bergeron is well known in international circles for being the only player ever to win gold at the senior World Championship before winning World Junior gold. The latter he achieved in large measure by teaming up with a young Sidney Crosby, but in the NHL he developed into a great two-way player over time. Consider that in 2006–07 he was a –28 on a team that missed the playoffs, and in 2011–12 he was a +36, the fifth year in a row he was a "plus" player. Yet for all his defensive acumen, his offence has barely been affected. This past season Bergeron still had 22 goals and 64 points.

JAROSLAV HALAK & BRIAN ELLIOTT—WILLIAM M. JENNINGS TROPHY

The St. Louis Blues seemed to change overnight when coach Ken Hitchcock took over the team. He implemented a stronger defensive system, and his goalies pitched in by becoming the stingiest duo in the league, allowing just 165 goals in 82 games, lowest in the league. They also combined for 15 shutouts to tie the modern-day record.

DANIEL ALFREDSSON—KING CLANCY MEMORIAL TROPHY

A career that is winding down was acknowledged in awarding this honour to Alfredsson, a career Senators forward who has made it clear he will live in Ottawa for many years after he retires (his younger brother is a firefighter in the city). As a result, "Alfie" has long held a special place in the hearts of Ottawans, and he has reciprocated, giving freely of his time to the less fortunate.

KEN HITCHCOCK—JACK ADAMS AWARD

It was November 6, 2011, scarcely a month into the season, that Blues coach Davis Payne was fired and replaced by Hitchcock. "Hitch" immediately transformed the team, taking it to second place overall with 109 points, a team record, thanks to another team record—49 wins.

TOP 10 LISTS

TOP 10 MOMENTS FROM INTERNATIONAL HOCKEY, 2011–12

1. Evgeni Malkin's sensational play leads Russia to World Championship gold for the third time in five years.
2. Slovakia defeats the Czech Republic 3–1 to advance to the gold-medal game of the World Championship for the first time since 2002.
3. Mika Zibanejad scores in overtime to give Sweden a 3–2 win over Russia and claim its first gold medal at the World Junior Championship since 1982.
4. Canada rallies to defeat the United States 5–4 to win gold at the World Women's Championship for the first time since 2007 and avenge a 9–1 loss in the preliminary round.
5. Goalie Florence Schelling is brilliant in leading Switzerland to its first-ever World Women's medal, a bronze, in 2012.
6. The IIHF honours Team Canada and the Soviet Union with the new Milestone Award on the eve of the 40th anniversary of the Summit Series.
7. The IIHF organizes a Hockey Forum in Barcelona in June 2012 to determine the direction of European hockey and its relationship with the NHL.
8. Canada falls behind Russia 6–1 in the semifinals of the World Juniors and storms back to make it 6–5, hitting the post late in the game and falling just short of the greatest comeback in international hockey history.
9. IIHF president Rene Fasel is voted to another term uncontested, continuing his reign, which began in 1994.
10. The KHL boldly announces plans to play two regular-season games in New York, turning the tables on the NHL and its recent forays into Europe.

TOP 10 WOMEN WHO SHOULD BE IN THE HOCKEY HALL OF FAME

1. Fran Rider
2. Shirley Cameron
3. Cassie Campbell
4. Danielle Goyette
5. Geraldine Heaney
6. Nancy Drolet
7. France St. Louis
8. Ben Smith
9. Vicky Sunohara
10. Krissy Wendell

TOP 10 GOALIES OF 2011–12

1. Jonathan Quick (Los Angeles)
2. Henrik Lundqvist (New York Rangers)
3. Ondrej Pavelec (Winnipeg)
4. Brian Elliott (St. Louis)
5. Martin Brodeur (New Jersey)
6. Mike Smith (Phoenix)
7. Craig Anderson (Ottawa)
8. Miikka Kiprusoff (Calgary)
9. Pekka Rinne (Nashville)
10. Kari Lehtonen (Dallas)

TOP 10 MOMENTS IN SIDNEY CROSBY'S CAREER

1. Scores the "golden goal" to give Canada victory at the 2010 Olympics.
2. Becomes the youngest captain to lead his team to the Stanley Cup (2009).
3. Youngest player to lead World Championships in scoring (2006).
4. Wins Art Ross Trophy at age 19, youngest player ever to do so (2007).
5. Leads Canada to World Junior gold over Alexander Ovechkin and Russia (2005).
6. Records four points in his first game after a 10-month absence because of post-concussion symptoms (2011).
7. Plays 26 games with owner and Hall of Famer Mario Lemieux (2005–06).
8. Named Pittsburgh team captain in the summer of 2007 at age 19.
9. Scores a "lacrosse goal" while playing in the QMJHL with Rimouski (2003).
10. Beats Montreal goalie Jose Theodore in his first shootout against his boyhood team (2006).

TOP 10 CURRENT PLAYERS WHO WEAR "CLASSIC" NUMBERS

1. Brian Elliott (St. Louis, #1)
2. Mark Streit (NY Islanders, #2)
3. Taylor Hall (Edmonton, #4)
4. Vincent Lecavalier (Tampa Bay, #4)
5. Mark Stuart (Winnipeg, #5)
6. Shea Weber (Nashville, #6)
7. Jack Johnson (Columbus, #7)
8. Matt Duchene (Colorado, #9)
9. Martin Havlat (San Jose, #9)
10. Zach Parise (Minnesota, #9)

NHL TEAM INFORMATION, 2012–13

ANAHEIM DUCKS

(name changed from Mighty Ducks of Anaheim on June 22, 2006)
First Game Played: October 8, 1993
Detroit Red Wings 7 at Mighty Ducks of Anaheim 2
Nickname Provenance: Owners, Disney, named team after a popular kids' movie, *The Mighty Ducks* (1992)
Mascot: Wild Thing
Arena History: Arrowhead Pond, 1993–2006; Honda Center, 2006–present (capacity 17,174)
Retired Numbers: none
Hall of Famers: Players (2): Jari Kurri, Adam Oates
Website: www.anaheimducks.com
Minor League Affiliate(s): Norfolk Admirals (AHL), Elmira Jackals (ECHL—shared with Ottawa)
Stanley Cups: (1) 2007
Hosted All-Star Game: none
1st Overall Draft Choices: none

BOSTON BRUINS

First Game Played: December 1, 1924
Montreal Maroons 1 at Boston Bruins 2
Nickname Provenance: Named by owner Art Ross for the brown bear
Mascot: Blades (b. October 9, 2000)
Arena History: Boston Arena, 1924–28; Boston Garden, 1928–95; FleetCenter, 1995–2003; TD Banknorth Garden (same building as the FleetCenter), 2005–2009; TD Garden, 2009–present (capacity 17,565)
Retired Numbers: Eddie Shore (2), Lionel Hitchman (3), Bobby Orr (4), Dit Clapper (5), Phil Esposito (7), Cam Neely (8), Johnny Bucyk (9), Milt Schmidt (15), Terry O'Reilly (24), Ray Bourque (77)
Hall of Famers: Players (48): Marty Barry, Bobby Bauer, Leo Boivin, Ray Bourque, Frank Brimsek, Johnny Bucyk, Billy Burch, Gerry Cheevers, Dit Clapper, Sprague Cleghorn, Paul Coffey, Roy Conacher, Bun Cook, Bill Cowley, Cy Denneny, Woody Dumart, Phil Esposito, Fern Flaman, Frank Frederickson, Harvey Jackson, Tom Johnson, Duke Keats, Guy Lapointe, Brian Leetch, Harry Lumley, Mickey MacKay, Sylvio Mantha, Joe Mullen, Cam Neely, Adam Oates, Harry Oliver, Bobby Orr, Bernie Parent, Brad Park, Jacques Plante, Babe Pratt, Bill Quackenbush, Jean Ratelle, Art Ross (inducted as Player, associated with Boston as Builder), Terry Sawchuk, Milt Schmidt, Eddie Shore, Babe Siebert, Hooley Smith, Allan Stanley, Nels Stewart, Tiny Thompson, Cooney Weiland

Builders (6): Charles Adams, Weston Adams, Walter Brown, Bud Poile (played with Boston, inducted as Builder), Glen Sather (played with Boston, inducted as Builder), Harry Sinden
Website: www.bostonbruins.com
Minor League Affiliate(s): Providence Bruins (AHL), South Carolina Stingrays (ECHL)
Stanley Cups: (6) 1928–29, 1938–39, 1940–41, 1969–70, 1971–72, 2010–11
Hosted All-Star Game: (2) 1971, 1996
1st Overall Draft Choices: 1982 (Gord Kluzak), 1997 (Joe Thornton)

BUFFALO SABRES

First Game Played: October 10, 1970
Buffalo Sabres 2 at Pittsburgh Penguins 1
Nickname Provenance: A contest determined the name Sabres
Mascot: Sabre-Tooth
Arena History: Memorial Auditorium ("The Aud"), 1970–96; Marine Midland Bank Arena, 1996–2000; HSBC Arena (same building as the Marine Midland Bank Arena), 2000–2011; First Niagara Centre (same building as HSBC Arena), 2011–present (capacity 18,890)
Retired Numbers: Tim Horton (2), Rick Martin (7), Gilbert Perreault (11), Rene Robert (14), Pat LaFontaine (16), Danny Gare (18)
Hall of Famers: Players (9): Dick Duff, Doug Gilmour, Tim Horton, Gilbert Perreault, Dale Hawerchuk, Clark Gillies, Grant Fuhr, Pat LaFontaine, Marcel Pronovost (inducted as Player, associated with Buffalo as Builder); Builders (4): Scotty Bowman, Punch Imlach, Seymour Knox III, Roger Neilson
Website: www.sabres.com
Minor League Affiliate(s): Rochester Americans (AHL), Gwinnett Gladiators (ECHL—shared with Phoenix)
Stanley Cups: none
Hosted All-Star Game: (1) 1978
1st Overall Draft Choices: 1970 (Gilbert Perreault), 1987 (Pierre Turgeon)

CALGARY FLAMES

First Game Played:
As Atlanta Flames: October 7, 1972
Atlanta Flames 3 at New York Islanders 2
As Calgary Flames: October 9, 1980
Quebec Nordiques 5 at Calgary Flames 5
Nickname Provenance: Flames was chosen by contest, representative of Atlanta during the Civil War, when much of it was burned to the ground
Mascot: Harvey the Hound
Arena History: The Omni (Atlanta), 1972–80; Stampede Corral, 1980–83; Olympic Saddledome, 1983–95; Canadian Airlines Saddledome, 1995–2001; Pengrowth

Saddledome, 2001–2010; Scotiabank Saddledome, 2010–present (same building as previous three Saddledomes—capacity 19,289)
Retired Numbers: Lanny McDonald (9), Mike Vernon (30)
Hall of Famers: Players (7): Lanny McDonald, Joe Mullen, Grant Fuhr, Brett Hull, Al MacInnis, Doug Gilmour, Joe Nieuwendyk; Builders (3): Cliff Fletcher, Harley Hotchkiss, Daryl "Doc" Seaman
Website: www.calgaryflames.com
Minor League Affiliate(s): Abbotsford Heat (AHL), Utah Grizzlies (ECHL)
Stanley Cups: (1) 1988–89
Hosted All-Star Game: (1) 1985
1st Overall Draft Choices: none

CAROLINA HURRICANES

First Game Played:
As Hartford Whalers: October 11, 1979
Hartford Whalers 1 at Minnesota North Stars 4
As Carolina Hurricanes: October 1, 1997
Carolina Hurricanes 2 at Tampa Bay Lightning 4
Nickname Provenance: Whalers adopted because it contained the letters of the WHA and it was emblematic of the region
Mascot: Stormy
Arena History: Springfield Civic Center (Springfield, Mass.), 1979–80; Hartford Civic Center (Hartford), 1980–97; Greensboro Coliseum, 1997–99; Raleigh Entertainment & Sports Arena, 1999–2003; RBC Center (same building as Raleigh Entertainment & Sports Arena), 2003–12; PNC Arena (same building as RBC Centre), 2012–present (capacity 18,176)
Retired Numbers: Glen Wesley (2), Ron Francis (10), Rod Brind'Amour (17)
Hall of Famers: Players (6): Paul Coffey (Hartford/Carolina), Gordie Howe (Hartford), Mark Howe (Hartford), Bobby Hull (Hartford), Dave Keon (Hartford), Ron Francis (Hartford/Carolina)
Website: www.carolinahurricanes.com
Minor League Affiliate(s): Charlotte Checkers (AHL), Florida Everblades (ECHL—shared with Tampa Bay)
Stanley Cups: (1) 2005–06
Hosted All-Star Game: (2) 1986 (as Hartford Whalers), 2011
1st Overall Draft Choices: none

CHICAGO BLACKHAWKS

First Game Played: November 17, 1926
Toronto St. Pats 1 at Chicago Black Hawks 4
Nickname Provenance: (Spelling changed from "Black Hawks" to "Blackhawks" in 1986)

Mascot: Tommy the Hawk
Arena History: Chicago Coliseum, 1926–29, 1932; Chicago Stadium, 1929–94; United Center, 1995–present (opening of United Center delayed by disruption of 1994–95 NHL season, capacity 19,717)
Retired Numbers: Glenn Hall (1), Keith Magnuson (3), Pierre Pilote (3), Bobby Hull (9), Denis Savard (18), Stan Mikita (21), Tony Esposito (35)
Hall of Famers: Players (40): Sid Abel, Ed Belfour, Doug Bentley, Max Bentley, George Boucher, Frank Brimsek, Billy Burch, Paul Coffey, Lionel Conacher, Roy Conacher, Art Coulter, Babe Dye, Phil Esposito, Tony Esposito, Bill Gadsby, Charlie Gardiner, Herb Gardiner, Doug Gilmour, Michel Goulet, Glenn Hall, George Hay, Bobby Hull, Duke Keats, Hugh Lehman, Ted Lindsay, Harry Lumley, Mickey MacKay, Stan Mikita, Howie Morenz, Bill Mosienko, Bert Olmstead, Bobby Orr, Pierre Pilote, Denis Savard, Earl Seibert, Clint Smith, Allan Stanley, Barney Stanley, Jack Stewart, Harry Watson; Builders (13): Al Arbour, Emile Francis (played for Chicago, inducted as Builder), Dick Irvin (played for Chicago, inducted as Builder), Tommy Ivan, John Mariucci (also played for Chicago), Major Frederic McLaughlin, James Norris, James Norris, Jr., Rudy Pilous, Bud Poile (played for Chicago, inducted as Builder), Carl Voss (played for Chicago, inducted as Builder), Arthur Wirtz, William Wirtz
Website: www.chicagoblackhawks.com
Minor League Affiliate(s): Rockford IceHogs (AHL), Toledo Walleye (ECHL—shared with Detroit)
Stanley Cups: (4) 1933–34, 1937–38, 1960–61, 2009–10
Hosted All-Star Game: (4) 1948, 1961, 1974, 1991
1st Overall Draft Choices: 2007 (Patrick Kane)

COLORADO AVALANCHE

First Game Played:
As Quebec Nordiques: October 10, 1979
Atlanta Flames 5 at Quebec Nordiques 3
As Colorado Avalanche: October 6, 1995
Detroit Red Wings 2 at Colorado Avalanche 3
Nickname Provenance: Team owners polled fans. Out of eight names offered, Avalanche was the most popular.
Mascot: Howler
Arena History: McNichols Sports Arena, 1995–99; Pepsi Center, 1999–present (capacity 18,007)
Retired Numbers: J-C Tremblay (3), Marc Tardif (8), Michel Goulet (16), Joe Sakic (19), Peter Stastny (26), Patrick Roy (33), Ray Bourque (77)
Hall of Famers: Players (8): Ray Bourque, Patrick Roy, Michel Goulet (Quebec), Jari Kurri, Guy Lafleur (Quebec), Peter Stastny (Quebec), Mats Sundin (Quebec), Joe Sakic (Quebec/Colorado)

Website: www.coloradoavalanche.com
Minor League Affiliate(s): Lake Erie Monsters (AHL), Denver Cutthroats (CHL)
Stanley Cups: (2) 1995–96, 2000–01
Hosted All-Star Game: (1) 2001
1st Overall Draft Choices: 1989 (Mats Sundin—Quebec Nordiques), 1990 (Owen Nolan—Quebec), 1991 (Eric Lindros—Quebec)

COLUMBUS BLUE JACKETS

First Game Played: October 7, 2000
Chicago Blackhawks 5 at Columbus Blue Jackets 3
Nickname Provenance: Reflects patriotism and history of the Civil War
Mascot: Stinger
Arena History: Nationwide Arena, 2000–present (capacity 18,144)
Retired Numbers: none
Hall of Famers: none
Website: www.bluejackets.com
Minor League Affiliate(s): Springfield Falcons (AHL), Evansville IceMen (ECHL)
Stanley Cups: none
Hosted All-Star Game: (1) 2013
1st Overall Draft Choices: 2002 (Rick Nash)

DALLAS STARS

First Game Played:
As Minnesota North Stars: October 11, 1967
Minnesota North Stars 2 at St. Louis Blues 2
As Dallas Stars: October 5, 1993
Detroit Red Wings 4 at Dallas Stars 6
Nickname Provenance: Shortening of North Stars, consistent with Texas as the Lone Star state
Mascot: none
Arena History: Metropolitan Sports Center (also known as the Met Center), 1967–93; Reunion Arena, 1993–2001; American Airlines Center, 2001–present (capacity 18,532)
Retired Numbers: Neal Broten (7), Bill Goldsworthy (8), Bill Masterton (19)
Hall of Famers: Players (9): Mike Gartner (Minnesota), Harry Howell (Minnesota), Brett Hull, Larry Murphy (Minnesota), Gump Worsley (Minnesota), Leo Boivin (Minnesota), Dino Ciccarelli (Minnesota), Ed Belfour, Joe Nieuwendyk; Builders (3): Herb Brooks (coached Minnesota), Glen Sather (played for University of Minnesota), John Mariucci
Website: www.dallasstars.com
Minor League Affiliate(s): Allen Americans (CHL), Idaho Steelheads (ECHL), Texas Stars (AHL)

Stanley Cups: (1) 1998–99
Hosted All-Star Game: (2) 1972 (as North Stars); 2007
1st Overall Draft Choices: 1978 (Bobby Smith—Minnesota North Stars), 1983
(Brian Lawton—Minnesota), 1988 (Mike Modano—Minnesota)

DETROIT RED WINGS

First Game Played:
As Detroit Cougars: November 18, 1926
Boston Bruins 2 at Detroit Cougars 0
As Detroit Falcons: November 13, 1930
New York Rangers 0 at Detroit Falcons 1
As Detroit Red Wings: November 10, 1932
Chicago Black Hawks 1 at Detroit Red Wings 3
Nickname Provenance: Owner James Norris, a Montreal native, used the Winged Wheel
from his hometown team and combined it with Detroit's place in America as a car-
making centre
Mascot: Al the Octopus
Arena History: Windsor Arena (Border Cities Arena), 1926–27; Olympia, 1927–79;
Joe Louis Arena, 1979–present (capacity 20,058)
Retired Numbers: Terry Sawchuk (1), Ted Lindsay (7), Gordie Howe (9), Alex
Delvecchio (10), Sid Abel (12), Steve Yzerman (19)
Hall of Famers: Players (54): Sid Abel, Jack Adams (inducted as Player, associated
with Detroit as Builder), Marty Barry, Andy Bathgate, Johnny Bucyk, Dino Ciccarelli,
Paul Coffey, Charlie Conacher, Roy Conacher, Alec Connell, Alex Delvecchio, Marcel
Dionne, Bernie Federko, Slava Fetisov, Frank Foyston, Frank Fredrickson, Bill Gadsby,
Ed Giacomin, Ebbie Goodfellow, Glenn Hall, Doug Harvey, George Hay, Harry Holmes,
Gordie Howe, Mark Howe, Syd Howe, Brett Hull, Duke Keats, Red Kelly, Brian Kilrea
(played for Detroit, inducted as Builder), Igor Larionov, Herbie Lewis, Ted Lindsay,
Harry Lumley, Frank Mahovlich, Larry Murphy, Reg Noble, Adam Oates, Brad Park,
Bud Poile (played for Detroit, inducted as Builder), Marcel Pronovost, Bill Quackenbush,
Luc Robitaille, Borje Salming, Terry Sawchuk, Earl Seibert, Darryl Sittler, Jack Stewart,
Tiny Thompson, Norm Ullman, Jack Walker, Harry Watson, Cooney Weiland, Steve
Yzerman; Builders (9): Al Arbour (played for Detroit, inducted as Builder), Leo Boivin
(played for Detroit, inducted as Builder), Scotty Bowman, Jimmy Devellano, Tommy
Ivan, Bruce Norris, James Norris, James Norris, Jr., Carl Voss (played for Detroit,
inducted as Builder)
Website: www.detroitredwings.com
Minor League Affiliate(s): Grand Rapids Griffins (AHL), Toledo Walleye
(ECHL—shared with Chicago)
Stanley Cups: (11) 1935–36, 1936–37, 1942–43, 1949–50, 1951–52, 1953–54,
1954–55, 1996–97, 1997–98, 2002–02, 2007–08

Hosted All-Star Game: (5) 1950, 1952, 1954, 1955, 1980
1st Overall Draft Choices: 1977 (Dale McCourt), 1986 (Joe Murphy)

EDMONTON OILERS

First Game Played: October 10, 1979
Edmonton Oilers 2 at Chicago Black Hawks 4
Nickname Provenance: From Alberta Oilers and later Edmonton Oilers of WHA, to refer to Alberta's place as an oil capital in Canada
Mascot: none
Arena History: Northlands Coliseum, 1979–99; Skyreach Centre, 1999–2003; Rexall Place, 2005–present (all three are the same building, capacity 16,839)
Retired Numbers: Al Hamilton (3), Paul Coffey (7), Glenn Anderson (9) Mark Messier (11), Jari Kurri (17), Grant Fuhr (31), Wayne Gretzky (99—leaguewide recognition)
Hall of Famers: Players (7): Glenn Anderson, Paul Coffey, Grant Fuhr, Wayne Gretzky, Jari Kurri, Mark Messier, Adam Oates; Builders (1): Glen Sather
Website: www.edmontonoilers.com
Minor League Affiliate(s): Oklahoma City Barons (AHL), Stockton Thunder (ECHL)
Stanley Cups: (5) 1983–84, 1984–85, 1986–87, 1987–88, 1989–90
Hosted All-Star Game: (1) 1989
1st Overall Draft Choices: 2010 (Taylor Hall), 2011 (Ryan Nugent-Hopkins), 2012 (Nail Yakupov)

FLORIDA PANTHERS

First Game Played: October 6, 1993
Florida Panthers 4 at Chicago Blackhawks 4
Nickname Provenance: Named for the animal, which is common in Florida
Mascot: Stanley C. Panther
Arena History: Miami Arena, 1993–99; National Car Rental Center, 1999–2002; Office Depot Center, 2002–05; BankAtlantic Center, 2005–present (previous three are the same building, capacity 17,040)
Retired Numbers: none
Hall of Famers: Players (5): Ed Belfour, Pavel Bure, Dino Ciccarelli, Igor Larionov, Joe Nieuwendyk
Website: www.floridapanthers.com
Minor League Affiliate(s): San Antonio Rampage (AHL), Cincinnati Cyclones (ECHL—shared with Nashville)
Stanley Cups: none
Hosted All-Star Game: (1) 2003
1st Overall Draft Choices: 1994 (Ed Jovanovski)

LOS ANGELES KINGS

First Game Played: October 14, 1967
Philadelphia Flyers 2 at Los Angeles Kings 4
Nickname Provenance: Named by owner Jack Kent Cooke to give the team a royal (i.e., important) sound to it
Mascot: Bailey
Arena History: Long Beach Arena, October 1967; Los Angeles Sports Arena, November–December 1967; The Forum, 1967–88; Great Western Forum, 1988–99 (same building as The Forum); Staples Center, 1999–present (capacity 18,118)
Retired Numbers: Marcel Dionne (16), Dave Taylor (18), Luc Robitaille (20), Rogie Vachon (30), Wayne Gretzky (99—leaguewide recognition)
Hall of Famers: Players (14): Paul Coffey, Marcel Dionne, Dick Duff, Grant Fuhr, Wayne Gretzky, Harry Howell, Jari Kurri, Larry Murphy, Bob Pulford, Larry Robinson, Luc Robitaille, Terry Sawchuk, Steve Shutt, Billy Smith; Builders (1): Brian Kilrea (played for Los Angeles, inducted as Builder)
Website: www.lakings.com
Minor League Affiliate(s): Manchester Monarchs (AHL), Ontario Reign (ECHL)
Stanley Cups: (1) 2011–12
Hosted All-Star Game: (2) 1981, 2002
1st Overall Draft Choices: none

MINNESOTA WILD

First Game Played: October 6, 2000
Minnesota Wild 1 at Mighty Ducks of Anaheim 3
Nickname Provenance: Selected by fan contest
Mascot: Nordy
Arena History: Xcel Energy Center, 2000–present (capacity 18,064)
Retired Numbers: none
Hall of Famers: none
Website: www.wild.com
Minor League Affiliate(s): Houston Aeros (AHL), Orlando Solar Bears (ECHL)
Stanley Cups: none
Hosted All-Star Game: (1) 2004
1st Overall Draft Choices: none

MONTREAL CANADIENS

First Game Played:
In NHA: January 19, 1910
Montreal Canadiens 4 at Renfrew Millionaires 9

In NHL: December 19, 1917

Ottawa Senators 4 at Montreal Canadiens 7

Nickname Provenance: As a Canadian team based in Quebec, simply called Canadians in French (they are also known as "the Habs," short for "*les habitants*," a name given to the early settlers of the province)

Mascot: Youppi

Arena History: Westmount Arena, 1909–1918; Jubilee Arena, 1918–20; Mount Royal Arena, 1920–24; Montreal Forum, 1924–96 (refurbished in 1968); Molson Centre, 1996–2002; Bell Centre, 2002–present (same building as Molson Centre, capacity 21,273)

Retired Numbers: Jacques Plante (1), Doug Harvey (2), Emile "Butch" Bouchard (3), Jean Beliveau (4), Bernie Geoffrion (5), Howie Morenz (7), Maurice Richard (9), Guy Lafleur (10), Yvan Cournoyer (12), Dickie Moore (12), Henri Richard (16), Elmer Lach (16), Serge Savard (18), Larry Robinson (19), Bob Gainey (23), Ken Dryden (29), Patrick Roy (33)

Hall of Famers: Players (51): Marty Barry, Harry Cameron, Gord Drillon, Dick Duff, Tony Esposito, Rod Langway, Roy Worters, Dick Irvin (inducted as Player, associated with Montreal as Builder), Howie Morenz, Georges Vezina, Aurel Joliat, Newsy Lalonde, Joe Malone, Sprague Cleghorn, Herb Gardiner, Sylvio Mantha, Joe Hall, George Hainsworth, Maurice Richard, Jack Laviolette, Didier Pitre, Bill Durnan, Babe Siebert, Toe Blake, Emile Bouchard, Elmer Lach, Ken Reardon, Tom Johnson, Jean Beliveau, Bernie Geoffrion, Doug Harvey, Dickie Moore, Jacques Plante, Henri Richard, Patrick Roy, Gump Worsley, Frank Mahovlich, Yvan Cournoyer, Ken Dryden, Jacques Lemaire, Bert Olmstead, Serge Savard, Jacques Laperriere, Guy Lafleur, Buddy O'Connor, Bob Gainey, Guy Lapointe, Steve Shutt, Larry Robinson, Denis Savard, Doug Gilmour; Builders (12): Cliff Fletcher, William Northey, Hon. Donat Raymond, Frank Selke, Ambrose O'Brien, Leo Dandurand, Tommy Gorman, Hon. Hartland de Montarville Molson, Joseph Cattarinich, Sam Pollock, Scotty Bowman, Glen Sather (played with Montreal, inducted as Builder)

Website: www.canadiens.com

Minor League Affiliate(s): Hamilton Bulldogs (AHL), Wheeling Nailers (ECHL—shared with Pittsburgh)

Stanley Cups: (23) 1923–24, 1929–30, 1930–31, 1943–44, 1945–46, 1952–53, 1955–56, 1956–57, 1957–58, 1958–59, 1959–60, 1964–65, 1065–66, 1967–68, 1968–69, 1970–71, 1972–73, 1975–76, 1976–77, 1977–78, 1978–79, 1985–86, 1992–93

Hosted All-Star Game: (12) 1953, 1956, 1957, 1958, 1959, 1960, 1965, 1967, 1969, 1975, 1993, 2009

1st Overall Draft Choices: 1969 (Rejean Houle), 1971 (Guy Lafleur), 1980 (Doug Wickenheiser)

NASHVILLE PREDATORS

First Game Played: October 10, 1998
Florida Panthers 1 at Nashville Predators 0
Nickname Provenance: Selected by fans
Mascot: Gnash
Arena History: Nashville Arena, 1998–99, 2007; Gaylord Entertainment Center, 1999–2007; Sommet Centre, 2007–2010; Bridgestone Arena, 2010–present (all refer to the same building, capacity 17,113)
Retired Numbers: none
Hall of Famers: none
Website: www.nashvillepredators.com
Minor League Affiliate(s): Milwaukee Admirals (AHL), Cincinnati Cyclones (ECHL—shared with Florida)
Stanley Cups: none
Hosted All-Star Game: none
1st Overall Draft Choices: none

NEW JERSEY DEVILS

First Game Played:
As Kansas City Scouts: October 9, 1974
Kansas City Scouts 2 at Toronto Maple Leafs 6
As Colorado Rockies: October 5, 1976
Toronto Maple Leafs 2 at Colorado Rockies 4
As New Jersey Devils: October 5, 1982
Pittsburgh Penguins 3 at New Jersey Devils 3
Nickname Provenance: Selected by fans in reference to legend of a demonic baby produced by one Mrs. Leeds in 1735, her 13th child
Mascot: The Devil
Arena History: Kemper Arena (Kansas City), 1974–76; McNichols Sports Arena (Colorado), 1976–82; Brendan Byrne Arena, 1982–83; Byrne Meadowlands Arena, 1983–92 (same building as Brendan Byrne Arena); Meadowlands Arena (same building as Byrne Meadowlands Arena), 1992–96; Continental Airlines Arena (same building as Meadowlands Arena), 1996–2007; Prudential Center, 2007–present (capacity 17,625)
Retired Numbers: Ken Daneyko (3), Scott Stevens (4), Scott Niedermayer (27)
Hall of Famers: Players (7): Slava Fetisov, Doug Gilmour, Igor Larionov, Lanny McDonald (Colorado Rockies), Joe Nieuwendyk, Peter Stastny, Scott Stevens; Builders (2): Herb Brooks, Lou Lamoriello
Website: www.newjerseydevils.com
Minor League Affiliate(s): Albany Devils (AHL), Kalamazoo Wings (ECHL—shared with Vancouver)

Stanley Cups: (3) 1994–95, 1999–2000, 2002–03
Hosted All-Star Game: (1) 1984
1st Overall Draft Choices: 1979 (Rob Ramage—Colorado Rockies)

NEW YORK ISLANDERS

First Game Played: October 7, 1972
Atlanta Flames 3 at New York Islanders 2
Nickname Provenance: Named, simply, because the team is located on Long Island, New York
Mascot: none
Arena History: Nassau Veterans' Memorial Coliseum, 1972–present (capacity 16,234)
Retired Numbers: Denis Potvin (5), Clark Gillies (9), Bryan Trottier (19), Mike Bossy (22), Bob Nystrom (23), Billy Smith (31)
Hall of Famers: Players (6): Mike Bossy, Pat LaFontaine, Denis Potvin, Billy Smith, Bryan Trottier, Clark Gillies; Builders (2): Al Arbour, Bill Torrey
Website: www.newyorkislanders.com
Minor League Affiliate(s): Bridgeport Sound Tigers (AHL)
Stanley Cups: (4) 1979–80, 1980–81, 1981–82, 1982–83
Hosted All-Star Game: (1) 1983
1st Overall Draft Choices: 1972 (Billy Harris), 1973 (Denis Potvin), 2000 (Rick DiPietro), 2009 (John Tavares)

NEW YORK RANGERS

First Game Played: November 16, 1926
Montreal Maroons 0 at New York Rangers 1
Nickname Provenance: Emerged when sportswriters in New York called the new franchise Tex's Rangers, in reference to Tex Rickard, the president of Madison Square Garden and the man who assembled the executive for the team in 1926
Mascot: none
Arena History: Madison Square Garden, 1926–68; Madison Square Garden, 1968–present (newly built, capacity 18,200)
Retired Numbers: Ed Giacomin (1), Brian Leetch (2), Harry Howell (3), Rod Gilbert (7), Andy Bathgate (9), Adam Graves (9) Mark Messier (11), Mike Richter (35)
Hall of Famers: Players (48): Glenn Anderson, Dick Duff, Howie Morenz, Lester Patrick, Bill Cook, Frank Boucher, Pavel Bure, Ching Johnson, Babe Siebert, Earl Seibert, Doug Bentley, Max Bentley, Babe Pratt, Neil Colville, Bryan Hextall, Bill Gadsby, Terry Sawchuk, Bernie Geoffrion, Doug Harvey, Charlie Rayner, Art Coulter, Johnny Bower, Tim Horton, Andy Bathgate, Jacques Plante, Harry Howell, Lynn Patrick, Pat LaFontaine, Harry Lumley, Gump Worsley, Allan Stanley, Rod Gilbert, Phil Esposito, Jean Ratelle, Ed Giacomin, Guy Lafleur, Buddy O'Connor, Brad Park,

Clint Smith, Marcel Dionne, Edgar Laprade, Bun Cook, Wayne Gretzky, Mike Gartner, Jari Kurri, Mark Messier, Brian Leetch, Luc Robitaille; Builders (9): Herb Brooks, Bud Poile (played with Rangers, inducted as Builder), Emile Francis (also played for Rangers), William Jennings, John Kilpatrick, Roger Neilson, Craig Patrick, Glen Sather (played with Rangers, inducted as Builder), Carl Voss (played with Rangers, inducted as Builder)
Website: www.newyorkrangers.com
Minor League Affiliate(s): Connecticut Whale (AHL), Greenville Road Warriors (ECHL)
Stanley Cups: (4) 1927–28, 1932–33, 1939–40, 1993–94
Hosted All-Star Game: (2) 1973, 1994
1st Overall Draft Choices: none

OTTAWA SENATORS

First Game Played: October 8, 1992
Montreal Canadiens 3 at Ottawa Senators 5
Nickname Provenance: From original team of same name from 1917–34
Mascot: Spartacat
Arena History: Civic Centre, 1992–96; Palladium, 1996; Corel Centre, 1996–2006; Scotiabank Place, 2006–present (same building as Palladium and Corel Centre, capacity 19,153)
Retired Numbers: Frank Finnigan (8)
Hall of Famers: none
Website: www.ottawasenators.com
Minor League Affiliate(s): Binghamton Senators (AHL), Elmira Jackals (ECHL)
Stanley Cups: none
Hosted All-Star Game: (1) 2012
1st Overall Draft Choices: 1993 (Alexandre Daigle), 1995 (Bryan Berard), 1996 (Chris Phillips)

PHILADELPHIA FLYERS

First Game Played: October 11, 1967
Philadelphia Flyers 1 at Oakland Seals 5
Nickname Provenance: Named by a nine-year-old in a fan contest
Mascot: none
Arena History: The Spectrum, 1967–96; CoreStates Center, 1996–98; First Union Center, 1998–2003 (same building as CoreStates Center); Wachovia Center, 2003–2010 (same building as First Union Center); Wells Fargo Center, 2010–present (same building as Wachovia Center, capacity 19,537)
Retired Numbers: Bernie Parent (1), Barry Ashbee (4), Bill Barber (7), Bobby Clarke (16)

Hall of Famers: Players (9): Paul Coffey, Adam Oates, Bernie Parent, Bobby Clarke, Bill Barber, Dale Hawerchuk, Mark Howe, Darryl Sittler, Allan Stanley; Builders (2): Ed Snider, Keith Allen
Website: www.philadelphiaflyers.com
Minor League Affiliate(s): Adirondack Phantoms (AHL), Trenton Titans (ECHL)
Stanley Cups: (2) 1973–74, 1974–75
Hosted All-Star Game: (2) 1976, 1992
1st Overall Draft Choices: 1975 (Mel Bridgman)

PHOENIX COYOTES

First Game Played:
As Winnipeg Jets: October 10, 1979
Winnipeg Jets 2 at Pittsburgh Penguins 4
As Phoenix Coyotes: October 5, 1996
Phoenix Coyotes 0 at Hartford Whalers 1
Nickname Provenance: Logo depicts a Kachina coyote, indigenous to the region
Mascot: Howler
Arena History: Winnipeg Arena (Winnipeg), 1979–96; America West Arena, 1996–98; Cellular One Ice Den (same building as America West Arena), 1998–99; America West Arena, 1999–2000; Alltel Ice Den, 2000–03 (same building as America West Arena); Glendale Arena, 2003–2008; Jobing.com Arena, 2008–present (same building as Glendale Arena, capacity 17,125)
Retired Numbers: Bobby Hull (9—Winnipeg), Dale Hawerchuk (10—Winnipeg), Thomas Steen (25—Winnipeg), Teppo Numminen (27)
Hall of Famers: Players (5): Mike Gartner, Brett Hull, Bobby Hull (Winnipeg), Dale Hawerchuk (Winnipeg), Serge Savard (Winnipeg)
Website: www.phoenixcoyotes.com
Minor League Affiliate(s): Portland Pirates (AHL), Gwinnett Gladiators (ECHL—shared with Buffalo), Arizona Sundogs (CHL)
Stanley Cups: none
Hosted All-Star Game: none
1st Overall Draft Choices: 1981 (Dale Hawerchuk—Winnipeg Jets)

PITTSBURGH PENGUINS

First Game Played: October 11, 1967
Montreal Canadiens 2 at Pittsburgh Penguins 1
Nickname Provenance: After the Pittsburgh arena opened in 1961, it was dubbed "The Igloo" for its shape. As a result, when Pittsburgh was awarded an NHL team in 1967, owners opted for a nickname compatible with "Igloo" and decided on "Penguins."
Mascot: Iceburgh

Arena History: Civic Arena ("The Igloo"), 1967–2000; Mellon Arena, 2000–2010 (same building as Civic Arena); Consol Energy Center, 2010–present (capacity 18,087)
Retired Numbers: Michel Briere (21), Mario Lemieux (66)
Hall of Famers: Players (11): Leo Boivin, Paul Coffey, Tim Horton, Red Kelly (inducted as Player, associated with Pittsburgh as Builder), Andy Bathgate, Mario Lemieux, Larry Murphy, Bryan Trottier, Joe Mullen, Ron Francis, Luc Robitaille; Builders (4): Scotty Bowman, Bob Johnson, Craig Patrick, Glen Sather (played for Pittsburgh, inducted as Builder)
Website: www.pittsburghpenguins.com
Minor League Affiliate(s): Wilkes-Barre/Scranton Penguins (AHL), Wheeling Nailers (ECHL—shared with Montreal)
Stanley Cups: (3) 1990–91, 1991–92, 2008–09
Hosted All-Star Game: (1) 1990
1st Overall Draft Choices: 1984 (Mario Lemieux), 2003 (Marc-Andre Fleury), 2005 (Sidney Crosby)

ST. LOUIS BLUES

First Game Played: October 11, 1967
Minnesota North Stars 2 at St. Louis Blues 2
Nickname Provenance: Named to remember the city's place in the history of music
Mascot: Louie
Arena History: St. Louis Arena, 1967–94; Kiel Center, 1994–2000; Savvis Center, 2000–2008, Scottrade Center, 2008–present (same building as Kiel Center and Savvis Center, capacity 19,150)
Retired Numbers: Al MacInnis (2), Bob Gassoff (3), Barclay Plager (8), Brian Sutter (11), Brett Hull (16), Bernie Federko (24)
Hall of Famers: Players (17): Glenn Anderson, Grant Fuhr, Bernie Federko, Doug Gilmour, Dale Hawerchuk, Joe Mullen, Wayne Gretzky, Peter Stastny, Guy Lapointe, Jacques Plante, Glenn Hall, Dickie Moore, Doug Harvey, Al MacInnis, Scott Stevens, Brett Hull, Adam Oates; Builders (7): Roger Neilson, Al Arbour, Scotty Bowman, Emile Francis, Craig Patrick (played for St. Louis, inducted as Builder), Lynn Patrick, Glen Sather (played for St. Louis, inducted as Builder)
Website: www.stlouisblues.com
Minor League Affiliate(s): Peoria Rivermen (AHL)
Stanley Cups: none
Hosted All-Star Game: (2) 1970, 1988
1st Overall Draft Choices: none

SAN JOSE SHARKS

First Game Played: October 4, 1991
San Jose Sharks 3 at Vancouver Canucks 4
Nickname Provenance: Named by team owners after a fan contest
Mascot: S.J. Sharkie (b. January 1992)
Arena History: Cow Palace, 1991–93; San Jose Arena, 1993–2001; Compaq Center, 2001–03; HP Pavilion, 2003–present (same building as Compaq Center and San Jose Arena, capacity 17,562)
Retired Numbers: none
Hall of Famers: (2) Ed Belfour, Igor Larionov
Website: www.sjsharks.com
Minor League Affiliate(s): Worcester Sharks (AHL), San Francisco Bulls (ECHL)
Stanley Cups: none
Hosted All-Star Game: 1997
1st Overall Draft Choices: none

TAMPA BAY LIGHTNING

First Game Played: October 7, 1992
Chicago Blackhawks 3 at Tampa Bay Lightning 7
Nickname Provenance: Tampa Bay is, statistically, the lightning capital of the world.
Mascot: Thunder Bug
Arena History: Expo Hall, 1992–93; ThunderDome, 1993–96 (five home games played at Orlando Arena); Ice Palace, 1998–2003; *St. Petersburg Times* Forum, 2003–12 (same building as Ice Palace); *Tampa Bay Times* Forum (same building as *St. Petersburg Times* Forum), 2012–present (capacity 19,758)
Retired Numbers: none
Hall of Famers: Players (2): Dino Ciccarelli, Denis Savard
Website: www.tampabaylightning.com
Minor League Affiliate(s): Syracuse Crunch (AHL), Florida Everblades (ECHL—shared with Carolina)
Stanley Cups: (1) 2003–04
Hosted All-Star Game: (1) 1999
1st Overall Draft Choices: 1992 (Roman Hamrlik), 1998 (Vincent Lecavalier), 2008 (Steve Stamkos)

TORONTO MAPLE LEAFS

First Game Played:
As Toronto Arenas: December 19, 1917
Toronto Arenas 9 at Montreal Wanderers 10

As Toronto St. Pats: December 23, 1919
Toronto St. Pats 0 at Ottawa Senators 3
As Toronto Maple Leafs: February 17, 1927
New York Americans 1 at Toronto Maple Leafs 4
Nickname Provenance: Named by owner Conn Smythe after a World War I regiment
Mascot: Carlton the Bear
Arena History: Arena Gardens (Mutual Street Arena), 1917–31; Maple Leaf Gardens, 1931–99; Air Canada Centre, 1999–present (capacity 18,819)
Retired Numbers: Bill Barilko (5), Ace Bailey (6)
Honoured Numbers: Turk Broda (1), Johnny Bower (1), Red Kelly (4), King Clancy (7), Tim Horton (7), Charlie Conacher (9), Ted Kennedy (9), Syl Apps (10), George Armstrong (10), Mats Sundin (13), Wendel Clark (17), Borje Salming (21), Frank Mahovlich (27), Darryl Sittler (27), Doug Gilmour (93)
Hall of Famers: Players (63): Jack Adams, Glenn Anderson, Syl Apps, Al Arbour, George Armstrong, Ace Bailey, Andy Bathgate, Ed Belfour, Max Bentley, Leo Boivin, Johnny Bower, Turk Broda, Harry Cameron, Gerry Cheevers, King Clancy, Sprague Cleghorn, Charlie Conacher, Rusty Crawford, Hap Day, Gord Drillon, Dick Duff, Babe Dye, Fern Flaman, Grant Fuhr, Mike Gartner, Eddie Gerard, Doug Gilmour, George Hainsworth, Harry Holmes, Red Horner, Tim Horton, Syd Howe, Harvey Jackson, Red Kelly, Ted Kennedy, Dave Keon, Brian Leetch, Harry Lumley, Frank Mahovlich, Lanny McDonald, Dickie Moore, Larry Murphy, Joe Nieuwendyk, Frank Nighbor, Reg Noble, Bert Olmstead, Bernie Parent, Pierre Pilote, Jacques Plante, Babe Pratt, Joe Primeau, Marcel Pronovost, Bob Pulford, Borje Salming, Terry Sawchuk, Sweeney Schriner, Darryl Sittler, Allan Stanley, Mats Sundin, Norm Ullman, Carl Voss, Harry Watson, Ron Francis; Builders (12): Harold Ballard, J.P. Bickell, Cliff Fletcher, Foster Hewitt, William Hewitt, Punch Imlach, Dick Irvin (played for Toronto, inducted as Builder), Frank Mathers (played for Toronto, inducted as Builder), Rudy Pilous, Bud Poile (played for Toronto, inducted as Builder), Frank Selke, Conn Smythe
Website: www.torontomapleleafs.com
Minor League Affiliate(s): Toronto Marlies (AHL), Reading Royals (ECHL—shared with Boston)
Stanley Cups: (13) 1917–18, 1921–22, 1931–32, 1941–42, 1944–45, 1946–47, 1947–48, 1948–49, 1950–51, 1961–62, 1962–63, 1963–64, 1966–67
Hosted All-Star Game: (8) 1947, 1949, 1951, 1962, 1963, 1964, 1968, 2000
1st Overall Draft Choices: 1985 (Wendel Clark)

VANCOUVER CANUCKS

First Game Played: October 9, 1970
Los Angeles Kings 3 at Vancouver Canucks 1
Nickname Provenance: Continuation of WHL franchise nickname
Mascot: Fin the Whale

Arena History: Pacific Coliseum, 1970–95; General Motors (GM) Place, 1995–2010; Rogers Arena, 2010–present (same building as GM Place, capacity 18,810)
Retired Numbers: Wayne Maki (11, unofficial, later worn by Mark Messier but not before or since), Stan Smyl (12), Trevor Linden (16), Markus Naslund (19)
Hall of Famers: (5) Igor Larionov, Cam Neely, Mark Messier, Mats Sundin, Pavel Bure
Website: www.canucks.com
Minor League Affiliate(s): Chicago Wolves (AHL), Kalamazoo Wings (ECHL—shared with New Jersey)
Stanley Cups: none
Hosted All-Star Game: (2) 1977, 1998
1st Overall Draft Choices: none

WASHINGTON CAPITALS

First Game Played: October 9, 1974
Washington Capitals 3 at New York Rangers 6
Nickname Provenance: So called because the team plays in the capital city of the USA
Mascot: Slapshot
Arena History: Capital Centre, 1974–93; US Air Arena, 1993–97 (same building as Capital Centre); US Airways Arena, 1997 (same building as US Air Arena); MCI Center, 1997–2006; Verizon Center, 2006–present (same building as MCI Center—capacity 18,506)
Retired Numbers: Rod Langway (6), Yvon Labre (7), Mike Gartner (11), Dale Hunter (32)
Hall of Famers: Players (5): Dino Ciccarelli, Mike Gartner, Rod Langway, Larry Murphy, Adam Oates, Scott Stevens; Builders (1): Craig Patrick (played for Washington, inducted as Builder)
Website: www.washingtoncaps.com
Minor League Affiliate(s): Hershey Bears (AHL), Reading Royals (ECHL)
Stanley Cups: none
Hosted All-Star Game: (1) 1982
1st Overall Draft Choices: 1974 (Greg Joly), 1976 (Rick Green), 2005 (Alexander Ovechkin)

WINNIPEG JETS

First Game Played:
As Atlanta Thrashers: October 2, 1999
New Jersey Devils 4 at Atlanta Thrashers 1
As Winnipeg Jets: October 9, 2011
Montreal Canadiens 5 at Winnipeg Jets 1
Nickname Provenance: Jets was the name of the previous WHA/NHL franchise
Arena History: Philips Arena, 1999–2011 (capacity 18,545); MTS Centre, 2011–present (capacity 15,015)

Retired Numbers: Dan Snyder (37, unofficial)
Hall of Famers: none
Website: www.winnipegjets.com
Minor League Affiliate(s): St. John's IceCaps (AHL), Colorado Eagles (ECHL)
Stanley Cups: none
Hosted All-Star Game: (1) 2008 (as Thrashers)
1st Overall Draft Choices: 1999 (Patrik Stefan), 2001 (Ilya Kovalchuk)

FINAL STANDINGS, REGULAR SEASON, 2011–12

(top eight teams in each conference qualify for the playoffs)

EASTERN CONFERENCE

	GP	W	L	OT	GF	GA	Pts
NY Rangers	82	51	24	7	226	187	109
Boston	82	49	29	4	269	202	102
Florida	82	38	26	18	203	227	94
Pittsburgh	82	51	25	6	282	221	108
Philadelphia	82	47	26	9	264	232	103
New Jersey	82	48	28	6	228	209	102
Washington	82	42	32	8	222	230	92
Ottawa	82	41	31	10	249	240	92
Buffalo	82	39	32	11	218	230	89
Tampa Bay	82	38	36	8	235	281	84
Winnipeg	82	37	35	10	225	246	84
Carolina	82	33	33	16	213	243	82
Toronto	82	35	37	10	231	264	80
NY Islanders	82	34	37	11	203	255	79
Montreal	82	31	35	16	212	226	78

WESTERN CONFERENCE

	GP	W	L	OT	GF	GA	Pts
Vancouver	82	51	22	9	249	198	111
St. Louis	82	49	22	11	210	165	109
Phoenix	82	42	27	13	216	204	97
Nashville	82	48	26	8	237	210	104
Detroit	82	48	28	6	248	203	102
Chicago	82	45	26	11	248	238	101
San Jose	82	43	29	10	228	210	96
Los Angeles	82	40	27	15	194	179	95
Calgary	82	37	29	16	202	226	90
Dallas	82	42	35	5	211	222	89
Colorado	82	41	35	6	208	220	88
Minnesota	82	35	36	11	177	226	81
Anaheim	82	34	36	12	204	231	80
Edmonton	82	32	40	10	212	239	74
Columbus	82	29	46	7	202	262	65

SCORING LEADERS & GOALIE LEADERS, 2011–12

(Nationality and NHL team in parentheses)

SCORING LEADERS, 2010–11

Points

Evgeni Malkin (RUS–PIT)	109
Steve Stamkos (CAN–TB)	97
Claude Giroux (CAN–PHI)	93
Jason Spezza (CAN–OTT)	84
Ilya Kovalchuk (RUS–NJ)	83
Phil Kessel (USA–TOR)	82
James Neal (USA–PIT)	81
Henrik Sedin (SWE–VAN)	81
John Tavares (CAN–NYI)	81
Patrik Elias (CZE–NJ)	78
Erik Karlsson (SWE–OTT)	78

Goals

Steve Stamkos (CAN–TB)	60
Evgeni Malkin (RUS–PIT)	50
Marian Gaborik (SVK–NYR)	41
James Neal (CAN–PIT)	40
Alexander Ovechkin (RUS–WAS)	38
Scott Hartnell (CAN–PHI)	37
Phil Kessel (USA–TOR)	37
Ilya Kovalchuk (RUS–NJ)	37
Corey Perry (CAN–ANA)	37
Matt Moulson (CAN–NYI)	36

Assists

Henrik Sedin (SWE–VAN)	67
Claude Giroux (CAN–PHI)	65
Erik Karlsson (SWE–OTT)	59
Evgeni Malkin (RUS–PIT)	59
Joe Thornton (CAN–SJ)	59
Ray Whitney (CAN–PHO)	53
Patrik Elias (CZE–NJ)	52
Anze Kopitar (SLO–LA)	51
Jason Spezza (CAN–OTT)	50
John Tavares (CAN–NYI)	50

Penalty Minutes

Derek Dorsett (CAN–CBJ)	235
Zac Rinaldo (CAN–PHI)	232
Zenon Konopka (CAN–OTT)	193
Chris Neil (CAN–OTT)	178
Cody McLeod (CAN–COL)	164
Steve Ott (CAN–DAL)	156
Brandon Prust (CAN–NYR)	156
Shawn Thornton (CAN–BOS)	154
David Clarkson (CAN–NJ)	138
Steve Downie (CAN–TB/COL)	137

WINS, GOALIE

Pekka Rinne (FIN–NAS)	43
Marc-Andre Fleury (CAN–PIT)	42
Henrik Lundqvist (SWE–NYR)	39
Mike Smith (CAN–PHO)	38
Jimmy Howard (USA–DET)	35
Miikka Kiprusoff (FIN–CAL)	35
Jonathan Quick (USA–LA)	35
Tim Thomas (USA–BOS)	35
Antti Niemi (FIN–SJ)	34
Craig Anderson (USA–OTT)	33
Ilya Bryzgalov (RUS–PHI)	33

LOSSES, GOALIE

Jonas Hiller (SUI–ANA)	30
Ondrej Pavelec (CZE–WIN)	28
Carey Price (CAN–MON)	28
Steve Mason (CAN–CBJ)	26
Semyon Varlamov (RUS–COL)	24
Cam Ward (CAN–CAR)	23
Craig Anderson (USA–OTT)	22
Miikka Kiprusoff (FIN–CAL)	22
Kari Lehtonen (FIN–DAL)	22
Antti Niemi (FIN–SJ)	22

MINUTES PLAYED

Jonas Hiller (SUI–ANA)	4,252:31
Pekka Rinne (FIN–NAS)	4,168:52
Miikka Kiprusoff (FIN–CAL)	4,128:00
Jonathan Quick (USA–LA)	4,099:26
Cam Ward (CAN–CAR)	3,988:03
Carey Price (CAN–MON)	3,944:06
Antti Niemi (FIN–SJ)	3,935:46
Ondrej Pavelec (CZE–WIN)	3,932:26
Mike Smith (CAN–PHO)	3,903:12
Marc-Andre Fleury (CAN–PIT)	3,896:13

SHUTOUTS

Jonathan Quick (USA–LA)	10
Brian Elliott (CAN–STL)	9
Henrik Lundqvist (SWE–NYR)	8
Mike Smith (CAN–PHO)	8
Ilya Bryzgalov (RUS–PHO)	6
Jaroslav Halak (SVK–STL)	6
Jimmy Howard (USA–DET)	6
Ryan Miller (USA–BUF)	6
Antti Niemi (FIN–CHI)	6

GOALS-AGAINST AVERAGE

Brian Elliott (CAN–STL)	1.56
Jonathan Quick (USA–LA)	1.95
Cory Schneider (USA–VAN)	1.96
Henrik Lundqvist (SWE–NYR)	1.97
Jaroslav Halak (SVK–STL)	1.97
Jimmy Howard (USA–DET)	2.13
Mike Smith (CAN–PHO)	2.21
Kari Lehtonen (FIN–DAL)	2.33
Miikka Kiprusoff (FIN–CAL)	2.35
Marc-Andre Fleury (CAN–PIT)	2.36

PLAYERS WHO PLAYED IN 2010–11, BUT NOT IN 2011–12

PLAYER	2011–12 STATUS
Andersson, Jonas	played for Moscow (KHL)
Arniel, Jamie	played for Providence (AHL)
Bagnall, Drew	played for Houston (AHL)
Bartulis, Oskars	played for Adirondack (AHL)
Begin, Steve	retired
Belak, Wade	deceased
Belle, Shawn	played for Mannheim (DEL)
Benoit, Andre	played for Moscow (KHL)
Betts, Blair	retired
Bliznak, Mario	played for Sparta Praha (CZE)
Bodie, Troy	played for Syracuse (AHL)
Boogaard, Derek	deceased
Boyd, Dustin	played for Astana Barys (KHL)
Boynton, Nick	retired
Brodeur, Mike	played in AHL & ECHL
Callahan, Joe	played for Hamilton (AHL)
Campanale, Matt	played in AHL & ECHL
Caputi, Luca	played for Toronto & Syracuse (AHL)
Clark, Chris	played for Providence (AHL)
Climie, Matt	played for Chicago (AHL)
Cohen, Colby	played for Providence (AHL)
Colliton, Jeremy	played for Bridgeport (AHL)
Comrie, Mike	retired
Conroy, Craig	retired
Corrente, Matt	played for Albany (AHL)
Craig, Ryan	played for Wilkes-Barre/Scranton (AHL)
Cullimore, Jassen	played for Iserlohn (DEL)
Cumiskey, Kyle	played for Syracuse (AHL)
Dawes, Nigel	played for Astana Barys (KHL)
Dekanich, Mark	played for Springfield (AHL)
Della Rovere, Stefan	played for Peoria (AHL)
Desjardins, Cedric	played for Lake Erie (AHL)
DiBenedetto, Justin	played for Bridgeport (AHL)
Doornbosch, Jamie	played for St. Mary's University (CAN)
Draper, Kris	retired
Drazenovic, Nick	played for Springfield (AHL)
Drury, Chris	retired
Dupont, Brodie	played for Milwaukee (AHL)

Dumont, J-P	played for Bern (SUI)
Earl, Robbie	played for Salzburg (AUT)
Eckford, Tyler	played for Portland (AHL)
Fahey, Brian	played for Rockford (AHL)
Foote, Adam	retired
Forsberg, Peter	retired
Frolov, Alexander	played for Omsk (KHL)
Gaunce, Cameron	played for Lake Erie (AHL)
Gerber, Martin	played for Vaxjo (SEL)
Godard, Eric	played for Texas (AHL)
Grier, Mike	retired
Hale, David	retired
Hanson, Christian	played for Hershey (AHL)
Harju, Johan	played for Lulea (SEL)
Hendry, Jordan	played for Houston (AHL)
Hensick, T.J.	played for Peoria (AHL)
Hnidy, Shane	retired
Holden, Nick	played for Springfield (AHL)
Hollweg, Ryan	played for Portland (AHL)
Holos, Jonas	played for Vaxjo (SEL)
Holzer, Korbinian	played for Toronto (AHL)
Hutchinson, Andrew	played for Astana Barys (KHL)
Jessiman, Hugh	played for Abbotsford (AHL)
Joensuu, Jesse	played for Jonkoping (SEL)
Johnson, Chad	played for Connecticut (AHL)
Johnson, Ryan	retired
Katic, Mark	played for Bridgeport (AHL)
Klasen, Linus	played for Malmo (SWE)
Koci, David	played for Sparta Praha (CZE)
Kolarik, Chad	did not play—injured
Koskinen, Mikko	played for Bridgeport (AHL)
Kotalik, Ales	played for Ceske Budejovice (CZE)
Kovalev, Alexei	played for Moscow (KHL)
Lalime, Patrick	retired
Lashoff, Matt	played for Toronto (AHL)
Lawson, Nathan	played for Hamilton (AHL)
Leach, Jay	played for Albany (AHL)
Leclaire, Pascal	retired
Leighton, Michael	played for Adirondack (AHL)
LeNeveu, David	played for Oklahoma City (AHL)
Lessard, Francis	played for Binghamton (AHL)
Liffiton, David	played for Lake Erie (AHL)

Locke, Corey	played for Binghamton (AHL)
Lukowich, Brad	played for Texas (AHL)
Macias, Ray	played in AHL & ECHL
Magnan, Olivier	played for Val Pusteria (ITA)
Mair, Adam	played for Springfield (AHL)
Mara, Paul	did not play—coaching high school
Marchant, Todd	retired
Mashinter, Brandon	played for Worcester (AHL)
Mauldin, Greg	played for Lake Erie (AHL)
McCabe, Bryan	retired
McCollum, Tom	played in AHL & ECHL
McKenna, Mike	played for Binghamton (AHL)
McRae, Philip	played for Peoria (AHL)
Meyer, Freddy	played for Modo (SEL)
Meyer, Stefan	played in AHL & SEL
Modano, Mike	retired
Modin, Fredrik	retired
Moller, Oscar	played for Skelleftea (SEL)
Moore, Mike	played for Worcester (AHL)
Morin, Travis	played for Texas (AHL)
Morrisonn, Shaone	played for Rochester (AHL)
Mueller, Marcel	played for Toronto (AHL)
Muzzin, Jake	played for Manchester (AHL)
Nash, Brendon	did not play—injured
Niedermayer, Rob	played for Lugano (SUI)
Niittymaki, Antero	played for Worcester & Syracuse (AHL)
Noreau, Maxim	played for Ambri-Piotta (SUI)
Ohlund, Mattias	did not play—injured
Osgood, Chris	retired
Oystrick, Nathan	played for Portland (AHL)
Parent, Ryan	played for Chicago (AHL)
Parrish, Mark	played for Binghamton (AHL)
Perrault, Joel	played for Langnau (SUI)
Petiot, Richard	played for Norfolk (AHL)
Pielmeier, Timo	played in AHL & ECHL
Pisani, Fernando	played for Sodertalje (SWE)
Poti, Tom	did not play—injured
Potulny, Ryan	played for Hershey (AHL)
Prucha, Petr	played for St. Petersburg (KHL)
Rafalski, Brian	retired
Recchi, Mark	retired
Reddox, Liam	played for Vaxjo (SEL)

Reinprecht, Steve	played for San Antonio & Chicago (AHL)
Rissmiller, Pat	played for Lake Erie (AHL)
Rivet, Craig	played for Elmira (ECHL)
Roy, Mathieu	played for Charlotte (AHL)
Ruutu, Jarkko	played for Jokerit (FIN)
Rypien, Rick	deceased
Salei, Ruslan	deceased
Salmela, Anssi	played for Avangard Omsk (KHL)
Samsonov, Sergei	did not play—unsigned
Sauve, Yann	played for Chicago (AHL)
Savard, Marc	did not play—post-concussion symptoms
Sawada, Raymond	played for Texas & St. John's (AHL)
Scatchard, Dave	retired
Sceviour, Colton	played for Texas (AHL)
Schaefer, Peter	did not play
Schremp, Rob	played for Modo (SEL)
Sexton, Dan	played for Syracuse (AHL)
Shirokov, Sergei	played for CSKA Moscow (KHL)
Sim, Jon	played in CZE & DEL
Sims, Shane	played for Gwinnett (ECHL)
Sjostrom, Fredrik	played for Farjestads & Vastra Frolunda (SEL)
Skrastins, Karlis	deceased
Sloan, Tyler	played for Milwaukee (AHL)
Smaby, Matt	played for Syracuse (AHL)
Sopel, Brent	played for Novokuznetsk (KHL)
Stafford, Garrett	played for Portland & Hamilton (AHL)
Stalock, Alex	played in AHL & ECHL
Stillman, Cory	retired
Stoa, Ryan	played for Lake Erie (AHL)
Strudwick, Jason	played for Sodertalje (SWE)
Sutherby, Brian	played for San Antonio (AHL)
Svatos, Marek	did not play
Sweatt, Lee	retired
Syvret, Danny	played for Peoria (AHL)
Tambellini, Jeff	played for Zurich (SUI)
Tatar, Tomas	played for Grand Rapids (AHL)
Thuresson, Andreas	played for Connecticut (AHL)
Timmins, Scott	played for San Antonio (AHL)
Vasyunov, Alexander	deceased
Vernace, Michael	played in AHL
Voros, Aaron	played for Connecticut (AHL)
Wallin, Niclas	played for Lulea (SEL)

Weight, Doug	retired
Welch, Noah	played for Jonkoping (SEL)
White, Todd	retired
Wick, Roman	played for Kloten (SUI)
Wiercioch, Patrick	played for Binghamton (AHL)
Williams, Jeremy	played for Salzburg (AUT)
Willsie, Brian	played for Hamilton (AHL)
Wright, James	played for San Antonio (AHL)
Zeiler, John	played for Augsburg (DEL)
Zherdev, Nikolai	played for Moscow (KHL)
Zigomanis, Mike	played for Toronto (AHL)
Zubarev, Andrei	played for Moscow (KHL)

PLAYERS SUSPENDED IN 2011–12

PRE-SEASON

September 20, 2011	P-L Letourneau-Leblond (Calgary)	5 games (boarding)
September 20, 2011	Jody Shelley (Philadelphia)	10 games (boarding)
September 23, 2011	James Wisniewski (Columbus)	12 games (hit to the head)
September 23, 2011	Brad Staubitz (Minnesota)	7 games (checking from behind)
September 24, 2011	Brad Boyes (Buffalo)	2 games (hit to the head)
September 24, 2011	J-F Jacques (Anaheim)	9 games (leaving bench to fight)
September 26, 2011	Tom Sestito (Philadelphia)	4 games (checking from behind)
September 28, 2011	Brendan Smith (Detroit)	8 games (hit to the head)
September 30, 2011	Clarke MacArthur (Toronto)	3 games (hit to the head)

REGULAR SEASON

October 8, 2011	P-M Bouchard (Minnesota)	2 games (high-sticking)
October 17, 2011	Kris Letang (Pittsburgh)	2 games (boarding)
October 28, 2011	Andy Sutton (Edmonton)	5 games (elbowing)
October 28, 2011	Daniel Carcillo (Chicago)	2 games (hit from behind)
November 2, 2011	Patrick Kaleta (Buffalo)	4 games (head-butting)
November 17, 2011	Chris Stewart (St. Louis)	3 games (checking from behind)
November 23, 2011	Andre Deveaux (NY Rangers)	3 games (hit to the head)
November 26, 2011	Max Pacioretty (Montreal)	3 games (hit to the head)
December 3, 2011	Jordin Tootoo (Nashville)	2 games (running goaltender)
December 3, 2011	Marc Fistric (Dallas)	3 games (charging)
December 6, 2011	Kevin Porter (Colorado)	4 games (kneeing)
December 7, 2011	Ville Leino (Buffalo)	1 game (elbowing)
December 7, 2011	Andy Sutton (Edmonton)	8 games (charging)
December 17, 2011	Milan Lucic (Boston)	1 game (hitting from behind)
December 18, 2011	Rene Bourque (Calgary)	2 games (hitting from behind)
December 20, 2011	Deryk Engelland (Pittsburgh)	3 games (hit to the head)
December 31, 2011	Ian Cole (St. Louis)	3 games (hit to the head)
December 31, 2011	Krys Barch (Florida)	1 game (inappropriate remarks)
December 31, 2011	Raffi Torres (Phoenix)	2 games (charging)
January 2, 2012	Daniel Carcillo (Chicago)	7 games (boarding)
January 3, 2012	Rene Bourque (Calgary)	5 games (elbowing)
January 7, 2012	Brad Marchand (Boston)	5 games (clipping)
January 8, 2012	J-F Jacques (Anaheim)	3 games (hit to the head)

January 14, 2012	Dane Byers (Columbus)	3 games (hit to the head)
January 21, 2012	Andrew Ference (Boston)	3 games (boarding)
January 22, 2012	Alex Ovechkin (Washington)	3 games (charging)
February 12, 2012	Zac Rinaldo (Philadelphia)	2 games (charging)
February 18, 2012	Warren Peters (Minnesota)	1 game (cross-checking)
March 8, 2012	Mike Green (Washington)	3 games (hit to the head)
March 12, 2012	Tyler Myers (Buffalo)	3 games (boarding)
March 15, 2012	Jeff Skinner (Carolina)	2 games (kicking)
March 20, 2012	Shane Doan (Phoenix)	3 games (elbowing)
March 21, 2012	Duncan Keith (Chicago)	5 games (elbowing)
April 1, 2012	Kyle Quincey (Detroit)	1 game (charging)
April 5, 2012	Nate Prosser (Minnesota)	1 game (head-butting)

PLAYOFFS

April 11, 2012	Byron Bitz (Vancouver)	2 games (boarding)
April 14, 2012	Carl Hagelin (NY Rangers)	3 games (elbowing)
April 14, 2012	Matt Carkner (Ottawa)	1 game (unsportsmanlike conduct)
April 14, 2012	Andrew Shaw (Chicago)	3 games (running goaltender)
April 14, 2012	Nicklas Backstrom (Washington)	1 game (cross-checking)
April 15, 2012	Craig Adams (Pittsburgh)	1 game (late-game instigator)
April 15, 2012	James Neal (Pittsburgh)	1 game (charging)
April 15, 2012	Arron Asham (Pittsburgh)	4 games (cross-checking)
April 17, 2012	Raffi Torres (Phoenix)	25 games (hit to the head)

MILESTONES TO WATCH FOR IN 2012–13

Daniel Alfredsson	18 points to 1,100
Jason Arnott	62 points to 1,000
Jay Bouwmeester	588 consecutive games and counting
Martin Brodeur	9 games to 1,200
Zdeno Chara	41 points to 500
Sidney Crosby	66 games to 500
Pavel Datsyuk	22 assists to 500
Shane Doan	12 points to 800
Radek Dvorak	9 games to 1,200
Patrik Elias	58 games to 1,100
Marc-Andre Fleury	66 games to 500
Hal Gill	30 games to 1,100
Sergei Gonchar	52 points to 800
Roman Hamrlik	21 games to 1,400
Tomas Holmstrom	74 games to 1,100
Jarome Iginla	27 points to 1,100
Jaromir Jagr	12 assists to 1,000
Olli Jokinen	8 goals to 300
Tomas Kaberle	26 games to 1,000
Pavel Kubina	30 games to 1,000
Vincent Lecavalier	2 games to 1,000
Henrik Lundqvist	32 games to 500
Patrick Marleau	13 goals to 400
Ethan Moreau	72 games to 1,000
Brendan Morrison	66 games to 1,000
Brad Richards	18 points to 800
Brian Rolston	44 games to 1,300
Teemu Selanne	37 goals to 700
Ryan Smyth	26 goals to 400
Martin St. Louis	69 games to 1,000
Marco Sturm	62 games to 1,000
Steve Sullivan	31 games to 1,000
Alex Tanguay	3 assists to 500
Joe Thornton	22 points to 1,100
Kimmo Timonen	30 games to 1,000
Dainius Zubrus	35 games to 1,000

2012 PLAYOFF RESULTS

EASTERN CONFERENCE QUARTERFINALS

(1) New York Rangers vs. (8) Ottawa

April 12	Ottawa 2 at NY Rangers 4
April 14	Ottawa 3 at NY Rangers 2 (Neil 1:17 OT)
April 16	NY Rangers 1 at Ottawa 0 (Boyle 7:35 3rd) [Lundqvist]
April 18	NY Rangers 2 at Ottawa 3 (Turris 2:24 OT)
April 21	Ottawa 2 at NY Rangers 0 [Anderson]
April 23	NY Rangers 3 at Ottawa 2
April 26	Ottawa 1 at NY Rangers 2

NY Rangers wins best-of-seven 4–3

(2) Boston vs. (7) Washington

April 12	Washington 0 at Boston 1 (Kelly 1:18 OT) [Thomas]
April 14	Washington 2 at Boston 1 (Backstrom 22:56 OT)
April 16	Boston 4 at Washington 3
April 19	Boston 1 at Washington 2
April 21	Washington 4 at Boston 3
April 22	Boston 4 at Washington 3 (Seguin 3:17 OT)
April 25	Washington 2 at Boston 1 (Ward 2:57 OT)

Washington wins best-of-seven 4–3

(3) Florida vs. (6) New Jersey

April 13	New Jersey 3 at Florida 2
April 15	New Jersey 2 at Florida 4
April 17	Florida 4 at New Jersey 3
April 19	Florida 0 at New Jersey 4 [Brodeur]
April 21	New Jersey 0 at Florida 3 [Theodore]
April 24	Florida 2 at New Jersey 3 (Zajac 5:39 OT)
April 26	New Jersey 3 at Florida 2 (Henrique 23:47 OT)

New Jersey wins best-of-seven 4–3

(4) Pittsburgh vs. (5) Philadelphia

April 11	Philadelphia 4 at Pittsburgh 3 (Voracek 2:23 OT)
April 13	Philadelphia 8 at Pittsburgh 5
April 15	Pittsburgh 4 at Philadelphia 8
April 18	Pittsburgh 10 at Philadelphia 3
April 20	Philadelphia 2 at Pittsburgh 3
April 22	Pittsburgh 1 at Philadelphia 5

Philadelphia wins best-of-seven 4–2

WESTERN CONFERENCE QUARTERFINALS

(1) Vancouver vs. (8) Los Angeles
April 11	Los Angeles 4 at Vancouver 2
April 13	Los Angeles 4 at Vancouver 2
April 15	Vancouver 0 at Los Angeles 1 [Quick]
April 18	Vancouver 3 at Los Angeles 1
April 22	Los Angeles 2 at Vancouver 1 (Stoll 4:27 OT)

Los Angeles wins best-of-seven 4–1

(2) St. Louis vs. (7) San Jose
April 12	San Jose 3 at St. Louis 2 (Havlat 23:34 OT)
April 14	San Jose 0 at St. Louis 3 [Halak/Elliott]
April 16	St. Louis 4 at San Jose 3
April 19	St. Louis 2 at San Jose 1
April 21	San Jose 1 at St. Louis 3

St. Louis wins best-of-seven 4–1

(3) Phoenix vs. (6) Chicago
April 12	Chicago 2 at Phoenix 3 (Hanzal 9:29 OT)
April 14	Chicago 4 at Phoenix 3 (Bickell 10:36 OT)
April 17	Phoenix 2 at Chicago 1 (Boedker 13:15 OT)
April 19	Phoenix 3 at Chicago 2 (Boedker 2:15 OT)
April 21	Chicago 2 at Phoenix 1 (Toews 2:44 OT)
April 23	Phoenix 4 at Chicago 0 [Smith]

Phoenix wins best-of-seven 4–2

(4) Nashville vs. (5) Detroit
April 11	Detroit 2 at Nashville 3
April 13	Detroit 3 at Nashville 2
April 15	Nashville 3 at Detroit 2
April 17	Nashville 3 at Detroit 1
April 20	Detroit 1 at Nashville 2

Nashville wins best-of-seven 4–1

EASTERN CONFERENCE SEMIFINALS

(1) NY Rangers vs. (7) Washington

April 28	Washington 1 at NY Rangers 3
April 30	Washington 3 at NY Rangers 2
May 2	NY Rangers 2 at Washington 1 (Gaborik 54:41 OT)
May 5	NY Rangers 2 at Washington 3
May 7	Washington 2 at NY Rangers 3 (M. Staal 1:35 OT)
May 9	NY Rangers 1 at Washington 2
May 12	Washington 1 at NY Rangers 2

NY Rangers win best-of-seven 4–3

(5) Philadelphia vs. (6) New Jersey

April 29	New Jersey 3 at Philadelphia 4 (Briere 4:36 OT)
May 1	New Jersey 4 at Philadelphia 1
May 3	Philadelphia 3 at New Jersey 4 (Ponikarovsky 17:21 OT)
May 6	Philadelphia 2 at New Jersey 4
May 8	New Jersey 3 at Philadelphia 1

New Jersey wins best-of-seven 4–1

WESTERN CONFERENCE SEMIFINALS

2) St. Louis vs. (8) Los Angeles

April 28	Los Angeles 3 at St. Louis 1
April 30	Los Angeles 5 at St. Louis 2
May 3	St. Louis 2 at Los Angeles 4
May 6	St. Louis 1 at Los Angeles 3

Los Angeles wins best-of-seven 4–0

(3) Phoenix vs. (4) Nashville

April 27	Nashville 3 at Phoenix 4 (Whitney 14:04 OT)
April 29	Nashville 3 at Phoenix 5
May 2	Phoenix 0 at Nashville 2 [Rinne]
May 4	Phoenix 1 at Nashville 0 (Morris 11:34 3rd) [Smith]
May 7	Nashville 1 at Phoenix 2

Phoenix wins best-of-seven 4–1

EASTERN CONFERENCE FINALS

(1) NY Rangers vs. (6) New Jersey

May 14	New Jersey 0 at NY Rangers 3 [Lundqvist]
May 16	New Jersey 3 at NY Rangers 2
May 19	NY Rangers 3 at New Jersey 0 [Lundqvist]
May 21	NY Rangers 1 at New Jersey 4
May 23	New Jersey 5 at NY Rangers 3
May 25	NY Rangers 2 at New Jersey 3 (Henrique 1:03 OT)

New Jersey wins best-of-seven 4–2

WESTERN CONFERENCE FINALS

(3) Phoenix vs. (8) Los Angeles

May 13	Los Angeles 4 at Phoenix 2
May 15	Los Angeles 4 at Phoenix 0 [Quick]
May 17	Phoenix 1 at Los Angeles 2
May 20	Phoenix 2 at Los Angeles 0 [Smith]
May 22	Los Angeles 4 at Phoenix 3 (Penner 17:42 OT)

Los Angeles wins best-of-seven 4–1

STANLEY CUP FINALS

(6) New Jersey vs. (8) Los Angeles

May 30	Los Angeles 2 at New Jersey 1 (Kopitar 8:13 OT)
June 2	Los Angeles 2 at New Jersey 1 (Carter 13:42 OT)
June 4	New Jersey 0 at Los Angeles 4 [Quick]
June 6	New Jersey 3 at Los Angeles 1
June 9	Los Angeles 1 at New Jersey 2
June 11	New Jersey 1 at Los Angeles 6

Los Angeles wins best-of-seven 4–2

PLAYER STATISTICS BY TEAM, 2012 PLAYOFFS

BOSTON BRUINS

	GP	G	A	P	Pim
Rich Peverley	7	3	2	5	4
Andrew Ference	7	1	3	4	0
Tyler Seguin	7	2	1	3	0
Johnny Boychuk	7	1	2	3	4
Zdeno Chara	7	1	2	3	8
Chris Kelly	7	1	2	3	4
David Krejci	7	1	2	3	4
Brian Rolston	7	1	2	3	0
Dennis Seidenberg	7	1	2	3	2
Milan Lucic	7	0	3	3	8
Brad Marchand	7	1	1	2	2
Benoit Pouliot	7	1	1	2	6
Patrice Bergeron	7	0	2	2	8
Gregory Campbell	7	0	2	2	0
Daniel Paille	7	1	0	1	2
Greg Zanon	7	0	1	1	0
Jordan Caron	2	0	0	0	0
Mike Mottau	2	0	0	0	0
Joe Corvo	5	0	0	0	0
Shawn Thornton	5	0	0	0	0
Tim Thomas	7	0	0	0	0

In Goal	GP	W-L	`Mins	GA	SO	GAA
Tim Thomas	7	3–4	448:03	16	1	2.14

CHICAGO BLACKHAWKS

	GP	G	A	P	Pim
Jonathan Toews	6	2	2	4	6
Patrick Kane	6	0	4	4	10
Michael Frolik	4	2	1	3	0
Nick Leddy	6	1	2	3	0
Brent Seabrook	6	1	2	3	0
Dave Bolland	6	0	3	3	2
Johnny Oduya	6	0	3	3	0
Bryan Bickell	6	2	0	2	4
Viktor Stalberg	6	0	2	2	8
Brendan Morrison	3	1	0	1	0
Brandon Bollig	4	1	0	1	19

Andrew Brunette	6	1	0	1	0
Patrick Sharp	6	1	0	1	4
Brandon Saad	2	0	1	1	0
Niklas Hjalmarsson	6	0	1	1	4
Duncan Keith	6	0	1	1	2
Dylan Olsen	1	0	0	0	0
Jimmy Hayes	2	0	0	0	15
Sean O'Donnell	2	0	0	0	0
Marian Hossa	3	0	0	0	0
Sami Lepisto	3	0	0	0	0
Jamal Myers	3	0	0	0	0
Andrew Shaw	3	0	0	0	15
Corey Crawford	6	0	0	0	0
Marcus Kruger	6	0	0	0	0

In Goal	**GP**	**W-L**	**Mins**	**GA**	**SO**	**GAA**
Corey Crawford	6	2–4	395:32	17	0	2.58

DETROIT RED WINGS

	GP	**G**	**A**	**P**	**Pim**
Henrik Zetterberg	5	2	1	3	4
Pavel Datsyuk	5	1	2	3	2
Jiri Hudler	5	2	0	2	4
Tomas Holmstrom	5	1	1	2	2
Valtteri Filppula	5	0	2	2	2
Niklas Kronwall	5	0	2	2	4
Kyle Quincey	5	0	2	2	6
Cory Emmerton	5	1	0	1	2
Johan Franzen	5	1	0	1	8
Ian White	5	1	0	1	0
Drew Miller	5	0	1	1	2
Brad Stuart	5	0	1	1	0
Darren Helm	1	0	0	0	0
Gustav Nyquist	4	0	0	0	0
Justin Abdelkader	5	0	0	0	2
Todd Bertuzzi	5	0	0	0	9
Daniel Cleary	5	0	0	0	2
Jonathan Ericsson	5	0	0	0	6
Jimmy Howard	5	0	0	0	0
Nicklas Lidstrom	5	0	0	0	0

In Goal	**GP**	**W-L**	**Mins**	**GA**	**SO**	**GAA**
Jimmy Howard	5	1–4	295:23	13	0	2.64

FLORIDA PANTHERS

	GP	G	A	P	Pim
Sean Bergenheim	7	3	3	6	4
Kris Versteeg	7	3	2	5	8
Stephen Weiss	7	3	2	5	6
Marcel Goc	7	2	3	5	0
Brian Campbell	7	1	4	5	2
Mikael Samuelsson	7	0	5	5	2
Jason Garrison	4	1	2	3	0
Tomas Fleischmann	7	1	2	3	2
Scottie Upshall	7	1	2	3	4
Tomas Kopecky	7	1	0	1	4
Mike Weaver	7	1	0	1	0
Tyson Strachan	2	0	1	1	0
Scott Clemmensen	3	0	1	1	0
Jerred Smithson	5	0	1	1	2
Dmitri Kulikov	7	0	1	1	4
Shawn Matthias	7	0	1	1	6
Keaton Ellerby	1	0	0	0	2
Wojtek Wolski	2	0	0	0	4
Jose Theodore	5	0	0	0	0
Erik Gudbranson	7	0	0	0	8
Ed Jovanovski	7	0	0	0	4
John Madden	7	0	0	0	0
Marco Sturm	7	0	0	0	4

In Goal	GP	W-L	Mins	GA	SO	GAA
Jose Theodore	5	2–2	268:24	11	1	2.46
Scott Clemmensen	3	1–2	179:23	7	0	2.35

LOS ANGELES KINGS

	GP	G	A	P	Pim
Dustin Brown	20	8	12	20	34
Anze Kopitar	20	8	12	20	9
Drew Doughty	20	4	12	16	14
Mike Richards	20	4	11	15	17
Justin Williams	20	4	11	15	12
Jeff Carter	20	8	5	13	4
Dustin Penner	20	3	8	11	32
Trevor Lewis	20	3	6	9	2
Dwight King	20	5	3	8	13
Matt Greene	20	2	4	6	12

Jarret Stoll	20	2	3	5	18
Alec Martinez	20	1	2	3	8
Willie Mitchell	20	1	2	3	16
Slava Voynov	20	1	2	3	4
Colin Fraser	18	1	1	2	4
Jordan Nolan	20	1	1	2	21
Brad Richardson	13	1	0	1	4
Rob Scuderi	20	0	1	1	4
Andrei Loktionov	2	0	0	0	0
Kyle Clifford	3	0	0	0	2
Simon Gagne	4	0	0	0	2
Jonathan Quick	20	0	0	0	0

In Goal	GP	W-L	Mins	GA	SO	GAA
Jonathan Quick	20	16–4	1,238:12	29	3	1.41

NASHVILLE PREDATORS

	GP	G	A	P	Pim
David Legwand	10	3	3	6	10
Alexander Radulov	8	1	5	6	4
Gabriel Bourque	10	3	2	5	4
Andrei Kostitsyn	8	3	1	4	2
Kevin Klein	10	2	2	4	2
Martin Erat	10	1	3	4	6
Mike Fisher	10	1	3	4	8
Patric Hornqvist	10	1	3	4	2
Ryan Suter	10	1	3	4	4
Shea Weber	10	2	1	3	9
Francis Bouillon	10	0	3	3	2
Nick Spaling	10	0	3	3	0
Brandon Yip	10	1	1	2	6
Paul Gaustad	10	1	1	2	5
Sergei Kostitsyn	10	1	1	2	4
Colin Wilson	4	1	0	1	0
Craig Smith	2	0	1	1	0
Matt Halischuk	5	0	1	1	4
Jack Hillen	2	0	0	0	2
Ryan Ellis	3	0	0	0	0
Jordin Tootoo	3	0	0	0	4
Hal Gill	5	0	0	0	0
Roman Josi	10	0	0	0	10
Pekka Rinne	10	0	0	0	2

In Goal	GP	W-L	Mins	GA	SO	GAA
Pekka Rinne	10	5–5	609:14	21	1	2.07

NEW JERSEY DEVILS

	GP	G	A	P	Pim
Ilya Kovalchuk	23	8	11	19	6
Zach Parise	24	8	7	15	4
Travis Zajac	24	7	7	14	4
Bryce Salvador	24	4	10	14	26
Adam Henrique	24	5	8	13	11
David Clarkson	24	3	9	12	32
Dainius Zubrus	24	3	7	10	18
Alexei Ponikarovsky	24	1	8	9	12
Marek Zidlicky	24	1	8	9	22
Patrik Elias	24	5	3	8	10
Ryan Carter	23	5	2	7	32
Stephen Gionta	24	3	4	7	4
Steve Bernier	24	2	5	7	27
Petr Sykora	18	2	3	5	6
Peter Harrold	17	0	4	4	6
Martin Brodeur	24	0	4	4	0
Mark Fayne	24	0	3	3	6
Anton Volchenkov	24	1	1	2	10
Adam Larsson	5	1	0	1	4
Jacob Josefson	6	0	1	1	0
Andy Greene	24	0	1	1	8
Johan Hedberg	1	0	0	0	0
Tim Sestito	1	0	0	0	0
Henrik Tallinder	3	0	0	0	0

In Goal	GP	W-L	Mins	GA	SO	GAA
Martin Brodeur	24	14–9	1,470:54	52	1	2.12
Johan Hedberg	1	0–1	36:20	1	0	1.67

NEW YORK RANGERS

	GP	G	A	P	Pim
Brad Richards	20	6	9	15	8
Dan Girardi	20	3	9	12	2
Marian Gaborik	20	5	6	11	2
Ryan Callahan	20	6	4	10	12
Artem Anisimov	20	3	7	10	4
Michael Del Zotto	20	2	8	10	12

Derek Stepan	20	1	8	9	4
Chris Kreider	18	5	2	7	6
Ruslan Fedotenko	20	2	5	7	8
Brian Boyle	17	3	3	6	15
Marc Staal	20	3	3	6	12
Anton Stralman	20	3	3	6	4
Ryan McDonagh	20	0	4	4	11
Carl Hagelin	17	0	3	3	17
Brandon Prust	19	1	1	2	31
Brandon Dubinsky	9	0	2	2	14
John Mitchell	18	0	1	1	2
Steve Eminger	4	0	0	0	0
Stu Bickel	18	0	0	0	16
Henrik Lundqvist	20	0	0	0	0
Mike Rupp	20	0	0	0	36

In Goal	**GP**	**W-L**	**Mins**	**GA**	**SO**	**GAA**
Henrik Lundqvist	20	10–10	1,250:49	38	3	1.82

OTTAWA SENATORS

	GP	**G**	**A**	**P**	**Pim**
Jason Spezza	7	3	2	5	8
Nick Foligno	7	1	3	4	8
Sergei Gonchar	7	1	3	4	6
Chris Neil	7	2	1	3	22
Kyle Turris	7	1	2	3	2
Daniel Alfredsson	4	2	0	2	0
Milan Michalek	7	1	1	2	4
Zenon Konopka	6	0	2	2	2
Filip Kuba	7	0	2	2	10
Erik Condra	7	1	0	1	0
Erik Karlsson	7	1	0	1	4
Mark Stone	1	0	1	1	0
Matt Carkner	4	0	1	1	21
Jared Cowen	7	0	1	1	4
Colin Greening	7	0	1	1	0
Jim O'Brien	7	0	1	1	0
Chris Phillips	7	0	1	1	4
Zack Smith	7	0	1	1	10
Kaspars Daugavins	1	0	0	0	0
Jakob Silfverberg	2	0	0	0	2
Bobby Butler	3	0	0	0	0

Matt Gilroy	3	0	0	0	0
Jesse Winchester	4	0	0	0	0
Craig Anderson	7	0	0	0	0

In Goal	**GP**	**W-L**	**Mins**	**GA**	**SO**	**GAA**
Craig Anderson	7	3–4	418:52	14	1	2.00

PHILADELPHIA FLYERS

	GP	**G**	**A**	**P**	**Pim**
Claude Giroux	10	8	9	17	13
Daniel Briere	11	8	5	13	4
Jakub Voracek	11	2	8	10	8
Brayden Schenn	11	3	6	9	8
Scott Hartnell	11	3	5	8	15
Jaromir Jagr	11	1	7	8	2
Maxime Talbot	11	4	2	6	10
Matt Carle	11	2	4	6	6
Wayne Simmonds	11	1	5	6	38
Matt Read	11	3	2	5	4
Sean Couturier	11	3	1	4	2
Kimmo Timonen	11	1	3	4	23
Braydon Coburn	11	0	4	4	8
Erik Gustafsson	7	1	1	2	2
James van Riemsdyk	7	1	1	2	4
Pavel Kubina	5	0	1	1	12
Nicklas Grossmann	9	0	1	1	8
Sergei Bobrovsky	1	0	0	0	0
Marc-Andre Bourdon	1	0	0	0	0
Andrej Meszaros	1	0	0	0	0
Zac Rinaldo	5	0	0	0	48
Andreas Lilja	10	0	0	0	6
Eric Wellwood	11	0	0	0	2
Ilya Bryzgalov	11	0	0	0	0

In Goal	**GP**	**W-L**	**Mins**	**GA**	**SO**	**GAA**
Ilya Bryzgalov	11	5–6	641:48	37	0	3.46
Sergei Bobrovsky	1	0–0	36:53	5	0	8.11

PHOENIX COYOTES

	GP	**G**	**A**	**P**	**Pim**
Antoine Vermette	16	5	5	10	24
Shane Doan	16	5	4	9	41
Keith Yandle	16	1	8	9	10

	GP	G	A	P	Pim
Mikkel Boedker	16	4	4	8	0
Rostislav Klesla	15	2	6	8	4
Ray Whitney	16	2	5	7	10
Daymond Langkow	16	1	6	7	4
Taylor Pyatt	16	4	2	6	2
Martin Hanzal	12	3	3	6	29
Derek Morris	16	2	4	6	24
Radim Vrbata	16	2	3	5	8
Kyle Chipchura	15	1	3	4	7
Oliver Ekman-Larsson	16	1	3	4	8
Gilbert Brule	12	2	1	3	0
Raffi Torres	3	1	1	2	2
Marc-Antoine Pouliot	8	1	1	2	2
Adrian Aucoin	11	0	2	2	10
Boyd Gordon	16	0	2	2	6
Mike Smith	16	0	1	1	14
Michael Stone	2	0	0	0	0
Paul Bissonnette	3	0	0	0	15
David Schlemko	5	0	0	0	0
Lauri Korpikoski	11	0	0	0	2
Michal Rozsival	15	0	0	0	2

In Goal	**GP**	**W-L**	**Mins**	**GA**	**SO**	**GAA**
Mike Smith	16	9–7	1,026:49	34	3	1.99

PITTSBURGH PENGUINS

	GP	G	A	P	Pim
Jordan Staal	6	6	3	9	2
Sidney Crosby	6	3	5	8	9
Evgeni Malkin	6	3	5	8	6
Tyler Kennedy	6	3	3	6	2
James Neal	5	2	4	6	12
Chris Kunitz	6	2	4	6	8
Steve Sullivan	6	2	4	6	4
Pascal Dupuis	6	2	4	6	0
Kris Letang	6	1	4	5	21
Matt Cooke	6	0	4	4	16
Matt Niskanen	4	1	2	3	6
Paul Martin	3	1	0	1	0
Richard Park	2	0	1	1	2
Eric Tangradi	2	0	1	1	0
Deryk Engelland	6	0	1	1	14

	GP	G	A	P	Pim
Marc-Andre Fleury	6	0	1	1	0
Zbynek Michalek	6	0	1	1	0
Brent Johnson	1	0	0	0	0
Ben Lovejoy	2	0	0	0	0
Arron Asham	3	0	0	0	10
Simon Despres	3	0	0	0	2
Brian Strait	3	0	0	0	0
Joe Vitale	4	0	0	0	12
Craig Adams	5	0	0	0	19
Brooks Orpik	6	0	0	0	4

In Goal	**GP**	**W-L**	**Mins**	**GA**	**SO**	**GAA**
Marc-Andre Fleury	6	2–4	337:08	26	0	4.63
Brent Johnson	1	0–0	20:00	2	0	6.00

SAN JOSE SHARKS

	GP	G	A	P	Pim
Joe Thornton	5	2	3	5	2
Logan Couture	5	1	3	4	0
Martin Havlat	5	2	1	3	8
Ryane Clowe	5	0	3	3	0
Brent Burns	5	1	1	2	4
Dan Boyle	5	0	2	2	4
Colin White	3	1	0	1	0
Andrew Desjardins	5	1	0	1	2
Torrey Mitchell	5	0	1	1	6
Tommy Wingels	5	0	1	1	7
Daniel Winnik	5	0	1	1	6
Brad Winchester	1	0	0	0	0
Michal Handzus	2	0	0	0	0
Jason Demers	3	0	0	0	2
T.J. Galiardi	3	0	0	0	6
Dominic Moore	3	0	0	0	5
Justin Braun	5	0	0	0	15
Patrick Marleau	5	0	0	0	4
Douglas Murray	5	0	0	0	19
Antti Niemi	5	0	0	0	0
Joe Pavelski	5	0	0	0	5
Marc-Eduard Vlasic	5	0	0	0	2

In Goal	**GP**	**W-L**	**Mins**	**GA**	**SO**	**GAA**
Antti Niemi	5	1–4	318:03	13	0	2.45

ST. LOUIS BLUES

	GP	G	A	P	Pim
Andy McDonald	9	5	5	10	8
Patrik Berglund	9	3	4	7	6
David Perron	9	1	4	5	10
Alex Pietrangelo	8	0	5	5	0
David Backes	9	2	2	4	18
Alexander Steen	9	1	2	3	6
Carlo Colaiacovo	7	0	3	3	16
T.J. Oshie	9	0	3	3	6
Kris Russell	9	0	3	3	5
Chris Stewart	7	2	0	2	12
Kevin Shattenkirk	9	1	1	2	6
Vladimir Sobotka	9	1	1	2	15
Matt D'Agostini	4	1	0	1	4
Jason Arnott	7	1	0	1	0
B.J. Crombeen	7	1	0	1	31
Jamie Langenbrunner	9	1	0	1	11
Barret Jackman	9	0	1	1	21
Scot Nichol	9	0	1	1	14
Jake Allen	1	0	0	0	0
Kent Huskins	1	0	0	0	2
Ian Cole	2	0	0	0	0
Jaroslav Halak	2	0	0	0	0
Ryan Reaves	2	0	0	0	0
Brian Elliott	8	0	0	0	2
Roman Polak	9	0	0	0	19

In Goal	GP	W-L	Mins	GA	SO	GAA
Brian Elliott	8	3–4	454:43	18	0	2.37
Jaroslav Halak	2	1–1	104:23	3	0	1.73
Jake Allen	1	0–0	1:07	0	0	0.00

VANCOUVER CANUCKS

	GP	G	A	P	Pim
Henrik Sedin	5	2	3	5	4
Dan Hamhuis	5	0	3	3	6
Ryan Kesler	5	0	3	3	6
Alexander Edler	5	2	0	2	8
Daniel Sedin	2	0	2	2	0
Kevin Bieksa	5	1	0	1	6
Alexandre Burrows	5	1	0	1	7

	GP	G	A	P	Pim
Jannik Hansen	5	1	0	1	14
Samuel Pahlsson	5	1	0	1	4
Keith Ballard	4	0	1	1	2
David Booth	5	0	1	1	0
Mason Raymond	5	0	1	1	0
Maxim Lapierre	5	0	1	1	16
Byron Bitz	1	0	0	0	0
Andrew Ebbett	1	0	0	0	0
Aaron Rome	1	0	0	0	0
Roberto Luongo	2	0	0	0	0
Dale Weise	2	0	0	0	0
Cory Schneider	3	0	0	0	0
Zack Kassian	4	0	0	0	2
Chris Higgins	5	0	0	0	2
Manny Malhotra	5	0	0	0	0
Sami Salo	5	0	0	0	2
Christopher Tanev	5	0	0	0	0

In Goal	GP	W-L	Mins	GA	SO	GAA
Cory Schneider	3	1–2	182:50	4	0	1.31
Roberto Luongo	2	0–2	117:05	7	0	3.59

WASHINGTON CAPITALS

	GP	G	A	P	Pim
Alexander Ovechkin	14	5	4	9	8
Nicklas Backstrom	13	2	6	8	18
Jason Chimera	14	4	3	7	6
Brooks Laich	14	2	5	7	6
John Carlson	14	2	3	5	8
Joel Ward	14	1	4	5	6
Alexander Semin	14	3	1	4	10
Troy Brouwer	14	2	2	4	8
Mike Green	14	2	2	4	10
Roman Hamrlik	14	1	3	4	12
Mike Knuble	11	2	1	3	6
Marcus Johansson	14	1	2	3	0
Dennis Wideman	14	0	3	3	2
Jay Beagle	12	1	1	2	4
Matt Hendricks	14	1	1	2	6
Karl Alzner	14	0	2	2	0
Keith Aucoin	14	0	2	2	2
John Erskine	4	0	1	1	0

Jeff Halpern	2	0	0	0	4
Mathieu Perreault	4	0	0	0	0
Jeff Schultz	10	0	0	0	2
Braden Holtby	14	0	0	0	2

In Goal	**GP**	**W-L**	**Mins**	**GA**	**SO**	**GAA**
Braden Holtby	14	7–7	921:56	30	0	1.95

ALL REGULAR-SEASON SCORES, 2011–12

OCTOBER 6, 2011

Philadelphia 2 at Boston 1 (all goals in 1st)
Montreal 0 at Toronto 2 [Reimer]
Pittsburgh 4 at Vancouver 3 (SO)

OCTOBER 8, 2011

NY Rangers 1 vs. Anaheim 2 (at Stockholm, Sweden) (SO)
Buffalo 4 vs. Los Angeles 2 (at Berlin, Germany)
Tampa Bay 1 at Boston 4 (game tied 1–1 early in 2nd)
Ottawa 5 at Toronto 6 (Kessel (TOR) hat trick)
Philadelphia 3 at New Jersey 0 [Bryzgalov]
Carolina 3 at Washington 4 (Green 2:24 OT)
Florida 2 at NY Islanders 0 [Theodore]
Nashville 4 at St. Louis 2 (game tied 2–2 midway through 3rd)
Columbus 2 at Minnesota 4 (Wild led 3–0 midway through game)
Dallas 2 at Chicago 5 (Bolland (CHI) two goals)
Detroit 3 at Colorado 0 [Conklin]
Pittsburgh 5 at Calgary 3 (eight different scorers)
Phoenix 3 at San Jose 6 (Sharks led 4–0 midway through game)

OCTOBER 9, 2011

Montreal 5 at Winnipeg 1 (first game in Winnipeg since 1995)
Pittsburgh 1 at Edmonton 2 (SO)

OCTOBER 10, 2011

Colorado 1 at Boston 0 (Hejduk 7:57 3rd) [Varlamov]
Carolina 2 at New Jersey 4 (Devils scored only two goals of 3rd)
Minnesota 1 at NY Islanders 2 (Isles led 2–0 after 1st & 2nd)
Calgary 2 at St. Louis 5 (game tied 1–1 after 1st)
Tampa Bay 5 at Washington 6 (SO)
Vancouver 3 at Columbus 2 (Jackets led 2–1 after 2nd)
Phoenix 1 at Dallas 2 (SO)

OCTOBER 11, 2011

Florida 2 at Pittsburgh 4 (Pens led 2–0 midway through game)
Minnesota 3 at Ottawa 4 (SO)

OCTOBER 12, 2011

Colorado 3 at Columbus 2 (SO)
Vancouver 4 at Philadelphia 5 (nine different scorers)
Boston 2 at Carolina 3 ('Canes led 2–0 early in 3rd)

OCTOBER 13, 2011

Los Angeles 1 at New Jersey 2 (SO)
Tampa Bay 1 at NY Islanders 5 (game tied 1–1 early in 1st)
Washington 3 at Pittsburgh 2 (Wideman 2:48 OT)
Calgary 4 at Montreal 1 (Habs scored first)
Colorado 7 at Ottawa 1 (Lindstrom (COL) two goals)
Vancouver 0 at Detroit 2 [Howard]
Phoenix 5 at Nashville 2 (Coyotes led 4–0 midway through game)
Edmonton 1 at Minnesota 2 (SO)
Winnipeg 3 at Chicago 4 (game tied 2–2 after 1st)
St. Louis 2 at Dallas 3 (Stars led 3–0 midway through game)

OCTOBER 14, 2011

Carolina 4 at Buffalo 3 (Sabres led 1–0 & 2–1)
San Jose 0 at Anaheim 1 (Macenauer 13:59 1st) [Hiller]

OCTOBER 15, 2011

Calgary 2 at Toronto 3 (Kessel (TOR) two goals)
Colorado 6 at Montreal 5 (SO)
NY Rangers 2 at NY Islanders 4 (game tied 2–2 after 2nd)
Los Angeles 3 at Philadelphia 2 (J. Johnson 1:39 OT)
Buffalo 3 at Pittsburgh 2 (Sabres led 2–0 after 1st)
Ottawa 1 at Washington 2 (all goals in 1st)
Winnipeg 1 at Phoenix 4 (first-ever game between old Winnipeg team and new)
Tampa Bay 2 at Florida 3 (SO)
New Jersey 3 at Nashville 2 (SO)
Detroit 3 at Minnesota 2 (Franzen 4:11 OT)
Columbus 2 at Dallas 4 (Jackets led 1–0 & 2–1)
Boston 3 at Chicago 2 (SO)

Vancouver 4 at Edmonton 3 (Oilers led 2–1 & 3–2)
St. Louis 4 at San Jose 2 (game tied 2–2 midway through 3rd)

OCTOBER 16, 2011

St. Louis 2 at Anaheim 4 (game tied 1–1 early in 2nd)

OCTOBER 17, 2011

Colorado 3 at Toronto 2 (D. Jones 1:11 OT)
Florida 7 at Tampa Bay 4 (Lightning led 2–1 late in 1st)
Pittsburgh 1 at Winnipeg 2 (no scoring in 3rd)
Nashville 1 at Edmonton 3 (Oilers had only three goals of 3rd)
Anaheim 3 at San Jose 2 (Selanne (ANA) two goals)

OCTOBER 18, 2011

Carolina 4 at Boston 1 ('Canes led 2–0 after 2nd)
Florida 0 at Washington 3 [Vokoun]
Dallas 3 at Columbus 2 (Stars led 2–0 early in 3rd)
Buffalo 3 at Montreal 1 (Habs led 1–0 midway through game)
Philadelphia 7 at Ottawa 2 (nine different scorers)
Pittsburgh 4 at Minnesota 2 (no scoring in 1st)
Edmonton 1 at Calgary 2 (Oilers led 1–0 after 1st & 2nd)
NY Rangers 4 at Vancouver 0 [Lundqvist]
Chicago 5 at Phoenix 2 (game tied 2–2 early in 2nd)
St. Louis 0 at Los Angeles 5 [Quick]

OCTOBER 19, 2011

Winnipeg 3 at Toronto 4 (SO)

OCTOBER 20, 2011

Toronto 2 at Boston 6 (Leafs scored first and last goals of game)
Washington 5 at Philadelphia 2 (Ovechkin (WAS) two goals)
Montreal 1 at Pittsburgh 3 (Habs scored late in 3rd)
Winnipeg 1 at Ottawa 4 (Jets led 1–0 early in 2nd)
NY Islanders 1 at Tampa Bay 4 (Lightning scored in each period)
Buffalo 3 at Florida 0 [Miller]
Chicago 3 at Colorado 1 (game tied 1–1 early in 3rd)
NY Rangers 3 at Calgary 2 (McDonagh 4:58 OT)

Minnesota 2 at Edmonton 1 (SO)
Nashville 1 at Vancouver 5 (both Sedin twins scored for VAN)
Los Angeles 2 at Phoenix 0 [Quick]

OCTOBER 21, 2011

San Jose 4 at New Jersey 3 (SO)
Columbus 2 at Detroit 5 (Franzen (DET) two goals)
Carolina 2 at St. Louis 3 (D'Agostini 3:58 OT)
Dallas 3 at Anaheim 1 (Stars led 2–0 after 1st)

OCTOBER 22, 2011

Nashville 2 at Calgary 0 [Rinne]
Minnesota 2 at Vancouver 3 (Salo 4:39 OT)
San Jose 4 at Boston 2 (game tied 2–2 midway through 3rd)
Toronto 5 at Montreal 4 (Grabovski 1:23 OT)
Columbus 3 at Ottawa 4 (M. Michalek broke 3–3 tie at 19:55 of 3rd)
St. Louis 4 at Philadelphia 2 (Blues led 2–0 after 1st)
New Jersey 1 at Pittsburgh 4 (game tied 1–1 early in 3rd)
Detroit 1 at Washington 7 (Green & Perreault (WAS) two goals)
Carolina 3 at Winnipeg 5 ('Canes led 2–0 early in 1st)
Buffalo 0 at Tampa Bay 3 [Garon]
NY Islanders 2 at Florida 4 (Panthers scored only two goals of 3rd)
Colorado 5 at Chicago 4 (SO)
NY Rangers 0 at Edmonton 2 [Khabibulin]
Dallas 0 at Los Angeles 1 (J. Johnson 15:02 3rd) [Quick]

OCTOBER 23, 2011

Phoenix 5 at Anaheim 4 (game tied 2–2 early in 2nd)

OCTOBER 24, 2011

Toronto 2 at Philadelphia 4 (Leafs led 1–0 early in 1st)
Florida 2 at Montreal 1 (game tied 1–1 after 1st & 2nd)
NY Rangers 2 at Winnipeg 1 (Rangers scored only goal of 3rd)

OCTOBER 25, 2011

Tampa Bay 4 at Buffalo 3 (Sabres led 2–0 early in 1st)
Pittsburgh 3 at NY Islanders 0 [Fleury]

Ottawa 3 at Carolina 2 (SO)
Detroit 1 at Columbus 4 (game tied 1–1 early in 1st)
San Jose 3 at Nashville 1 (Pavelski scored two goals to break 1–1 tie in 3rd)
Anaheim 2 at Chicago 3 (SO)
Vancouver 2 at Edmonton 3 (Oilers scored all goals early in 2nd)
Dallas 3 at Phoenix 2 (SO)
New Jersey 3 at Los Angeles 0 [Hedberg]

OCTOBER 26, 2011

Philadelphia 1 at Montreal 5 (game tied 1–1 midway through 2nd)
Colorado 2 at Calgary 4 (game tied 1–1 after 1st)
St. Louis 3 at Vancouver 0 [Elliott]

OCTOBER 27, 2011

Montreal 2 at Boston 1 (Bruins led 1–0 midway through game)
Columbus 2 at Buffalo 4 (game tied 2–2 midway through 3rd)
Toronto 4 at NY Rangers 2 (Leafs scored four in a row)
Winnipeg 9 at Philadelphia 8 (Jets led 5–1 & 6–2, trailed 7–6; Ladd broke 8–8 tie at 18:54 of 3rd)
NY Islanders 2 at Pittsburgh 3 (SO)
Florida 3 at Ottawa 4 (Foligno broke 3–3 tie at 19:56 of 3rd)
Tampa Bay 3 at Nashville 5 (Stamkos (TB) two goals)
Anaheim 3 at Minnesota 2 (Ducks led 2–0 midway through game)
Los Angeles 5 at Dallas 3 (game tied 3–3 midway through 3rd)
Washington 1 at Edmonton 2 (no scoring last 27 minutes of game)
New Jersey 3 at Phoenix 5 (Ray Whitney (PHO) two goals)

OCTOBER 28, 2011

Chicago 0 at Carolina 3 [Ward]
San Jose 4 at Detroit 2 (game tied 2–2 late in 2nd)
Edmonton 3 at Colorado 1 (no scoring in 1st)
St. Louis 1 at Calgary 3 (no scoring first 34 minutes of game)

OCTOBER 29, 2011

Ottawa 5 at NY Rangers 4 (SO)
Florida 3 at Buffalo 2 (Garrison broke 2–2 tie at 18:17 of 3rd)
Pittsburgh 3 at Toronto 4 (Leafs led 1–0, 2–1, 3–2)
Boston 2 at Montreal 4 (Habs led 3–0 midway through game)

San Jose 3 at NY Islanders 2 (Burns 1:07 OT)
Carolina 1 at Philadelphia 5 (Flyers scored only four goals of 3rd)
Winnipeg 0 at Tampa Bay 1 (Lecavalier 19:20 2nd) [Roloson]
Anaheim 0 at Nashville 3 [Rinne]
Detroit 0 at Minnesota 1 (Heatley 10:51 1st) [Harding]
New Jersey 1 at Dallas 3 (game tied 1–1 midway through 3rd)
Columbus 2 at Chicago 5 (Stalberg (CHI) two goals)
Los Angeles 2 at Phoenix 3 (Langkow 4:16 OT)
Washington 4 at Vancouver 7 (four players had two goals)

OCTOBER 30, 2011

Anaheim 1 at Columbus 3 (no scoring in 3rd)
Toronto 2 at Ottawa 3 (Leafs led 1–0 midway through 1st)
Los Angeles 2 at Colorado 3 (Avs scored only goal of 3rd)
St. Louis 2 at Edmonton 4 (Oilers scored three goals in 2nd)

OCTOBER 31, 2011

San Jose 2 at NY Rangers 5 (game tied 2–2 midway through 2nd)
Winnipeg 4 at Florida 3 (SO)
Nashville 4 at Chicago 5 (Stalberg 2:18 OT)

NOVEMBER 1, 2011

Ottawa 3 at Boston 5 (game tied 3–3 early in 3rd)
Anaheim 4 at Washington 5 (Backstrom 2:18 OT)
Tampa Bay 2 at Carolina 4 (Skinner (CAR) two goals)
Minnesota 2 at Detroit 1 (Setoguchi 1:33 OT)
Vancouver 5 at Calgary 1 (Flames scored only goal of 3rd)

NOVEMBER 2, 2011

Philadelphia 3 at Buffalo 2 (Flyers led 3–0 after 1st)
Toronto 5 at New Jersey 3 (no scoring in 3rd)
Phoenix 4 at Colorado 1 (Coyotes led 2–1 after 2nd)

NOVEMBER 3, 2011

Winnipeg 3 at NY Islanders 0 [Pavelec]
Anaheim 1 at NY Rangers 2 (SO)
New Jersey 4 at Philadelphia 3 (SO)

Toronto 4 at Columbus 1 (MacArthur two goals)
Chicago 3 at Florida 2 (SO)
Calgary 4 at Detroit 1 (Flames scored in each period)
Vancouver 1 at Minnesota 5 (Matt Cullen only two goals of 3rd)
Nashville 3 at Phoenix 0 [Rinne]
Edmonton 3 at Los Angeles 0 [Khabibulin]
Pittsburgh 3 at San Jose 4 (SO)

NOVEMBER 4, 2011

Washington 5 at Carolina 1 ('Canes led 1–0 after 1st)
Calgary 1 at Buffalo 2 (Sabres led 1–0 after 1st & 2nd)
Montreal 2 at Ottawa 1 (no scoring in 1st)
Chicago 4 at Tampa Bay 5 (Lecavalier 4:06 OT)
Vancouver 2 at St. Louis 3 (game tied 2–2 early in 3rd)
Colorado 6 at Dallas 7 (Eriksson 3:55 OT)

]NOVEMBER 5, 2011

Boston 7 at Toronto 0 [Thomas]
Buffalo 3 at Ottawa 2 (SO)
Winnipeg 2 at New Jersey 3 (Henrique 1:28 OT)
Washington 3 at NY Islanders 5 (eight different scorers)
Montreal 3 at NY Rangers 5 (Rangers led 3–0 after 1st)
Columbus 2 at Philadelphia 9 (Flyers led 8–0 after 2nd)
Anaheim 0 at Detroit 5 [Howard]
St. Louis 1 at Minnesota 2 (no scoring in first half of game)
Edmonton 2 at Phoenix 4 (Coyotes led 2–0 after 2nd)
Pittsburgh 3 at Los Angeles 2 (SO)
Nashville 4 at San Jose 3 (Legwand 2:53 OT)

NOVEMBER 6, 2011

Dallas 5 at Carolina 2 (Benn (DAL) two goals)
Tampa Bay 4 at Florida 3 (SO)
Winnipeg 0 at NY Rangers 3 [Biron]
Vancouver 6 at Chicago 2 (game tied 1–1 after 1st)
Calgary 2 at Colorado 1 (no scoring final 34 minutes)

NOVEMBER 7, 2011

NY Islanders 2 at Boston 6 (game tied 1–1 early in 1st)
Los Angeles 2 at San Jose 4 (Kings scored first goal)

NOVEMBER 8, 2011

Winnipeg 5 at Buffalo 6 (Vanek 4:35 OT)
Florida 5 at Toronto 1 (Panthers led 4–0 early in 3rd)
Carolina 2 at New Jersey 3 (Henrique broke 2–2 tie with late goal)
Dallas 5 at Washington 2 (Ryder (DAL) two goals in 1st)
Edmonton 3 at Montreal 1 (no scoring in 1st)
Colorado 2 at Detroit 5 (Franzen hat trick)
Chicago 0 at St. Louis 3 [Halak]
Minnesota 3 at Calgary 0 [Backstrom]
Nashville 3 at Los Angeles 4 (Kings scored only two goals of 2nd)

NOVEMBER 9, 2011

NY Rangers 3 at Ottawa 2 (Sens led 1–0 midway through game)
Philadelphia 1 at Tampa Bay 2 (Connolly 2:30 OT)
Nashville 4 at Anaheim 2 (Craig Smith (NAS) two goals)

NOVEMBER 10, 2011

Edmonton 3 at Boston 6 (game tied 2–2 after 1st)
Chicago 6 at Columbus 3 (Toews (CHI) two goals in 1st)
Toronto 3 at St. Louis 2 (SO)
Florida 5 at Winnipeg 2 (Panthers led 4–0 after 2nd)
NY Islanders 3 at Colorado 4 (Quincey 2:39 OT)
Montreal 3 at Phoenix 2 (Gorges 1:45 OT)
Vancouver 3 at Los Angeles 2 (Canucks scored all goals in 1st)
Minnesota 1 at San Jose 3 (Wild scored only goal of 3rd)

NOVEMBER 11, 2011

Washington 3 at New Jersey 1 (Caps scored only two goals of 3rd)
Carolina 1 at NY Rangers 5 (game tied 1–1 after 2nd)
Dallas 1 at Pittsburgh 3 (Neal two goals)
Ottawa 1 at Buffalo 5 (Sabres led 2–0 at 2:25 of 1st)
Edmonton 0 at Detroit 3 [Howard]
Calgary 1 at Chicago 4 (Hawks led 1–0 after 1st, 2–0 after 2nd)
Vancouver 3 at Anaheim 4 (Ducks scored all goals in 2nd, Canucks all goals in 3rd)

NOVEMBER 12, 2011

Buffalo 2 at Boston 6 (Seguin (BOS) two goals)
Ottawa 5 at Toronto 2 (Leafs led 1–0 after 1st)

New Jersey 3 at Washington 2 (SO)
Pittsburgh 3 at Carolina 5 (game tied 3–3 midway through 3rd)
Dallas 2 at Detroit 5 (Wings scored only three goals of 3rd)
Winnipeg 1 at Columbus 2 (Johansen two goals)
Montreal 2 at Nashville 1 (Pacioretty 2:31 OT)
Tampa Bay 0 at St. Louis 3 [Elliott]
Calgary 4 at Colorado 3 (Flames led 4–0 midway through game)
Minnesota 2 at Los Angeles 5 (Wild scored only two goals of 3rd)
Phoenix 3 at San Jose 0 [Smith]

NOVEMBER 13, 2011

Philadelphia 3 at Florida 2 (Flyers led 2–0 midway through game)
Edmonton 3 at Chicago 6 (Montador (CHI) two goals in 1st)
Minnesota 3 at Anaheim 2 (Fowler both Ducks goals)
NY Islanders 1 at Vancouver 4 (Canucks scored only two goals of 3rd)

NOVEMBER 14, 2011

Philadelphia 5 at Carolina 3 (Giroux (PHI) two goals)
Buffalo 3 at Montreal 2 (SO)
Tampa Bay 2 at Winnipeg 5 (seven different scorers)

NOVEMBER 15, 2011

New Jersey 3 at Boston 4 (Bruins trailed 1–0, led 2,1 & 3–2)
Phoenix 3 at Toronto 2 (SO)
NY Rangers 4 at NY Islanders 2 (Rangers broke 2–2 tie with two late goals)
Colorado 3 at Pittsburgh 6 (nine different scorers)
Minnesota 4 at Columbus 2 (Jackets led 2–0 after 1st)
Detroit 1 at St. Louis 2 (no scoring last 29 minutes)
Washington 1 at Nashville 3 (all goals in 3rd)
Florida 6 at Dallas 0 [Clemmensen]
Ottawa 3 at Calgary 1 (game tied 1–1 after 2nd)

NOVEMBER 16, 2011

Carolina 0 at Montreal 4 [Price]
New Jersey 5 at Buffalo 3 (Myers (BUF) two goals)
Chicago 5 at Vancouver 1 (Canucks led 1–0 early in 2nd)
Anaheim 1 at Los Angeles 2 (SO)

NOVEMBER 17, 2011

Columbus 1 at Boston 2 (SO)
Montreal 3 at NY Islanders 4 (six goals in 2nd)
Phoenix 1 at Philadelphia 2 (Read broke 1–1 game at 19:41 of 3rd)
Pittsburgh 1 at Tampa Bay 4 (Lecavalier (TB) two goals)
Florida 1 at St. Louis 4 (game tied 1–1 after 1st)
Toronto 1 at Nashville 4 (Erat two goals)
Colorado 0 at Minnesota 1 (Setoguchi 17:29 3rd) [Backstrom]
Washington 1 at Winnipeg 4 (no scoring in 3rd)
Ottawa 5 at Edmonton 2 (Sens scored only three goals of 1st)
Los Angeles 5 at Anaheim 3 (Cogliano (ANA) two goals)
Detroit 2 at San Jose 5 (game tied 1–1 after 1st)

NOVEMBER 18, 2011

Buffalo 1 at Carolina 0 (Pominville 13:04 1st) [Enroth]
Dallas 0 at Colorado 3 [Giguere]
Chicago 2 at Calgary 5 (Glencross (CAL) two goals)

NOVEMBER 19, 2011

Philadelphia 4 at Winnipeg 6 (Jets led 5–1 midway through game)
Detroit 4 at Los Angeles 1 (game tied 1–1 early in 2nd)
Phoenix 4 at Buffalo 2 (game tied 2–2 midway through 2nd)
Washington 1 at Toronto 7 (Leafs scored only four goals of 3rd)
NY Rangers 0 at Montreal 4 [Price]
Boston 6 at NY Islanders 0 [Thomas]
New Jersey 4 at Tampa Bay 2 (Devils led 3–0 after 2nd)
Pittsburgh 2 at Florida 3 (Panthers scored only goal of 3rd)
Columbus 4 at Nashville 3 (Wisniewski 2:43 OT)
St. Louis 2 at Minnesota 3 (SO)
San Jose 4 at Dallas 1 (Stars scored final goal of game)
Chicago 2 at Edmonton 9 (game tied 1–1 early in 1st)

NOVEMBER 20, 2011

Toronto 2 at Carolina 3 (Kessel (TOR) two goals in 3rd)
San Jose 4 at Colorado 1 (game tied 1–1 early in 2nd)
Detroit 4 at Anaheim 2 (Wings led 3–0 early in 2nd)
Ottawa 1 at Vancouver 2 (Higgins 2:18 OT)

NOVEMBER 21, 2011

Carolina 4 at Philadelphia 2 (no scoring in 3rd)
NY Islanders 0 at Pittsburgh 5 [Fleury]
Phoenix 3 at Washington 4 (game tied 2–2 after 2nd)
Calgary 1 at Columbus 4 (Jackets led 3–0 early in 2nd)
Boston 1 at Montreal 0 (Ference 15:41 1st) [Thomas]
New Jersey 3 at Florida 4 (Versteeg (FLO) two goals in 2nd)
Edmonton 1 at Dallas 4 (Stars led 2–0 early in 2nd)

NOVEMBER 22, 2011

Toronto 7 at Tampa Bay 1 (game tied 1–1 midway through 1st)
Los Angeles 3 at St. Louis 2 (Mitchell broke 2–2 tie late in 3rd)
Edmonton 6 at Nashville 2 (Eberle & Horcoff (EDM) two goals)

NOVEMBER 23, 2011

Boston 4 at Buffalo 3 (SO)
Columbus 1 at New Jersey 2 (SO)
Philadelphia 4 at NY Islanders 3 (Briere 2:34 OT)
St. Louis 3 at Pittsburgh 2 (Pietrangelo 4:07 OT)
Winnipeg 3 at Washington 4 (Chimera 1:52 OT)
Montreal 4 at Carolina 3 (SO)
Calgary 3 at Detroit 5 (Flames led 2–1 early in 2nd)
NY Rangers 1 at Florida 2 (no scoring in final 35 minutes)
Nashville 2 at Minnesota 3 (Predators led 1–0 after 1st & 2nd)
Los Angeles 2 at Dallas 3 (Ott 2:56 OT)
Vancouver 3 at Colorado 0 [Schneider]
Anaheim 2 at Phoenix 4 (Vrbata (PHO) two goals)
Chicago 0 at San Jose 1 (Demers 17:08 2nd) [Niemi]

NOVEMBER 24, 2011

No games scheduled

NOVEMBER 25, 2011

Detroit 3 at Boston 2 (SO)
New Jersey 1 at NY Islanders 0 (Sykora 14:13 2nd) [Hedberg]
Montreal 1 at Philadelphia 3 (Habs led 1–0 after 1st)
Edmonton 5 at Minnesota 2 (Nugent-Hopkins (EDM) two goals)
NY Rangers 6 at Washington 3 (no scoring in 1st)

Chicago 6 at Anaheim 5 (Hawks trailed 4–2, scored four goals in 3rd)
Ottawa 3 at Pittsburgh 6 (Penguins trailed 1–0, scored five in a row)
Winnipeg 3 at Carolina 1 (game tied 1–1 early in 2nd)
Buffalo 1 at Columbus 5 (no scoring in 3rd)
Tampa Bay 2 at Florida 1 (Stamkos 2:29 OT)
Calgary 0 at St. Louis 2 [Elliott]
Toronto 4 at Dallas 3 (SO)
Vancouver 5 at Phoenix 0 [Schneider]

NOVEMBER 26, 2011

NY Islanders 3 at New Jersey 2 (Islanders led 1–0 & 2–1)
Philadelphia 0 at NY Rangers 2 [Lundqvist]
Edmonton 2 at Colorado 5 (Avs trailed 2–1 after 2nd)
Winnipeg 2 at Boston 4 (Jets led 2–0 midway through 1st)
Washington 1 at Buffalo 5 (Luke Adam two goals)
Pittsburgh 4 at Montreal 3 (Letang 2:09 OT)
Florida 1 at Tampa Bay 5 (Stamkos two goals)
Nashville 1 at Detroit 4 (Predators scored final goal)
Dallas 0 at Phoenix 3 [Lehtonen/Smith]
Vancouver 3 at San Jose 2 (game tied 1–1 after 1st)
Chicago 2 at Los Angeles 1 (no scoring in 3rd)

NOVEMBER 27, 2011

Carolina 3 at Ottawa 4 (Spezza (OTT) two goals in 1st)
St. Louis 2 at Columbus 1 (no scoring in 1st)
Calgary 5 at Minnesota 2 (Flames led 3–2 after 1st & 2nd)
Toronto 5 at Anaheim 2 (Ducks led 1–0 midway through 1st)

NOVEMBER 28, 2011

Tampa Bay 1 at Minnesota 3 (no scoring in 1st)
Dallas 3 at Colorado 1 (Stars led 2–0 late in 3rd)
Nashville 2 at Edmonton 1 (one goal in each period)
San Jose 0 at Los Angeles 2 [Quick]

NOVEMBER 29, 2011

NY Islanders 2 at Buffalo 1 (game tied 1–1 early in 3rd)
Pittsburgh 3 at NY Rangers 4 (Rangers scored four goals in 2nd)
St. Louis 2 at Washington 1 (no scoring final 31 minutes)

Florida 3 at Carolina 1 (Matthias two goals in 3rd)
Ottawa 6 at Winnipeg 4 (Senators led 1–0, trailed 2–1, led 3–2, trailed 4–3)
Phoenix 4 at Chicago 1 (Hawks scored only goal late in 3rd)
Nashville 0 at Calgary 1 (D. Smith 18:50 1st) [Kiprusoff]
Columbus 1 at Vancouver 4

NOVEMBER 30, 2011

Boston 6 at Toronto 3 (Lucic (BOS) two goals)
Tampa Bay 2 at Detroit 4 (two goals in each period)
New Jersey 1 at Colorado 6 (Devils scored only goal of 2nd)
Minnesota 3 at Edmonton 2 (SO)
Montreal 1 at Anaheim 4 (game tied 1–1 after 1st)

DECEMBER 1, 2011

Pittsburgh 2 at Washington 1 (one goal in each period)
NY Rangers 5 at Carolina 3 ('Canes led 2–1 after 1st)
Phoenix 0 at Winnipeg 1 (Little 6:53 1st) [Pavelec]
Ottawa 2 at Dallas 3 (Nystrom broke 2–2 tie at 17:40 of 3rd)
Columbus 4 at Calgary 3 (SO)
Nashville 6 at Vancouver 5 (Predators led 2–0, 3–1, trailed 5–3)
Florida 1 at Los Angeles 2 (no scoring in 3rd)
Montreal 3 at San Jose 4 (SO)

DECEMBER 2, 2011

Detroit 4 at Buffalo 1 (Wings led 3–0 after 1st & 2nd)
New Jersey 2 at Minnesota 4 (five goals in 1st)
NY Islanders 4 at Chicago 5 (SO)
St. Louis 2 at Colorado 3 (SO)
Columbus 3 at Edmonton 6 (R. Jones (EDM) hat trick in 3rd)
Philadelphia 4 at Anaheim 3 (Giroux 3:29 OT)

DECEMBER 3, 2011

Montreal 2 at Los Angeles 1 (no scoring in 3rd)
Toronto 1 at Boston 4 (game tied 1–1 early in 2nd)
Ottawa 2 at Washington 3 (Laich 0:12 OT)
Pittsburgh 3 at Carolina 2 (McBain both 'Canes goals)
New Jersey 2 at Winnipeg 4 (Jets scored only two goals of 3rd)
NY Rangers 4 at Tampa Bay 2 (Rangers scored only three goals of 3rd)

Chicago 5 at St. Louis 2 (Blues led 1–0, 2–1)
Buffalo 3 at Nashville 2 (Sabres led 2–0 after 1st & 2nd)
Philadelphia 4 at Phoenix 2 (Flyers led 4–0 early in 2nd)
NY Islanders 5 at Dallas 4 (Islanders led 3–0, 4–3)
Calgary 5 at Edmonton 3 (O. Jokinen (CAL) two goals)
Florida 5 at San Jose 3 (Panthers trailed 1–0, 2–1)

DECEMBER 4, 2011

Detroit 2 at Colorado 4 (game tied 2–2 early in 3rd)
Minnesota 5 at Anaheim 3 (Wild scored final two goals late in 3rd to break 3–3 tie)
Calgary 1 at Vancouver 5 (Flames led 1–0 early in 2nd)

DECEMBER 5, 2011

Toronto 4 at NY Rangers 2 (Leafs led 3–0 early in 2nd)
Boston 3 at Pittsburgh 1 (Penguins scored last goal)
Tampa Bay 2 at Ottawa 4 (no scoring in 1st)
Washington 4 at Florida 5 (Panthers led 5–1 late in 2nd)
Phoenix 4 at Chicago 3 (SO)

DECEMBER 6, 2011

New Jersey 3 at Toronto 2 (Clarkson 2:40 OT)
Tampa Bay 1 at NY Islanders 5 (Lightning led 1–0 early in 1st)
Columbus 3 at Montreal 2 (SO)
Detroit 2 at St. Louis 3 (no scoring in 1st)
Phoenix 3 at Nashville 2 (Yandle broke 2–2 tie at 18:15 of 3rd)
Boston 1 at Winnipeg 2 (Jets led 1–0 after 1st & 2nd)
Carolina 6 at Calgary 7 (teams combined for seven goals in 3rd)
Colorado 0 at Vancouver 6 [Luongo/Schneider]
Los Angeles 2 at Anaheim 3 (Ryan (ANA) scored first and last goals of game)
Minnesota 2 at San Jose 1 (all scoring in 1st)

DECEMBER 7, 2011

Washington 5 at Ottawa 3 (eight different scorers)
Philadelphia 5 at Buffalo 4 (Giroux 2:37 OT)
Carolina 5 at Edmonton 3 (eight different scorers)

DECEMBER 8, 2011

Florida 2 at Boston 0 [Theodore]
Ottawa 4 at New Jersey 5 (SO)
Chicago 3 at NY Islanders 2 (Sharp 1:34 OT)
Tampa Bay 3 at NY Rangers 2 (SO)
Pittsburgh 2 at Philadelphia 3 (Flyers led 3–0 midway through game)
Nashville 4 at Columbus 3 (C. Wilson 1:45 OT)
Vancouver 4 at Montreal 3 (SO)
Phoenix 2 at Detroit 5 (Red Wings led 5–0 after 1st)
Anaheim 2 at St. Louis 4 (game tied 1–1 late in 1st)
Colorado 2 at Calgary 3 (no scoring for first 35 minutes)
Minnesota 4 at Los Angeles 2 (Wild led 3–0 after 2nd)
Dallas 2 at San Jose 5 (no scoring in 3rd)

DECEMBER 9, 2011

Toronto 2 at Washington 4 (Wideman (WAS) scored first two goals)
Florida 1 at Buffalo 2 (Pominville 2:19 OT)
Carolina 2 at Winnipeg 4 (Jets led 4–0 midway through game)
Colorado 1 at Edmonton 4 (no scoring in 3rd)

DECEMBER 10, 2011

Montreal 2 at New Jersey 1 (Habs never trailed)
NY Rangers 4 at Buffalo 1 (Hagelin two goals)
Vancouver 4 at Ottawa 1 (Kesler two goals)
Pittsburgh 6 at NY Islanders 3 (Neal (PIT) two goals)
Tampa Bay 2 at Philadelphia 5 (Lightning led 1–0 early in 2nd)
Winnipeg 1 at Detroit 7 (Jets scored at 0:35 of 1st)
Boston 5 at Columbus 3 (Jackets led 2–0 late in 1st)
San Jose 0 at St. Louis 1 (Shattenkirk 19:34 1st) [Elliott]
Anaheim 2 at Nashville 3 (game tied 1–1 after 2nd)
Minnesota 4 at Phoenix 1 (Coyotes scored final goal)
Edmonton 0 at Calgary 3 [Kiprusoff]
Dallas 2 at Los Angeles 1 (game tied 1–1 midway through 2nd)

DECEMBER 11, 2011

Florida 1 at NY Rangers 6 (Stepan two goals)
San Jose 2 at Chicago 3 (Sharp 4:26 OT)

DECEMBER 12, 2011

New Jersey 5 at Tampa Bay 4 (Devils led 2–0, 5–2)

DECEMBER 13, 2011

Los Angeles 0 at Boston 3 [Rask]
Ottawa 3 at Buffalo 2 (Cowen 0:45 OT)
Carolina 1 at Toronto 2 (Connolly 0:44 OT)
Dallas 1 at NY Rangers 0 (Daley 15:01 3rd) [Bachman]
Detroit 4 at Pittsburgh 1 (Penguins led 1–0 after 1st)
Philadelphia 5 at Washington 1 (Caps scored final goal late in 3rd)
Vancouver 1 at Columbus 2 (SO)
NY Islanders 3 at Montreal 5 (eight different scorers)
New Jersey 3 at Florida 2 (SO)
Calgary 1 at Nashville 2 (Predators scored only goal of 3rd)
Minnesota 1 at Winnipeg 2 (Wild led 1–0 early in 2nd)
San Jose 3 at Colorado 4 (SO)

]DECEMBER 14, 2011

Boston 5 at Ottawa 2 (Bruins scored three goals in 3rd)
Chicago 4 at Minnesota 3 (SO)
Phoenix 1 at Anaheim 4 (Ducks never trailed)

DECEMBER 15, 2011

Dallas 3 at NY Islanders 2 (Stars scored only two goals of 3rd)
Vancouver 3 at Carolina 4 (Canucks led 2–0 midway through game)
Los Angeles 2 at Columbus 1 (Jackets led 1–0 early in 3rd)
Philadelphia 4 at Montreal 3 (Flyers led 1–0, 2–1, 3–2)
Calgary 4 at Tampa Bay 5 (Stamkos 0:30 OT)
NY Rangers 1 at St. Louis 4 (Blues scorfed only two goals of 1st & 3rd)
Detroit 3 at Nashville 4 (Predators scored final three goals of game)
Washington 1 at Winnipeg 0 (Ovechkin 18:46 3rd) [Neuvirth]
Edmonton 2 at Phoenix 4 (game tied 2–2 midway through 3rd)
Colorado 4 at San Jose 5 (Sharks scored only three goals of 3rd)

DECEMBER 16, 2011

Dallas 3 at New Jersey 6 (Devils scored four goals in a row in middle of game)
Toronto 4 at Buffalo 5 (Sabres scored four goals in 2nd)
Pittsburgh 4 at Ottawa 6 (teams combined for eight goals in 2nd)

Calgary 2 at Florida 3 (SO)
Anaheim 1 at Chicago 4 (Ducks scored late in 3rd)

DECEMBER 17, 2011

Boston 6 at Philadelphia 0 [Thomas]
Vancouver 5 at Toronto 3 (eight different scorers)
New Jersey 5 at Montreal 3 (Devils led 1–0, 2–1, trailed 3–2)
Buffalo 3 at Pittsburgh 8 (Penguins led 6–1 after 2nd)
Anaheim 3 at Winnipeg 5 (Perry (ANA) two goals)
Los Angeles 2 at Detroit 8 (Miller (DET) two goals)
Tampa Bay 3 at Columbus 2 (no scoring in 3rd)
St. Louis 1 at Nashville 2 (SO)
NY Islanders 2 at Minnesota 1 (SO)
NY Rangers 3 at Phoenix 2 (Rangers scored only two goals of 3rd)
Washington 1 at Colorado 2 (no scoring in 3rd)
Edmonton 2 at San Jose 3 (game tied 2–2 after 2nd)

DECEMBER 18, 2011

Carolina 2 at Florida 3 (Versteeg 3:08 OT)
Calgary 2 at Chicago 4 (Hawks led 3–0 after 2nd)
Columbus 4 at St. Louis 6 (Blues led 1–0, trailed 2–1, led 3–2 after 2nd)

DECEMBER 19, 2011

Montreal 2 at Boston 3 (Bruins scored in each period)
Los Angeles 3 at Toronto 2 (SO)
Anaheim 3 at Dallas 5 (eight different scorers)
Philadelphia 2 at Colorado 3 (SO)
Detroit 3 at Edmonton 2 (Red Wings scored only goal of 3rd)
Minnesota 0 at Vancouver 4 [Luongo]

DECEMBER 20, 2011

NY Rangers 4 at New Jersey 1 (Devils led 1–0 after 1st)
Chicago 2 at Pittsburgh 3 (Penguins led 3–0 early in 3rd)
Nashville 1 at Washington 4 (Capitals led 2–0 after 1st & 2nd)
Buffalo 1 at Ottawa 4 (game tied 1–1 after 2nd)
Phoenix 2 at Florida 1 (no scoring in 3rd)
NY Islanders 3 at Winnipeg 2 (SO)
Minnesota 1 at Calgary 2 (no scoring in final 34 minutes)

DECEMBER 21, 2011

Phoenix 4 at Carolina 3 (Coyotes led 1–0, trailed 3–1)
Montreal 1 at Chicago 5 (Habs led 1–0 midway through game)
Philadelphia 4 at Dallas 1 (Stars scored at 0:56 of 1st)
St. Louis 2 at Colorado 3 (no scoring in 3rd)
Detroit 2 at Vancouver 4 (Canucks scored twice in 21 seconds in 1st)
Tampa Bay 2 at San Jose 7 (Couture (SJ) two goals in 1st)

DECEMBER 22, 2011

Buffalo 2 at Toronto 3 (no scoring in first 31 minutes)
NY Islanders 2 at NY Rangers 4 (game tied 1–1 early in 2nd)
Florida 3 at Ottawa 4 (Butler 2:02 OT)
Columbus 5 at Nashville 6 (Predators trailed 5–2 midway through game)
Montreal 0 at Winnipeg 4 [Pavelec]
Detroit 2 at Calgary 3 (Glencross (CAL) two goals)
Minnesota 1 at Edmonton 4 (Wild scored only goal of 3rd)
Anaheim 2 at Los Angeles 3 (SO)

DECEMBER 23, 2011

Florida 0 at Boston 8 [Rask]
Washington 3 at New Jersey 4 (SO)
Toronto 5 at NY Islanders 3 (eight different scorers)
Philadelphia 2 at NY Rangers 4 (no scoring in first half of game)
Ottawa 1 at Carolina 2 (T. Ruutu 1:36 OT)
Pittsburgh 4 at Winnipeg 1 (game tied 1–1 midway through 2nd)
Nashville 3 at Dallas 6 (nine different scorers)
Tampa Bay 1 at Colorado 2 (Duchene 3:38 OT)
St. Louis 3 at Phoenix 2 (no scoring in 1st)
Calgary 3 at Vancouver 1 (all goals in 3rd)
Los Angeles 1 at San Jose 2 (SO)

DECEMBER 24, 2011

No games scheduled

DECEMBER 25, 2011

No games scheduled

DECEMBER 26, 2011

Colorado 4 at Minnesota 2 (Wild led 1–0, 2–1)
Washington 2 at Buffalo 4 (Sabres led 4–0 after 1st)
NY Islanders 0 at NY Rangers 3 [Lundqvist]
New Jersey 2 at Carolina 4 ('Canes led 3–0 after 2nd)
Dallas 3 at St. Louis 5 (C. Stewart (STL) two goals)
Detroit 4 at Nashville 1 (Filppula (DET) two goals)
Columbus 1 at Chicago 4 (Stalberg (CHI) two goals in 2nd)
Edmonton 3 at Vancouver 5 (Canucks led 3–0 after 1st)
Phoenix 3 at Los Angeles 4 (game tied 2–2 after 1nd)
Anaheim 3 at San Jose 2 (no scoring final 27 minutes)

DECEMBER 27, 2011

Carolina 2 at Pittsburgh 4 (game tied 1–1 after 2nd)
Calgary 2 at Columbus 1 (SO)
Montreal 6 at Ottawa 2 (Habs scored five goals in a row in middle of game)
Philadelphia 1 at Tampa Bay 5 (Stamkos two goals)
Toronto 3 at Florida 5 (game tied 1–1 early in 2nd)
St. Louis 2 at Detroit 3 (Blues led 2–0 late in 2nd)
Winnipeg 4 at Colorado 1 (Kane two goals)

DECEMBER 28, 2011

Buffalo 1 at New Jersey 3 (no scoring in final 32 minutes)
NY Rangers 1 at Washington 4 (Semin two goals)
Minnesota 1 at Nashville 2 (SO)
Los Angeles 2 at Chicago 0 [Quick]
Boston 2 at Phoenix 1 (Seidenberg 0:58 OT)
Vancouver 3 at San Jose 2 (Ebbett 3:23 OT)

DECEMBER 29, 2011

Calgary 1 at NY Islanders 3 (Flames led 1–0 after 1st)
Philadelphia 4 at Pittsburgh 2 (Flyers scored in each period)
Toronto 3 at Carolina 4 (E. Staal 3:09 OT)
Montreal 3 at Tampa Bay 4 (Habs led 3–1 late in 2nd)
Edmonton 3 at Minnesota 4 (Oilers scored only goal of 3rd)
Los Angeles 0 at Winnipeg 1 (Kane 1:09 OT) [C. Mason]
Columbus 4 at Dallas 1 (Nash two goals)
Phoenix 2 at Colorado 3 (Avs scored only goal of 3rd)
Vancouver 5 at Anaheim 2 (Sedin twins combined for three goals)

DECEMBER 30, 2011

Buffalo 1 at Washington 3 (Ovechkin two goals)
Calgary 3 at Ottawa 4 (Alfredsson 3:31 OT)
NY Rangers 4 at Florida 1 (no scoring in last half of game)
Nashville 2 at St. Louis 1 (SO)
Detroit 2 at Chicago 3 (Red Wings led 1–0, 2–1)

DECEMBER 31, 2011

Pittsburgh 1 at New Jersey 3 (Devils led 2–0 after 1st & 2nd)
Edmonton 1 at NY Islanders 4 (no scoring in final 35 minutes)
Carolina 2 at Tampa Bay 5 (Stamkos hat trick)
Montreal 2 at Florida 3 (Habs led 1–0 early in 2nd)
Phoenix 4 at Minnesota 2 (Vrbata (PHO) two goals in 3rd)
Ottawa 3 at Buffalo 2 (SO)
Toronto 2 at Winnipeg 3 (Leafs led 1–0 early in 2nd)
St. Louis 0 at Detroit 3 [Howard]
Washington 4 at Columbus 2 (Ovechkin (WAS) two goals in 3rd)
Boston 2 at Dallas 4 (game tied 1–1 late in 1st)
Colorado 4 at Anaheim 2 (Hejduk (COL) two goals)
Vancouver 1 at Los Angeles 4 (Canucks led 1–0 early in 1st)

JANUARY 1, 2012

Calgary 3 at Nashville 5 (S. Kostitsyn (NAS) hat trick)

JANUARY 2, 2012

NY Rangers 3 at Philadelphia 2 (game played outdoors)
New Jersey 2 at Ottawa 3 (Alfredsson 4:00 OT)
Edmonton 4 at Chicago 3 (Oilers scored three goals in 2nd)
San Jose 3 at Vancouver 2 (SO)
Colorado 2 at Los Angeles 1 (SO)

JANUARY 3, 2012

Edmonton 3 at Buffalo 4 (game tied 2–2 after 2nd)
Tampa Bay 3 at Toronto 7 (ten different scorers)
Calgary 1 at Washington 3 (no scoring in 3rd)
NY Islanders 4 at Carolina 3 (SO)
Phoenix 1 at St. Louis 4 (Blues scored in each period)
Detroit 5 at Dallas 4 (Hudler (DET) & Ryder (DAL) two goals)

JANUARY 4, 2012

Winnipeg 3 at Montreal 7 (Eller four goals)
Boston 6 at New Jersey 1 (Bergeron two goals)
Minnesota 0 at Vancouver 3 [Luongo]
San Jose 3 at Anaheim 1 (Ducks scored at 2:37 of 1st)

JANUARY 5, 2012

Calgary 0 at Boston 9 [Rask]
Winnipeg 0 at Toronto 4 [Gustavsson]
Florida 2 at NY Rangers 3 (Gaborik 3:29 OT)
Chicago 4 at Philadelphia 5 (Van Riemsdyk (PHI) two goals)
Tampa Bay 1 at Ottawa 4 (Senators led 2–0 after 2nd)
Edmonton 3 at St. Louis 4 (Blues scored only three goals of 3rd)
Dallas 4 at Nashville 1 (game tied 1–1 midway through 1st)
Phoenix 0 at Los Angeles 1 (Doughty 0:38 OT) [Quick]
Columbus 1 at San Jose 2 (Jackets scored at 2:13 of 1st)

JANUARY 6, 2012

Florida 2 at New Jersey 5 (Devils scored only three goals of 3rd)
NY Rangers 3 at Pittsburgh 1 (Penguins led 1–0 early in 1st)
Buffalo 2 at Carolina 4 (game tied 2–2 early in 3rd)
Colorado 4 at Chicago 0 [Varlamov]
NY Islanders 2 at Anaheim 4 (Ryan (ANA) two goals)

JANUARY 7, 2012

Vancouver 4 at Boston 3 (Bruins led 2–1 late in 2nd)
Ottawa 2 at Philadelphia 3 (Briere 4:54 OT)
Edmonton 1 at Dallas 4 (Stars scored only three goals of 3rd)
Columbus 1 at Los Angeles 0 (Clitsome 11:25 2nd) [Sanford]
Winnipeg 2 at Buffalo 1 (Oduya 0:57 OT)
Detroit 3 at Toronto 4 (Leafs led 3–0 midway through 1st)
Tampa Bay 1 at Montreal 3 (Lightning scored at 3:24 of 1st)
New Jersey 3 at Pittsburgh 1 (Penguins led 1–0 early in 1st)
Colorado 0 at St. Louis 4 [Elliott]
Carolina 2 at Nashville 5 (Hornqvist (NAS) two goals)
NY Islanders 1 at Phoenix 5 (Doan hat trick)
Minnesota 1 at Calgary 3 (all goals in 3rd)
Washington 2 at San Jose 5 (game tied 2–2 early in 3rd)

JANUARY 8, 2012

Philadelphia 4 at Ottawa 6 (Senators led 1–0, 2–1, trailed 4–2, scored only four goals of 3rd)
Detroit 3 at Chicago 2 (Datsyuk 3:08 OT)
Columbus 4 at Anaheim 7 (Perry (ANA) hat trick)

JANUARY 9, 2012

Vancouver 1 at Florida 2 (no scoring in 3rd)
Washington 2 at Los Angeles 5 (Johansson (WAS) two goals)

JANUARY 10, 2012

Winnipeg 3 at Boston 5 (Jets led 1–0, 2–1, 3–2)
Buffalo 0 at Toronto 2 [Gustavsson]
Detroit 1 at NY Islanders 5 (Moulson two goals)
Phoenix 1 at NY Rangers 2 (SO)
Ottawa 5 at Pittsburgh 1 (M. Michalek two goals)
Philadelphia 2 at Carolina 1 (Flyers scored only goal of 3rd)
St. Louis 3 at Montreal 0 [Halak]
Vancouver 5 at Tampa Bay 4 (SO)
San Jose 4 at Minnesota 5 (SO)
Columbus 2 at Chicago 5 (Stalberg hat trick)
Nashville 4 at Colorado 1 (Predators led 3–0 after 1st)
New Jersey 3 at Calgary 6 (Flames led 4–0 after 2st)
Dallas 2 at Anaheim 5 (S. Koivu hat trick)

JANUARY 11, 2012

Pittsburgh 0 at Washington 1 (Chimera 15:25 1st) [Vokoun]
New Jersey 2 at Edmonton 1 (Parise 1:06 OT)

JANUARY 12, 2012

Montreal 1 at Boston 2 (Bruins led 1–0 after 1st & 2nd)
Philadelphia 3 at NY Islanders 2 (Flyers led 2–0 after 2nd)
Ottawa 3 at NY Rangers 0 [Anderson]
Carolina 5 at Tampa Bay 2 (Tlusty (CAR) two goals)
Phoenix 2 at Detroit 3 (SO)
Vancouver 3 at St. Louis 2 (D. Sedin 0:46 OT)
Colorado 2 at Nashville 3 (Legwand 0:34 OT)
San Jose 2 at Winnipeg 0 [Niemi]

Minnesota 2 at Chicago 5 (Hawks scored four straight in middle of game)
Anaheim 0 at Calgary 1 (B. Jones 1:51 OT) [Kiprusoff]
Dallas 5 at Los Angeles 4 (SO)

JANUARY 13, 2012

Tampa Bay 3 at Washington 4 (Brouwer (WAS) hat trick)
Phoenix 3 at Columbus 4 (Coyotes opened scoring at 1:49 of 1st)
Toronto 2 at Buffalo 3 (no scoring in 3rd)
Pittsburgh 4 at Florida 1 (Penguins led 3–0 early in 3rd)
Anaheim 5 at Edmonton 0 [Hiller]

JANUARY 14, 2012

Chicago 2 at Detroit 3 (Bertuzzi 4:21 OT)
Colorado 2 at Dallas 1 (Avs led 1–0 after 1st & 2nd)
NY Rangers 3 at Toronto 0 [Biron]
Ottawa 3 at Montreal 2 (SO)
Buffalo 2 at NY Islanders 4 (Grabner (NYI) two goals in 3rd)
Boston 2 at Carolina 4 ('Canes scored final three goals of game in 3rd)
New Jersey 2 at Winnipeg 1 (Jets led 1–0 after 1st & 2nd)
San Jose 2 at Columbus 1 (Marleau broke 1–1 tie late in 3rd)
Minnesota 2 at St. Louis 3 (SO)
Philadelphia 2 at Nashville 4 (Predators led 2–0 midway through game)
Los Angeles 4 at Calgary 1 (Kings led 3–0 late in 2nd)

JANUARY 15, 2012

Pittsburgh 6 at Tampa Bay 3 (Malkin (PIT) hat trick in 3rd)
Carolina 1 at Washington 2 (Caps scored only goal of 3rd)
NY Rangers 1 at Montreal 4 (Pacioretty two goals)
San Jose 3 at Chicago 4 (Hawks led 2–0 after 1st, 3–2 after 2nd)
Los Angeles 1 at Edmonton 2 (Hall 3:06 OT)
Anaheim 4 at Vancouver 2 (Blake (ANA) two goals)

JANUARY 16, 2012

Nashville 3 at NY Islanders 1 (Predators led 3–0 after 1st & 2nd)
Colorado 1 at Phoenix 6 (Doan and Gordon (PHO) two goals)
Winnipeg 2 at Ottawa 0 [Mason]
Boston 3 at Florida 2 (SO)
Buffalo 0 at Detroit 5 [Howard]
Dallas 0 at St. Louis 1 (Oshie 11:26 3rd) [Halak]

JANUARY 17, 2012

Ottawa 3 at Toronto 2 (Leafs led 2–0 late in 1st)
Winnipeg 1 at New Jersey 5 (Kovalchuk two goals)
Nashville 0 at NY Rangers 3 [Lundqvist]
Minnesota 1 at Philadelphia 5 (Flyers scored three goals in 2nd)
Carolina 1 at Pittsburgh 2 (SO)
NY Islanders 3 at Washington 0 [Nabokov]
Edmonton 2 at Columbus 4 (Oilers led 2–0 after 1st)
Boston 3 at Tampa Bay 5 (Lightning led 1–0, 2–1, 3–2)
Detroit 3 at Dallas 2 (SO)
Los Angeles 3 at Vancouver 2 (SO)
Calgary 1 at San Jose 2 (SO)

JANUARY 18, 2012

Washington 3 at Montreal 0 [Neuvirth]
Buffalo 2 at Chicago 6 (Hawks scored two goals in each period)
Florida 3 at Colorado 4 (R. O'Reilly 3:55 OT)
Phoenix 2 at Anaheim 6 (Beauchemin (ANA) two goals)

JANUARY 19, 2012

Minnesota 1 at Toronto 4 (Wild scored final goal of game)
Boston 4 at New Jersey 1 (Devils led 1–0 after 1st & 2nd)
Pittsburgh 4 at NY Rangers 1 (Penguins scored only three goals of 3rd)
NY Islanders 4 at Philadelphia 1 (Islanders led 3–0 early in 3rd)
Nashville 3 at Columbus 0 [Rinne]
Edmonton 0 at St. Louis 1 (Pietrangelo 14:46 3rd) [Halak]
Buffalo 1 at Winnipeg 4 (game tied 1–1 midway through 2nd)
Detroit 3 at Phoenix 2 (SO)
Calgary 2 at Los Angeles 1 (SO)
Ottawa 4 at San Jose 1 (Sharks led 1–0 at 3:10 of 1st)

JANUARY 20, 2012

Montreal 4 at Pittsburgh 5 (SO)
Washington 0 at Carolina 3 [Ward]
Florida 1 at Chicago 3 (Panthers scored only goal of 3rd)
Tampa Bay 2 at Dallas 1 (Purcell both Lightning goals)

JANUARY 21, 2012

NY Rangers 3 at Boston 2 (Gaborik 4:56 OT)
Philadelphia 4 at New Jersey 1 (Hartnell two goals)
San Jose 3 at Vancouver 4 (Canucks led 1–0, trailed 2–1)
Montreal 3 at Toronto 1 (game tied 1–1 after 1st & 2nd)
Carolina 1 at NY Islanders 2 (Tavares 3:58 OT)
Columbus 2 at Detroit 3 (SO)
Ottawa 1 at Anaheim 2 (Ducks led 2–0 after 2nd)
Florida 4 at Winnipeg 3 (SO)
Buffalo 2 at St. Louis 4 (Backes (STL) two goals)
Chicago 2 at Nashville 5 (game tied 1–1 after 1st)
Tampa Bay 4 at Phoenix 3 (Coyotes scored only two goals of 3rd)
Dallas 2 at Minnesota 5 (Wild scored final four goals)
Calgary 6 at Edmonton 2 (Stempniak hat trick)
Colorado 3 at Los Angeles 1 (Kings led 1–0 early in 2nd)

JANUARY 22, 2012

Boston 6 at Philadelphia 5 (SO)
Washington 3 at Pittsburgh 4 (Malkin 1:31 OT)
Colorado 2 at Anaheim 3 (Ryan (ANA) two goals)

JANUARY 23, 2012

NY Islanders 0 at Toronto 3 [Gustavsson]
Winnipeg 1 at Carolina 2 ('Canes led 2–0 midway through 1st)
St. Louis 1 at Detroit 3 (Blues led 1–0 after 1st)
Columbus 1 at Nashville 4 (Predators led 1–0 midway through 1st)
San Jose 1 at Edmonton 2 (SO)
Ottawa 1 at Los Angeles 4 (Senators scored only goal of 3rd)

JANUARY 24, 2012

Buffalo 2 at New Jersey 1 (SO)
Toronto 4 at NY Islanders 3 (MacArthur 2:06 OT)
Winnipeg 0 at NY Rangers 3 [Lundqvist]
Boston 3 at Washington 5 (Perreault (WAS) two goals)
Columbus 2 at Tampa Bay 4 (game tied 1–1 after 1st)
Philadelphia 3 at Florida 2 (SO)
Pittsburgh 3 at St. Louis 2 (SO)
Nashville 3 at Chicago 1 (Predators led 2–0 after 1st & 2nd)

Anaheim 0 at Dallas 1 (Goligoski 16:41 1st) [Lehtonen]
Minnesota 3 at Colorado 2 (Wild scored only goal of 3rd)
San Jose 1 at Calgary 0 (Ferreiro 11:35 3rd) [Niemi]
Ottawa 2 at Phoenix 3 (Coyotes scored in each period)
Edmonton 2 at Vancouver 3 (SO)

JANUARY 25, 2012

Detroit 2 at Montreal 7 (Desharnais (MON) & Hudler (DET) two goals)

JANUARY 26–30, 2012

NHL All-Star Game break

JANUARY 31, 2012

Ottawa 3 at Boston 4 (Senators led 3–1 midway through game)
NY Rangers 3 at New Jersey 4 (SO)
Winnipeg 2 at Philadelphia 1 (SO)
Toronto 4 at Pittsburgh 5 (SO)
NY Islanders 5 at Carolina 2 (Tavares (NYI) two goals in 3rd)
Buffalo 3 at Montreal 1 (Habs led 1–0 early in 2nd)
Washington 3 at Tampa Bay 4 (Stamkos 2:45 OT)
Nashville 5 at Minnesota 4 (Wild led 4–1 midway through 3rd)
Detroit 3 at Calgary 1 (game tied 1–1 after 2nd)
Anaheim 4 at Phoenix 1 (Cogliano 2nd period hat trick)
Colorado 2 at Edmonton 3 (Oilers led 2–1 after 2nd)
Chicago 2 at Vancouver 3 (D. Sedin 3:37 OT)
Columbus 0 at San Jose 6 [Niemi]

FEBRUARY 1, 2012

NY Rangers 1 at Buffalo 0 (SO)
Pittsburgh 0 at Toronto 1 (MacArthur 13:35 3rd) [Reimer]
Washington 2 at Florida 4 (Samuelsson (FLO) two goals)
Dallas 6 at Anaheim 2 (eight different scorers)
Columbus 2 at Los Angeles 3 (Doughty broke 2–2 tie at 19:59 of 3rd)

FEBRUARY 2, 2012

Carolina 3 at Boston 0 [Ward]
Montreal 3 at New Jersey 5 (Parise & Clarkson (NJ) two goals)

Nashville 1 at Philadelphia 4 (Simmonds two goals)
Winnipeg 2 at Tampa Bay 1 (Wellwood 3:14 OT)
Minnesota 1 at Colorado 0 (Zanon 6:04 1st) [Backstrom]
Chicago 4 at Edmonton 8 (Gagner four goals, four assists)
Detroit at Vancouver (SO)
Dallas 2 at San Jose 5 (Sharks led 2–0 midway through game)

FEBRUARY 3, 2012

NY Islanders 2 at Ottawa 1 (Eaton 2:35 OT)
Winnipeg 1 at Florida 2 (no scoring in 3rd)
Los Angeles 0 at St. Louis 1 (Langenbrunner 8:38 2nd) [Halak]
Chicago 1 at Calgary 3 (game tied 1–1 late in 2nd)
Columbus 3 at Anaheim 2 (Brassard 3:55 OT)

FEBRUARY 4, 2012

Pittsburgh 2 at Boston 1 (no scoring in 2nd)
New Jersey 6 at Philadelphia 4 (Devils led 6–0 after 2nd)
Washington 3 at Montreal 0 [Vokoun]
Vancouver 3 at Colorado 2 (SO)
Toronto 5 at Ottawa 0 [Reimer]
Buffalo 4 at NY Islanders 3 (SO)
Los Angeles 1 at Carolina 2 (Kings led 1–0 late in 2nd)
Florida 3 at Tampa Bay 6 (St. Louis (TB) hat trick)
St. Louis 1 at Nashville 3 (Predators led 2–0 after 1st & 2nd)
Minnesota 1 at Dallas 2 (SO)
San Jose 3 at Phoenix 5 (game tied 2–2 late in 2nd)
Detroit 4 at Edmonton 5 (SO)

FEBRUARY 5, 2012

Boston 4 at Washington 1 (Bruins led 2–0 after 1st & 2nd)
Pittsburgh 2 at New Jersey 5 (Devils never trailed)
Philadelphia 2 at NY Rangers 5 (game tied 2–2 early in 3rd)
Winnipeg 0 at Montreal 3 [Price]

FEBRUARY 6, 2012

Edmonton 3 at Toronto 6 (Leafs scored three goals in 2nd)
Detroit 1 at Phoenix 3 (Hanzal two goals)
Calgary 2 at Anaheim 3 (SO)

FEBRUARY 7, 2012

New Jersey 1 at NY Rangers 0 (Clarkson 8:14 1st) [Brodeur]
NY Islanders 1 at Philadelphia 0 (SO)
Florida 0 at Washington 4 [Vokoun]
Minnesota 1 at Columbus 3 (game tied 1–1 late in 2nd)
Pittsburgh 2 at Montreal 3 (SO)
St. Louis 3 at Ottawa 1 (Perron two goals)
Los Angeles 3 at Tampa Bay 1 (no scoring in 3rd)
Vancouver 4 at Nashville 3 (SO)
Toronto 1 at Winnipeg 2 (no scoring in last half of game)
Phoenix 4 at Dallas 1 (game tied 1–1 late in 2nd)
Chicago 2 at Colorado 5 (Avs scored only three goals of 3rd)

FEBRUARY 8, 2012

Boston 0 at Buffalo 6 [Miller]
Edmonton 2 at Detroit 4 (Gagner (EDM) two goals)
Carolina 2 at Anaheim 3 (Perry 2:14 OT)
Calgary 4 at San Jose 3 (O. Jokinen (CAL) hat trick)

FEBRUARY 9, 2012

St. Louis 4 at New Jersey 3 (SO)
Montreal 4 at NY Islanders 2 (Pacioretty hat trick)
Tampa Bay 3 at NY Rangers 4 (Richards 2:37 OT)
Toronto 3 at Philadelphia 4 (teams combined for six goals in 2nd)
Winnipeg 3 at Washington 2 (SO)
Dallas 4 at Columbus 2 (Benn (DAL) two goals)
Nashville 3 at Ottawa 4 (Spezza (OTT) two goals)
Los Angeles 1 at Florida 3 (Panthers led 2–0 after 2nd)
Vancouver 5 at Minnesota 2 (both Sedins (VAN) scored)
Calgary 1 at Phoenix 2 (Doan 3:05 OT)

FEBRUARY 10, 2012

Dallas 2 at Buffalo 3 (SO)
Anaheim 1 at Detroit 2 (SO)
Carolina 3 at Colorado 4 (R. O'Reilly 4:58 OT)
Chicago 3 at San Jose 5 (Krueger (CHI) two goals in 2nd)

FEBRUARY 11, 2012

Nashville 3 at Boston 4 (SO)
Florida 3 at New Jersey 1 (Devils scored at 1:39 of 1st)
Los Angeles 1 at NY Islanders 2 (Streit 1:36 OT)
NY Rangers 5 at Philadelphia 2 (Callahan hat trick)
Winnipeg 5 at Pittsburgh 8 (Letang (PIT) two goals; 12 different scorers)
Edmonton 4 at Ottawa 3 (Hall 0:17 OT)
Tampa Bay 2 at Buffalo 1 (Lightning led 2–0 after 2nd)
Montreal 5 at Toronto 0 [Price]
Colorado 2 at St. Louis 3 (Colaiacovo 3:18 OT)
Columbus 3 at Minnesota 1 (Wild led 1–0 late in 1st)
Chicago 0 at Phoenix 3 [Smith]
Vancouver 2 at Calgary 3 (SO)

FEBRUARY 12, 2012

Florida 4 at NY Islanders 1 (Islanders led 1–0 at 3:35 of 1st)
Washington 2 at NY Rangers 3 (game tied 1–1 midway through 2nd)
Philadelphia 3 at Detroit 4 (Red Wings led 1–0, trailed 2–1, 3–2)
Anaheim 5 at Columbus 3 (Perry (ANA) hat trick)
Los Angeles 4 at Dallas 2 (game tied 2–2 midway through 3rd)
Tampa Bay 2 at Pittsburgh 4 (Downie (TB) two goals in 1st)
San Jose 0 at St. Louis 3 [Halak]

FEBRUARY 13, 2012

San Jose 5 at Washington 3 (Pavelski (SJ) scored first two goals of game)
Carolina 5 at Montreal 3 ('Canes scored only three goals of 3rd)
Vancouver 1 at Phoenix 2 (SO)

FEBRUARY 14, 2012

NY Rangers 3 at Boston 0 [Lundqvist]
New Jersey 4 at Buffalo 1 (Kovalchuk hat trick)
St. Louis 1 at Columbus 2 (Blues led 1–0 late in 1st)
Ottawa 4 at Tampa Bay 0 [Anderson]
Dallas 1 at Detroit 3 (Stars scored in final minute)
Chicago 2 at Nashville 3 (Predators scored in each period)
Anaheim 2 at Minnesota 1 (Wild led 1–0 after 1st & 2nd)
NY Islanders 3 at Winnipeg 1 (Jets led 1–0 after 1st)
Toronto 1 at Calgary 5 (Leafs scored late in 1st)

FEBRUARY 15, 2012

Anaheim 2 at Pittsburgh 1 (one goal in each period)
Boston 4 at Montreal 3 (SO)
Ottawa 6 at Florida 2 (game tied 1–1 early in 2nd)
Toronto 4 at Edmonton 3 (Connolly 1:39 OT)
Colorado 1 at Vancouver 3 (game tied 1–1 midway through 3rd)

FEBRUARY 16, 2012

Chicago 4 at NY Rangers 2 (Hawks led 4–0 midway through 1st)
Buffalo 2 at Philadelphia 7 (Sabres led 2–0 after 1st)
San Jose 5 at Tampa Bay 6 (St. Louis 4:27 OT)
NY Islanders 1 at St. Louis 5 (no scoring in 3rd)
Winnipeg 4 at Minnesota 3 (SO)
Calgary 2 at Dallas 3 (Ribeiro 2:01 OT)
Phoenix 1 at Los Angeles 0 (Vrbata 15:59 2nd) [Smith]

FEBRUARY 17, 2012

Anaheim 2 at New Jersey 3 (SO)
San Jose 2 at Carolina 3 ('Canes led 2–0 after 1st & 2nd)
Montreal 4 at Buffalo 3 (SO)
Washington 2 at Florida 1 (Panthers scored 1–0 after 1st & 2nd)
Nashville 1 at Detroit 2 (one goal in each period)
Boston 2 at Winnipeg 4 (Little (WIN) two goals in 3rd)
Colorado 3 at Edmonton 1 (no scoring in final 25 minutes)

FEBRUARY 18, 2012

Pittsburgh 6 at Philadelphia 4 (Penguins led 1–0, trailed 2–1, game tied 3–3 after 2nd)
Chicago 6 at Columbus 1 (Hawks scored two goals in each period)
Minnesota 0 at St. Louis 4 [Elliott]
Carolina 3 at NY Islanders 4 (Islanders scored only goal of 3rd)
Washington 1 at Tampa Bay 2 (no scoring last half of game)
Toronto 2 at Vancouver 6 (Burrows (VAN) two goals)
Dallas 1 at Phoenix 2 (Vrbata 1:15 OT)
Calgary 1 at Los Angeles 0 (Cammalleri 4:03 3rd) [Kiprusoff]

FEBRUARY 19, 2012

Pittsburgh 2 at Buffalo 6 (Sabres led 3–0 early in 2nd)
San Jose 2 at Detroit 3 (Red Wings scored in each period)
St. Louis 1 at Chicago 3 (Blues led 1–0 after 1st & 2nd)

Boston 0 at Minnesota 2 [Backstrom]
New Jersey 3 at Montreal 1 (Devils led 2–0 after 2nd)
Anaheim 2 at Florida 0 [Hiller]
Columbus 2 at NY Rangers 3 (Stepan 0:22 OT)
Nashville 3 at Dallas 2 (Predators scored three goals in a row in middle of game)
Vancouver 5 at Edmonton 2 (both Sedin twins (VAN) scored)
Colorado 1 at Winnipeg 5 (Little two goals)

FEBRUARY 20, 2012

Ottawa 6 at NY Islanders 0 [Anderson]
Washington 0 at Carolina 5 [Peters]

FEBRUARY 21, 2012

NY Islanders 1 at Buffalo 2 (one goal in each period)
New Jersey 4 at Toronto 3 (Fayne 1:18 OT)
NY Rangers 0 at Pittsburgh 2 [Fleury]
San Jose 3 at Columbus 6 (Carter (CBJ) hat trick)
Dallas 3 at Montreal 0 [Lehtonen]
Anaheim 2 at Tampa Bay 3 (Stamkos (TB) two goals in 1st)
Vancouver 1 at Nashville 3 (no scoring in 1st)
Philadelphia 5 at Winnipeg 4 (Jagr 4:16 OT)
Detroit 1 at Chicago 2 (one goal in each period)
Edmonton 6 at Calgary 1 (Flames led 1–0 midway through 1st)
Los Angeles 4 at Phoenix 5 (SO)

FEBRUARY 22, 2012

Washington 2 at Ottawa 5 (Senators led 4–0 after 2nd)
Boston 4 at St. Louis 2 (no scoring in middle 30 minutes of game)
Los Angeles 1 at Colorado 4 (Kings scored only goal of 3rd)

FEBRUARY 23, 2012

San Jose 2 at Toronto 1 (Sharks led 2–0 after 1st)
Anaheim 3 at Carolina 2 (SO)
Minnesota 3 at Florida 2 (SO)
Vancouver 4 at Detroit 3 (SO)
St. Louis 3 at Nashville 2 (SO)
Tampa Bay 3 at Winnipeg 4 (Jets led 4–0 after 2nd)
Dallas 3 at Chicago 1 (Hawks led 1–0 after 2nd)
Phoenix 4 at Calgary 3 (SO)
Philadelphia 0 at Edmonton 2 [Dubnyk]

FEBRUARY 24, 2012

Vancouver 2 at New Jersey 1 (no scoring last 28 minutes of game)
NY Rangers 3 at NY Islanders 4 (SO)
Montreal 1 at Washington 4 (Capitals led 3–0 after 2nd)
Colorado 5 at Columbus 0 [Varlamov]
Boston 1 at Buffalo 2 (SO)
Minnesota 1 at Dallas 4 (Wandell two goals)

FEBRUARY 25, 2012

Tampa Bay 1 at Pittsburgh 8 (Malkin hat trick)
St. Louis 3 at Winnipeg 2 (SO)
Phoenix 3 at Edmonton 1 (Coyotes led 2–0 after 1st & 2nd)
Chicago 0 at Los Angeles 4 [Quick]
Washington 4 at Toronto 2 (Capitals led 4–0 after 2nd)
Boston 5 at Ottawa 3 (Alfredsson (OTT) two goals in 3rd)
Buffalo 2 at NY Rangers 3 (Callahan 2:59 OT)
Florida 3 at Carolina 2 (SO)
Colorado 4 at Detroit 3 (Avs led 3–0 after 2nd)
San Jose 2 at Nashville 6 (Weber (NAS) two goals)
Philadelphia 5 at Calgary 4 (SO)

FEBRUARY 26, 2012

Tampa Bay 4 at New Jersey 3 (St. Louis (TB) hat trick)
Columbus 2 at Pittsburgh 4 (no scoring in first half of game)
Vancouver 2 at Dallas 3 (Eriksson 3:52 OT)
NY Islanders 2 at Ottawa 5 (Isles led 1–0 after 1st)
Montreal 2 at Florida 4 (Habs led 2–0 midway through 1st)
San Jose 3 at Minnesota 4 (Sharks led 3–2 midway through 3rd)
Chicago 1 at Anaheim 3 (game tied 1–1 after 1st)

FEBRUARY 27, 2012

New Jersey 0 at NY Rangers 2 [Lundqvist]
Los Angeles 1 at Nashville 2 (Predators led 2–0 after 2nd)
Edmonton 5 at Winnipeg 3 (Oilers scored four goals in a row in 3rd)
Anaheim 1 at Colorado 4 (Avs scored only three goals of 3rd)
St. Louis 3 at Calgary 1 (Arnott two goals)

FEBRUARY 28, 2012

Ottawa 1 at Boston 0 (Karlsson 14:44 1st) [Lehner]
Florida 5 at Toronto 3 (Santorelli (FLO) two goals)
NY Islanders 2 at Washington 3 (Ovechkin 1:35 OT)
Nashville 3 at Carolina 4 (Predators led 1–0, 2–1)
Detroit 5 at Columbus 2 (Blue Jackets led 2–1 early in 3rd)
Montreal 1 at Tampa Bay 2 (no scoring final 39 minutes)
Los Angeles 4 at Minnesota 0 [Bernier]
Vancouver 1 at Phoenix 2 (SO)
Philadelphia 0 at San Jose 1 (Clowe 1:22 1st) [Niemi]

FEBRUARY 29, 2012

Pittsburgh 4 at Dallas 3 (SO)
Toronto 4 at Chicago 5 (Hossa (CHI) two goals)
St. Louis 5 at Edmonton 2 (Blues led 3–0 early in 2nd)
Buffalo 2 at Anaheim 0 [Miller]

MARCH 1, 2012

New Jersey 3 at Boston 4 (Krejci 2:59 OT)
Minnesota 4 at Montreal 5 (SO)
NY Islanders 3 at Philadelphia 6 (game tied 2–2 early in 2nd)
NY Rangers 3 at Carolina 2 (no scoring in 1st)
Florida 0 at Winnipeg 7 [Pavelec]
Columbus 2 at Colorado 0 [Mason]
Calgary 4 at Phoenix 2 (Flames led 3–0 after 1st)
St. Louis 0 at Vancouver 2 [Luongo]
Buffalo 1 at San Jose 0 (Stafford 18:51 1st) [Miller]

MARCH 2, 2012

New Jersey 5 at Washington 0 [Hedberg]
Chicago 2 at Ottawa 1 (no scoring in last 30 minutes)
NY Rangers 3 at Tampa Bay 4 (Malone 1:58 OT)
Minnesota 0 at Detroit 6 [Howard]
Dallas 3 at Edmonton 1 (Oilers scored in final minute)
Calgary 2 at Anaheim 3 (Getzlaf broke 2–2 tie at 19:14 of 3rd)

MARCH 3, 2012

NY Islanders 3 at Boston 2 (Islanders scored in each period)
Toronto 3 at Montreal 1 (Habs led 1–0 early in 2nd)
Tampa Bay 4 at Carolina 3 (Stamkos 2:41 OT)
Nashville 3 at Florida 1 (Predators led 2–0 early in 2nd)
Columbus 5 at Phoenix 2 (Nash (CBJ) two goals)
Pittsburgh 5 at Colorado 1 (Penguins led 4–0 after 2nd)
Buffalo 5 at Vancouver 3 (Leino (BUF) scored first two goals early in 1st)
Anaheim 4 at Los Angeles 2 (Carter (LA) two goals in 2nd)
St. Louis 3 at San Jose 1 (no scoring in 3rd)

MARCH 4, 2012

New Jersey 0 at NY Islanders 1 (Okposo 2:39 2nd) [Nilsson]
Boston 3 at NY Rangers 4 (Rangers led 2–0, 3–2)
Chicago 2 at Detroit 1 (no scoring in 3rd)
Ottawa 2 at Florida 4 (Senators led 2–0 after 1st)
Dallas 3 at Calgary 2 (SO)
Philadelphia 1 at Washington 0 (E. Wellwood 7:51 2nd) [Bryzgalov]
Colorado 2 at Minnesota 0 [Varlamov]

MARCH 5, 2012

Phoenix 1 at Pittsburgh 2 (Penguins led 2–0 after 1st & 2nd)
Buffalo 1 at Winnipeg 3 (game tied 1–1 after 2nd)
Edmonton 2 at Anaheim 4 (Perry (ANA) two goals in 3rd)

MARCH 6, 2012

Boston 5 at Toronto 4 (Leafs led 1–0, 2–1)
NY Rangers 1 at New Jersey 4 (Devils scored only three goals of 3rd)
Detroit 2 at Philadelphia 3 (Red Wings led 1–0 early in 1st)
Carolina 4 at Washington 3 (Faulk 3:38 OT)
Phoenix 2 at Columbus 3 (Blue Jackets led 2–0 at 3:54 of 1st)
Ottawa 7 at Tampa Bay 3 (M. Michalek (OTT) natural hat trick in 3rd)
Chicago 1 at St. Louis 5 (McDonald two goals)
Los Angeles 5 at Nashville 4 (Williams (LA) two goals in 1st)
Minnesota 2 at Colorado 7 (eight different scorers)
Montreal 4 at Calgary 5 (Flames led 2–0, 5–2)
Dallas 5 at Vancouver 2 (Canucks led 1–0 early in 2nd)
Edmonton 3 at San Jose 2 (SO)

MARCH 7, 2012

Carolina 2 at Buffalo 3 (Pominville 0:56 OT)
Toronto 2 at Pittsburgh 3 (Leafs led 2–0 early in 2nd)

MARCH 8, 2012

Buffalo 1 at Boston 3 (Bruins scored only two goals of 3rd)
NY Islanders 1 at New Jersey 5 (Kovalchuk hat trick)
Florida 0 at Philadelphia 5 [Bryzgalov]
Tampa Bay 2 at Washington 3 (Ovechkin 4:09 OT)
Los Angeles 1 at Columbus 3 (game tied 1–1 midway through 1st)
NY Rangers 1 at Ottawa 4 (Rangers led 1–0 early in 1st)
Anaheim 1 at St. Louis 3 (Backes two goals)
Colorado 2 at Nashville 4 (Avs led 1–0 at 1:14 of 1st)
San Jose 3 at Dallas 4 (SO)
Minnesota 3 at Phoenix 2 (SO)
Montreal 5 at Edmonton 3 (both teams scored in all periods)
Winnipeg 2 at Vancouver 3 (Jets led 2–1 early in 3rd)

MARCH 9, 2012

Florida 1 at Pittsburgh 2 (SO)
Los Angeles 3 at Detroit 4 (Kings led 1–0, 2–1, 3–2)
NY Rangers 3 at Chicago 4 (game tied 2–2 midway through 3rd)
Winnipeg 3 at Calgary 5 (Flames led 3–0 midway through 1st)

MARCH 10, 2012

Washington 4 at Boston 3 (game tied 2–2 early in 2nd)
Edmonton 2 at Colorado 3 (SO)
Philadelphia 1 at Toronto 0 (SO) [Bryzgalov/Gustavsson]
Buffalo 4 at Ottawa 3 (SO)
New Jersey 2 at NY Islanders 1 (all goals in 3rd)
Carolina 4 at Tampa Bay 2 (Skinner (CAR) two goals)
Columbus 1 at St. Louis 4 (game tied 1–1 early in 2nd)
Detroit 2 at Nashville 3 (A. Kostitsyn (NAS) two goals)
Anaheim 0 at Dallas 2 [Lehtonen]
San Jose 0 at Phoenix 3 [Smith]
Montreal 4 at Vancouver 1 (Cole (MON) two goals in 3rd)

MARCH 11, 2012

Boston 2 at Pittsburgh 5 (Krejci (BOS) two goals in 2nd)
Toronto 0 at Washington 2 [Neuvirth]
Carolina 0 at Florida 2 [Theodore]
St. Louis 2 at Columbus 1 (Blues scored only goal of 3rd)
Calgary 4 at Minnesota 3 (teams combined for six goals in 3rd)
Philadelphia 1 at New Jersey 4 (Devils led 1–0 after 1st & 2nd)
NY Islanders 3 at NY Rangers 4 (Gaborik 4:54 OT)
Los Angeles 3 at Chicago 2 (SO)

MARCH 12, 2012

Montreal 2 at Buffalo 3 (Myers 2:01 OT)
Anaheim 2 at Colorado 3 (Landeskog 1:52 OT)
San Jose 3 at Edmonton 2 (Sharks scored in each period)
Nashville 5 at Phoenix 4 (SO)

MARCH 13, 2012

Washington 5 at NY Islanders 4 (SO)
Carolina 2 at NY Rangers 4 (Richards (NYR) two goals in 2nd)
New Jersey 0 at Philadelphia 3 [Bryzgalov]
Boston 1 at Tampa Bay 6 (Stamkos two goals)
Toronto 2 at Florida 5 (Bergenheim (FLO) two goals)
Dallas 1 at Minnesota 0 (Benn 3:46 3rd) [Lehtonen]
St. Louis 3 at Chicago 4 (SO)
San Jose 2 at Calgary 3 (Stajan 4:20 OT)
Detroit 2 at Los Angeles 5 (Kings led 2–0 after 2nd)

MARCH 14, 2012

Colorado 5 at Buffalo 4 (SO)
Ottawa 2 at Montreal 3 (SO)
Dallas 2 at Winnipeg 5 (Jets scored four goals in 2nd)
Columbus 0 at Edmonton 3 [Dubnyk]
Phoenix 5 at Vancouver 4 (Canucks led 2–0 midway through 1st)
Detroit 0 at Anaheim 4 [Hiller]

MARCH 15, 2012

Colorado 0 at New Jersey 1 (SO) [Giguere/Brodeur]
Philadelphia 3 at NY Islanders 2 (Islanders scored only two goals of 3rd)
Pittsburgh 5 at NY Rangers 2 (Cooke (PIT) two goals)
St. Louis 0 at Carolina 2 [Ward]
Toronto 3 at Tampa Bay 1 (Lightning scored in final minute)
Boston 2 at Florida 6 (eight different scorers)
Phoenix 1 at Calgary 4 (Flames led 2–0 early in 2nd)
Nashville 1 at San Jose 2 (SO)

MARCH 16, 2012

Montreal 1 at Ottawa 2 (Kuba 3:07 OT)
Washington 2 at Winnipeg 3 (Jets scored in each period)
Chicago 4 at Dallas 1 (Sharp two goals)
Calgary 1 at Edmonton 3 (Nugent-Hopkins two goals)
Los Angeles 4 at Anaheim 2 (Kings led 3–0 after 1st)

MARCH 17, 2012

Philadelphia 2 at Boston 3 (SO)
Pittsburgh 5 at New Jersey 2 (Penguins scored only three goals of 2nd)
Carolina 5 at Minnesota 3 (Wild led 3–2 after 2nd)
NY Islanders 3 at Montreal 2 (SO)
Toronto 3 at Ottawa 1 (Senators scored late in 3rd)
Colorado 3 at NY Rangers 1 (game tied 1–1 after 1st)
St. Louis 3 at Tampa Bay 1 (Lightning scored only goal of 3rd)
Buffalo 2 at Florida 3 (SO)
Columbus 3 at Vancouver 4 (D. Sedin (VAN) two goals)
Nashville 2 at Los Angeles 4 (game tied 1–1 after 2nd)
Detroit 2 at San Jose 3 (Havlat 3:23 OT)

MARCH 18, 2012

Pittsburgh 2 at Philadelphia 3 (Hartnell 4:59 OT)
Washington 2 at Chicago 5 (Hawks led 2–0 after 1st)
Columbus 2 at Calgary 1 (SO)
Phoenix 3 at Edmonton 2 (SO)
Nashville 3 at Anaheim 1 (Ducks led 1–0 after 1st & 2nd)
Carolina 4 at Winnipeg 3 (Miettinen (WIN) two goals in 2nd)

MARCH 19, 2012

Toronto 0 at Boston 8 [Thomas]
New Jersey 2 at NY Rangers 4 (Rangers led 2–0 early in 2nd)
Buffalo 7 at Tampa Bay 3 (Pominville & Foligno (BUF) two goals)
Washington 5 at Detroit 3 (Ovechkin (WAS) two goals in 1st)
Vancouver 0 at Minnesota 2 [Harding]
Anaheim 5 at San Jose 3 (eight different scorers)

MARCH 20, 2012

NY Islanders 5 at Toronto 2 (Leafs led 2–1 early in 2nd)
Florida 2 at Philadelphia 1 (no scoring in last 32 minutes)
Winnipeg 4 at Pittsburgh 8 (Neal (PIT) hat trick)
Chicago 5 at Columbus 1 (Sharp two goals)
New Jersey 1 at Ottawa 0 (Kovalchuk 17:20 2nd) [Hedberg]
Edmonton 6 at Nashville 3 (Hemsky (EDM) hat trick)
Phoenix 3 at Dallas 4 (SO)
Calgary 1 at Colorado 2 (D. Jones 3:51 OT)
San Jose 2 at Los Angeles 5 (game tied 1–1 after 1st)

MARCH 21, 2012

Montreal 0 at Buffalo 3 [Miller]
Florida 1 at Carolina 3 (E. Staal two goals)
Detroit 1 at NY Rangers 2 (Callahan 2:42 OT)
Vancouver 1 at Chicago 2 (Shaw 2:42 OT)
St. Louis 3 at Anaheim 4 (Blues led 1–0, 2–1, 3–2)

MARCH 22, 2012

Washington 1 at Philadelphia 2 (SO)
Nashville 1 at Pittsburgh 5 (Malkin two goals)
Edmonton 2 at Tampa Bay 3 (SO)
Calgary 2 at Minnesota 3 (SO)
Vancouver 2 at Dallas 1 (Canucks led 1–0 after 1st & 2nd)
Colorado 2 at Phoenix 3 (Coyotes led 3–0 after 2nd)
St. Louis 0 at Los Angeles 1 (SO)
Boston 1 at San Jose 2 (Bruins scored late in 3rd)

MARCH 23, 2012

Toronto 4 at New Jersey 3 (SO)
Buffalo 4 at NY Rangers 1 (Stafford two goals)
Winnipeg 4 at Washington 3 (Stapleton 2:37 OT)
Carolina 1 at Columbus 5 (Umberger two goals)
Ottawa 1 at Montreal 5 (Cole hat trick in 1st)
Edmonton 2 at Florida 1 (SO)

MARCH 24, 2012

Calgary 1 at Dallas 4 (Stars led 2–1 after 1st & 2nd)
Boston 4 at Los Angeles 2 (game tied 1–1 after 2nd)
Minnesota 1 at Buffalo 3 (Sabres scored only two goals of 3rd)
NY Rangers 4 at Toronto 3 (SO)
Pittsburgh 4 at Ottawa 8 (Penguins led 2–1 after 1st)
Montreal 1 at Philadelphia 4 (Briere two goals in 2nd)
NY Islanders 3 at Tampa Bay 4 (Stamkos (TB) scored first two goals of game)
Carolina 4 at Detroit 5 ('Canes led 2–1, 4–2)
Winnipeg 1 at Nashville 3 (Predators led 2–0 after 2nd)
Vancouver 3 at Colorado 2 (Higgins 1:40 OT)
Phoenix 3 at San Jose 4 (SO)

MARCH 25, 2012

Edmonton 6 at Columbus 3 (nine different scorers)
Minnesota 0 at Washington 3 [Holtby]
NY Islanders 3 at Florida 2 (SO)
New Jersey 2 at Pittsburgh 5 (game tied 1–1 early in 1st)
Nashville 6 at Chicago 1 (Predators led 4–0 early in 3rd)
Boston 3 at Anaheim 2 (no scoring in 1st)
St. Louis 4 at Phoenix 0 [Elliott]

MARCH 26, 2012

Tampa Bay 5 at Philadelphia 3 (game tied 2–2 after 2nd)
Columbus 2 at Detroit 7 (Blue Jackets scored final two goals of game)
Ottawa 6 at Winnipeg 4 (Senators led 2–0, 3–2, 4–3)
Dallas 4 at Calgary 5 (Stars led 1–0, 2–1)
Los Angeles 0 at Vancouver 1 (Malhotra 3:05 1st) [Luongo]
Colorado 1 at San Jose 5 (Pavelski two goals)

MARCH 27, 2012

Tampa Bay 2 at Boston 5
Carolina 3 at Toronto 0 [Ward]
Chicago 1 at New Jersey 2 (SO)
NY Islanders 5 at Pittsburgh 3 (game tied 2–2 midway through 2nd)
Buffalo 5 at Washington 1 (Stafford two goals)
Florida 3 at Montreal 2 (SO)
Nashville 0 at St. Louis 3 [Elliott]
NY Rangers 3 at Minnesota 2 (Rangers scored only goal of 3rd)

MARCH 28, 2012

NY Rangers 4 at Winnipeg 2 (Jets led 2–0 early in 2nd)
Detroit 2 at Columbus 4 (Red Wings scored only goal of 3rd)
Los Angeles 3 at Calgary 0 [Quick]
Dallas 3 at Edmonton 1 (Oilers scored last goal of game)
Colorado 0 at Vancouver 1 (Higgins 17:04 1st) [Schneider]
San Jose 1 at Anaheim 3 (game tied 1–1 after 2nd)

MARCH 29, 2012

Washington 3 at Boston 2 (SO)
Philadelphia 7 at Toronto 1 (B. Schenn (PHI) two goals in 1st)
Tampa Bay 4 at New Jersey 6 (Malone (TB) hat trick)
Pittsburgh 3 at NY Islanders 5 (game tied 1–1 midway through 2nd)
Florida 2 at Minnesota 3 (M. Koivu 0:15 OT)
St. Louis 3 at Chicago 4 (SO)
San Jose 0 at Phoenix 2 [Smith]

MARCH 30, 2012

Montreal 1 at NY Rangers 4 (Habs scored late in 3rd)
Winnipeg 4 at Carolina 3 (Ladd 0:16 OT)
Florida 1 at Columbus 4 (Nikitin two goals)
Pittsburgh 5 at Buffalo 3 (eight different scorers)
Nashville 4 at Detroit 1 (no scoring in first 33 minutes)
Colorado 4 at Calgary 1 (Avs led 3–0 after 2nd)
Los Angeles 4 at Edmonton 1 (Kings scored in each period)
Dallas 2 at Vancouver 5 (game tied 1–1 midway through 2nd)

MARCH 31, 2012

Boston 6 at NY Islanders 3 (both teams scored in all periods)
Ottawa 4 at Philadelphia 3 (SO)
Buffalo 3 at Toronto 4 (Leafs led 3–1 after 2nd)
Montreal 2 at Washington 3 (SO)
New Jersey 5 at Carolina 0 [Brodeur]
Winnipeg 2 at Tampa Bay 3 (Stamkos 0:45 OT)
Columbus 5 at St. Louis 2 (Umberger (CBJ) two goals)
Chicago 5 at Nashville 4 (Hawks led 4–0, Predators tied game, 4–4)
Los Angeles 3 at Minnesota 4 (SO)
Anaheim 0 at Phoenix 4 [Smith]
Calgary 2 at Vancouver 3 (Ebbett 3:58 OT)
Dallas 0 at San Jose 3 [Niemi]

APRIL 1, 2012

Ottawa 5 at NY Islanders 1 (Islanders led 1–0 early in 1st)
Boston 2 at NY Rangers 1 (no scoring in final 28 minutes)
Florida 1 at Detroit 2 (SO)
Minnesota 5 at Chicago 4 (SO)
Philadelphia 6 at Pittsburgh 4 (Penguins led 2–0 early in 1st)
Edmonton 2 at Anaheim 1 (all goals in 1st)

APRIL 2, 2012

Washington 2 at Tampa Bay 4 (Stamkos two late goals in 3rd to break 2–2 tie)
Edmonton 2 at Los Angeles 0 [Dubnyk]

APRIL 3, 2012

Pittsburgh 5 at Boston 3 (Crosby (PIT) two goals)
Toronto 5 at Buffalo 6 (Roy 3:29 OT)
NY Islanders 1 at New Jersey 3 (Devils scored in each period)
NY Rangers 5 at Philadelphia 3 (Rangers led 4–0 after 1st)
Carolina 2 at Ottawa 1 (Senators scored in final minute)
Winnipeg 5 at Florida 4 (Ladd 3:12 OT)
Minnesota 1 at Nashville 2 (SO)
San Jose 5 at Dallas 2 (Stars led 2–1 midway through game)
Anaheim 4 at Vancouver 5 (SO)
Columbus 0 at Phoenix 2 [Smith]

APRIL 4, 2012

Tampa Bay 2 at Montreal 5 (Pacioretty (MON) two goals in 3rd)
Detroit 3 at St. Louis 2 (SO)

APRIL 5, 2012

Tampa Bay 2 at Toronto 3 (Phaneuf 4:01 OT)
Winnipeg 4 at NY Islanders 5 (Islanders led 2–0, 3–2, 4–3)
Buffalo 1 at Philadelphia 2 (no scoring in first 37 minutes)
NY Rangers 2 at Pittsburgh 5 (game tied 1–1 early in 1st)
Florida 2 at Washington 4 (Capitals led 3–0 midway through game)
Montreal 1 at Carolina 2 (SO)
Boston 3 at Ottawa 1 (Bruins scored in each period)
New Jersey 2 at Detroit 1 (one goal in each period)
Dallas 0 at Nashville 2 [Rinne]
Chicago 1 at Minnesota 2 (SO)
Columbus 5 at Colorado 2 (Atkinson hat trick)
Vancouver 2 at Calgary 3 (Canucks led 1–0 after 1st & 2nd)
Anaheim 3 at Edmonton 2 (Getzlaf 1:12 OT)
San Jose 6 at Los Angeles 5 (SO)

APRIL 6, 2012

Phoenix 4 at St. Louis 1 (game tied 1–1 early in 2nd)

APRIL 7, 2012

Buffalo 3 at Boston 4 (SO)
Ottawa 2 at New Jersey 4 (Senators led 2–1 late in 2nd)
Washington 4 at NY Rangers 1 (Capitals led 4–0 early in 2nd)
Philadelphia 2 at Pittsburgh 4 (game tied 2–2 midway through 2nd)
Chicago 3 at Detroit 2 (SO)
Anaheim 2 at Calgary 5 (Aliu (CAL) two goals)
Toronto 1 at Montreal 4 (Habs scored in each period)
Tampa Bay 4 at Winnipeg 3 (Purcell 1:08 OT)
NY Islanders 3 at Columbus 7 (Atkinson (CBJ) two goals)
Carolina 1 at Florida 4 (Panthers led 3–0 after 2nd)
Phoenix 4 at Minnesota 1 (Pyatt two goals)
St. Louis 3 at Dallas 2 (Blues led 2–0 early in 3rd)
Nashville 6 at Colorado 1 (game tied 1–1 early in 1st)
Edmonton 0 at Vancouver 3 [Luongo]
Los Angeles 2 at San Jose 3 (Boyle 3:58 OT)

2012 NHL ALL-STAR GAME

TEAM CHARA

Zdeno Chara (capt.)
Jamie Benn
Brian Campbell
Pavel Datsyuk
Jordan Eberle
Marian Gaborik
Marian Hossa
Jimmy Howard
Jarome Iginla
Patrick Kane
Phil Kessel
Joffrey Lupul
Evgeni Malkin
Corey Perry
Dion Phaneuf
Carey Price
Tyler Seguin
Ryan Suter
Tim Thomas
Kimmo Timonen
Dennis Wideman

TEAM ALFREDSSON

Daniel Alfredsson (capt.)
Logan Couture
Alexander Edler
Brian Elliott
Dan Girardi
Claude Giroux
Scott Hartnell
Erik Karlsson
Kris Letang
Henrik Lundqvist
Milan Michalek
James Neal
Jason Pominville
Johnathan Quick
Daniel Sedin

Henrik Sedin
Jason Spezza
Steve Stamkos
John Tavares
Shea Weber
Keith Yandle

ROOKIES

Team Chara—Luke Adam, Raphael Diaz, Colin Greening, Cody Hodgson, Ryan Johansen, Gabriel Landeskog
Team Alfredsson—Sean Couturier, Justin Faulk, Carl Hagelin, Nick Johnson, Matt Read, Craig Smith

GAME SUMMARY

January 29, 2012
Scotiabank Centre, Ottawa

First Period

1. Team Chara, Gaborik (Datsyuk)	4:34
2. Team Chara, Malkin (Iginla)	5:38
3. Team Chara, Gaborik (Hossa, Suter)	10:09
4. Team Alfredsson, Spezza (Girardi, M. Michalek)	10:36
5. Team Alfredsson, H. Sedin (Hartnell, Letang)	12:51
6. Team Alfredsson, Tavares (Pominville, Yandle)	13:49

Penalties: none

Second Period

7. Team Chara, Gaborik (Hossa, Datsyuk)	1:23
8. Team Chara, Lupul (Kessel)	3:33
9. Team Alfredsson, Pominville (Neal, Stamkos)	7:17
10. Team Alfredsson, Alfredsson (unassisted)	14:33
11. Team Alfredsson, Alfredsson (D. Sedin, H. Sedin)	16:04
12. Team Chara, Kane (Eberle)	18:24

Penalties: none

Third Period

13. Team Chara, Kessel (Campbell)	4:12
14. Team Alfredsson, M. Michalek (Tavares, Spezza)	5:21
15. Team Chara, Iginla (Malkin, Perry)	7:45
16. Team Alfredsson, Giroux (Hartnell, Couture)	9:40
17. Team Chara, Hossa (Datsyuk)	12:04

18. Team Chara, Chara (Gaborik)   12:20
19. Team Chara, Perry (Iginla, Wideman)   13:26
20. Team Alfredsson, D. Sedin (H. Sedin, Alfredsson)   14:20
21. Team Chara, Lupul (Seguin, Kessel)   15:33
Penalties: none

GOALIES

Team Chara
1st period—Howard (3 goals)
2nd period—Price (3 goals)
3rd period—Thomas (3 goals)

Team Alfredsson
1st period—Quick (3 goals)
2nd period—Lundqvist (3 goals)
3rd period—Elliott (6 goals)

SHOTS ON GOAL

Team Chara	12	13	19	44
Team Alfredsson	14	15	21	50

Referees—Eric Furlatt and Tim Peel
Linesmen—Brad Kovacik and Derek Amell

MVP—Marian Gaborik

Attendance—20,510

SHOOTOUT LEADERS, 2011–12

SKATERS

Shots

Zach Parise (NJ)	16
Matt Cullen (MIN)	16
Ilya Kovalchuk (NJ)	14
T.J. Oshie (STL)	14
Max Pacioretty (MON)	13
Jason Pominville (BUF)	13
Radim Vrbata (PHO)	13
Brad Boyes (BUF)	12
David Desharnais (MON)	12
Jordan Eberle (EDM)	12
Patrik Elias (NJ)	12
Jiri Hudler (DET)	12
Patrick Kane (CHI)	12
Mikko Koivu (MIN)	12
Tyler Seguin (BOS)	12

Goals

Ilya Kovalchuk (NJ)	11
Evgeni Malkin (PIT)	8
Zach Parise (NJ)	8
Matt Cullen (MIN)	7
Frans Nielsen (NYI)	7
Alexandre Burrows (VAN)	6
Patrik Elias (NJ)	6
Sam Gagner (EDM)	6
Milan Hejduk (COL)	6
Patrick Kane (CHI)	6
Tyler Seguin (BOS)	6
Jason Spezza (OTT)	6
Ray Whitney (PHO)	6

Shooting Percentage (minimum 5 shots)

Daniel Alfredsson (OTT)	83.3% (5/6)
Matt Hendricks (WAS)	83.3% (5/6)
Ilya Kovalchuk (NJ)	78.6% (11/14)
Evgeni Malkin (PIT)	72.7% (8/11)
Sam Gagner (EDM)	66.7% (6/9)

Chris Kunitz (PIT)	66.7% (4/6)
Matt Read (PHI)	66.7% (4/6)
Blake Wheeler (WIN)	66.7% (4/6)
Frans Nielsen (NYI)	63.6% (7/11)
Patrice Bergeron (BOS)	62.5% (5/8)

Worst Shooting Percentage (minimum 5 shots)

Viktor Stalberg (CHI)	0.00% (0/5)
Anze Kopitar (LA)	11.1% (1/9)
Brad Richards (NYR)	11.1% (1/9)
Patrick Sharp (CHI)	12.5% (1/8)
Alex Tanguay (COL)	12.5% (1/8)
Kris Versteeg (FLO)	12.5% (1/8)
Marcel Goc (FLO)	14.3% (1/7)
Phil Kessel (TOR)	14.3% (1/7)
David Perron (STL)	14.3% (1/7)
Michael Ryder (DAL)	14.3% (1/7)

GOALIES

Wins

Marc-Andre Fleury (PIT)	9 (11 SO)
Semyon Varlamov (COL)	8 (8 SO)
Antti Niemi (SJ)	8 (12 SO)
Tim Thomas (BOS)	7 (8 SO)
Martin Brodeur (NJ)	7 (9 SO)
Kari Lehtonen (DAL)	7 (9 SO)
Corey Crawford (CHI)	6 (7 SO)
Craig Anderson (OTT)	6 (10 SO)
Roberto Luongo (VAN)	6 (10 SO)
Jonathan Quick (LA)	6 (14 SO)
Mike Smith (PHO)	6 (14 SO)

Save Percentage (minimum 15 shots faced)

Semyon Varlamov (COL)	91.7% (22/24)
Jimmy Howard (DET)	81.5% (22/27)
Corey Crawford (CHI)	81.3% (26/32)
Josh Harding (MIN)	78.3% (18/23)
Evgeni Nabokov (NYI)	77.8% (14/18)
Antti Niemi (SJ)	77.5% (31/40)
Marc-Andre Fleury (PIT)	76.9% (30/39)
Kari Lehtonen (DAL)	76.9% (30/39)

Tim Thomas (BOS)	76.9% (20/26)		
Devan Dubnyk (EDM)	74.1% (20/27)		

TEAM RECORDS

Most Shootouts

Team	SO	W	L
Minnesota	20	11	9
Florida	17	6	11
Montreal	17	5	12
New Jersey	16	12	4
Phoenix	16	6	10
Vancouver	15	8	7
Los Angeles	15	6	9

Fewest Shootouts

Team	SO	W	L
Tampa Bay	6	3	3
Carolina	7	1	6
Washington	8	4	4
Winnipeg	8	4	4
Columbus	9	4	5
NY Rangers	9	4	5
Toronto	9	4	5

NATIONALITY OF ALL PLAYERS, 2011–12

SUMMARY

(figures in parentheses show leaguewide representation as a percentage)

TOTAL	**985**	
CANADA	522	(53.0%)
Alberta	78	
British Columbia	56	
Manitoba	34	
New Brunswick	3	
Newfoundland	7	
Nova Scotia	9	
Ontario	212	
Prince Edward Island	6	
Quebec	71	
Saskatchewan	46	
UNITED STATES	234	(23.8%)
SWEDEN	67	(6.8%)
CZECH REPUBLIC	43	(4.4%)
RUSSIA	30	(3.0%)
FINLAND	29	(2.9%)
SLOVAKIA	12	(1.2%)
GERMANY	9	(0.9%)
SWITZERLAND	7	(0.7%)
DENMARK	6	(0.6%)
AUSTRIA	3	(0.3%)
LATVIA	3	(0.3%)
BELARUS	2	(0.2%)
FRANCE	2	(0.2%)
KAZAKHSTAN	2	(0.2%)
SLOVENIA	2	(0.2%)
UKRAINE	2	(0.2%)
BAHAMAS	1	(0.1%)
BRAZIL	1	(0.1%)
BRUNEI	1	(0.1%)
ITALY	1	(0.1%)
JAPAN	1	(0.1%)
LITHUANIA	1	(0.1%)
NIGERIA	1	(0.1%)

NORWAY	1	(0.1%)
POLAND	1	(0.1%)
SOUTH KOREA	1	(0.1%)

NATIONALITY BREAKDOWN

CANADA	**522**	
Alberta	78	
Airdrie	2	Zach Boychuk, Dana Tyrell
Banff	1	Ryan Smyth
Barrhead	1	Leland Irving
Beaverlodge	1	Matt Walker
Calgary	14	Cody Almond, Jay Beagle, Braydon Coburn, Joe Colborne, Mike Connolly, Patrick Eaves, Kris Foucault, T.J. Galiardi, Mike Green, Taylor Hall, Nick Johnson, Krys Kolanos, Chris Phillips, Jeff Schultz
Camrose	1	Josh Green
Caroline	3	Kris Russell, Ryan Russell, Jim Vandermeer
Cochrane	1	Mason Raymond
Cold Lake	1	Alexander Auld
Consort	1	Riley Nash
Edmonton	21	Jay Bouwmeester, Johnny Boychuk, Gilbert Brule, Jason Chimera, Erik Christensen, Deryk Engelland, Tyler Ennis, Andrew Ference, Vernon Fiddler, Mark Fistric, Matt Frattin, Jarome Iginla, Matt Kassian, Daymond Langkow, Bryan Little, Joffrey Lupul, Derek Morris, Scott Nichol, Dion Phaneuf, David Schlemko, Jared Spurgeon
Elk Point	2	Mark Letestu, Sheldon Souray
Forestburg	1	Evan Oberg
Fort McMurray	1	Scottie Upshall
Fort Saskatchewan	2	Mike Commodore, Ray Whitney
Halkirk	1	Shane Doan
Lac La Biche	1	Rene Bourque
Lethbridge	3	Rob Klinkhammer, Spencer Machacek, Kris Versteeg
Lloydminster	1	Clarke MacArthur
Medicine Hat	2	Brooks Laich, Zack Smith
Olds	1	Jay Rosehill
Provost	1	Lance Bouma
Red Deer	4	Matt Fraser, Trent Hunter, Chris Mason, Paul Postma
Rimbey	1	Jason Jaffray
Rocky Mountain House	1	Brad Stuart

St. Paul	1	Kyle Brodziak
Sherwood Park	1	Cam Ward
Spruce Grove	1	Ben Scrivens
Strathmore	1	Keaton Ellerby
Taber	1	Devin Setoguchi
Vermilion	1	Jeff Woywitka
Viking	1	Brett Sutter
Wetaskiwin	1	Allen York
Westlock	1	Kyle Chipchura
British Columbia	**56**	
Abbotsford	1	David van der Gulik
Aldergrove	1	Brad Thiessen
Burnaby	5	Karl Alzner, Jason LaBarbera, Ryan Nugent-Hopkins, Mark Olver, Greg Zanon
Campbell River	2	Brett Connolly, Kris Fredheim
Kelowna	1	Josh Gorges
Kitimat	1	Rod Pelley
Maple Ridge	1	Andrew Ladd
New Westminster	2	Brenden Dillon, Kyle Turris
North Vancouver	1	Ben Maxwell
Osoyoos	1	Chuck Kobasew
Pitt Meadows	1	Brendan Morrison
Port McNeill	2	Willie Mitchell, Clayton Stoner
Port Moody	1	Ryan Johansen
Prince George	2	Brett Bulmer, Brandon Manning
Quesnel	2	Brett Festerling, Aaron Gagnon
Revelstoke	1	Aaron Volpatti
Richmond	4	Scott Hannan, Brandon McMillan, Brent Seabrook, Brandon Segal
Salmon Arm	1	Cody Franson
Sicamous	2	Colin Fraser, Shea Weber
Smithers	1	Dan Hamhuis
Terrace	1	Bradley Mills
Trail	2	Shawn Horcoff, Barret Jackman
Vancouver	10	Troy Brouwer, Stefan Elliott, Zach Hamill, Evander Kane, Bracken Kearns, Milan Lucic, Steve Montador, Carey Price, Mike Santorelli, Brandon Yip
Vernon	3	Eric Brewer, Andrew Ebbett, Jerred Smithson
Victoria	4	Tyson Barrie, Jamie Benn, Jordie Benn, Ryan O'Byrne
White Rock	3	Jason Garrison, Colton Gillies, Colten Teubert

Manitoba	34	
Binscarth	1	Cody McLeod
Brandon	5	Matt Calvert, Carson McMillan, Alex Plante, Bryce Salvador, Ryan White
Churchill	1	Jordin Tootoo
Dauphin	1	Colby Robak
Nesbitt	1	Aaron Rome
Portage La Prairie	1	Arron Asham
Selkirk	1	Andrew Murray
Snowflake	1	Justin Falk
Swan River	1	Chay Genoway
Thompson	1	Jody Shelley
Winkler	2	Eric Fehr, Dustin Penner
Winnipeg	18	Carter Ashton, Cam Barker, Cody Eakin, Ryan Garbutt, Travis Hamonic, Darren Helm, Duncan Keith, Frazer McLaren, Derek Meech, Colton Orr, Ryan Reaves, James Reimer, Alexander Steen, Michael Stone, Jonathan Toews, Dale Weise, Ian White, Travis Zajac
Ontario	212	
Ajax	1	Brent Burns
Alfred	1	Benoit Pouliot
Almonte	1	Kent Huskins
Amherstburg	1	Kevin Westgarth
Ayr	1	Kyle Clifford
Barrie	1	John Madden
Bayfield	1	Jeremy Welsh
Belleville	6	Matt Cooke, Andrew Raycroft, Brad Richardson, Andrew Shaw, Derek Smith, Ty Wishart
Blyth	1	Justin Peters
Bowmanville	1	Bryan Bickell
Bramalea	1	Mike Weaver
Brampton	3	Rick Nash, Kris Newbury, Tyler Seguin
Brantford	2	Adam Henrique, Paul Szczechura
Brights Grove	1	Brad Staubitz
Cambridge	2	Tim Brent, Trevor Gillies
Carp	1	Kurtis Foster
Chatham	2	T.J. Brodie, Ryan Jones
Clinton	1	Ryan O'Reilly
Cobourg	1	Justin Williams
Collingwood	1	Jason Arnott

Courtice	1	Greg Nemisz
Dryden	1	Chris Pronger
Elliot Lake	1	Zack Stortini
Fergus	1	Jamie McGinn
Gloucester	1	Grant Clitsome
Grimsby	1	Kevin Bieksa
Guelph	4	Krys Barch, Logan Couture, David Jones, Rich Peverley
Haliburton	1	Matt Duchene
Hamilton	4	Ryan Ellis, Ray Emery, Brian McGrattan, Steve Staios
Hearst	1	Claude Giroux
Huntsville	1	Ethan Moreau
Ilderton	1	Matt Read
Kenora	1	Mike Richards
King City	2	Daniel Carcillo, Alex Pietrangelo
Kingston	6	Bryan Allen, John Erskine, Jay McClement, Mike Murphy, Mike Smith, Andy Sutton
Kitchener	6	Evan Brophey, Mike Hoffman, Kevin Klein, Kyle Quincey, Mark Scheifele, Dennis Wideman
LaSalle	1	Dalton Prout
Lively	1	Andrew Desjardins
London	13	Gregory Campbell, Jeff Carter, Drew Doughty, Sam Gagner, Matt Hackett, Nazem Kadri, Mark Mancari, Cody McCormick, Curtis McElhinney, Brandon Prust, Bryan Rodney, Joe Thornton, Jason Williams
Long Sault	1	Jesse Winchester
Markdale	1	Chris Neil
Markham	2	Jeff Skinner, Steve Stamkos
Mississauga	9	Brad Boyes, Cody Goloubef, Tom Kostopoulos, Manny Malhotra, Shawn Matthias, Zac Rinaldo, Jason Spezza, Matt Stajan, John Tavares
Newmarket	2	Steve Downie, Brian Elliott
Niagara-on-the-Lake	1	Zenon Konopka
Oakville	4	Scott Glennie, Steve Mason, David McIntyre, Kyle Wilson
Oshawa	6	Josh Bailey, Michael Haley, Ryan Hamilton, Jay Harrison, James Neal, Shawn Thornton
Ottawa	14	Adrian Aucoin, Brendan Bell, Mark Borowiecki, Dan Boyle, Paul Byron, Calvin De Haan, Ben Eager, Mark Fraser, Erik Gudbranson, Jon Matsumoto, Marc Methot, Sean O'Donnell, Derek Roy, Trevor Smith
Owen Sound	2	Cody Bass, Curtis Sanford
Palmerston	1	Nick Spaling
Paris	1	Zac Dalpe

Peterborough	2	Mike Fisher, Corey Perry
Pickering	1	Sean Avery
Port Elgin	1	Brett MacLean
Port Hope	1	Shane O'Brien
Richmond Hill	3	Mike Cammalleri, Derek Joslin, Theo Peckham
Sarnia	1	Dustin Jeffrey
Sault Ste. Marie	4	Matt D'Agostini, Tyler Kennedy, Chris Thorburn, Marty Turco
Simcoe	1	Dwayne Roloson
St. Catharines	3	Jordan Nolan, John Scott, Riley Sheahan
St. Isidore	1	Francis Wathier
St. Pauls	1	Mark Bell
St. Thomas	1	Cory Emmerton
Stittsville	1	Matt Bradley
Stouffville	1	Michael del Zotto
Strathroy	2	Brian Campbell, Andy McDonald
Sudbury	3	Todd Bertuzzi, Andrew Brunette, Derek MacKenzie
Thornhill	1	Dominic Moore
Thunder Bay	8	Robert Bortuzzo, Taylor Chorney, Taylor Pyatt, Tom Pyatt, Patrick Sharp, Eric Staal, Jordan Staal, Marc Staal
Timmins	1	Steve Sullivan
Toronto	34	Mike Blunden, Dave Bolland, Chris Campoli, Casey Cizikas, David Clarkson, Andrew Cogliano, Carlo Colaiacovo, Tyler Cuma, Trevor Daley, Mike Duco, Mark Giordano, Matt Halischuk, Cody Hodgson, Peter Holland, Chris Kelly, Mike Knuble, Jamal Mayers, Kenndal McArdle, Matt Moulson, Cal O'Reilly, Brandon Pirri, Chris Porter, Wayne Simmonds, Brendan Smith, Reilly Smith, Devante Smith-Pelly, Chris Stewart, P.K. Subban, Chris Tanev, Raffi Torres, Joel Ward, Stephen Weiss, Daniel Winnick, Harry Zolnierczyk
Waterloo	1	John Mitchell
Welland	6	Paul Bissonnette, Cal Clutterbuck, Matt Ellis, Daniel Girardi, Nathan Horton, Daniel Paille
Winchester	1	Matt Carkner
Whitby	1	Victor Oreskevich
Windsor	8	Matt Beleskey, Cam Fowler, Ed Jovanovski, Zack Kassian, Matt Martin, Eric Wellwood, Kyle Wellwood, Ryan Wilson
Woodbridge	2	Mike Angelidis, Steve Eminger

New Brunswick	3	
Miramichi	1	Brad Malone
Moncton	1	Patrice Cormier
Quispamsis	1	Randy Jones

Newfoundland	7	
Bonavista	1	Adam Pardy
Carbonear	1	Daniel Cleary
St. John's	5	Luke Adam, Ryane Clowe, Colin Greening, Teddy Purcell, Michael Ryder

Nova Scotia	9	
Halifax	5	Eric Boulton, Sidney Crosby, Andrew Gordon, Andrew Joudrey, Brad Marchand
Judique	1	Andrew MacDonald
New Glasgow	1	Colin White
Pictou	1	Joey MacDonald
Port Hawkesbury	1	Aaron Johnson

Prince Edward Island	6	
Charlottetown	3	Mark Flood, Drew MacIntyre, Adam McQuaid
Murray Harbour	1	Brad Richards
Summerside	2	Darryl Boyce, Steve Ott

Quebec	71	
Alma	1	Guillaume Desbiens
Amqui	1	Sebastien Caron
L'Ancienne-Lorette	1	Patrice Bergeron
Baie-Comeau	1	Pierre-Cedric Labrie
Beauceville	1	Stephane Veilleux
Chandler	1	Mathieu Garon
Dorval	1	Jason Demers
Boucherville	1	Kevin Marshall
Dégelis	1	Gabriel Dumont
Drummondville	1	Mathieu Perreault
Gatineau	2	Daniel Briere, Alexandre Picard (b. Jul '85)
Greenfield Park	2	Jerome Samson, Frederic St. Denis
Hull	2	Derick Brassard, P-A Parenteau
Île-Bizard	1	Vincent Lecavalier
Lac-St-Charles	1	Martin Biron
Lafontaine	1	Yann Danis

LaSalle	1	Anthony Stewart
Laval	7	Jonathan Bernier, Simon Despres, Pascal Dupuis, Philippe Dupuis, Maxime Macenauer, Martin St. Louis, Jose Theodore
Lemoyne	1	Maxime Talbot
Lévis	1	Pierre-Luc Letourneau-Leblond
Longueuil	1	Bruno Gervais
Montreal	14	Alexandre Bolduc, Martin Brodeur, Corey Crawford, Mathieu Darche, J-S Giguere, Marc-Andre Gragnani, Kris Letang, Matt Lombardi, Roberto Luongo, Torrey Mitchell, Kevin Poulin, Mike Ribeiro, Marco Scandella, Marc-Edouard Vlasic
Pointe-Claire	2	Alex Burrows, Louis Leblanc
Quebec City	5	Steve Bernier, David Desharnais, Alexandre Giroux, Marc-Antoine Pouliot, Paul Stastny
Repentigny	1	Jason Pominville
Rimouski	1	Gabriel Bourque
St-Agapit	1	Antoine Vermette
Ste-Cathérine	1	Guillaume Latendresse
Ste-Foy	1	Simon Gagne
St. Jean Richelieu	1	Jeff Deslauriers
Ste-Justine	1	Alex Tanguay
St-Hyacinthe	2	Marc-Andre Bourdon, David Savard
St-Léonard	1	Maxim Lapierre
St-Louis-de-France	1	Marc-Andre Bergeron
Sayabec	1	Jordan Caron
Sherbrooke	4	Eric Belanger, Pierre-Marc Bouchard, David Perron, Stephane Robidas
Sorel	2	Francois Beauchemin, Marc-Andre Fleury
Terrebonne	1	J-F Jacques
Val-Senneville	1	Philippe Cornet
Saskatchewan	**46**	
Aneroid	1	Patrick Marleau
Aylesbury	1	Matt Watkins
Brock	1	Steve MacIntyre
Carlyle	1	Brenden Morrow
Central Butte	1	Blair Jones
Estevan	1	Trent Whitfield
Humboldt	1	Dustin Tokarski
Kamsack	1	Darcy Hordichuk
Kindersley	2	Derek Dorsett, Curtis Glencross

Lanigan	1	Sheldon Brookbank
Lloydminster	2	Colby Armstrong, Braden Holtby
Meadow Lake	3	Blake Comeau, D.J. King, Dwight King
Melfort	2	Jaden Schwartz, Tyson Strachan
Melville	1	Jarret Stoll
Nipawin	1	Dane Byers
Prince Albert	1	Adam Cracknell
Punnichy	1	Nolan Yonkman
Regina	11	Keith Aulie, Tyler Bozak, Brett Carson, Devan Dubnyk, Jordan Eberle, Ryan Getzlaf, Tanner Glass, Josh Harding, Scott Hartnell, Chris Kunitz, Brendan Mikkelson
Saskatoon	9	Byron Bitz, Jared Cowen, Dan Ellis, Brayden McNabb, Warren Peters, Darroll Powe, Cory Sarich, Brayden Schenn, Luke Schenn
Stewart Valley	1	Travis Moen
Strasbourg	1	Nick Schultz
Unity	1	Boyd Gordon
Wapella	1	Brett Clark
UNITED STATES	**234**	
Alaska	7	Matt Carle, Ty Conklin, Joey Crabb, Brandon Dubinsky, Scott Gomez, Nate Thompson, Tim Wallace
Arizona	1	Sean Couturier
California	6	Jonathon Blum, Brooks Orpik, Rhett Rakhshani, Brett Sterling, Casey Wellman, Jason Zucker
Colorado	4	Ben Bishop, Mat Clark, B.J. Crombeen, Ben Holmstrom
Connecticut	10	Cam Atkinson, Nick Bonino, Ron Hainsey, Lane MacDermid, Colin McDonald, Max Pacioretty, Jonathan Quick, Ryan Shannon, Kevin Shattenkirk, Colin Wilson
Delaware	1	Mark Eaton
Florida	1	Blake Geoffrion
Illinois	12	Craig Anderson, Jarred Boll, Mike Brown, Joe Corvo, Brett Lebda, Al Montoya, John Moore, Greg Rallo, Tim Stapleton, Bill Sweatt, Ryan Thang, Tommy Wingels
Indiana	2	Jack Johnson, John-Michael Liles
Iowa	1	Scott Clemmensen
Maine	1	Jon Disalvatore
Maryland	1	Jeff Halpern

Massachusetts	18	Keith Aucoin, Brian Boyle, Bobby Butler, John Carlson, Rick DiPietro, Benn Ferriero, Hal Gill, Jimmy Hayes, Josh Hennessy, Doug Janik, Chris Kreider, John McCarthy, Mike Mottau, Jay Pandolfo, Cory Schneider, Brian Strait, Ryan Whitney, Keith Yandle
Michigan	37	Justin Abdelkader, David Booth, Drayson Bowman, Ian Cole, Sean Collins, Erik Condra, Chris Conner, Nathan Gerbe, Tim Gleason, Andy Greene, Matt Greene, Adam Hall, Matt Hunwick, Shawn Hunwick, Brent Johnson, Steven Kampfer, Ryan Kesler, Torey Krug, Chad LaRose, David Legwand, Peter Mannino, Alec Martinez, Andy Miele, Ryan Miller, David Moss, Aaron Palushaj, Scott Parse, Jeff Petry, Kevin Porter, Corey Potter, Brian Rolston, Jim Slater, Chris Summers, Matt Taormina, Tim Thomas, Corey Tropp, James Wisniewski
Minnesota	47	Andrew Alberts, David Backes, Keith Ballard, Stu Bickel, Jason Blake, Justin Braun, J.T. Brown, Dustin Byfuglien, Ryan Carter, Mark Cullen, Matt Cullen, Cade Fairchild, Justin Faulk, Joe Finley, Jake Gardiner, Tom Gilbert, Alex Goligoski, Matt Hendricks, Erik Johnson, Jamie Langenbrunner, Nick Leddy, Brian Lee, Jordan Leopold, Mike Lundin, Paul Martin, Jamie McBain, Ryan McDonagh, Peter Mueller, Aaron Ness, Matt Niskanen, Jim O'Brien, Kyle Okposo, Jarod Palmer, Zach Parise, Toby Petersen, Nate Prosser, Chad Rau, Mike Sauer, Carl Sneep, Derek Stepan, Colin Stuart, Mark Stuart, Jeff Taffe, Chris Vande Velde, Blake Wheeler, Clay Wilson, J.T. Wyman
Missouri	6	Brandon Bollig, Chris Butler, Cam Janssen, Patrick Maroon, Travis Turnbull, Joe Vitale
Nebraska	1	Jed Ortmeyer
New Hampshire	3	Mark Fayne, Brian Foster, Ben Lovejoy
New Jersey	5	T.J. Brennan, Drew Miller, Bobby Ryan, Bobby Sanguinetti, James van Riemsdyk
New York	31	Zach Bogosian, Francis Bouillon, Dustin Brown, Ryan Callahan, Erik Cole, Tim Connolly, Tim Erixon, Marcus Foligno, Nick Foligno, Matt Gilroy, Brian Gionta, Stephen Gionta, Chris Higgins, Jimmy Howard, Patrick Kaleta, Patrick Kane, Tim Kennedy, Mike Komisarek, Jeremy Morin, Chris Mueller, Eric Nystrom, Kyle Palmieri, Nick Palmieri, Marty Reasoner, Rob

		Scuderi, Tim Sestito, Tom Sestito, Lee Stempniak, Brandon Sutter, Derek Whitmore, Steven Zalewski
North Carolina	2	Patrick O'Sullivan, Ben Smith
North Dakota	2	Paul Gaustad, Tim Jackman
Ohio	3	Carter Camper, Peter Harrold, Mike Rupp
Oklahoma	1	Matt Donovan
Oregon	1	Jack Hillen
Pennsylvania	10	Matt Bartkowski, Nate Guenin, Ryan Malone, George Parros, Dylan Reese, Brandon Saad, Eric Tangradi, Bill Thomas, R.J. Umberger, Mike Weber
Rhode Island	1	Brian Boucher
Texas	1	Tyler Myers
Utah	3	Richard Bachman, Trevor Lewis, Dylan Olsen
Washington	2	Pat Dwyer, T.J. Oshie
Wisconsin	13	Adam Burish, Jake Dowell, Davis Drewiske, Phil Kessel, Joe Pavelski, Joe Piskula, Joel Rechlicz, Jack Skille, Craig Smith, Drew Stafford, David Steckel, Ryan Suter, Brad Winchester

REST OF THE WORLD

SWEDEN	67	Daniel Alfredsson, Joakim Andersson, Mikael Backlund, Nicklas Backstrom, Niklas Bergfors, Patrik Berglund, Fabian Brunnstrom, Alexander Edler, Mattias Ekholm, Oliver Ekman-Larsson, Andreas Engqvist, Jhonas Enroth, Tobias Enstrom, Jonathan Ericsson, Loui Eriksson, Johan Franzen, Nicklas Grossman, Carl Gunnarsson, Erik Gustafsson, Jonas Gustavsson, Carl Hagelin, Johan Hedberg, Viktor Hedman, Niklas Hjalmarsson, Tomas Holmstrom, Patrik Hornqvist, Kristian Huselius, Marcus Johansson, Jacob Josefson, Eric Karlsson, Henrik Karlsson, Carl Klingberg, Niklas Kronwall, Marcus Kruger, Anton Lander, Gabriel Landeskog, Adam Larsson, Robin Lehner, Anders Lindback, Nicklas Lidstrom, Joakim Lindstrom, Andreas Lilja, Henrik Lundqvist, Jacob Markstrom, Doug Murray, Anders Nilsson, Gustav Nyquist, John Oduya, Linus Omark, Magnus Paajarvi, Samuel Pahlsson, Andre Petersson, Mattias Ritola, David Rundblad, Mikael Samuelsson, Daniel Sedin, Henrik Sedin, Jakov Silfverberg, Viktor Stalberg, Anton Stralman, Henrik Tallinder, Mattias Tedenby, David Ullstrom, Alexander Urbom, Tom Wandell, Henrik Zetterberg, Mika Zibanejad

CZECH REPUBLIC   43   Radek Dvorak, Patrik Elias, Martin Erat, Tomas Fleischmann, Michael Frolik, Roman Hamrlik, Martin Hanzal, Martin Havlat, Jan Hejda, Milan Hejduk, Ales Hemsky, Roman Horak, Jiri Hudler, Jaromir Jagr, Tomas Kaberle, Jakub Kindl, Rostislav Klesla, David Krejci, Filip Kuba, Tomas Kubalik, Pavel Kubina, Tomas Kundratek, Radek Martinek, Milan Michalek, Zbynek Michalek, Michal Neuvirth, Rostislav Olesz, Ondrej Pavelec, Tomas Plekanec, Roman Polak, Vaclav Prospal, Michal Repik, Michal Rozsival, Ladislav Smid, Vladimir Sobotka, Jaroslav Spacek, Petr Sykora, Jiri Tlusty, Tomas Vincour, Tomas Vokoun, Jakub Voracek, Radim Vrbata, Marek Zidlicky

RUSSIA   30   Artem Anisimov, Anton Babchuk, Sergei Bobrovsky, Ilya Bryzgalov, Alexander Burmistrov, Evgeni Dadonov, Pavel Datsyuk, Alexei Emelin, Nikita Filatov, Sergei Gonchar, Evgeni Grachev, Nikolai Khabibulin, Antonin Khudobin, Ilya Kovalchuk, Nikolai Kulemin, Dmitri Kulikov, Andrei Loktionov, Evgeni Malkin, Andrei Markov, Maxim Mayorov, Nikita Nikitin, Dmitri Orlov, Alexander Ovechkin, Alexander Radulov, Alexander Semin, Fedor Tyutin, Simeon Varlamov, Anton Volchenkov, Slava Voynov, Vladimir Zharkov

FINLAND   29   Niklas Backstrom, Sean Bergenheim, Valtteri Filppula, Niklas Hagman, Teemu Hartikainen, Jussi Jokinen, Olli Jokinen, Miikka Kiprusoff, Mikko Koivu, Saku Koivu, Lauri Korpikoski, Teemu Laakso, Kari Lehtonen, Ville Leino, Sami Lepisto, Toni Lydman, Antti Miettinen, Antti Niemi, Petteri Nokelainen, Lennart Petrell, Joni Pitkanen, Tuukka Rask, Pekka Rinne, Tuomo Ruutu, Jussi Rynnas, Sami Salo, Teemu Selanne, Iiro Tarkki, Kimmo Timonen

SLOVAKIA   12   Peter Budaj, Zdeno Chara, Marian Gaborik, Jaroslav Halak, Michal Handzus, Marian Hossa, Milan Jurcina, Tomas Kopecky, Milan Kytnar, Andrei Meszaros, Andrej Sekera, Lubomir Visnovsky

GERMANY   9   Christian Ehrhoff, Marcel Goc, Mikhail Grabovski, Thomas Greiss, Dany Heatley, Jochen Hecht, Dennis Seidenberg, Marco Sturm, Alexander Sulzer

SWITZERLAND	7	Sven Bartschi, Raphael Diaz, Jonas Hiller, Roman Josi, Nino Niederreiter, Mark Streit, Yannick Weber
DENMARK	6	Mikkel Boedker, Lars Eller, Jannik Hansen, Philip Larsen, Frans Nielsen, Peter Regin
LATVIA	3	Kaspars Daugavins, Raitis Ivanins, Arturs Kulda
AUSTRIA	3	Michael Grabner, Andreas Nodl, Thomas Vanek
BELARUS	2	Andrei Kostitsyn, Sergei Kostitsyn
FRANCE	2	Stephane da Costa, Max Sauve
KAZAKHSTAN	2	Nik Antropov, Evgeni Nabokov
SLOVENIA	2	Anze Kopitar, Jan Mursak
UKRAINE	2	Ruslan Fedotenko, Alexei Ponikarovsky
BAHAMAS	1	Andre Deveaux
BRAZIL	1	Robyn Regehr
BRUNEI	1	Craig Adams
ITALY	1	Luca Sbisa
JAPAN	1	Ryan O'Marra
LITHUANIA	1	Dainius Zubrus
NIGERIA	1	Akim Aliu
NORWAY	1	Mats Zuccarello
POLAND	1	Wojtek Wolski
SOUTH KOREA	1	Richard Park

FIRST GAMES PLAYED, 2011–12

Skater (NAT)	Team (date)	G	A	P	Pim
Goalie (NAT)	**Team (date)**	**Mins**	**GA**	**W/L**	
Aliu, Akim (NIG)	CAL (Apr. 5)	0	1	1	2
Andersson, Joakim (SWE)	DET (Dec. 27)	0	0	0	0
Angelidis, Mike (CAN)	TB (Jan. 24)	1	0	1	0
Ashton, Carter (CAN)	TOR (Mar. 7)	0	0	0	0
Atkinson, Cam (USA)	CBJ (Oct. 7)	0	0	0	0
Barrie, Tyson (CAN)	COL (Feb. 7)	0	0	0	0
Bartschi, Sven (SUI)	CAL (Mar. 9)	0	0	0	2
Benn, Jordie (CAN)	DAL (Jan. 3)	0	1	1	0
Bickel, Stu (USA)	NYR (Dec. 20)	0	1	1	2
Bollig, Brandon (USA)	CHI (Feb. 29)	0	0	0	5
Borowiecki, Mark (CAN)	OTT (Jan. 19)	0	0	0	0
Bortuzzo, Robert (CAN)	PIT (Nov. 5)	0	0	0	2
Bourdon, Marc-Andre (CAN)	PHI (Nov. 21)	0	0	0	2
Bourque, Gabriel (CAN)	NAS (Dec. 28)	0	0	0	0
Brennan, T.J. (USA)	BUF (Nov. 23)	1	0	1	0
Brown, J.T. (USA)	TB (Mar. 31)	0	0	0	0
Bulmer, Brett (CAN)	MIN (Oct. 8)	0	0	0	0
Camper, Carter (USA)	BOS (Feb. 22)	0	0	0	0
Cizikas, Casey (CAN)	NYI (Feb. 24)	0	0	0	2
Clark, Mat (USA)	ANA (Apr. 1)	0	0	0	0
Connolly, Brett (CAN)	TB (Oct. 7)	0	0	0	2
Connolly, Mike (CAN)	COL (Mar. 4)	0	0	0	2
Cornet, Philippe (CAN)	EDM (Jan. 31)	0	1	1	0
Couturier, Sean (USA)	PHI (Oct. 6)	0	0	0	0
Cuma, Tyler (CAN)	MIN (Apr. 5)	0	0	0	2
De Haan, Calvin (CAN)	NYI (Dec. 15)	0	0	0	0
Despres, Simon (CAN)	PIT (Dec. 1)	0	1	1	2
Diaz, Raphael (SUI)	MON (Oct. 6)	0	0	0	0
Dillon, Brenden (CAN)	DAL (Apr. 7)	0	0	0	2
Donovan, Matt (USA)	NYI (Apr. 3)	0	0	0	2
Dumont, Gabriel (CAN)	MON (Apr. 4)	0	0	0	0
Eakin, Cody (CAN)	WAS (Nov. 1)	0	0	0	0
Ekholm, Mattias (SWE)	NAS (Oct. 13)	0	0	0	0
Elliott, Stefan (CAN)	COL (Nov. 26)	1	0	1	0
Ellis, Ryan (CAN)	NAS (Dec. 26)	0	0	0	2
Emelin, Alexei (RUS)	MON (Oct. 9)	0	0	0	2
Erixon, Tim (USA)	NYR (Oct. 7)	0	0	0	2

Fairchild, Cade (USA)	STL (Nov. 29)	0	0	0	0
Faulk, Justin (USA)	MIN (Oct. 22)	0	0	0	0
Finley, Joe (USA)	BUF (Dec. 2)	0	0	0	0
Foligno, Marcus (USA)	BUF (Dec. 20)	0	0	0	0
Foster, Brian (USA)	FLO (Feb. 4)	4:52	0	ND	
Foucault, Kris (CAN)	MIN (Feb. 14)	0	0	0	0
Fraser, Matt (CAN)	DAL (Jan. 24)	0	0	0	0
Fredheim, Kris (CAN)	MIN (Nov. 17)	0	0	0	0
Garbutt, Ryan (CAN)	WIN (Feb. 18)	0	0	0	0
Gardiner, Jake (USA)	TOR (Oct. 6)	0	0	0	0
Genoway, Chay (CAN)	MIN (Apr. 7)	0	1	1	0
Glennie, Scott (CAN)	DAL (Apr. 7)	0	0	0	2
Goloubef, Cody (CAN)	CBJ (Mar. 31)	0	0	0	0
Gudbranson, Erik (CAN)	FLO (Oct. 8)	0	0	0	0
Hackett, Matt (CAN)	MIN (Dec. 6)	58:49	0	W	
Hagelin, Carl (SWE)	NYR (Nov. 25)	0	1	1	0
Hayes, Jimmy (USA)	CHI (Dec. 30)	0	0	0	2
Hoffman, Mike (CAN)	OTT (Dec. 23)	0	0	0	0
Holland, Peter (CAN)	ANA (Nov. 5)	0	0	0	0
Horak, Roman (CZE)	CAL (Oct. 8)	0	1	1	0
Hunwick, Shawn (USA)	CBJ (Apr. 7)	2:33	0	ND	
Irving, Leland (CAN)	CAL (Dec. 16)	64:58	2	OTL	
Johansen, Ryan (CAN)	CBJ (Oct. 7)	0	0	0	0
Josi, Roman (SUI)	NAS (Nov. 26)	0	0	0	0
Joudrey, Andrew (CAN)	CBJ (Feb. 1)	0	0	0	0
Kassian, Zack (CAN)	BUF (Nov. 25)	0	1	1	0
Kearns, Bracken (CAN)	FLO (Oct. 20)	0	0	0	0
Kreider, Chris (USA)	NYR (Apr. 16)	0	0	0	0
Krug, Torey (USA)	BOS (Apr. 3)	0	0	0	0
Kundratek, Tomas (CZE)	WAS (Jan. 11)	0	0	0	0
Kytnar, Milan (SVK)	EDM (Jan. 11)	0	0	0	0
Labrie, Pierre-Cedric (CAN)	TB (Jan. 7)	0	0	0	0
Lander, Anton (SWE)	EDM (Oct. 9)	0	0	0	0
Landeskog, Gabriel (SWE)	COL (Oct. 8)	0	0	0	0
Larsson, Adam (SWE)	NJ (Oct. 8)	0	0	0	0
Leblanc, Louis (CAN)	MON (Nov. 30)	0	0	0	0
MacDermid, Lane (USA)	BOS (Mar. 4)	0	0	0	5
Macenauer, Maxime (CAN)	ANA (Oct. 7)	0	1	1	0
Malone, Brad (CAN)	COL (Dec. 9)	0	0	0	0
Manning, Brandon (CAN)	PHI (Mar. 8)	0	0	0	0
Maroon, Patrick (USA)	ANA (Oct. 25)	0	0	0	2
Marshall, Kevin (CAN)	PHI (Nov. 21)	0	0	0	0

Name	Team (Date)				
McIntyre, David (CAN)	MIN (Nov. 28)	0	0	0	0
McNabb, Brayden (CAN)	BUF (Nov. 26)	0	0	0	0
Miele, Andy (USA)	PHO (Oct. 23)	0	0	0	2
Murphy, Mike (CAN)	CAR (Dec. 6)	8:37	0	L	
Nash, Riley (CAN)	CAR (Dec. 21)	0	0	0	0
Ness, Aaron (USA)	NYI (Feb. 7)	0	0	0	0
Nilsson, Anders (SWE)	NYI (Nov. 19)	39:41	3	ND	
Nolan, Jordan (CAN)	LA (Feb. 11)	0	0	0	2
Nugent-Hopkins, Ryan (CAN)	EDM (Oct. 9)	1	0	1	2
Nyquist, Gustav (SWE)	DET (Nov. 1)	0	0	0	0
Olsen, Dylan (USA)	CHI (Jan. 5)	0	0	0	0
Orlov, Dmitri (RUS)	WAS (Nov. 21)	0	0	0	0
Palmer, Jarod (USA)	MIN (Dec. 17)	0	0	0	0
Petersson, Andre (SWE)	OTT (Jan. 21)	0	0	0	0
Petrell, Lennart (FIN)	EDM (Oct. 13)	0	0	0	0
Prout, Dalton (CAN)	CBJ (Mar. 30)	0	0	0	0
Rallo, Greg (USA)	FLO (Dec. 18)	0	0	0	0
Rau, Chad (USA)	MIN (Jan. 21)	1	0	1	0
Read, Matt (CAN)	PHI (Oct. 6)	0	0	0	0
Rinaldo, Zac (CAN)	PHI (Oct. 6)	0	0	0	2
Robak, Colby (CAN)	FLO (Feb. 12)	0	0	0	0
Rundblad, David (SWE)	OTT (Oct. 11)	0	0	0	0
Russell, Ryan (CAN)	CBJ (Jan. 7)	0	0	0	0
Rynnas, Jussi (FIN)	TOR (Mar. 27)	39:23	0	ND	
Saad, Brandon (USA)	CHI (Oct. 7)	0	0	0	0
Sauve, Max (FRA)	BOS (Mar. 11)	0	0	0	0
Savard, David (CAN)	CBJ (Oct. 7)	0	0	0	0
Scheifele, Mark (CAN)	WIN (Oct. 9)	0	0	0	0
Schwartz, Jaden (CAN)	STL (Mar. 17)	1	0	1	0
Scrivens, Ben (CAN)	TOR (Nov. 3)	60:00	1	W	
Shaw, Andrew (CAN)	CHI (Jan. 5)	1	0	1	5
Sheahan, Riley (CAN)	DET (Apr. 7)	0	0	0	4
Silfverberg, Jakob (SWE)	OTT (Apr. 23)	0	0	0	2
Smith, Brendan (CAN)	DET (Nov. 17)	0	0	0	0
Smith, Craig (USA)	NAS (Oct. 7)	1	0	1	2
Smith, Reilly (CAN)	DAL (Mar. 28)	0	0	0	0
Smith-Pelly, Devante (CAN)	ANA (Oct. 7)	0	0	0	0
Sneep, Carl (USA)	PIT (Dec. 17)	0	1	1	0
St. Denis, Frederic (CAN)	MON (Nov. 16)	0	0	0	4
Stone, Michael (CAN)	PHO (Feb. 18)	0	0	0	0
Sweatt, Bill (USA)	VAN (Dec. 8)	0	0	0	0
Tarkki, Iiro (FIN)	ANA (Jan. 8)	40:51	3	W	

Teubert, Colten (CAN)	EDM (Nov. 3)	0	0	0	0
Thang, Ryan (USA)	NAS (Oct. 31)	0	0	0	0
Thiessen, Brad (CAN)	PIT (Feb. 26)	59:41	2	W	
Tropp, Corey (USA)	BUF (Nov. 4)	0	0	0	0
Turnbull, Travis (USA)	BUF (Mar. 21)	0	0	0	0
Ullstrom, David (SWE)	NYI (Nov. 21)	0	0	0	0
Voynov, Slava (RUS)	LA (Oct. 18)	0	0	0	0
Watkins, Matt (CAN)	PHO (Feb. 21)	0	0	0	0
Welsh, Jeremy (CAN)	CAR (Apr. 7)	0	0	0	4
Whitmore, Derek (USA)	BUF (Dec. 20)	0	0	0	0
York, Allen (CAN)	CBJ (Oct. 25)	2:33	0	ND	
Zibanejad, Mika (SWE)	OTT (Oct. 7)	0	1	1	0
Zolnierczyk, Harry (CAN)	PHI (Oct. 18)	1	0	1	0
Zucker, Jason (USA)	MIN (Mar. 29)	0	0	0	0

BY NATION

Canada	71
United States	37
Sweden	13
Finland	3
Russia	3
Switzerland	3
Czech Republic	2
France	1
Slovakia	1
Nigeria	1
TOTAL	135

BY NHL TEAM

Anaheim	6
Boston	4
Buffalo	8
Calgary	4
Carolina	3
Chicago	5
Colorado	5
Columbus	9
Dallas	5
Detroit	4
Edmonton	6

Florida	5
Los Angeles	2
Minnesota	11
Montreal	5
Nashville	6
New Jersey	1
NY Islanders	6
NY Rangers	4
Ottawa	6
Philadelphia	7
Phoenix	3
Pittsburgh	4
St. Louis	2
San Jose	0
Tampa Bay	4
Toronto	4
Vancouver	1
Washington	3
Winnipeg	2

PLAYER REGISTER, REGULAR SEASON, 2011–12

Skater YEAR	GP	G	A	P	Pim		
Goalie YEAR	**GP**	**W-L-OTL-T**	**Mins**	**GA**	**SO**	**GAA**	

Abdelkader, Justin b. Muskegon, Michigan, February 25, 1987

	GP	G	A	P	Pim
2011–12 DET	81	8	14	22	62
NHL Totals	209	18	29	47	160

Adam, Luke b. St. John's, Newfoundland, June 18, 1990

	GP	G	A	P	Pim
2011–12 BUF	52	10	10	20	14
NHL Totals	71	13	11	24	26

Adams, Craig b. Seria, Brunei, April 26, 1977

	GP	G	A	P	Pim
2011–12 PIT	82	5	13	18	34
NHL Totals	751	46	87	133	565

Alberts, Andrew b. Minneapolis, Minnesota, June 30, 1981

	GP	G	A	P	Pim
2011–12 VAN	44	2	1	3	40
NHL Totals	425	8	46	54	460

Alfredsson, Daniel b. Gothenburg, Sweden, December 11, 1972

	GP	G	A	P	Pim
2011–12 OTT	75	27	32	59	18
NHL Totals	1,131	416	666	1,082	467

Aliu, Akim b. Okene, Nigeria, April 24, 1989

	GP	G	A	P	Pim
2011–12 CAL	2	2	1	3	12
NHL Totals	2	2	1	3	12

Allen, Bryan b. Kingston, Ontario, August 21, 1980

	GP	G	A	P	Pim
2011–12 CAR	82	1	13	14	76
NHL Totals	601	29	89	118	724

Almond, Cody b. Calgary, Alberta, July 24, 1989

	GP	G	A	P	Pim
2011–12 MIN	10	1	0	1	15
NHL Totals	25	2	0	2	26

Alzner, Karl b. Burnaby, British Columbia, September 24, 1988

2011–12 WAS	82	1	16	17	29
NHL Totals	215	4	35	39	63

Anderson, Craig b. Park Ridge, Illinois, May 21, 1981

2011–12 OTT	63	33–22–6	3,492	165	3	2.84
NHL Totals	294	131–110–2–30	16,409	764	19	2.79

Andersson, Joakim b. Munkedal, Sweden, February 5, 1989

2011–12 DET	5	0	0	0	0
NHL Totals	5	0	0	0	0

Angelidis, Mike b. Woodbridge, Ontario, June 27, 1985

2011–12 TB	6	1	0	1	5
NHL Totals	6	1	0	1	5

Anisimov, Artem b. Yaroslavl, Soviet Union (Russia), May 24, 1988

2011–12 NYR	79	16	20	36	34
NHL Totals	244	46	62	108	86

Antropov, Nik b. Vost, Soviet Union (Kazakhstan), February 18, 1980

2011–12 WIN	69	15	20	35	42
NHL Totals	748	187	260	447	611

Armstrong, Colby b. Lloydminster, Saskatchewan, November 23, 1982

2011–12 TOR	29	1	2	3	9
NHL Totals	439	87	117	204	364

Arnott, Jason b. Collingwood, Ontario, October 11, 1974

2011–12 STL	72	17	17	34	26
NHL Totals	1,244	417	521	938	1,242

Asham, Arron b. Portage La Prairie, Manitoba, April 13, 1978

2011–12 PIT	64	5	11	16	76
NHL Totals	756	92	114	206	940

Ashton, Carter b. Winnipeg, Manitoba, April 1, 1991

2011–12 TOR	15	0	0	0	13
NHL Totals	15	0	0	0	13

Atkinson, Cam b. Riverside, Connecticut, June 5, 1989

2011–12 CBJ	27	7	7	14	14
NHL Totals	27	7	7	14	14

Aucoin, Adrian   b. Ottawa, Ontario, July 3, 1973

2011–12 PHO	64	2	7	9	42	
NHL Totals	1,072	121	274	395	777	

Aucoin, Keith   b. Waltham, Massachusetts, November 6, 1978

2011–12 WAS	27	3	8	11	0
NHL Totals	102	11	26	37	18

Auld, Alexander   b. Cold Lake, Alberta, January 7, 1981

2011–12 OTT	14	2–4–2	645	36	0	3.35
NHL Totals	237	91–88–2–32	12,985	606	6	2.80

Aulie, Keith   b. Regina, Saskatchewan, June 11, 1989

2011–12 TOR/TB	36	0	3	3	29
NHL Totals	76	2	3	5	61

• traded by Toronto to Tampa Bay on February 27, 2012, for Carter Ashton

Avery, Sean   b. Pickering, Ontario, April 10, 1980

2011–12 NYR	15	3	0	3	21
NHL Totals	580	90	157	247	1,533

Babchuk, Anton   b. Kiev, Soviet Union (Russia), May 6, 1984

2011–12 CAL	32	2	8	10	6
NHL Totals	282	36	70	106	108

Bachman, Richard   b. Salt Lake City, Utah, July 25, 1987

2011–12 DAL	18	8–5–1	933	43	1	2.77
NHL Totals	19	8–5–1	943	43	1	2.74

Backes, David   b. Blaine, Minnesota, May 1, 1984

2011–12 STL	82	24	30	54	101
NHL Totals	446	126	146	272	601

Backlund, Mikael   b. Vasteras, Sweden, March 17, 1989

2011–12 CAL	41	4	7	11	16
NHL Totals	138	15	31	46	40

Backstrom, Nicklas   b. Gavle, Sweden, November 23, 1987

2011–12 WAS	42	14	30	44	24
NHL Totals	365	101	266	367	184

Backstrom, Niklas b. Helsinki, Finland, February 13, 1978

2011–12 MIN	46	19–18–7	2,590	105	4	2.43
NHL Totals	327	160–109–0–42	18,780	758	26	2.42

Bailey, Josh b. Oshawa, Ontario, October 2, 1989

2011–12 NYI	80	13	19	32	32
NHL Totals	291	47	73	120	103

Ballard, Keith b. Baudette, Minnesota, November 26, 1982

2011–12 VAN	47	1	6	7	64
NHL Totals	509	36	127	163	520

Barch, Krys b. Guelph, Ontario, March 26, 1980

2011–12 DAL/FLO	51	2	3	5	114
NHL Totals	304	12	19	31	669

• traded by Dallas to Florida on December 7, 2011, with a 6th-round draft choice in 2012 for Jake Hauswirth and a 5th-round draft choice in 2012

Barker, Cam b. Winnipeg, Manitoba, April 4, 1986

2011–12 EDM	25	2	0	2	23
NHL Totals	296	21	73	94	286

Barrie, Tyson b. Victoria, British Columbia, July 26, 1991

2011–12 COL	10	0	0	0	0
NHL Totals	10	0	0	0	0

Bartkowski, Matt b. Pittsburgh, Pennsylvania, June 4, 1988

2011–12 BOS	3	0	0	0	0
NHL Totals	9	0	0	0	4

Bartschi, Sven b. Bern, Switzerland, October 5, 1992

2011–12 CAL	5	3	0	3	4
NHL Totals	5	3	0	3	4

Bass, Cody b. Owen Sound, Ontario, January 7, 1987

2011–12 CBJ	14	0	1	1	32
NHL Totals	48	2	3	5	66

Beagle, Jay b. Calgary, Alberta, October 16, 1985

2011–12 WAS	41	4	1	5	23
NHL Totals	82	7	3	10	35

Beauchemin, Francois   b. Sorel, Quebec, June 4, 1980

2011–12 ANA	82	8	14	22	48
NHL Totals	491	39	116	155	285

Belanger, Eric   b. Sherbrooke, Quebec, December 16, 1977

2011–12 EDM	78	4	12	16	32
NHL Totals	794	138	217	355	351

Beleskey, Matt   b. Windsor, Ontario, June 7, 1988

2011–12 ANA	70	4	11	15	72
NHL Totals	167	18	25	43	143

Bell, Brendan   b. Ottawa, Ontario, March 31, 1983

2011–12 NYR	1	0	0	0	0
NHL Totals	102	7	21	28	51

Bell, Mark   b. St. Pauls, Ontario, August 5, 1980

2011–12 ANA	5	0	0	0	5
NHL Totals	450	87	95	182	602

Benn, Jamie   b. Victoria, British Columbia, July 18, 1989

2011–12 DAL	71	26	37	63	55
NHL Totals	222	70	90	160	152

Benn, Jordie   b. Victoria, British Columbia, July 26, 1987

2011–12 DAL	3	0	2	2	0
NHL Totals	3	0	2	2	0

Bergenheim, Sean   b. Helsinki, Finland, February 8, 1984

2011–12 FLO	62	17	6	23	48
NHL Totals	388	71	61	132	299

Bergeron, Marc-Andre   b. St-Louis-de-France, Quebec, October 13, 1980

2011–12 TB	43	4	20	24	20
NHL Totals	465	81	145	226	205

Bergeron, Patrice   b. L'Ancienne-Lorette, Quebec, July 24, 1985

2011–12 BOS	81	22	42	64	20
NHL Totals	537	143	258	401	162

Bergfors, Niclas   b. Sodertalje, Sweden, March 7, 1987

2011–12 NAS	11	1	1	2	2
NHL Totals	173	35	48	83	20

Berglund, Patrik   b. Vasteras, Sweden, June 2, 1988

2011–12 STL	82	19	19	38	30
NHL Totals	310	75	88	163	88

Bernier, Jonathan   b. Laval, Quebec, August 7, 1988

2011–12 LA	16	5–6–2	890	35	1	2.36
NHL Totals	48	20–17–0–5	2,692	112	5	2.50

Bernier, Steve   b. Quebec City, Quebec, March 31, 1985

2011–12 NJ	32	1	5	6	16
NHL Totals	417	77	88	165	213

Bertuzzi, Todd   b. Sudbury, Ontario, February 2, 1975

2011–12 DET	71	14	24	38	64
NHL Totals	1,093	303	448	751	1,436

Bickel, Stu   b. Chanhassen, Minnesota, October 2, 1986

2011–12 NYR	51	0	9	9	0
NHL Totals	51	0	9	9	0

Bickell, Bryan   b. Bowmanville, Ontario, March 9, 1986

2011–12 CHI	71	9	15	24	48
NHL Totals	172	31	36	67	95

Bieksa, Kevin   b. Grimsby, Ontario, June 16, 1981

2011–12 VAN	78	8	36	44	94
NHL Totals	425	42	149	191	650

Biron, Martin   b. Lac-St-Charles, Quebec, August 15, 1977

2011–12 NYR	21	12–6–2	1,220	50	2	2.46
NHL Totals	500	228–188–25–34	28,206	1,225	28	2.61

Bishop, Ben   b. Denver, Colorado, November 21, 1986

2011–12 OTT	10	3–3–2	532	22	0	2.48
NHL Totals	23	7–8–0–3	1,145	51	1	2.67

Bissonnette, Paul   b. Welland, Ontario, March 11, 1985

2011–12 PHO	31	1	0	1	41
NHL Totals	135	5	3	8	251

Bitz, Byron b. Saskatoon, Saskatchewan, July 21, 1984

2011–12 VAN	10	1	3	4	14
NHL Totals	97	10	12	22	65

Blake, Jason b. Moorhead, Minnesota, September 2, 1973

2011–12 ANA	45	7	5	12	6
NHL Totals	871	213	273	486	455

Blum, Jonathan b. Long Beach, California, January 30, 1989

2011–12 NAS	33	3	4	7	6
NHL Totals	56	6	9	15	14

Blunden, Mike b. Toronto, Ontario, December 15, 1986

2011–12 MON	39	2	2	4	27
NHL Totals	90	4	4	8	96

Bobrovsky, Sergei b. Novokuznetsk, Soviet Union (Russia), September 20, 1988

2011–12 PHI	29	14–10–2	1,550	78	0	3.02
NHL Totals	83	42–23–0–10	4,567	208	0	2.73

Boedker, Mikkel b. Brondby, Denmark, December 16, 1989

2011–12 PHO	82	11	13	24	12
NHL Totals	208	27	42	69	38

Bogosian, Zach b. Massena, New York, July 15, 1990

2011–12 WIN	65	5	25	30	71
NHL Totals	264	29	60	89	208

Bolduc, Alexandre b. Montreal, Quebec, June 26, 1985

2011–12 PHO	2	0	0	0	2
NHL Totals	48	2	3	5	40

Boll, Jarred b. Crystal Lake, Illinois, May 13, 1986

2011–12 CBJ	54	2	1	3	126
NHL Totals	345	22	24	46	863

Bolland, Dave b. Toronto, Ontario, June 5, 1986

2011–12 CHI	76	19	18	37	47
NHL Totals	297	63	91	154	189

Bollig, Brandon b. St. Charles, Missouri, January 31, 1987

2011–12 CHI	18	0	0	0	58
NHL Totals	18	0	0	0	58

Bonino, Nick b. Hartford, Connecticut, April 20, 1988

2011–12 ANA	50	5	13	18	8
NHL Totals	85	6	14	20	18

Booth, David b. Detroit, Michigan, November 24, 1984

2011–12 FLO/VAN	62	16	14	30	34
NHL Totals	365	103	93	196	159

• traded by Florida to Vancouver on October 22, 2011, with Steve Reinprecht and a 3rd-round draft choice in 2013 for Mikael Samuelsson and Marco Sturm

Borowiecki, Mark b. Ottawa, Ontario, July 12, 1989

2011–12 OTT	2	0	0	0	2
NHL Totals	2	0	0	0	2

Bortuzzo, Robert b. Thunder Bay, Ontario, March 18, 1989

2011–12 PIT	6	0	0	0	2
NHL Totals	6	0	0	0	2

Bouchard, Pierre-Marc b. Sherbrooke, Quebec, April 27, 1984

2011–12 MIN	37	9	13	22	18
NHL Totals	522	98	229	327	170

Boucher, Brian b. Woonsocket, Rhode Island, January 2, 1977

2011–12 CAR	10	1–6–1	546	31	0	3.41
NHL Totals	324	120–137–30–25	18,075	816	17	2.71

Bouillon, Francis b. New York, New York, October 17, 1975

2011–12 NAS	66	4	7	11	33
NHL Totals	676	29	105	134	481

Boulton, Eric b. Halifax, Nova Scotia, August 17, 1976

2011–12 NJ	51	0	0	0	115
NHL Totals	600	27	46	73	1,265

Bouma, Lance b. Provost, Alberta, March 25, 1990

2011–12 CAL	27	1	2	3	11
NHL Totals	43	1	3	4	13

Bourdon, Marc-Andre   b. St-Hyacinthe, Quebec, September 17, 1989

2011–12 PHI	45	4	3	7	52
NHL Totals	45	4	3	7	52

Bourque, Gabriel   b. Rimouski, Quebec, September 23, 1990

2011–12 NAS	43	7	12	19	6
NHL Totals	43	7	12	19	6

Bourque, Rene   b. Lac La Biche, Alberta, December 10, 1981

2011–12 CAL/MON	76	18	6	24	68
NHL Totals	470	126	121	247	404

• traded by Calgary to Montreal on January 12, 2012, with Patrick Holland and a 2nd-round draft choice in 2013 for Mike Cammalleri, Karri Ramo and a 5th-round draft choice in 2012

Bouwmeester, Jay   b. Edmonton, Alberta, September 27, 1983

2011–12 CAL	82	5	24	29	26
NHL Totals	717	65	220	285	447

Bowman, Drayson   b. Grand Rapids, Michigan, March 8, 1989

2011–12 CAR	37	6	17	13	4
NHL Totals	69	8	8	16	20

Boyce, Darryl   b. Summerside, Prince Edward Island, July 7, 1984

2011–12 TOR/CBJ	37	1	4	5	35
NHL Totals	84	6	12	18	68

• claimed off waivers on February 25, 2012, by Columbus from Toronto

Boychuk, Johnny   b. Edmonton, Alberta, January 19, 1984

2011–12 BOS	77	5	10	15	53
NHL Totals	202	13	33	46	141

Boychuk, Zach   b. Airdrie, Alberta, October 4, 1989

2011–12 CAR	16	0	2	2	0
NHL Totals	72	7	11	18	6

Boyes, Brad   b. Mississauga, Ontario, April 17, 1982

2011–12 BUF	65	8	15	23	6
NHL Totals	558	158	214	372	175

Boyle, Brian   b. Dorchester, Massachusetts, December 18, 1984

2011–12 NYR	82	11	15	26	59
NHL Totals	271	44	33	77	226

Boyle, Dan b. Ottawa, Ontario, July 12, 1976

2011–12 SJ	81	9	39	48	57
NHL Totals	833	125	380	505	584

Bozak, Tyler b. Regina, Saskatchewan, March 19, 1986

2011–12 TOR	73	18	29	47	22
NHL Totals	192	41	65	106	42

Bradley, Matt b. Stittsville, Ontario, June 13, 1978

2011–12 FLO	45	3	5	8	31
NHL Totals	675	59	90	149	562

Brassard, Derick b. Hull, Quebec, September 22, 1987

2011–12 CBJ	74	14	27	41	42
NHL Totals	275	51	100	151	168

Braun, Justin b. St. Paul, Minnesota, February 10, 1987

2011–12 SJ	66	2	9	11	23
NHL Totals	94	4	18	22	25

Brennan, T.J. b. Willingboro, New Jersey, April 3, 1989

2011–12 BUF	11	1	0	1	6
NHL Totals	11	1	0	1	6

Brent, Tim b. Cambridge, Ontario, March 10, 1984

2011–12 CAR	79	12	12	24	27
NHL Totals	177	21	24	45	68

Brewer, Eric b. Vernon, British Columbia, April 17, 1979

2011–12 TB	82	1	20	21	49
NHL Totals	840	66	165	231	667

Briere, Daniel b. Gatineau, Quebec, October 6, 1977

2011–12 PHI	70	16	33	49	69
NHL Totals	813	280	363	643	686

Brodeur, Martin b. Montreal, Quebec, May 6, 1972

2011–12 NJ	59	31–21–4	3,392	136	3	2.41
NHL Totals	1,191	656–371–105–58	70,028	2,603	119	2.23

Brodie, T.J. b. Chatham, Ontario, June 7, 1990

2011–12 CAL	54	2	12	14	14
NHL Totals	57	2	12	14	16

Brodziak, Kyle   b. St. Paul, Alberta, May 25, 1984

2011–12 MIN	82	22	22	44	66	
NHL Totals	419	73	99	172	204	

Brookbank, Sheldon   b. Lanigan, Saskatchewan, October 3, 1980

2011–12 ANA	80	3	11	14	72	
NHL Totals	277	4	32	36	400	

Brophey, Evan   b. Kitchener, Ontario, December 3, 1986

2011–12 COL	3	0	0	0	0	
NHL Totals	4	0	0	0	0	

Brouwer, Troy   b. Vancouver, British Columbia, August 17, 1985

2011–12 WAS	82	18	15	33	61	
NHL Totals	320	67	69	136	222	

Brown, Dustin   b. Ithaca, New York, November 4, 1984

2011–12 LA	82	22	32	54	53	
NHL Totals	595	163	196	359	430	

Brown, J.T.   b. Burnsville, Minnesota, July 2, 1990

2011–12 TB	5	0	1	1	0	
NHL Totals	5	0	1	1	0	

Brown, Mike   b. Northbrook, Illinois, June 24, 1985

2011–12 TOR	50	2	2	4	74	
NHL Totals	242	14	10	24	449	

Brule, Gilbert   b. Edmonton, Alberta, January 1, 1987

2011–12 PHO	33	5	9	14	11	
NHL Totals	296	43	52	95	154	

Brunette, Andrew   b. Sudbury, Ontario, August 24, 1973

2011–12 CHI	78	12	15	27	4	
NHL Totals	1,110	268	465	733	314	

Brunnstrom, Fabian   b. Jonstorp, Sweden, February 6, 1985

2011–12 DET	5	0	1	1	4	
NHL Totals	104	19	22	41	22	

Bryzgalov, Ilya   b. Togliatti, Soviet Union (Russia), June 22, 1980

2011–12 PHI	59	33–16–7	3,415	141	6	2.48
NHL Totals	385	189–132–0–42	22,110	930	29	2.52

Budaj, Peter b. Banska Bystrica, Czechoslovakia (Slovakia), September 18, 1982

2011–12 MON	17	5–7–5	1,037	44	0	2.55
NHL Totals	259	106–98–0–32	14,348	671	9	2.81

Bulmer, Brett b. Prince George, British Columbia, April 26, 1992

2011–12 MIN	9	0	3	3	6
NHL Totals	9	0	3	3	6

Burish, Adam b. Madison, Wisconsin, January 6, 1983

2011–12 DAL	65	6	13	19	76
NHL Totals	297	25	29	54	490

Burmistrov, Alexander   b. Kazan, Soviet Union (Russia), October 21, 1991

2011–12 WIN	76	13	15	28	42
NHL Totals	150	19	29	48	69

Burns, Brent b. Ajax, Ontario, March 9, 1985

2011–12 SJ	81	11	26	37	34
NHL Totals	534	66	154	220	359

Burrows, Alex b. Pointe-Claire, Quebec, April 11, 1981

2011–12 VAN	80	28	24	52	90
NHL Totals	522	139	131	270	771

Butler, Bobby b. Marlborough, Massachusetts, April 26, 1987

2011–12 OTT	56	6	10	16	12
NHL Totals	94	16	21	37	22

Butler, Chris b. St. Louis, Missouri, October 27, 1986

2011–12 CAL	68	2	13	15	34
NHL Totals	223	7	44	51	100

Byers, Dane b. Nipawin, Saskatchewan, February 21, 1986

2011–12 CBJ	8	0	0	0	29
NHL Totals	14	1	0	1	60

Byfuglien, Dustin b. Minneapolis, Minnesota, March 27, 1985

2011–12 WIN	66	12	41	53	72
NHL Totals	407	87	128	215	433

Byron, Paul b. Ottawa, Ontario, April 27, 1989

2011–12 CAL	22	3	2	5	2
NHL Totals	30	4	3	7	4

Callahan, Ryan   b. Rochester, New York, March 21, 1985

| 2011–12 NYR | 76 | 29 | 25 | 54 | 61 |
| NHL Totals | 360 | 105 | 93 | 198 | 240 |

Calvert, Matt   b. Brandon, Manitoba, December 24, 1989

| 2011–12 CAL | 13 | 0 | 3 | 3 | 16 |
| NHL Totals | 55 | 11 | 12 | 23 | 28 |

Cammalleri, Mike   b. Richmond Hill, Ontario, June 8, 1982

| 2011–12 MON/CAL | 66 | 20 | 21 | 41 | 66 |
| NHL Totals | 562 | 197 | 228 | 425 | 289 |

• traded by Montreal to Calgary on January 12, 2012, with Karri Ramo and a 5th-round draft choice in 2012 for Rene Bourque, Patrick Holland and a 2nd-round draft choice in 2013

Campbell, Brian   b. Strathroy, Ontario, May 23, 1979

| 2011–12 FLO | 82 | 4 | 49 | 53 | 6 |
| NHL Totals | 708 | 58 | 307 | 365 | 173 |

Campbell, Gregory   b. London, Ontario, December 17, 1983

| 2011–12 BOS | 78 | 8 | 8 | 16 | 80 |
| NHL Totals | 521 | 50 | 80 | 130 | 485 |

Camper, Carter   b. Rocky River, Ohio, July 6, 1988

| 2011–12 BOS | 3 | 1 | 0 | 1 | 0 |
| NHL Totals | 3 | 1 | 0 | 1 | 0 |

Campoli, Chris   b. North York (Toronto), Ontario, July 9, 1984

| 2011–12 MON | 43 | 2 | 9 | 11 | 8 |
| NHL Totals | 440 | 35 | 111 | 146 | 200 |

Carcillo, Daniel   b. King City, Ontario, January 28, 1985

| 2011–12 CHI | 28 | 2 | 9 | 11 | 82 |
| NHL Totals | 310 | 38 | 46 | 84 | 1,068 |

Carkner, Matt   b. Winchester, Ontario, November 3, 1980

| 2011–12 OTT | 29 | 1 | 2 | 3 | 33 |
| NHL Totals | 162 | 4 | 18 | 22 | 361 |

Carle, Matt   b. Anchorage, Alaska, September 25, 1984

| 2011–12 PHI | 82 | 4 | 34 | 38 | 36 |
| NHL Totals | 471 | 32 | 170 | 202 | 167 |

Carlson, John b. Natick, Massachusetts, January 10, 1990

2011–12 WAS	82	9	23	32	22
NHL Totals	186	17	58	75	74

Caron, Jordan b. Sayabec, Quebec, November 2, 1990

2011–12 BOS	48	7	8	15	14
NHL Totals	71	10	12	22	20

Caron, Sebastien b. Amqui, Quebec, June 25, 1980

2011–12 TB	3	1–1–0	135	7	0	3.11
NHL Totals	95	26–48–7–7	5,156	296	4	3.44

Carson, Brett b. Regina, Saskatchewan, November 29, 1985

2011–12 CAL	2	0	0	0	0
NHL Totals	80	2	10	12	20

Carter, Jeff b. London, Ontario, January 1, 1985

2011–12 CBJ/LA	55	21	13	34	16
NHL Totals	516	202	175	377	304

• traded by Columbus to Los Angeles on February 23, 2012, for Jack Johnson and a 1st-round draft choice in either 2012 or 2013

Carter, Ryan b. White Bear Lake, Minnesota, August 3, 1983

2011–12 FLO/NJ	72	4	4	8	90
NHL Totals	254	18	25	43	275

• claimed off waivers on October 26, 2011, by New Jersey from Florida

Chara, Zdeno b. Trencin, Czechoslovakia (Slovakia), March 18, 1977

2011–12 BOS	79	12	40	52	86
NHL Totals	1,007	137	322	459	1,471

Chimera, Jason b. Edmonton, Alberta, May 2, 1979

2011–12 WAS	82	20	19	39	78
NHL Totals	663	118	136	254	658

Chipchura, Kyle b. Westlock, Alberta, February 19, 1986

2011–12 PHO	53	3	13	16	42
NHL Totals	216	13	31	44	161

Chorney, Taylor b. Thunder Bay, Ontario, April 27, 1987

2011–12 STL/EDM	5	0	0	0	0
NHL Totals	61	1	6	7	16

• claimed off waivers on November 10, 2011, by Edmonton from St. Louis

Christensen, Erik   b. Edmonton, Alberta, December 17, 1983

2011–12 NYR/MIN	49	7	5	12	8
NHL Totals	387	68	95	163	162

• traded by NY Rangers to Minnesota on February 3, 2012, with a conditional 7th-round draft choice in 2013 for Casey Wellman

Cizikas, Casey   b. Toronto, Ontario, February 27, 1991

2011–12 NYI	15	0	4	4	6
NHL Totals	15	0	4	4	6

Clark, Brett   b. Wapella, Saskatchewan, December 23, 1976

2011–12 TB	82	2	13	15	20
NHL Totals	681	45	140	185	293

Clark, Mat   b. Lakewood, Colorado, October 17, 1990

2011–12 ANA	2	0	0	0	0
NHL Totals	2	0	0	0	0

Clarkson, David   b. Toronto, Ontario, March 31, 1984

2011–12 NJ	80	30	16	46	138
NHL Totals	378	82	64	146	692

Cleary, Daniel   b. Carbonear, Newfoundland, December 18, 1978

2011–12 DET	75	12	21	33	30
NHL Totals	821	151	211	362	415

Clemmensen, Scott   b. Des Moines, Iowa, July 23, 1977

2011–12 FLO	30	14–6–6	1,566	67	1	2.57
NHL Totals	152	64–45–0–20	8,178	360	7	2.64

Clifford, Kyle   b. Ayr, Ontario, January 13, 1991

2011–12 LA	81	5	7	12	123
NHL Totals	157	12	14	26	264

Clitsome, Grant   b. Gloucester, Ontario, April 14, 1985

2011–12 CBJ/WIN	63	4	13	17	32
NHL Totals	105	9	30	39	54

• claimed off waivers on February 27, 2012, by Winnipeg from Columbus

Clowe, Ryane   b. St. John's, Newfoundland, September 30, 1982

2011–12 SJ	76	17	28	45	97
NHL Totals	395	101	159	260	488

Clutterbuck, Cal b. Welland, Ontario, November 18, 1987

2011–12 MIN	74	15	12	27	103
NHL Totals	304	58	42	100	310

Coburn, Braydon b. Calgary, Alberta, February 27, 1985

2011–12 PHI	81	4	20	24	56
NHL Totals	460	30	105	135	384

Cogliano, Andrew b. Toronto, Ontario, June 14, 1987

2011–12 ANA	82	13	13	26	15
NHL Totals	410	70	102	172	152

Colaiacovo, Carlo b. Toronto, Ontario, January 27, 1983

2011–12 STL	64	2	17	19	22
NHL Totals	370	30	109	139	191

Colborne, Joe b. Calgary, Alberta, January 30, 1990

2011–12 TOR	10	1	4	5	4
NHL Totals	11	1	5	6	4

Cole, Erik b. Oswego, New York, November 6, 1978

2011–12 MON	82	35	26	61	48
NHL Totals	702	219	232	451	605

Cole, Ian b. Ann Arbor, Michigan, February 21, 1989

2011–12 STL	26	1	5	6	22
NHL Totals	52	2	8	10	57

Collins, Sean b. Troy, Michigan, October 30, 1983

2011–12 WAS	2	0	0	0	0
NHL Totals	21	2	1	3	12

Comeau, Blake b. Meadow Lake, Saskatchewan, February 18, 1986

2011–12 NYI/CAL	74	5	10	15	30
NHL Totals	319	61	75	136	167

• claimed off waivers on November 25, 2011, by Calgary from NY Islanders

Commodore, Mike b. Fort Saskatchewan, Alberta, November 7, 1979

2011–12 DET/TB	30	0	2	2	38
NHL Totals	484	23	83	106	683

• traded by Detroit to Tampa Bay on February 27, 2012, for a conditional 7th-round draft choice in 2013

Condra, Eric b. Trenton, Michigan, August 6, 1986

2011–12 OTT	81	8	17	25	30
NHL Totals	107	14	22	36	42

Conklin, Ty b. Anchorage, Alaska, March 30, 1976

2011–12 DET	15	5–6–1	805	44	1	3.28
NHL Totals	215	96–67–4–19	11,527	516	17	2.69

Conner, Chris b. Westland, Michigan, December 23, 1983

2011–12 DET	8	1	2	3	0
NHL Totals	147	17	26	43	30

Connolly, Brett b. Campbell River, British Columbia, May 2, 1992

2011–12 TB	68	4	11	15	30
NHL Totals	68	4	11	15	30

Connolly, Mike b. Calgary, Alberta, July 3, 1989

2011–12 COL	2	0	0	0	2
NHL Totals	2	0	0	0	2

Connolly, Tim b. Syracuse, New York, May 7, 1981

2011–12 TOR	70	13	23	36	40
NHL Totals	697	131	300	431	300

Cooke, Matt b. Belleville, Ontario, September 7, 1978

2011–12 PIT	82	19	19	38	44
NHL Totals	887	145	194	339	1,032

Cormier, Patrice b. Moncton, New Brunswick, June 14, 1990

2011–12 WIN	9	0	0	0	0
NHL Totals	30	1	1	2	4

Cornet, Philippe b. Val Senneville, Quebec, March 28, 1990

2011–12 EDM	2	0	1	1	0
NHL Totals	2	0	1	1	0

Corvo, Joe b. Oak Park, Illinois, June 20, 1977

2011–12 BOS	75	4	21	25	13
NHL Totals	643	83	200	283	217

Couture, Logan b. Guelph, Ontario, March 28, 1989

2011–12 SJ	80	31	34	65	16
NHL Totals	184	68	62	130	63

Couturier, Sean b. Phoenix, Arizona, December 7, 1992

2011–12 PHI	77	13	14	27	14
NHL Totals	77	13	14	27	14

Cowen, Jared b. Saskatoon, Saskatchewan, January 25, 1991

2011–12 OTT	82	5	12	17	56
NHL Totals	83	5	12	17	58

Crabb, Joey b. Anchorage, Alaska, April 3, 1983

2011–12 TOR	67	11	15	26	33
NHL Totals	144	18	32	50	85

Cracknell, Adam b. Prince Albert, Saskatchewan, July 15, 1985

2011–12 STL	2	1	0	1	0
NHL Totals	26	4	4	8	8

Crawford, Corey b. Montreal, Quebec, December 31, 1984

2011–12 CHI	57	30–17–7	3,218	146	0	2.72
NHL Totals	122	64–38–0–14	6,925	290	5	2.51

Crombeen, B.J. b. Denver, Colorado, July 10, 1985

2011–12 STL	40	1	2	3	71
NHL Totals	288	27	29	56	580

Crosby, Sidney b. Halifax, Nova Scotia, August 7, 1987

2011–12 PIT	22	8	29	37	14
NHL Totals	434	223	386	609	401

Cullen, Mark b. Moorhead, Minnesota, October 28, 1978

2011–12 FLO	6	0	1	1	2
NHL Totals	38	7	10	17	4

Cullen, Matt b. Virginia, Minnesota, November 2, 1976

2011–12 MIN	73	14	21	35	24
NHL Totals	1,031	195	340	535	450

Cuma, Tyler b. Toronto, Ontario, January 19, 1990

2011–12 MIN	1	0	0	0	2
NHL Totals	1	0	0	0	2

Da Costa, Stephane   b. Paris, France, July 11, 1989

2011–12 OTT	22	3	2	5	8
NHL Totals	26	3	2	5	8

Dadonov, Evgeni   b. Chelyabinsk, Soviet Union (Russia), March 12, 1989

2011–12 FLO	15	2	1	3	2
NHL Totals	55	10	10	20	16

D'Agostini, Matt   b. Sault Ste. Marie, Ontario, October 23, 1986

2011–12 STL	55	9	9	18	27
NHL Totals	238	44	45	89	113

Daley, Trevor   b. Toronto, Ontario, October 9, 1983

2011–12 DAL	79	4	21	25	42
NHL Totals	577	38	117	155	423

Dalpe, Zac   b. Paris, Ontario, November 1, 1989

2011–12 CAR	16	1	2	3	4
NHL Totals	31	4	3	7	4

Danis, Yann   b. Lafontaine, Quebec, June 21, 1981

2011–12 EDM	1	0–0–0	32	2	0	3.75
NHL Totals	50	16–21–0–4	2,572	116	3	2.71

Darche, Mathieu   b. Montreal, Quebec, November 26, 1976

2011–12 MON	61	5	7	12	18
NHL Totals	250	40	32	72	58

Datsyuk, Pavel   b. Sverdlovsk, Soviet Union (Russia), July 20, 1978

2011–12 DET	70	19	48	67	14
NHL Totals	732	240	478	718	186

Daugavins, Kaspars   b. Riga, Soviet Union (Latvia), May 18, 1988

2011–12 OTT	65	5	6	11	12
NHL Totals	66	5	6	11	12

De Haan, Calvin   b. Ottawa, Ontario, May 9, 1991

2011–12 NYI	1	0	0	0	0
NHL Totals	1	0	0	0	0

Del Zotto, Michael   b. Stouffville, Ontario, June 24, 1990

2011–12 NYR	77	10	31	41	36
NHL Totals	204	21	68	89	88

Demers, Jason   b. Dorval, Quebec, June 9, 1988

2011–12 SJ	57	4	9	13	22
NHL Totals	183	10	48	58	71

Desbiens, Guillaume   b. Alma, Quebec, April 20, 1985

2011–12 CAL	10	0	0	0	25
NHL Totals	23	0	0	0	37

Desharnais, David   b. Quebec City, Quebec, September 14, 1986

2011–12 MON	81	16	44	60	24
NHL Totals	130	24	59	83	36

Desjardins, Andrew   b. Lively, Ontario, July 27, 1986

2011–12 SJ	76	4	13	17	47
NHL Totals	93	5	15	20	51

Deslauriers, Jeff   b. St. Jean Richelieu, Quebec, May 15, 1984

2011–12 ANA	4	3–1–0	241	11	0	2.74
NHL Totals	62	23–32–0–4	3,578	193	3	3.24

Despres, Simon   b. Laval, Quebec, July 27, 1991

2011–12 PIT	18	1	3	4	10
NHL Totals	18	1	3	4	10

Deveaux, Andre   b. Freeport, Bahamas, February 23, 1984

2011–12 NYR	9	0	1	1	29
NHL Totals	31	0	2	2	104

Diaz, Raphael   b. Baar, Switzerland, January 9, 1986

2011–12 MON	59	3	13	16	30
NHL Totals	59	3	13	16	30

Dillon, Brenden   b. New Westminster, British Columbia, November 13, 1990

2011–12 DAL	1	0	0	0	0
NHL Totals	1	0	0	0	0

DiPietro, Rick   b. Winthrop, Massachusetts, September 19, 1981

2011–12 NYI	8	3–2–3	354	22	0	3.73
NHL Totals	315	130–133–8–31	18,023	859	16	2.86

Disalvatore, Jon   b. Bangor, Maine, March 30, 1981

2011–12 MIN	1	0	0	0	2
NHL Totals	6	0	0	0	4

Doan, Shane   b. Halkirk, Alberta, October 10, 1976

2011–12 PHO	79	22	28	50	48
NHL Totals	1,198	318	470	788	1,071

Donovan, Matt   b. Edmond, Oklahoma, May 9, 1990

2011–12 NYI	3	0	0	0	0
NHL Totals	3	0	0	0	0

Dorsett, Derek   b. Kindersley, Saskatchewan, December 20, 1986

2011–12 CBJ	77	12	8	20	235
NHL Totals	256	24	32	56	674

Doughty, Drew   b. London, Ontario, December 8, 1989

2011–12 LA	77	10	26	36	69
NHL Totals	316	43	119	162	247

Dowell, Jake   b. Eau Claire, Wisconsin, March 4, 1985

2011–12 DAL	52	2	5	7	53
NHL Totals	154	11	22	33	133

Downie, Steve   b. Newmarket, Ontario, April 3, 1987

2011–12 TB/COL	75	14	27	41	137
NHL Totals	272	55	82	137	654

• traded by Tampa Bay to Colorado on February 21, 2012, for Kyle Quincey

Drewiske, Davis   b. Hudson, Wisconsin, November 22, 1984

2011–12 LA	9	2	0	2	2
NHL Totals	106	3	15	18	53

Dubinsky, Brandon   b. Anchorage, Alaska, April 29, 1986

2011–12 NYR	77	10	24	34	110
NHL Totals	393	81	132	213	457

Dubnyk, Devan   b. Regina, Saskatchewan, May 4, 1986

2011–12 EDM	47	20–20–3	2,653	118	2	2.67
NHL Totals	101	36–43–0–13	5,790	275	4	2.85

Duchene, Matt   b. Haliburton, Ontario, January 16, 1991

2011–12 COL	58	14	14	28	8
NHL Totals	219	65	85	150	57

Duco, Mike b. Toronto, Ontario, July 8, 1987

2011–12 VAN	6	0	2	2	5
NHL Totals	18	0	2	2	65

Dumont, Gabriel b. Dégelis, Quebec, October 6, 1990

2011–12 MON	3	0	0	0	0
NHL Totals	3	0	0	0	0

Dupuis, Pascal b. Laval, Quebec, April 7, 1979

2011–12 PIT	82	25	34	59	34
NHL Totals	750	155	181	336	337

Dupuis, Philippe b. Laval, Quebec, April 24, 1985

2011–12 TOR	30	0	0	0	16
NHL Totals	116	6	12	18	62

Dvorak, Radek b. Tabor, Czechoslovakia (Czech Republic), March 9, 1977

2011–12 DAL	73	4	17	21	12
NHL Totals	1,191	219	358	577	406

Dwyer, Pat b. Spokane, Washington, June 22, 1983

2011–12 CAR	73	5	7	12	23
NHL Totals	224	21	22	43	41

Eager, Ben b. Ottawa, Ontario, January 22, 1984

2011–12 EDM	63	8	5	13	107
NHL Totals	386	42	40	82	848

Eakin, Cody b. Winnipeg, Manitoba, May 24, 1991

2011–12 WAS	30	4	4	8	4
NHL Totals	30	4	4	8	4

Eaton, Mark b. Wilmington, Delaware, May 6, 1977

2011–12 NYI	62	1	3	4	10
NHL Totals	627	24	61	85	238

Eaves, Patrick b. Calgary, Alberta, May 1, 1984

2011–12 DET	10	0	1	1	2
NHL Totals	380	70	63	133	141

Ebbett, Andrew b. Vernon, British Columbia, January 2, 1983

2011–12 EDM	18	5	1	6	6
NHL Totals	163	24	34	58	44

Eberle, Jordan b. Regina, Saskatchewan, May 15, 1990

2011–12 EDM	78	34	42	76	10
NHL Totals	147	52	67	119	32

Edler, Alexander b. Stockholm, Sweden, April 21, 1986

2011–12 VAN	82	11	38	49	34
NHL Totals	386	43	141	184	200

Ehrhoff, Christian b. Moers, West Germany (Germany), July 6, 1982

2011–12 BUF	66	5	27	32	47
NHL Totals	566	58	200	258	385

Ekholm, Mattias b. Borlange, Sweden, May 24, 1990

2011–12 NAS	2	0	0	0	0
NHL Totals	2	0	0	0	0

Ekman-Larsson, Oliver b. Karlskrona, Sweden, July 17, 1991

2011–12 PHO	82	13	19	32	32
NHL Totals	130	14	29	43	56

Elias, Patrik b. Trebic, Czechoslovakia (Czech Republic), April 13, 1976

2011–12 NJ	81	26	52	78	16
NHL Totals	1,042	361	533	894	475

Eller, Lars b. Herlev, Denmark, May 8, 1989

2011–12 MON	79	16	12	28	66
NHL Totals	163	25	22	47	118

Ellerby, Keaton b. Strathmore, Alberta, November 5, 1988

2011–12 FLO	40	0	5	5	10
NHL Totals	116	2	15	17	34

Elliott, Brian b. Newmarket, Ontario, April 9, 1985

2011–12 STL	38	23–10–4	2,235	58	9	1.56
NHL Totals	180	84–63–0–20	9,982	432	18	2.60

Elliott, Stefan b. Vancouver, British Columbia, January 30, 1991

2011–12 COL	39	4	9	13	8
NHL Totals	39	4	9	13	8

Ellis, Dan b. Saskatoon, Saskatchewan, June 19, 1980

2011–12 ANA	10	1–5–0	419	19	0	2.72
NHL Totals	165	72–57–0–15	8,795	393	12	2.68

Ellis, Matt b. Welland, Ontario, August 31, 1981

2011–12 BUF	60	3	5	8	25
NHL Totals	261	16	25	41	81

Ellis, Ryan b. Hamilton, Ontario, January 3, 1991

2011–12 NAS	32	3	8	11	4
NHL Totals	32	3	8	11	4

Emelin, Alexei b. Togliatti, Soviet Union (Russia), April 25, 1986

2011–12 MON	67	3	4	7	30
NHL Totals	67	3	4	7	30

Emery, Ray b. Hamilton, Ontario, September 28, 1982

2011–12 CHI	34	15–9–0–4	1,774	83	0	2.81
NHL Totals	207	109–62–0–19	11,404	512	11	2.69

Eminger, Steve b. Woodbridge, Ontario, October 31, 1983

2011–12 NYR	42	2	3	5	28
NHL Totals	453	19	77	96	351

Emmerton, Cory b. St. Thomas, Ontario, June 1, 1988

2011–12 DET	71	6	4	10	14
NHL Totals	73	7	4	11	14

Engelland, Deryk b. Edmonton, Alberta, April 3, 1982

2011–12 PIT	73	4	13	17	56
NHL Totals	145	7	22	29	196

Engqvist, Andreas b. Stockholm, Sweden, December 23, 1987

2011–12 MON	12	0	0	0	4
NHL Totals	15	0	0	0	4

Ennis, Tyler b. Edmonton, Alberta, October 6, 1989

2011–12 BUF	48	15	19	34	14
NHL Totals	140	38	54	92	50

Enroth, Jhonas b. Stockholm, Sweden, June 25, 1988

2011–12 BUF	26	8–11–4	1,399	63	1	2.70
NHL Totals	41	17–14–0–6	2,227	102	2	2.75

Enstrom, Tobias b. Nordingra, Sweden, November 5, 1984

2011–12 WIN	62	6	27	33	38
NHL Totals	380	32	172	204	216

Erat, Martin   b. Trebic, Czechoslovakia (Czech Republic), August 28, 1981

2011–12 NAS	71	19	39	58	30
NHL Totals	687	159	301	460	400

Ericsson, Jonathan   b. Karlskrona, Sweden, March 2, 1984

2011–12 DET	69	1	10	11	47
NHL Totals	232	10	34	44	197

Eriksson, Loui   b. Gothenburg, Sweden, July 17, 1985

2011–12 DAL	82	26	45	71	12
NHL Totals	453	138	190	328	106

Erixon, Tim   b. Port Chester, New York, February 24, 1991

2011–12 NYR	18	0	2	2	8
NHL Totals	18	0	2	2	8

Erskine, John   b. Kingston, Ontario, June 26, 1980

2011–12 WAS	28	0	2	2	51
NHL Totals	424	11	33	44	775

Fairchild, Cade   b. Duluth, Minnesota, January 15, 1989

2011–12 STL	5	0	1	1	0
NHL Totals	5	0	1	1	0

Falk, Justin   b. Snowflake, Manitoba, October 11, 1988

2011–12 MIN	47	1	8	9	54
NHL Totals	47	1	8	9	54

Faulk, Justin   b. South St. Paul, Minnesota, March 20, 1992

2011–12 CAR	66	8	14	22	29
NHL Totals	66	8	14	22	29

Fayne, Mark   b. Nashua, New Hampshire, May 15, 1987

2011–12 NJ	82	4	13	17	26
NHL Totals	139	8	23	31	53

Fedotenko, Ruslan   b. Kiev, Soviet Union (Ukraine), January 18, 1979

2011–12 NYR	73	9	11	20	16
NHL Totals	816	169	184	353	460

Fehr, Eric   b. Winkler, Manitoba, September 7, 1985

2011–12 WIN	35	2	1	3	12
NHL Totals	265	48	48	96	90

Ference, Andrew   b. Edmonton, Alberta, March 17, 1979

2011–12 BOS	72	6	18	24	46
NHL Totals	712	33	147	180	610

Ferriero, Benn   b. Boston, Massachusetts, April 29, 1987

2011–12 SJ	35	7	1	8	8
NHL Totals	92	14	8	22	25

Festerling, Brett   b. Quesnel, British Columbia, March 3, 1986

2011–12 WIN	5	0	0	0	2
NHL Totals	88	0	8	8	35

Fiddler, Vernon   b. Edmonton, Alberta, May 9, 1980

2011–12 DAL	82	8	13	21	60
NHL Totals	534	67	99	166	342

Filatov, Nikita   b. Moscow, Soviet Union (Russia), May 25, 1990

2011–12 OTT	9	0	1	1	4
NHL Totals	53	6	8	14	20

Filppula, Valtteri   b. Vantaa, Finland, March 20, 1984

2011–12 DET	81	23	43	66	14
NHL Totals	442	91	143	234	152

Finley, Joe   b. Edina, Minnesota, June 29, 1987

2011–12 BUF	5	0	0	0	12
NHL Totals	5	0	0	0	12

Fisher, Mike   b. Peterborough, Ontario, June 5, 1980

2011–12 NAS	72	24	27	51	33
NHL Totals	774	196	215	411	597

Fistric, Mark   b. Edmonton, Alberta, June 1, 1986

2011–12 DAL	60	0	2	2	41
NHL Totals	257	3	20	23	220

Fleischmann, Tomas   b. Koprivnice, Czechoslovakia (Czech Republic), May 16, 1984

2011–12 FLO	82	27	34	61	26
NHL Totals	387	95	125	220	118

Fleury, Marc-Andre   b. Sorel, Quebec, November 28, 1984

2011–12 PIT	67	42–17–4	3,896	153	3	2.36
NHL Totals	434	226–143–2–41	24,757	1,104	22	2.68

Flood, Mark b. Charlottetown, Prince Edward Island, September 29, 1984

2011–12 WIN	33	3	4	7	10
NHL Totals	39	3	5	8	10

Foligno, Marcus b. Buffalo, New York, August 10, 1991

2011–12 BUF	14	6	7	13	9
NHL Totals	14	6	7	13	9

Foligno, Nick b. Buffalo, New York, October 31, 1987

2011–12 OTT	82	15	32	47	124
NHL Totals	351	61	87	148	299

Foster, Brian b. Pembroke, New Hampshire, February 4, 1987

2011–12 FLO	1	0–0–0	5	0	0	0.00
NHL Totals	1	0–0–0	5	0	0	0.00

Foster, Kurtis b. Carp, Ontario, November 24, 1981

2011–12 NJ/MIN	51	4	10	14	35
NHL Totals	382	41	114	155	283

• traded by New Jersey to Minnesota on February 24, 2012, with Nick Palmieri, Stephane Veilleux, a 2nd-round draft choice in 2012 and a conditional 3rd-round draft choice in 2013 for Marek Zidlicky

Foucault, Kris b. Calgary, Alberta, December 12, 1990

2011–12 MIN	1	0	0	0	0
NHL Totals	1	0	0	0	0

Fowler, Cam b. Windsor, Ontario, December 5, 1991

2011–12 ANA	82	5	24	29	18
NHL Totals	158	15	54	69	38

Franson, Cody b. Salmon Arm, British Columbia, August 8, 1987

2011–12 TOR	57	5	16	21	22
NHL Totals	198	19	52	71	68

Franzen, Johan b. Landsbro, Sweden, December 23, 1979

2011–12 DET	77	29	27	56	40
NHL Totals	472	150	125	275	288

Fraser, Colin b. Sicamous, British Columbia, January 28, 1985

2011–12 LA	67	2	6	8	67
NHL Totals	291	18	31	49	235

Fraser, Mark b. Ottawa, Ontario, September 29, 1986

2011–12 NJ	4	0	0	0	14
NHL Totals	98	3	5	8	86

Fraser, Matt b. Red Deer, Alberta, May 20, 1990

2011–12 DAL	1	0	0	0	0
NHL Totals	1	0	0	0	0

Frattin, Matt b. Edmonton, Alberta, January 3, 1988

2011–12 TOR	56	8	7	15	25
NHL Totals	57	8	7	15	25

Fredheim, Kris b. Campbell River, British Columbia, February 23, 1987

2011–12 MIN	3	0	0	0	2
NHL Totals	3	0	0	0	2

Frolik, Michael b. Kladno, Czechoslovakia (Czech Republic), February 17, 1988

2011–12 CHI	63	5	10	15	22
NHL Totals	304	58	83	141	117

Gaborik, Marian b. Trencin, Czechoslovakia (Slovakia), February 14, 1982

2011–12 NYR	82	41	35	76	34
NHL Totals	722	324	323	647	390

Gagne, Simon b. Ste-Foy, Quebec, February 29, 1980

2011–12 LA	34	7	10	17	18
NHL Totals	761	283	298	581	316

Gagner, Sam b. London, Ontario, August 10, 1989

2011–12 EDM	75	18	29	47	36
NHL Totals	366	77	143	220	180

Gagnon, Aaron b. Quesnel, British Columbia, April 24, 1986

2011–12 WIN	7	0	0	0	0
NHL Totals	28	0	2	2	0

Galiardi, T.J. b. Calgary, Alberta, April 22, 1988

2011–12 COL/SJ	69	9	6	15	53
NHL Totals	185	34	39	73	99

• traded by Colorado to San Jose on February 27, 2012, with a 7th-round draft choice in 2013 for Mike Connolly, Jamie McGinn and Michael Sgarbossa

Garbutt, Ryan   b. Winnipeg, Manitoba, August 12, 1985

2011–12 DAL	20	2	1	3	22
NHL Totals	20	2	1	3	22

Gardiner, Jake   b. Deephaven, Minnesota, July 4, 1990

2011–12 TOR	75	7	23	30	18
NHL Totals	75	7	23	30	18

Garrison, Jason   b. White Rock, British Columbia, November 13, 1984

2011–12 FLO	77	16	17	33	32
NHL Totals	190	23	36	59	81

Garon, Mathieu   b. Chandler, Quebec, January 9, 1978

2011–12 TB	48	23–16–4	2,484	118	1	2.85
NHL Totals	323	139–122–3–28	17,431	821	20	2.83

Gaustad, Paul   b. Fargo, North Dakota, February 3, 1982

2011–12 BUF/NAS	70	7	14	21	76
NHL Totals	493	71	114	185	591

• traded by Buffalo to Nashville on February 27, 2012, with a 4th-round draft choice in 2013 for a 1st-round draft choice in 2012

Genoway, Chay   b. Swan River, Manitoba, December 20, 1986

2011–12 MIN	1	0	1	1	0
NHL Totals	1	0	1	1	0

Geoffrion, Blake   b. Plantation, Florida, February 3, 1988

2011–12 NAS/MON	35	2	3	5	27
NHL Totals	55	8	5	13	34

• traded by Nashville to Montreal on February 17, 2012, with Robert Slaney and a 2nd-round draft choice in 2012 for Hal Gill and a conditional 5th-round draft choice in 2013

Gerbe, Nathan   b. Oxford, Michigan, July 24, 1987

2011–12 BUF	62	6	19	25	32
NHL Totals	146	24	38	62	74

Gervais, Bruno   b. Longueuil, Quebec, October 3, 1984

2011–12 TB	50	6	7	13	8
NHL Totals	381	15	66	81	172

Getzlaf, Ryan   b. Regina, Saskatchewan, May 10, 1985

2011–12 ANA	82	11	46	57	75
NHL Totals	512	137	335	472	492

Giguere, Jean-Sebastien   b. Montreal, Quebec, May 16, 1977

2011–12 COL	32	15–11–3	1,820	69	2	2.27
NHL Totals	557	246–206–25–59	31,599	1,327	36	2.52

Gilbert, Tom   b. Minneapolis, Minnesota, January 10, 1983

2011–12 EDM/MIN	67	3	19	22	20
NHL Totals	404	33	130	163	114

• traded by Edmonton to Minnesota on February 27, 2012, for Nick Schultz

Gill, Hal   b. Concord, Massachusetts, April 6, 1975

2011–12 MON/NAS	76	1	12	13	37
NHL Totals	1,070	36	148	184	948

• traded by Montreal to Nashville on February 17, 2012, with a conditional 5th-round draft choice in 2013 for Robert Slaney and a 2nd-round draft choice in 2012

Gillies, Colton   b. White Rock, British Columbia, February 12, 1989

2011–12 MIN/CBJ	75	2	6	8	35
NHL Totals	127	5	11	16	55

• claimed off waivers on January 14, 2012, by Columbus from Minnesota

Gillies, Trevor   b. Cambridge, Ontario, January 30, 1979

2011–12 NYI	3	0	0	0	0
NHL Totals	57	2	1	3	261

Gilroy, Matt   b. North Bellmore, New York, July 30, 1984

2011–12 TB/OTT	67	3	17	20	18
NHL Totals	194	10	36	46	55

• traded by Tampa Bay to Ottawa on February 27, 2012, for Brian Lee

Gionta, Brian   b. Rochester, New York, January 18, 1979

2011–12 MON	31	8	7	15	16
NHL Totals	647	217	202	419	293

Gionta, Stephen   b. Rochester, New York, October 9, 1983

2011–12 NJ	1	1	0	1	0
NHL Totals	13	1	0	1	6

Giordano, Mark   b. Toronto, Ontario, March 10, 1983

2011–12 CAL	61	9	18	27	75
NHL Totals	338	37	98	135	326

Girardi, Dan   b. Welland, Ontario, April 29, 1984

2011–12 NYR	82	5	24	29	20
NHL Totals	442	29	111	140	185

Giroux, Alexandre b. Quebec City, Quebec, June 16, 1981

2011–12 CBJ	9	1	0	1	8
NHL Totals	48	6	6	12	26

Giroux, Claude b. Hearst, Ontario, January 12, 1988

2011–12 PHI	77	28	65	93	29
NHL Totals	285	78	165	243	113

Glass, Tanner b. Regina, Saskatchewan, November 29, 1983

2011–12 WIN	78	5	11	16	73
NHL Totals	262	13	26	39	306

Gleason, Tim b. Southfield, Michigan, January 29, 1983

2011–12 CAR	82	1	17	18	71
NHL Totals	557	15	103	118	541

Glencross, Curtis b. Kindersley, Saskatchewan, December 28, 1982

2011–12 CAL	67	26	22	48	62
NHL Totals	358	94	96	190	276

Glennie, Scott b. Oakville, Ontario, February 22, 1991

2011–12 DAL	1	0	0	0	2
NHL Totals	1	0	0	0	2

Goc, Marcel b. Calw, West Germany (Germany), August 24, 1983

2011–12 FLO	57	11	16	27	10
NHL Totals	446	52	83	135	106

Goligoski, Alex b. Grand Rapids, Minnesota, July 30, 1985

2011–12 DAL	71	9	21	30	16
NHL Totals	271	37	98	135	96

Goloubef, Cody b. Mississauga, Ontario, November 30, 1989

2011–12 CBJ	1	0	0	0	0
NHL Totals	1	0	0	0	0

Gomez, Scott b. Anchorage, Alaska, December 23, 1979

2011–12 MON	38	2	3	5	6
NHL Totals	902	169	517	686	580

Gonchar, Sergei b. Chelyabinsk, Soviet Union (Russia), April 13, 1974

2011–12 OTT	74	5	32	37	55
NHL Totals	1,132	214	534	748	917

Gordon, Andrew b. Halifax, Nova Scotia, December 13, 1985

2011–12 ANA	37	2	3	5	6
NHL Totals	49	3	4	7	6

Gordon, Boyd b. Unity, Saskatchewan, October 19, 1983

2011–12 PHO	75	8	15	23	10
NHL Totals	438	35	73	108	92

Gorges, Josh b. Kelowna, British Columbia, August 14, 1984

2011–12 MON	82	2	14	16	39
NHL Totals	446	11	64	75	222

Grabner, Michael b. Villach, Austria, October 5, 1987

2011–12 NYI	78	20	12	32	12
NHL Totals	174	59	36	95	30

Grabovski, Mikhail b. Potsdam, East Germany (Germany), January 31, 1984

2011–12 TOR	74	23	28	51	51
NHL Totals	319	85	116	201	221

Grachev, Evgeni b. Khabarovsk, Soviet Union (Russia), February 21, 1990

2011–12 STL	26	1	3	4	2
NHL Totals	34	1	3	4	2

Gragnani, Marc-Andre b. Montreal, Quebec, March 11, 1987

2011–12 BUF/VAN	58	2	13	15	26
NHL Totals	73	3	15	18	34

• traded by Buffalo to Vancouver on February 27, 2012, with Zack Kassian for Cody Hodgson and Alexander Sulzer

Green, Josh b. Camrose, Alberta, November 16, 1977

2011–12 EDM	7	1	1	2	7
NHL Totals	341	36	40	76	206

Green, Mike b. Calgary, Alberta, October 12, 1985

2011–12 WAS	32	3	4	7	12
NHL Totals	398	82	169	251	298

Greene, Andy b. Trenton, Michigan, October 30, 1982

2011–12 NJ	56	1	15	16	16
NHL Totals	347	16	85	101	102

Greene, Matt   b. Grand Ledge, Michigan, May 13, 1983

| 2011–12 LA | 82 | 4 | 11 | 15 | 58 |
| NHL Totals | 461 | 11 | 51 | 62 | 527 |

Greening, Colin   b. St. John's, Newfoundland, March 9, 1986

| 2011–12 OTT | 82 | 17 | 20 | 37 | 46 |
| NHL Totals | 106 | 23 | 27 | 50 | 56 |

Greiss, Thomas   b. Fussen, West Germany (Germany), January 29, 1986

| 2011–12 SJ | 19 | 9–7–1 | 1,043 | 40 | 0 | 2.30 |
| NHL Totals | 38 | 16–12–0–3 | 1,954 | 82 | 0 | 2.52 |

Grossman, Nicklas   b. Stockholm, Sweden, January 22, 1985

| 2011–12 DAL/PHI | 74 | 0 | 11 | 11 | 36 |
| NHL Totals | 355 | 3 | 44 | 47 | 180 |

• traded by Dallas to Philadelphia on February 16, 2012, for a 2nd-round draft choice in 2012 and a 3rd-round draft choice in 2013

Gudbranson, Erik   b. Ottawa, Ontario, January 7, 1992

| 2011–12 FLO | 72 | 2 | 6 | 8 | 78 |
| NHL Totals | 72 | 2 | 6 | 8 | 78 |

Guenin, Nate   b. Sewickley, Pennsylvania, December 10, 1982

| 2011–12 ANA | 15 | 2 | 0 | 2 | 6 |
| NHL Totals | 32 | 2 | 2 | 4 | 14 |

Gunnarsson, Carl   b. Orebro, Sweden, November 9, 1986

| 2011–12 TOR | 76 | 4 | 15 | 19 | 20 |
| NHL Totals | 187 | 11 | 43 | 54 | 44 |

Gustafsson, Erik   b. Kvissleby, Sweden, December 15, 1988

| 2011–12 PHI | 30 | 1 | 4 | 5 | 2 |
| NHL Totals | 33 | 1 | 4 | 5 | 6 |

Gustavsson, Jonas   b. Stockholm, Sweden, October 24, 1984

| 2011–12 TOR | 42 | 17–17–4 | 2,301 | 112 | 4 | 2.92 |
| NHL Totals | 107 | 39–45–0–15 | 5,882 | 292 | 5 | 2.98 |

Hackett, Matt   b. London, Ontario, March 7, 1990

| 2011–12 MIN | 12 | 3–6–0 | 556 | 22 | 0 | 2.37 |
| NHL Totals | 12 | 3–6–0 | 556 | 22 | 0 | 2.37 |

Hagelin, Carl b. Sodertalje, Sweden, August 23, 1988

2011–12 NYR	64	14	24	38	24
NHL Totals	64	14	24	38	24

Hagman, Niklas b. Espoo, Finland, December 5, 1979

2011–12 CAL/ANA	71	9	14	23	14
NHL Totals	770	147	154	301	220

• claimed off waivers on November 14, 2011, by Anaheim from Calgary

Hainsey, Ron b. Bolton, Connecticut, March 24, 1981

2011–12 WIN	56	0	10	10	23
NHL Totals	544	34	145	179	261

Halak, Jaroslav b. Bratislava, Czechoslovakia (Slovakia), May 13, 1985

2011–12 STL	46	26–12–7	2,747	90	6	1.97
NHL Totals	204	109–67–0–21	11,798	477	22	2.43

Haley, Michael b. Oshawa, Ontario, March 30, 1986

2011–12 NYI	14	0	0	0	57
NHL Totals	43	2	1	3	151

Halischuk, Matt b. Toronto, Ontario, June 1, 1988

2011–12 NAS	73	15	13	28	27
NHL Totals	121	20	23	43	31

Hall, Adam b. Kalamazoo, Michigan, August 14, 1980

2011–12 TB	57	2	5	7	17
NHL Totals	565	65	78	143	236

Hall, Taylor b. Calgary, Alberta, November 14, 1991

2011–12 EDM	61	27	26	53	36
NHL Totals	126	49	46	95	63

Halpern, Jeff b. Potomac, Maryland, May 3, 1976

2011–12 WAS	69	4	12	16	24
NHL Totals	861	146	212	358	607

Hamhuis, Dan b. Smithers, British Columbia, December 13, 1982

2011–12 VAN	82	4	33	37	46
NHL Totals	629	42	179	221	455

Hamill, Zach   b. Vancouver, British Columbia, September 23, 1988

2011–12 BOS	16	0	2	2	4
NHL Totals	20	0	4	4	4

Hamilton, Ryan   b. Oshawa, Ontario, April 15, 1985

2011–12 TOR	2	0	1	1	2
NHL Totals	2	0	1	1	2

Hamonic, Travis   b. Winnipeg, Manitoba, August 16, 1990

2011–12 NYI	73	2	22	24	73
NHL Totals	135	7	43	50	176

Hamrlik, Roman   b. Zlin, Czechoslovakia (Czech Republic), April 12, 1974

2011–12 WAS	68	2	11	13	34
NHL Totals	1,379	155	482	637	1,400

Handzus, Michal   b. Banska Bystrica, Czechoslovakia (Slovakia), March 11, 1977

2011–12 SJ	67	7	17	24	18
NHL Totals	911	179	280	459	466

Hannan, Scott   b. Richmond, British Columbia, January 23, 1979

2011–12 CAL	78	2	10	12	38
NHL Totals	908	33	164	197	522

Hansen, Jannick   b. Herlev, Denmark, March 15, 1986

2011–12 VAN	82	16	23	39	34
NHL Totals	271	40	64	104	123

Hanzal, Martin   b. Pisek, Czechoslovakia (Czech Republic), February 20, 1987

2011–12 PHO	64	8	26	34	63
NHL Totals	352	54	105	159	289

Harding, Josh   b. Regina, Saskatchewan, June 18, 1984

2011–12 MIN	34	13–12–4	1,855	81	2	2.62
NHL Totals	117	41–51–0–9	6,141	271	6	2.65

Harrison, Jay   b. Oshawa, Ontario, November 3, 1982

2011–12 CAR	72	9	14	23	60
NHL Totals	202	13	28	41	200

Harrold, Peter   b. Kirtland Hills, Ohio, June 8, 1983

2011–12 NJ	11	0	2	2	0
NHL Totals	175	8	20	28	50

Hartikainen, Teemu   b. Kuopio, Finland, May 3, 1990

2011–12 EDM	17	2	3	5	6
NHL Totals	29	5	5	10	10

Hartnell, Scott   b. Regina, Saskatchewan, April 18, 1982

2011–12 PHI	82	37	30	67	136
NHL Totals	843	222	252	474	1,279

Havlat, Martin   b. Mlada Bolslav, Czechoslovakia (Czech Republic), April 19, 1981

2011–12 SJ	39	7	20	27	22
NHL Totals	660	216	323	539	354

Hayes, Jimmy   b. Boston, Massachusetts, November 21, 1989

2011–12 CHI	31	5	4	9	16
NHL Totals	31	5	4	9	16

Heatley, Dany   b. Freiburg, West Germany (Germany), January 21, 1981

2011–12 MIN	82	24	29	53	28
NHL Totals	751	349	393	742	594

Hecht, Jochen   b. Mannheim, West Germany (Germany), June 21, 1977

2011–12 BUF	22	4	4	8	6
NHL Totals	786	181	268	449	440

Hedberg, Johan   b. Leksand, Sweden, May 3, 1973

2011–12 NJ	27	17–7–2	1,591	59	4	2.23
NHL Totals	354	155–133–14–27	19,650	926	21	2.83

Hedman, Victor   b. Ornskoldsvik, Sweden, December 18, 1990

2011–12 TB	61	5	18	23	65
NHL Totals	214	12	57	69	214

Hejda, Jan   b. Prague, Czechoslovakia (Czech Republic), June 18, 1978

2011–12 COL	81	5	14	19	24
NHL Totals	422	17	78	95	207

Hejduk, Milan   b. Usti-nad-Labem, Czechoslovakia (Czech Republic), February 14, 1976

2011–12 COL	81	14	23	37	14
NHL Totals	991	371	423	794	316

Helm, Darren   b. Winnipeg, Manitoba, January 21, 1987

2011–12 DET	68	9	17	26	12
NHL Totals	248	32	51	83	52

Hemsky, Ales   b. Pardubice, Czechoslovakia (Czech Republic), August 13, 1983

2011–12 EDM	69	10	26	36	43
NHL Totals	559	124	307	431	267

Hendricks, Matt   b. Blaine, Minnesota, June 17, 1981

2011–12 WAS	78	4	5	9	95
NHL Totals	215	22	28	50	292

Hennessy, Josh   b. Brockton, Massachusetts, February 7, 1985

2011–12 BOS	3	0	0	0	2
NHL Totals	23	1	0	1	6

Henrique, Adam   b. Brantford, Ontario, February 6, 1990

2011–12 NJ	74	16	35	51	7
NHL Totals	75	16	35	51	7

Higgins, Chris   b. Smithtown, New York, June 2, 1983

2011–12 VAN	71	18	25	43	16
NHL Totals	482	123	116	239	160

Hillen, Jack   b. Portland, Oregon, January 24, 1986

2011–12 NAS	55	2	4	6	20
NHL Totals	230	10	46	56	129

Hiller, Jonas   b. Felben Wellhausen, Switzerland, February 12, 1982

2011–12 ANA	73	29–30–12	4,253	182	4	2.57
NHL Totals	250	118–91–0–21	13,971	589	15	2.53

Hjalmarsson, Niklas   b. Eksjo, Sweden, June 6, 1987

2011–12 CHI	69	1	14	15	14
NHL Totals	260	7	39	46	86

Hodgson, Cody   b. Toronto, Ontario, February 18, 1990

2011–12 VAN/BUF	83	19	22	41	10
NHL Totals	91	20	23	43	10

• traded by Vancouver to Buffalo on February 27, 2012, with Alexander Sulzer for Zack Kassian and Marc-Andre Gragnani

Hoffman, Mike b. Kitchener, Ontario, November 24, 1989

2011–12 OTT	1	0	0	0	0
NHL Totals	1	0	0	0	0

Holland, Peter b. Toronto, Ontario, January 14, 1991

2011–12 ANA	4	1	0	1	2
NHL Totals	4	1	0	1	2

Holmstrom, Ben b. Colorado Springs, Colorado, April 9, 1987

2011–12 PHI	5	0	0	0	2
NHL Totals	7	0	0	0	7

Holmstrom, Tomas b. Pitea, Sweden, January 23, 1973

2011–12 DET	74	11	13	24	40
NHL Totals	1,026	243	287	530	769

Holtby, Braden b. Lloydminster, Saskatchewan, September 16, 1989

2011–12 WAS	7	4–2–1	361	15	1	2.49
NHL Totals	21	14–4–0–3	1,097	37	3	2.02

Horak, Roman b. Ceske Budejovice, Czechoslovakia (Czech Republic), May 21, 1991

2011–12 CAL	61	3	8	11	14
NHL Totals	61	3	8	11	14

Horcoff, Shawn b. Trail, British Columbia, September 17, 1978

2011–12 EDM	81	13	21	34	24
NHL Totals	765	155	280	435	487

Hordichuk, Darcy b. Kamsack, Saskatchewan, August 10, 1980

2011–12 EDM	43	1	2	3	64
NHL Totals	538	20	21	41	1,138

Hornqvist, Patric b. Sollentuna, Sweden, January 1, 1987

2011–12 NAS	76	27	16	43	28
NHL Totals	263	80	69	149	131

Horton, Nathan b. Welland, Ontario, May 29, 1985

2011–12 BOS	46	17	15	32	54
NHL Totals	548	185	195	380	521

Hossa, Marian b. Stara Lubovna, Czechoslovakia (Slovakia), January 12, 1979

2011–12 CHI	81	29	48	77	20
NHL Totals	978	417	487	904	528

Howard, Jimmy   b. Syracuse, New York, March 26, 1984

2011–12 DET	57	35–17–4	3,360	119	6	2.13
NHL Totals	192	110–54–0–19	11,172	449	11	2.41

Hudler, Jiri   b. Olomouc, Czechoslovakia (Czech Republic), January 4, 1984

2011–12 DET	81	25	25	50	42
NHL Totals	409	87	127	214	160

Hunter, Trent   b. Red Deer, Alberta, July 5, 1980

2011–12 LA	38	2	5	7	8
NHL Totals	497	101	135	236	209

Hunwick, Matt   b. Warren, Michigan, May 21, 1985

2011–12 COL	33	3	3	6	8
NHL Totals	248	16	45	61	100

Hunwick, Shawn   b. Sterling Heights, Michigan, April 9, 1987

2011–12 CBJ	1	0–0–0	3	0	0	0.00
NHL Totals	1	0–0–0	3	0	0	0.00

Huselius, Kristian   b. Osterhaninge, Sweden, November 10, 1978

2011–12 CBJ	2	0	0	0	2
NHL Totals	662	190	261	451	256

Huskins, Kent   b. Almonte, Ontario, May 4, 1979

2011–12 STL	25	2	5	7	10
NHL Totals	299	13	54	67	169

Iginla, Jarome   b. Edmonton, Alberta, July 1, 1977

2011–12 CAL	82	32	35	67	43
NHL Totals	1,188	516	557	1,073	809

Irving, Leland   b. Barrhead, Alberta, April 11, 1988

2011–12 CAL	7	1–3–0	394	21	0	3.20
NHL Totals	7	1–3–0	394	21	0	3.20

Ivanans, Raitis   b. Riga, Soviet Union (Latvia), January 1, 1979

2011–12 CAL	1	0	0	0	0
NHL Totals	282	12	6	18	569

Jackman, Barret   b. Trail, British Columbia, March 5, 1981

2011–12 STL	81	1	12	13	57
NHL Totals	598	20	119	139	843

Jackman, Tim b. Minot, North Dakota, November 14, 1981

2011–12 CAL	75	1	6	7	94
NHL Totals	348	22	36	58	537

Jacques, Jean-Francois b. Terrebonne, Quebec, April 29, 1985

2011–12 ANA	6	0	0	0	12
NHL Totals	166	9	8	17	197

Jaffray, Jason b. Rimbey, Alberta, June 30, 1981

2011–12 WIN	13	0	1	1	7
NHL Totals	49	4	7	11	40

Jagr, Jaromir b. Kladno, Czechoslovakia (Czech Republic), February 15, 1972

2011–12 PHI	73	19	35	54	30
NHL Totals	1,346	665	988	1,653	937

Janik, Doug b. Agawam, Massachusetts, March 26, 1980

2011–12 DET	9	0	1	1	6
NHL Totals	190	3	16	19	154

Janssen, Cam b. St. Louis, Missouri, April 15, 1984

2011–12 NJ	48	0	1	1	75
NHL Totals	308	3	8	11	750

Jeffrey, Dustin b. Sarnia, Ontario, February 27, 1988

2011–12 PIT	26	4	2	6	2
NHL Totals	66	12	9	21	6

Johansen, Ryan b. Vancouver, British Columbia, July 31, 1992

2011–12 CBJ	67	9	12	21	24
NHL Totals	67	9	12	21	24

Johansson, Marcus b. Landskrona, Sweden, October 6, 1990

2011–12 WAS	80	14	32	46	8
NHL Totals	149	27	46	73	18

Johnson, Aaron b. Port Hawkesbury, Nova Scotia, April 30, 1983

2011–12 CBJ	53	3	13	16	26
NHL Totals	281	17	45	62	217

Johnson, Brent b. Farmington, Michigan, March 12, 1977

2011–12 PIT	16	6–7–2	811	42	0	3.11
NHL Totals	309	140–112–13–27	16,978	744	14	2.63

Johnson, Erik   b. Bloomington, Minnesota, March 21, 1988

2011–12 COL	73	4	22	26	26
NHL Totals	298	27	100	127	189

Johnson, Jack   b. Indianapolis, Indiana, January 13, 1987

2011–12 LA/CBJ	82	12	26	38	39
NHL Totals	364	34	104	138	271

• traded by Los Angeles to Columbus on February 23, 2012, with a 1st-round draft choice in either 2012 or 2013 for Jeff Carter

Johnson, Nick   b. Calgary, Alberta, December 24, 1985

2011–12 MIN	77	8	18	26	45
NHL Totals	87	10	21	31	52

Jokinen, Jussi   b. Kalajoki, Finland, April 11, 1983

2011–12 CAR	79	12	34	46	54
NHL Totals	536	115	220	335	208

Jokinen, Olli   b. Kuopio, Finland, December 5, 1978

2011–12 CAL	82	23	38	61	54
NHL Totals	1,042	292	391	683	967

Jones, Blair   b. Central Butte, Saskatchewan, September 27, 1986

2011–12 TB/CAL	43	3	5	8	18
NHL Totals	99	5	9	14	32

• traded by Tampa Bay to Calgary on January 6, 2012, for Brendan Mikkelson

Jones, David   b. Guelph, Ontario, August 10, 1984

2011–12 COL	72	20	17	37	32
NHL Totals	239	67	50	117	78

Jones, Randy   b. Quispamsis, New Brunswick, July 23, 1981

2011–12 WIN	39	1	1	2	8
NHL Totals	365	20	85	105	185

Jones, Ryan   b. Chatham, Ontario, June 14, 1984

2011–12 EDM	79	17	16	33	42
NHL Totals	255	50	37	87	124

Josefson, Jacob   b. Stockholm, Sweden, March 2, 1991

2011–12 NJ	41	2	7	9	6
NHL Totals	69	5	14	19	12

Josi, Roman b. Bern, Switzerland, June 1, 1990

2011–12 NAS	52	5	11	16	14
NHL Totals	52	5	11	16	14

Joslin, Derek b. Richmond Hill, Ontario, March 17, 1987

2011–12 CAR	44	2	2	4	35
NHL Totals	114	4	12	16	63

Joudrey, Andrew b. Halifax, Nova Scotia, July 15, 1984

2011–12 CBJ	1	0	0	0	0
NHL Totals	1	0	0	0	0

Jovanovski, Ed b. Windsor, Ontario, June 26, 1976

2011–12 FLO	66	3	10	13	31
NHL Totals	1,085	136	358	494	1,452

Jurcina, Milan b. Liptovsky Mikulas, Czechoslovakia (Slovakia), June 7, 1983

2011–12 NYI	65	3	8	11	30
NHL Totals	430	22	59	81	280

Kaberle, Tomas b. Rakovnik, Czechoslovakia (Czech Republic), March 2, 1978

2011–12 CAR/MON	72	3	28	31	12
NHL Totals	974	87	473	560	260

• traded by Carolina to Montreal on December 9, 2011, for Jaroslav Spacek

Kadri, Nazem b. London, Ontario, October 6, 1990

2011–12 TOR	21	5	2	7	8
NHL Totals	51	8	11	19	16

Kaleta, Patrick b. Buffalo, New York, June 8, 1986

2011–12 BUF	63	5	5	10	116
NHL Totals	267	26	24	50	434

Kampfer, Steven b. Ann Arbor, Michigan, September 24, 1988

2011–12 BOS/MIN	23	2	3	5	6
NHL Totals	61	7	8	15	18

• traded by Boston to Minnesota on February 27, 2012, for Greg Zanon

Kane, Evander b. Vancouver, British Columbia, August 2, 1991

2011–12 WIN	74	30	27	57	53
NHL Totals	213	63	63	126	183

Kane, Patrick b. Buffalo, New York, November 19, 1988

2011–12 CHI	82	23	43	66	40
NHL Totals	399	126	243	369	182

Karlsson, Erik b. Landsbro, Sweden, May 31, 1990

2011–12 OTT	81	19	59	78	42
NHL Totals	216	37	112	149	116

Karlsson, Henrik b. Stockholm, Sweden, November 27, 1983

2011–12 CAL	9	1–4–2	454	24	0	3.17
NHL Totals	26	5–9–0–8	1,292	60	0	2.79

Kassian, Matt b. Edmonton, Alberta, October 28, 1986

2011–12 MIN	24	2	0	2	55
NHL Totals	28	2	0	2	67

Kassian, Zack b. Windsor, Ontario, January 24, 1991

2011–12 BUF/VAN	44	4	6	10	51
NHL Totals	44	4	6	10	51

• traded by Buffalo to Vancouver on February 27, 2012, with Marc-Andre Gragnani for Alexander Sulzer and Cody Hodgson

Kearns, Bracken b. North Vancouver, British Columbia, May 12, 1981

2011–12 FLO	5	0	0	0	10
NHL Totals	5	0	0	0	10

Keith, Duncan b. Winnipeg, Manitoba, July 16, 1983

2011–12 CHI	74	4	36	40	42
NHL Totals	560	56	226	282	386

Kelly, Chris b. Toronto, Ontario, November 11, 1980

2011–12 BOS	82	20	19	39	41
NHL Totals	569	97	123	220	296

Kennedy, Tim b. Buffalo, New York, April 30, 1986

2011–12 FLO	27	1	1	2	4
NHL Totals	112	11	18	29	54

Kennedy, Tyler b. Sault Ste. Marie, Ontario, July 15, 1986

2011–12 PIT	60	11	22	33	29
NHL Totals	326	70	87	157	162

Kesler, Ryan b. Detroit, Michigan, August 31, 1984

2011–12 VAN	77	22	27	49	56
NHL Totals	561	153	184	337	501

Kessel, Phil b. Madison, Wisconsin, October 2, 1987

2011–12 TOR	82	37	45	82	20
NHL Totals	456	165	162	327	121

Khabibulin, Nikolai b. Sverdlovsk, Soviet Union (Russia), January 13, 1973

2011–12 EDM	40	12–20–7	2,261	100	2	2.65
NHL Totals	783	328–328–58–58	44,755	2,028	45	2.72

Khudobin, Anton b. Ust-Kamenogorsk, Soviet Union (Russia), May 7, 1986

2011–12 BOS	1	1–0–0	60	1	0	1.00
NHL Totals	7	5–1–0–0	318	7	1	1.32

Kindl, Jakub b. Sumperk, Czechoslovakia (Czech Republic), February 10, 1987

2011–12 DET	55	1	12	13	25
NHL Totals	106	3	14	17	61

King, D.J. b. Meadow Lake, Saskatchewan, June 27, 1984

2011–12 WAS	1	0	0	0	0
NHL Totals	118	4	7	11	215

King, Dwight b. Meadow Lake, Saskatchewan, July 5, 1989

2011–12 LA	27	5	9	14	10
NHL Totals	33	5	9	14	12

Kiprusoff, Miikka b. Turku, Finland, October 26, 1976

2011–12 CAL	70	35–22–11	4,128	162	4	2.35
NHL Totals	599	311–199–7–67	34,825	1,423	44	2.45

Klein, Kevin b. Kitchener, Ontario, December 13, 1984

2011–12 NAS	66	4	17	21	4
NHL Totals	309	12	53	65	80

Klesla, Rostislav b. Novy Jicin, Czechoslovakia (Czech Republic), March 21, 1982

2011–12 PHO	65	3	10	13	54
NHL Totals	596	45	102	147	574

Klingberg, Carl b. Gothenburg, Sweden, January 28, 1991

2011–12 WIN	6	0	0	0	4
NHL Totals	7	0	0	0	4

Klinkhammer, Rob b. Lethbridge, Alberta, August 12, 1986

2011–12 OTT	15	0	2	2	2
NHL Totals	16	0	2	2	2

Knuble, Mike b. Toronto, Ontario, July 4, 1972

2011–12 WAS	72	6	12	18	32
NHL Totals	1,040	274	266	540	621

Kobasew, Chuck b. Osoyoos, British Columbia, April 17, 1982

2011–12 COL	58	7	7	14	51
NHL Totals	531	103	96	199	358

Koivu, Mikko b. Turku, Finland, March 12, 1983

2011–12 MIN	55	12	32	44	28
NHL Totals	488	108	253	361	334

Koivu, Saku b. Turku, Finland, November 23, 1974

2011–12 ANA	74	11	27	38	50
NHL Totals	1,012	236	540	776	745

Kolanos, Krys b. Calgary, Alberta, July 27, 1981

2011–12 CAL	13	0	1	1	2
NHL Totals	149	20	22	42	94

Komisarek, Mike b. Islip Terrace, New York, January 19, 1982

2011–12 TOR	45	1	4	5	41
NHL Totals	515	14	63	77	663

Konopka, Zenon b. Niagara-on-the-Lake, Ontario, January 2, 1981

2011–12 OTT	55	3	2	5	193
NHL Totals	250	11	16	27	877

Kopecky, Tomas b. Ilava, Czechoslovakia (Slovakia), February 5, 1982

2011–12 FLO	80	10	22	32	32
NHL Totals	418	47	80	127	233

Kopitar, Anze b. Jesenice, Yugoslavia (Slovenia), August 24, 1987

2011–12 LA	82	25	51	76	20
NHL Totals	475	163	271	434	134

Korpikoski, Lauri b. Turku, Finland, July 28, 1986

2011–12 PHO	82	17	20	37	14
NHL Totals	300	47	55	102	64

Kostitsyn, Andrei b. Novopolosk, Soviet Union (Belarus), February 3, 1985

2011–12 MON/NAS	72	16	20	36	26
NHL Totals	398	103	119	222	181

• traded by Montreal to Nashville on February 27, 2012, for a 2nd-round draft choice and a conditional 5th-round draft choice in 2013

Kostitsyn, Sergei b. Novopolosk, Soviet Union (Belarus), March 20, 1987

2011–12 NAS	75	17	26	43	34
NHL Totals	307	64	97	161	177

Kostopoulos, Tom b. Mississauga, Ontario, January 24, 1979

2011–12 CAL	81	4	8	12	57
NHL Totals	615	60	96	156	705

Kovalchuk, Ilya b. Tver, Soviet Union (Russia), April 15, 1983

2011–12 NJ	77	37	46	83	33
NHL Totals	779	406	379	785	498

Kreider, Chris b. Boxford, Massachusetts, April 30, 1991

2011–12 NYR	0	0	0	0	0
NHL Totals	0	0	0	0	0

• made NHL debut in the playoffs this season

Krejci, David b. Sternberk, Czechoslovakia (Czech Republic), April 28, 1986

2011–12 BOS	79	23	39	62	36
NHL Totals	377	81	195	276	138

Kronwall, Niklas b. Stockholm, Sweden, January 12, 1981

2011–12 DET	82	15	21	36	38
NHL Totals	467	49	168	217	298

Krug, Torey b. Livonia, Michigan, April 12, 1991

2011–12 BOS	2	0	1	1	0
NHL Totals	2	0	1	1	0

Kruger, Marcus b. Stockholm, Sweden, May 27, 1990

2011–12 CHI	71	9	17	26	22
NHL Totals	78	9	17	26	26

Kuba, Filip b. Ostrava, Czechoslovakia (Czech Republic), December 29, 1976

2011–12 OTT	73	6	26	32	26
NHL Totals	792	69	254	323	337

Kubalik, Tomas   b. Plzen, Czechoslovakia (Czech Republic), May 1, 1990

2011–12 CBJ	8	1	1	2	6
NHL Totals	12	1	3	4	6

Kubina, Pavel   b. Celadna, Czechoslovakia (Czech Republic), April 15, 1977

2011–12 TB/PHI	69	3	12	15	74
NHL Totals	970	110	276	386	1,123

• traded by Tampa Bay to Philadelphia on February 18, 2012, for Jon Kalinski, a conditional 2nd-round draft choice in 2012 or 2013, and a 4th-round draft choice in 2013

Kulda, Arturs   b. Riga, Soviet Union (Latvia), July 25, 1988

2011–12 WIN	9	0	0	0	4
NHL Totals	15	0	2	2	8

Kulemin, Nikolai   b. Magnitogorsk, Soviet Union (Russia), July 14, 1986

2011–12 TOR	70	7	21	28	6
NHL Totals	303	68	84	152	66

Kulikov, Dmitri   b. Lipetsk, Soviet Union (Russia), October 29, 1990

2011–12 FLO	58	4	24	28	36
NHL Totals	198	13	57	70	113

Kundratek, Tomas   b. Prerov, Czech Republic, December 26, 1989

2011–12 WAS	5	0	0	0	2
NHL Totals	5	0	0	0	2

Kunitz, Chris   b. Regina, Saskatchewan, September 26, 1979

2011–12 PIT	82	26	35	61	49
NHL Totals	533	150	201	351	450

Kytnar, Milan   b. Topolcany, Czechoslovakia (Slovakia), May 19, 1989

2011–12 EDM	1	0	0	0	0
NHL Totals	1	0	0	0	0

Laakso, Teemu   b. Tuusula, Finland, August 27, 1987

2011–12 NAS	9	0	0	0	8
NHL Totals	17	0	0	0	10

LaBarbera, Jason   b. Burnaby, British Columbia, January 18, 1980

2011–12 PHO	19	3–9–3	1,015	43	0	2.54
NHL Totals	160	55–64–0–17	8,333	397	6	2.86

Labrie, Pierre-Cedric b. Baie-Comeau, Quebec, December 6, 1986

2011–12 TB	14	0	2	2	15
NHL Totals	14	0	2	2	15

Ladd, Andrew b. Maple Ridge, British Columbia, December 12, 1985

2011–12 WIN	82	28	22	50	64
NHL Totals	484	120	138	258	283

Laich, Brooks b. Medicine Hat, Alberta, June 23, 1983

2011–12 WAS	82	16	25	41	34
NHL Totals	557	116	162	278	237

Lander, Anton b. Sundsvall, Sweden, April 24, 1991

2011–12 EDM	56	2	4	6	12
NHL Totals	56	2	4	6	12

Landeskog, Gabriel b. Stockholm, Sweden, November 23, 1992

2011–12 COL	82	22	30	52	51
NHL Totals	82	22	30	52	51

Langenbrunner, Jamie b. Duluth, Minnesota, July 24, 1975

2011–12 STL	70	6	18	24	32
NHL Totals	1,105	253	419	662	837

Langkow, Daymond b. Edmonton, Alberta, September 27, 1976

2011–12 PHO	73	11	19	30	14
NHL Totals	1,090	270	402	672	547

Lapierre, Maxim b. St-Léonard, Quebec, March 29, 1985

2011–12 VAN	82	9	10	19	130
NHL Totals	415	50	53	103	431

LaRose, Chad b. Fraser, Michigan, March 27, 1982

2011–12 CAR	67	19	13	32	48
NHL Totals	473	83	93	176	257

Larsen, Philip b. Esbjerg, Denmark, December 7, 1989

2011–12 DAL	55	3	8	11	16
NHL Totals	63	3	11	14	16

Larsson, Adam b. Skelleftea, Sweden, November 12, 1992

2011–12 NJ	65	2	16	18	20
NHL Totals	65	2	16	18	20

Latendresse, Guillaume b. Ste-Cathérine, Quebec, May 24, 1987

2011–12 MIN	16	5	4	9	20
NHL Totals	314	81	56	137	177

Lebda, Brett b. Buffalo Grove, Illinois, January 15, 1982

2011–12 CBJ	30	1	3	4	14
NHL Totals	397	20	56	76	229

Leblanc, Louis b. Pointe-Claire, Quebec, January 26, 1991

2011–12 MON	42	5	5	10	28
NHL Totals	42	5	5	10	28

Lecavalier, Vincent b. Île-Bizard, Quebec, April 21, 1980

2011–12 TB	64	22	27	49	50
NHL Totals	998	373	469	842	717

Leddy, Nick b. Eden Prairie, Minnesota, March 20, 1991

2011–12 CHI	82	3	34	37	10
NHL Totals	128	7	37	44	14

Lee, Brian b. Moorhead, Minnesota, March 26, 1987

2011–12 OTT/TB	55	1	15	16	35
NHL Totals	187	5	31	36	108

• traded by Ottawa to Tampa Bay on February 27, 2012, for Matt Gilroy

Legwand, David b. Detroit, Michigan, August 17, 1980

2011–12 NAS	78	19	34	53	26
NHL Totals	846	188	313	501	424

Lehner, Robin b. Gothenburg, Sweden, July 24, 1991

2011–12 OTT	5	3–2–0	299	10	1	2.01
NHL Totals	13	4–6–0–0	640	30	1	2.81

Lehtonen, Kari b. Helsinki, Finland, November 16, 1983

2011–12 DAL	59	32–22–4	3,497	136	4	2.33
NHL Totals	344	166–133–0–32	19,949	901	21	2.71

Leino, Ville b. Savonlinna, Finland, October 6, 1983

2011–12 BUF	71	8	17	25	16
NHL Totals	220	38	60	98	54

Leopold, Jordan   b. Golden Valley, Minnesota, August 3, 1980

2011–12 BUF	79	10	14	24	28
NHL Totals	586	63	131	194	254

Lepisto, Sami   b. Espoo, Finland, October 17, 1984

2011–12 CHI	26	1	2	3	4
NHL Totals	176	6	29	35	137

Letang, Kris   b. Montreal, Quebec, April 24, 1987

2011–12 PIT	51	10	32	42	34
NHL Totals	350	39	132	171	237

Letestu, Mark   b. Elk Point, Alberta, February 4, 1985

2011–12 PIT/CBJ	62	11	14	25	8
NHL Totals	136	26	27	53	23

• traded by Pittsburgh to Columbus on November 8, 2011, for a 4th-round draft choice in 2012

Letourneau-Leblond, Pierre-Luc   b. Lévis, Quebec, June 4, 1985

2011–12 CAL	3	0	0	0	10
NHL Totals	40	0	3	3	101

Lewis, Trevor   b. Salt Lake City, Utah, January 8, 1987

2011–12 LA	72	3	4	7	26
NHL Totals	155	7	16	23	32

Lidstrom, Nicklas   b. Vasteras, Sweden, April 28, 1970

2011–12 DET	70	11	23	34	28
NHL Totals	1,564	264	878	1,142	514

• retired at season's end

Liles, John-Michael   b. Zionsville, Indiana, November 25, 1980

2011–12 TOR	66	7	20	27	20
NHL Totals	589	75	227	302	238

Lilja, Andreas   b. Helsingborg, Sweden, July 13, 1975

2011–12 PHI	46	0	6	6	34
NHL Totals	576	16	71	87	563

Lindback, Anders   b. Gavle, Sweden, May 3, 1988

2011–12 NAS	16	5–8–0	792	32	0	2.42
NHL Totals	38	16–13–0–2	1,923	81	2	2.53

Lindstrom, Joakim b. Skelleftea, Sweden, December 5, 1983

2011–12 COL	16	2	3	5	0
NHL Totals	97	15	18	33	46

Little, Bryan b. Edmonton, Alberta, November 12, 1987

2011–12 WIN	74	24	22	46	26
NHL Totals	356	92	103	195	121

Loktionov, Andrei b. Voskresensk, Soviet Union (Russia), May 30, 1990

2011–12 LA	39	3	4	7	2
NHL Totals	59	7	7	14	4

Lombardi, Matt b. Montreal, Quebec, March 18, 1982

2011–12 TOR	62	8	10	18	10
NHL Totals	508	97	157	254	285

Lovejoy, Ben b. Concord, New Hampshire, February 20, 1984

2011–12 PIT	34	1	4	5	13
NHL Totals	95	4	21	25	63

Lucic, Milan b. Vancouver, British Columbia, June 7, 1988

2011–12 BOS	81	26	35	61	135
NHL Totals	359	90	122	212	525

Lundin, Mike b. Burnsville, Minnesota, September 24, 1984

2011–12 MIN	17	0	2	2	4
NHL Totals	241	4	31	35	54

Lundqvist, Henrik b. Are, Sweden, March 2, 1982

2011–12 NYR	62	39–18–5	3,754	123	8	1.97
NHL Totals	468	252–155–0–54	27,642	1,046	43	2.27

Luongo, Roberto b. Montreal, Quebec, April 4, 1979

2011–12 VAN	55	31–14–8	3,162	127	5	2.41
NHL Totals	727	339–283–33–68	41,690	1,749	60	2.52

Lupul, Joffrey b. Edmonton, Alberta, September 23, 1983

2011–12 TOR	66	25	42	67	48
NHL Totals	515	151	172	323	313

Lydman, Toni b. Lahti, Finland, September 25, 1977

2011–12 ANA	74	0	13	13	46
NHL Totals	812	36	200	236	539

MacArthur, Clarke b. Lloydminster, Alberta, April 6, 1985

2011–12 TOR	73	20	23	43	37
NHL Totals	363	85	108	193	203

MacDermid, Lane b. Hartford, Connecticut, August 25, 1989

2011–12 BOS	5	0	0	0	5
NHL Totals	5	0	0	0	5

MacDonald, Andrew b. Judique, Nova Scotia, September 7, 1986

2011–12 NYI	75	5	14	19	26
NHL Totals	184	10	43	53	85

MacDonald, Joey b. Pictou, Nova Scotia, February 7, 1980

2011–12 DET	14	8–5–1	806	29	0	2.16
NHL Totals	101	31–48–0–13	5,584	283	2	3.04

Macenauer, Maxime b. Laval, Quebec, January 4, 1989

2011–12 WIN	29	1	3	4	18
NHL Totals	29	1	3	4	18

Machacek, Spencer b. Lethbridge, Alberta, October 14, 1988

2011–12 WIN	13	2	7	9	7
NHL Totals	25	2	7	9	7

MacIntyre, Drew b. Charlottetown, Prince Edward Island, June 24, 1983

2011–12 BUF	2	0–0–0	43	1	0	1.40
NHL Totals	4	0–1–0–0	105	4	0	2.29

MacIntyre, Steve b. Brock, Saskatchewan, August 8, 1980

2011–12 PIT	12	0	0	0	6
NHL Totals	90	2	2	4	163

MacKenzie, Derek b. Sudbury, Ontario, June 11, 1981

2011–12 CBJ	66	7	7	14	40
NHL Totals	193	19	26	45	92

MacLean, Brett b. Port Elgin, Ontario, December 24, 1988

2011–12 WIN	5	0	2	2	2
NHL Totals	18	2	3	5	4

Madden, John b. Barrie, Ontario, May 4, 1973

2011–12 FLO	31	3	0	3	4
NHL Totals	898	165	183	348	219

Malhotra, Manny b. Mississauga, Ontario, May 18, 1980

2011–12 VAN	78	7	11	18	14
NHL Totals	855	108	170	278	421

Malkin, Evgeni b. Magnitogorsk, Soviet Union (Russia), July 31, 1986

2011–12 PIT	75	50	59	109	70
NHL Totals	427	208	319	527	426

Malone, Brad b. Miramichi, New Brunswick, May 20, 1989

2011–12 COL	9	0	2	2	0
NHL Totals	9	0	2	2	0

Malone, Ryan b. Pittsburgh, Pennsylvania, December 1, 1979

2011–12 TB	68	20	28	48	82
NHL Totals	560	168	179	347	600

Mancari, Mark b. London, Ontario, July 11, 1985

2011–12 VAN	6	0	0	0	0
NHL Totals	42	3	10	13	22

Manning, Brandon b. Prince George, British Columbia, June 4, 1990

2011–12 PHI	4	0	0	0	0
NHL Totals	4	0	0	0	0

Mannino, Peter b. Farmington Hills, Michigan, February 17, 1984

2011–12 WIN	1	0–0–0	20	0	0	0.00
NHL Totals	6	1–1–0–0	226	15	0	3.99

Marchand, Brad b. Halifax, Nova Scotia, May 11, 1988

2011–12 BOS	76	28	27	55	87
NHL Totals	173	49	48	97	158

Markov, Andrei b. Voskresensk, Soviet Union (Russia), December 20, 1978

2011–12 MON	13	0	3	3	4
NHL Totals	636	81	288	369	365

Markstrom, Jacob b. Gavle, Sweden, January 31, 1990

2011–12 FLO	7	2–4–1	383	17	0	2.66
NHL Totals	8	2–5–0–1	423	19	0	2.69

Marleau, Patrick b. Aneroid, Saskatchewan, September 15, 1979

2011–12 SJ	82	30	34	64	26
NHL Totals	1,117	387	443	830	367

Maroon, Patrick   b. St. Louis, Missouri, April 23, 1988

2011–12 ANA	2	0	0	0	2
NHL Totals	2	0	0	0	2

Marshall, Kevin   b. Boucherville, Quebec, March 10, 1989

2011–12 WAS	10	0	0	0	8
NHL Totals	10	0	0	0	8

Martin, Matt   b. Windsor, Ontario, May 8, 1989

2011–12 NYI	80	7	7	14	121
NHL Totals	153	12	18	30	294

Martin, Paul   b. Minneapolis, Minnesota, March 5, 1981

2011–12 PIT	73	2	25	27	18
NHL Totals	550	31	183	214	148

Martinek, Radek   b. Havlickuv Brod, Czechoslovakia (Czech Republic), August 31, 1976

2011–12 CBJ	7	1	0	1	0
NHL Totals	460	22	82	104	272

Martinez, Alec   b. Rochester Hills, Michigan, July 26, 1987

2011–12 LA	51	6	6	12	8
NHL Totals	115	11	17	28	28

Mason, Chris   b. Red Deer, Alberta, April 20, 1976

2011–12 WIN	20	8–7–1	995	43	2	2.59
NHL Totals	306	136–106–1–34	16,535	725	23	2.63

Mason, Steve   b. Oakville, Ontario, May 29, 1988

2011–12 CBJ	46	16–26–3	2,534	143	1	3.39
NHL Totals	219	93–93–0–26	12,425	599	19	2.89

Matsumoto, Jon   b. Ottawa, Ontario, October 13, 1986

2011–12 FLO	1	0	0	0	0
NHL Totals	14	2	0	2	4

Matthias, Shawn   b. Mississauga, Ontario, February 19, 1988

2011–12 FLO	79	10	14	24	49
NHL Totals	205	25	35	60	79

Maxwell, Ben   b. North Vancouver, British Columbia, March 30, 1988

2011–12 WIN/ANA/WIN	15	1	5	6	2
NHL Totals	47	2	6	8	19

• claimed off waivers on November 10, 2011, by Anaheim from Winnipeg; claimed off waivers on December 6, 2011, by Winnipeg from Anaheim

Mayers, Jamal   b. Toronto, Ontario, October 24, 1974

2011–12 CHI	81	6	9	15	91
NHL Totals	896	90	127	217	1,184

Mayorov, Maxim   b. Andizhan, Soviet Union (Russia), March 26, 1989

2011–12 CBJ	10	1	1	2	2
NHL Totals	22	2	1	3	2

McArdle, Kenndal   b. Toronto, Ontario, January 4, 1987

2011–12 WIN	9	0	0	0	4
NHL Totals	42	1	2	3	51

McBain, Jamie   b. Edina, Minnesota, February 25, 1988

2011–12 CAR	76	8	19	27	4
NHL Totals	166	18	49	67	36

McCarthy, John   b. Boston, Massachusetts, August 9, 1986

2011–12 SJ	10	0	0	0	10
NHL Totals	51	2	2	4	18

McClement, Jay   b. Kingston, Ontario, March 2, 1983

2011–12 COL	80	10	7	17	31
NHL Totals	553	63	114	177	223

McCormick, Cody   b. London, Ontario, April 18, 1983

2011–12 BUF	50	1	3	4	56
NHL Totals	321	18	36	54	448

McDonagh, Ryan   b. St. Paul, Minnesota, June 13, 1989

2011–12 NYR	82	7	25	32	44
NHL Totals	122	8	33	41	58

McDonald, Andy   b. Strathroy, Ontario, August 25, 1977

2011–12 STL	25	10	12	22	2
NHL Totals	648	175	293	468	264

McDonald, Colin b. New Haven, Connecticut, September 30, 1984

2011–12 PIT	5	0	0	0	0
NHL Totals	7	1	0	1	0

McElhinney, Curtis b. London, Ontario, May 23, 1983

2011–12 PHO	2	1–0–0	72	2	0	1.67
NHL Totals	69	19–26–0–4	3,158	163	2	3.10

McGinn, Jamie b. Fergus, Ontario, August 5, 1988

2011–12 SJ/COL	78	20	17	37	37
NHL Totals	221	35	27	62	110

• traded by San Jose to Colorado on February 27, 2012, with Mike Connolly and Michael Sgarbossa for Daniel Winnick, T.J. Galiardi and a 7th-round draft choice in 2013

McGrattan, Brian b. Hamilton, Ontario, September 2, 1981

2011–12 NAS	30	0	2	2	61
NHL Totals	212	3	13	16	456

McIntyre, David b. Oakville, Ontario, February 4, 1987

2011–12 MIN	7	1	1	2	2
NHL Totals	7	1	1	2	2

McLaren, Frazer b. Winnipeg, Manitoba, October 29, 1987

2011–12 SJ	7	0	0	0	9
NHL Totals	39	1	5	6	85

McLeod, Cody b. Binscarth, Manitoba, June 26, 1984

2011–12 COL	75	6	5	11	164
NHL Totals	348	37	29	66	773

McMillan, Brandon b. Richmond, British Columbia, March 22, 1990

2011–12 ANA	25	0	4	4	20
NHL Totals	85	11	14	25	38

McMillan, Carson b. Brandon, Manitoba, September 10, 1988

2011–12 MIN	11	1	2	3	11
NHL Totals	15	2	3	5	11

McNabb, Brayden b. Saskatoon, Saskatchewan, January 21, 1991

2011–12 BUF	25	1	7	8	15
NHL Totals	25	1	7	8	15

McQuaid, Adam   b. Charlottetown, Prince Edward Island, October 12, 1986

2011–12 BOS	72	2	8	10	99
NHL Totals	158	6	20	26	216

Meech, Derek   b. Winnipeg, Manitoba, April 21, 1984

2011–12 WIN	2	0	0	0	4
NHL Totals	128	4	12	16	43

Meszaros, Andrei   b. Povazska Bystrica, Czechoslovakia (Slovakia), October 13, 1985

2011–12 PHI	62	7	18	25	38
NHL Totals	522	49	151	200	379

Methot, Marc   b. Ottawa, Ontario, June 21, 1985

2011–12 CBJ	46	1	6	7	24
NHL Totals	275	7	44	51	208

Michalek, Milan   b. Jindrichuv Hradec, Czechoslovakia (Czech Republic), December 7, 1984

2011–12 OTT	77	35	25	60	32
NHL Totals	526	166	175	341	283

Michalek, Zbynek   b. Jindrichuv Hradec, Czechoslovakia (Czech Republic), December 23, 1982

2011–12 PIT	62	2	11	13	24
NHL Totals	550	34	113	147	246

Miele, Andy   b. Grosse Pointe Woods, Michigan, April 15, 1988

2011–12 PHO	7	0	0	0	6
NHL Totals	7	0	0	0	6

Miettinen, Antti   b. Hameenlinna, Finland, July 3, 1980

2011–12 WIN	45	5	8	13	0
NHL Totals	517	94	131	225	232

Mikkelson, Brendan   b. Regina, Saskatchewan, June 22, 1987

2011–12 TB	41	1	2	3	13
NHL Totals	127	1	8	9	53

Miller, Drew   b. Dover, New Jersey, February 17, 1984

2011–12 DET	80	14	11	25	20
NHL Totals	280	40	37	77	68

Miller, Ryan b. East Lansing, Michigan, July 17, 1980

2011–12 BUF	61	31–21–7	3,536	150	6	2.55
NHL Totals	460	252–147–1–50	26,975	1,154	28	2.57

Mills, Brad b. Terrace, British Columbia, May 3, 1983

2011–12 NJ	27	0	1	1	32
NHL Totals	31	1	1	2	37

Mitchell, John b. Waterloo, Ontario, January 22, 1985

2011–12 NYR	63	5	11	16	8
NHL Totals	222	25	46	71	84

Mitchell, Torrey b. Montreal, Quebec, January 30, 1985

2011–12 SJ	76	9	10	19	29
NHL Totals	280	30	43	73	152

Mitchell, Willie b. Port McNeill, British Columbia, April 23, 1977

2011–12 LA	76	5	19	24	44
NHL Totals	719	29	123	152	686

Moen, Travis b. Stewart Valley, Saskatchewan, April 6, 1982

2011–12 MON	48	9	7	16	41
NHL Totals	570	52	55	107	681

Montador, Steve b. Vancouver, British Columbia, December 21, 1979

2011–12 CHI	52	5	9	14	45
NHL Totals	571	33	98	131	807

Montoya, Al b. Chicago, Illinois, February 13, 1985

2011–12 NYI	31	9–11–0–5	1,720	89	0	3.10
NHL Totals	56	21–17–0–10	3,133	144	2	2.76

Moore, Dominic b. Thornhill, Ontario, August 3, 1980

2011–12 TB/SJ	79	4	21	25	54
NHL Totals	530	67	118	185	349

• traded by Tampa Bay to San Jose on February 16, 2012, with a 7th-round draft choice in 2012 for a 2nd-round draft choice in 2012

Moore, John b. Winnetka, Illinois, November 19, 1990

2011–12 CBJ	67	2	5	7	8
NHL Totals	69	2	5	7	8

Moreau, Ethan b. Huntsville, Ontario, September 22, 1975

2011–12 LA	28	1	3	4	20
NHL Totals	928	147	140	287	1,110

Morin, Jeremy b. Auburn, New York, April 16, 1991

2011–12 CHI	3	0	0	0	0
NHL Totals	12	2	1	3	9

Morris, Derek b. Edmonton, Alberta, August 24, 1978

2011–12 PHO	59	2	9	11	38
NHL Totals	1,005	87	309	396	927

Morrison, Brendan b. Pitt Meadows, British Columbia, August 15, 1975

2011–12 CAL/CHI	39	4	7	11	12
NHL Totals	934	200	401	601	452

• traded by Calgary to Chicago on January 27, 2012, for Brian Connelly

Morrow, Brenden b. Carlyle, Saskatchewan, January 16, 1979

2011–12 DAL	57	11	15	26	97
NHL Totals	806	237	280	517	1,185

Moss, David b. Dearborn, Michigan, December 28, 1981

2011–12 CAL	32	2	7	9	12
NHL Totals	317	61	63	124	94

Mottau, Mike b. Quincy, Massachusetts, March 19, 1978

2011–12 NYI/BOS	35	0	2	2	15
NHL Totals	313	7	51	58	160

• traded by NY Islanders to Boston on February 27, 2012, with Brian Rolston for Yannick Riendeau and Mark Cantin

Moulson, Matt b. North York (Toronto), Ontario, November 1, 1983

2011–12 NYI	82	36	33	69	6
NHL Totals	275	103	77	180	52

Mueller, Chris b. West Seneca, New York, March 6, 1986

2011–12 NAS	4	0	0	0	0
NHL Totals	19	0	3	3	2

Mueller, Peter b. Bloomington, Minnesota, April 14, 1988

2011–12 COL	32	7	9	16	8
NHL Totals	254	55	88	143	80

Murphy, Mike b. Kingston, Ontario, January 15, 1989

2011–12 CAR	2	0–1–0	36	0	0	0.00
NHL Totals	2	0–1–0	36	0	0	0.00

Murray, Andrew b. Selkirk, Manitoba, November 6, 1981

2011–12 SJ	39	1	3	4	4
NHL Totals	220	24	16	40	36

Murray, Doug b. Bromma, Sweden, March 12, 1980

2011–12 SJ	60	0	4	4	31
NHL Totals	422	6	50	56	335

Mursak, Jan b. Maribor, Yugoslavia (Slovenia), January 20, 1988

2011–12 DET	25	1	2	3	0
NHL Totals	44	2	2	4	4

Myers, Tyler b. Houston, Texas, February 1, 190

2011–12 BUF	55	8	15	23	33
NHL Totals	217	29	79	108	105

Nabokov, Evgeni b. Kamenogorsk, Soviet Union (Kazakhstan), July 25, 1975

2011–12 NYI	42	19–18–3	2,378	101	2	2.55
NHL Totals	605	312–196–29–54	34,868	1,395	52	2.40

Nash, Rick b. Brampton, Ontario, June 16, 1984

2011–12 CBJ	82	30	29	59	40
NHL Totals	674	289	258	547	568

Nash, Riley b. Consort, Alberta, May 9, 1989

2011–12 CAR	5	0	1	1	2
NHL Totals	5	0	1	1	2

Neal, James b. Oshawa, Ontario, September 3, 1987

2011–12 PIT	80	40	41	81	87
NHL Totals	314	113	105	218	268

Neil, Chris b. Markdale, Ontario, June 18, 1979

2011–12 OTT	72	13	15	28	178
NHL Totals	731	90	110	200	1,861

Nemisz, Greg b. Courtice, Ontario, June 5, 1990

2011–12 CAL	9	0	0	0	0
NHL Totals	15	0	1	1	0

Ness, Aaron   b. Roseau, Minnesota, May 18, 1990

2011–12 NYI	9	0	0	0	2
NHL Totals	9	0	0	0	2

Neuvirth, Michal   b. Usti nad Labem, Czechoslovakia (Czech Republic), March 23, 1988

2011–12 WAS	38	13–13–5	2,020	95	3	2.82
NHL Totals	108	51–30–0–9	5,802	256	7	2.65

Newbury, Kris   b. Brampton, Ontario, February 19, 1982

2011–12 NYR	7	0	0	0	24
NHL Totals	66	4	4	8	123

Nichol, Scott   b. Edmonton, Alberta, December 31, 1974

2011–12 STL	80	3	5	8	83
NHL Totals	632	55	71	126	891

Niederreiter, Nino   b. Chur, Switzerland, September 8, 1992

2011–12 NYI	55	1	0	1	12
NHL Totals	64	2	1	3	20

Nielsen, Frans   b. Herning, Denmark, April 24, 1984

2011–12 NYI	82	17	30	47	6
NHL Totals	319	54	113	167	68

Niemi, Antti   b. Vantaa, Finland, August 29, 1983

2011–12 SJ	68	34–22–9	3,936	159	6	2.42
NHL Totals	170	96–48–0–20	9,791	389	19	2.38

Nikitin, Nikita   b. Omsk, Soviet Union (Russia), June 16, 1986

2011–12 STL/CBJ	61	7	25	32	18
NHL Totals	102	8	33	41	28

• traded by St. Louis to Columbus on November 10, 2011, for Kris Russell

Nilsson, Anders   b. Lulea, Sweden, March 19, 1990

2011–12 NYI	4	1–2–0	218	10	1	2.75
NHL Totals	4	1–2–0	218	10	1	2.75

Niskanen, Matt   b. Virginia, Minnesota, December 6, 1986

2011–12 PIT	75	4	17	21	47
NHL Totals	370	21	86	107	203

Nodl, Andreas b. Vienna, Austria, February 28, 1987

2011–12 PHI/CAR	60	3	5	8	8
NHL Totals	175	15	20	35	26

• claimed off waivers on November 29, 2011, by Carolina from Philadelphia

Nokelainen, Petteri b. Imatra, Finland, January 16, 1986

2011–12 PHO/MON	56	3	4	7	37
NHL Totals	245	20	21	41	103

• traded by Phoenix to Montreal on October 23, 2011, with Garrett Stafford for Brock Trotter and a 7th-round draft choice in 2012

Nolan, Jordan b. St. Catharines, Ontario, June 23, 1989

2011–12 LA	26	2	2	4	28
NHL Totals	26	2	2	4	28

Nugent-Hopkins, Ryan b. Burnaby, British Columbia, April 12, 1993

2011–12 EDM	62	18	34	52	16
NHL Totals	62	18	34	52	16

Nyquist, Gustav b. Halmstad, Sweden, September 1, 1989

2011–12 DET	18	1	6	7	2
NHL Totals	18	1	6	7	2

Nystrom, Eric b. Syosset, New York, February 14, 1983

2011–12 DAL	74	16	5	21	24
NHL Totals	360	39	33	72	245

Oberg, Evan b. Forestburg, Alberta, February 16, 1988

2011–12 TB	3	0	0	0	0
NHL Totals	7	0	0	0	0

O'Brien, Jim b. Maplewood, Minnesota, January 29, 1989

2011–12 OTT	28	3	3	6	4
NHL Totals	34	3	3	6	6

O'Brien, Shane b. Port Hope, Ontario, August 9, 1983

2011–12 COL	76	3	17	20	105
NHL Totals	455	13	71	84	793

O'Byrne, Ryan b. Victoria, British Columbia, July 19, 1984

2011–12 COL	74	1	6	7	57
NHL Totals	266	3	30	33	309

O'Donnell, Sean   b. Ottawa, Ontario, October 13, 1971

2011–12 CHI	51	0	7	7	23
NHL Totals	1,224	31	198	229	1,809

Oduya, John   b. Stockholm, Sweden, October 1, 1981

2011–12 WIN/CHI	81	3	15	18	33
NHL Totals	463	23	91	114	222

• traded by Winnipeg to Chicago on February 27, 2012, for a 2nd- and 3rd-round draft choice in 2013

Okposo, Kyle   b. St. Paul, Minnesota, April 16, 1988

2011–12 NYI	79	24	21	45	46
NHL Totals	271	68	93	161	158

Olesz, Rostislav   b. Bilovec, Czechoslovakia (Czech Republic), October 10, 1985

2011–12 CHI	6	0	0	0	6
NHL Totals	355	57	75	132	118

Olsen, Dylan   b. Salt Lake City, Utah, January 3, 1991

2011–12 CHI	28	0	1	1	6
NHL Totals	28	0	1	1	6

Olver, Mark   b. Burnaby, British Columbia, January 1, 1988

2011–12 COL	24	4	3	7	15
NHL Totals	42	6	10	16	33

Omark, Linus   b. Overtornea, Sweden, February 5, 1987

2011–12 EDM	14	3	0	3	8
NHL Totals	65	8	22	30	34

O'Marra, Ryan   b. Tokyo, Japan, June 9, 1987

2011–12 EDM/ANA	9	0	1	1	4
NHL Totals	33	1	6	7	17

• traded by Edmonton to Anaheim on February 16, 2012, for Bryan Rodney

O'Reilly, Cal   b. Toronto, Ontario, September 30, 1986

2011–12 NAS/PHO/PIT	33	2	5	7	4
NHL Totals	113	13	28	41	12

• traded by Nashville to Phoenix on October 28, 2011, for a 4th-round draft choice in 2012; claimed off waivers on February 1, 2012, by Pittsburgh from Phoenix

O'Reilly, Ryan b. Clinton, Ontario, February 7, 1991

2011–12 COL	81	18	37	55	12
NHL Totals	236	39	68	107	46

Oreskovich, Victor b. Whitby, Ontario, August 15, 1986

2011–12 VAN	1	0	0	0	7
NHL Totals	67	2	7	9	41

Orlov, Dmitri b. Novokuznetsk, Russia, July 23, 1991

2011–12 WAS	60	3	16	19	18
NHL Totals	60	3	16	19	18

Orpik, Brooks b. San Francisco, California, September 26, 1980

2011–12 PIT	73	2	16	18	61
NHL Totals	585	11	100	111	656

Orr, Colton b. Winnipeg, Manitoba, March 3, 1982

2011–12 TOR	5	1	0	1	5
NHL Totals	378	11	9	20	921

Ortmeyer, Jed b. Omaha, Nebraska, September 3, 1978

2011–12 MIN	35	1	1	2	14
NHL Totals	345	22	31	53	161

Oshie, T.J. b. Mount Vernon, Washington, December 23, 1986

2011–12 STL	80	19	35	54	50
NHL Totals	262	63	112	175	131

O'Sullivan, Patrick b. Winston-Salem, North Carolina, February 1, 1985

2011–12 PHO	23	2	2	4	2
NHL Totals	334	58	103	161	116

Ott, Steve b. Summerside, Prince Edward Island, August 19, 1982

2011–12 DAL	74	11	28	39	156
NHL Totals	566	85	135	220	1,170

Ovechkin, Alexander b. Moscow, Soviet Union (Russia), September 17, 1985

2011–12 WAS	78	38	27	65	26
NHL Totals	553	339	340	679	372

Paajarvi, Magnus b. Norrkoping, Sweden, April 12, 1991

2011–12 EDM	41	2	6	8	4
NHL Totals	121	17	25	42	20

Pacioretty, Max   b. New Canaan, Connecticut, November 20, 1988

2011–12 MON	79	33	32	65	56
NHL Totals	202	53	61	114	142

Pahlsson, Samuel   b. Ornskoldsvik, Sweden, December 17, 1977

2011–12 CBJ/VAN	80	4	13	17	34
NHL Totals	798	68	131	199	356

• traded by Columbus to Vancouver on February 27, 2012, for two 4th-round draft choices in 2012

Paille, Daniel   b. Welland, Ontario, April 15, 1984

2011–12 BOS	69	9	6	15	15
NHL Totals	381	60	64	124	109

Palmer, Jarod   b. Fridley, Minnesota, February 10, 1986

2011–12 MIN	6	1	0	1	4
NHL Totals	6	1	0	1	4

Palmieri, Kyle   b. Smithtown, New York, February 1, 1991

2011–12 ANA	18	4	3	7	6
NHL Totals	28	5	3	8	6

Palmieri, Nick   b. Utica, New York, July 12, 1989

2011–12 NJ/MIN	38	4	3	7	14
NHL Totals	87	13	12	25	20

• traded by New Jersey to Minnesota on February 24, 2012, with Kurtis Foster, Stephane Veilleux, a 2nd-round draft choice in 2012 and a conditional 3rd-round draft choice in 2013 for Marek Zidlicky

Palushaj, Aaron   b. Livonia, Michigan, September 7, 1989

2011–12 MON	38	1	4	5	8
NHL Totals	41	1	4	5	10

Pandolfo, Jay   b. Winchester, Massachusetts, December 27, 1974

2011–12 NYI	62	1	2	3	8
NHL Totals	881	100	126	226	162

Pardy, Adam   b. Bonavista, Newfoundland, March 29, 1984

2011–12 DAL	36	0	3	3	16
NHL Totals	183	4	25	29	157

Parenteau, P-A   b. Hull, Quebec, March 24, 1983

2011–12 NYI	80	18	49	67	89
NHL Totals	188	41	88	129	141

Parise, Zach   b. Minneapolis, Minnesota, July 28, 1984

2011–12 NJ	82	31	38	69	32
NHL Totals	502	194	216	410	177

Park, Richard   b. Seoul, South Korea, May 27, 1976

2011–12 PIT	54	7	7	14	12
NHL Totals	738	102	139	241	266

Parros, George   b. Washington, Pennsylvania, December 29, 1979

2011–12 ANA	46	1	3	4	85
NHL Totals	413	17	16	33	950

Parse, Scott   b. Portage, Michigan, September 5, 1984

2011–12 LA	9	2	0	2	14
NHL Totals	73	14	16	30	36

Pavelec, Ondrej   b. Kladno, Czechoslovakia (Czech Republic), August 31, 1987

2011–12 WIN	68	29–28–9	3,932	191	4	2.91
NHL Totals	187	70–79–0–25	10,421	519	10	2.99

Pavelski, Joe   b. Plover, Wisconsin, July 11, 1984

2011–12 SJ	82	31	30	61	31
NHL Totals	431	134	171	305	173

Peckham, Theo   b. Richmond Hill, Ontario, November 10, 1987

2011–12 EDM	54	1	2	3	16
NHL Totals	156	4	13	17	382

Pelley, Rod   b. Kitimat, British Columbia, September 1, 1984

2011–12 NJ/ANA	52	2	1	3	16
NHL Totals	256	9	20	29	102

• traded by New Jersey to Anaheim on December 12, 2011, with Mark Fraser and a 7th-round draft choice in 2012 for Kurtis Foster and Timo Pielmeier

Penner, Dustin   b. Winkler, Manitoba, September 28, 1982

2011–12 LA	65	7	10	17	43
NHL Totals	489	135	127	262	306

Perreault, Mathieu   b. Drummondville, Quebec, January 5, 1988

2011–12 WAS	64	16	14	30	24
NHL Totals	120	27	26	53	50

Perron, David   b. Sherbrooke, Quebec, May 28, 1988

2011–12 STL	57	21	21	42	28	
NHL Totals	292	74	99	173	188	

Perry, Corey   b. Peterborough, Ontario, May 16, 1985

2011–12 ANA	80	37	23	60	127	
NHL Totals	530	205	224	429	664	

Peters, Justin   b. Blyth, Ontario, August 30, 1986

2011–12 CAR	7	2–3–2	387	16	1	2.48
NHL Totals	28	11–11–0–3	1,523	82	1	3.23

Peters, Warren   b. Saskatoon, Saskatchewan, July 10, 1982

2011–12 MIN	58	1	4	5	54	
NHL Totals	96	4	4	8	72	

Petersen, Toby   b. Minneapolis, Minnesota, October 27, 1978

2011–12 DAL	39	2	3	5	6	
NHL Totals	397	33	48	81	50	

Petersson, Andre   b. Olofstrom, Sweden, September 11, 1990

2011–12 OTT	1	0	0	0	0	
NHL Totals	1	0	0	0	0	

Petrell, Lennart   b. Helsinki, Finland, April 13, 1984

2011–12 EDM	60	4	5	9	45	
NHL Totals	60	4	5	9	45	

Petry, Jeff   b. Ann Arbor, Michigan, December 9, 1987

2011–12 EDM	73	2	23	25	26	
NHL Totals	108	3	27	30	36	

Peverley, Rich   b. Guelph, Ontario, July 8, 1982

2011–12 BOS	57	11	31	42	22	
NHL Totals	333	71	122	193	136	

Phaneuf, Dion   b. Edmonton, Alberta, April 10, 1985

2011–12 TOR	82	12	32	44	92	
NHL Totals	552	97	215	312	736	

Phillips, Chris   b. Calgary, Alberta, March 9, 1978

2011–12 OTT	80	5	14	19	16	
NHL Totals	1,025	65	191	256	671	

Picard, Alexandre   b. Gatineau, Quebec, July 5, 1985

2011–12 PIT	17	0	4	4	4
NHL Totals	253	19	50	69	86

Pietrangelo, Alex   b. King City, Ontario, January 18, 1990

2011–12 STL	81	12	39	51	36
NHL Totals	177	24	73	97	63

Pirri, Brandon   b. Toronto, Ontario, April 10, 1991

2011–12 CHI	5	0	2	2	0
NHL Totals	6	0	2	2	0

Piskula, Joe   b. Antigo, Wisconsin, July 5, 1984

2011–12 CAL	5	0	0	0	2
NHL Totals	10	0	0	0	8

Pitkanen, Joni   b. Oulu, Finland, September 19, 1983

2011–12 CAR	30	5	12	17	16
NHL Totals	513	56	217	273	472

Plante, Alex   b. Brandon, Manitoba, May 9, 1989

2011–12 EDM	3	0	1	1	2
NHL Totals	10	0	2	2	15

Plekanec, Tomas   b. Kladno, Czechoslovakia (Czech Republic), October 31, 1982

2011–12 MON	81	17	35	52	56
NHL Totals	551	142	221	363	330

Polak, Roman   b. Ostrava, Czechoslovakia (Czech Republic), April 28, 1986

2011–12 STL	77	0	11	11	57
NHL Totals	304	8	52	60	200

Pominville, Jason   b. Repentigny, Quebec, November 30, 1982

2011–12 BUF	82	30	43	73	12
NHL Totals	541	175	256	431	139

Ponikarovsky, Alexei   b. Kiev, Soviet Union (Ukraine), April 9, 1980

2011–12 CAR/NJ	82	14	19	33	34
NHL Totals	636	135	179	314	405

• traded by Carolina to New Jersey on January 20, 2012, for Joe Sova and a 4th-round draft choice in 2012

Porter, Chris b. Toronto, Ontario, May 29, 1984

2011–12 STL	47	4	3	7	11	
NHL Totals	98	8	8	16	27	

Porter, Kevin b. Detroit, Michigan, March 12, 1986

2011–12 COL	35	4	3	7	17	
NHL Totals	163	25	20	45	48	

Postma, Paul b. Red Deer, Alberta, February 22, 1989

2011–12 WIN	3	0	0	0	0	
NHL Totals	4	0	0	0	0	

Potter, Corey b. Lansing, Michigan, January 5, 1984

2011–12 EDM	62	4	17	21	24	
NHL Totals	71	5	18	23	26	

Poulin, Kevin b. Montreal, Quebec, April 12, 1990

2011–12 NYI	6	2–4–0	296	15	0	3.04
NHL Totals	16	6–6–0–1	788	35	0	2.67

Pouliot, Benoit b. Alfred, Ontario, September 29, 1986

2011–12 BOS	74	16	16	32	38	
NHL Totals	257	53	51	104	186	

Pouliot, Marc-Antoine b. Quebec City, Quebec, May 22, 1985

2011–12 PHO	13	0	4	4	2	
NHL Totals	192	21	36	57	76	

Powe, Darroll b. Saskatoon, Saskatchewan, June 22, 1985

2011–12 MIN	82	6	7	13	57	
NHL Totals	286	28	28	56	187	

Price, Carey b. Vancouver, British Columbia, August 16, 1987

2011–12 MON	65	26–28–11	3,944	160	4	2.43
NHL Totals	271	124–104–0–35	15,958	680	16	2.56

Pronger, Chris b. Dryden, Ontario, October 10, 1974

2011–12 PHI	13	1	11	12	10	
NHL Totals	1,167	157	541	698	1,590	

• missed most of the season with post-concussion symptoms

Prospal, Vaclav   b. Ceske Budejovice, Czechoslovakia (Czech Republic), February 17, 1975

2011–12 CBJ	82	16	39	55	36	
NHL Totals	1,060	243	492	735	549	

Prosser, Nate   b. Elk River, Minnesota, May 7, 1986

2011–12 MIN	51	1	11	12	57
NHL Totals	56	1	12	13	65

Prout, Dalton   b. LaSalle, Ontario, March 13, 1990

2011–12 CBJ	5	0	0	0	0
NHL Totals	5	0	0	0	0

Prust, Brandon   b. London, Ontario, March 16, 1984

2011–12 NYR	82	5	12	17	156
NHL Totals	279	24	39	63	612

Purcell, Teddy   b. St. John's, Newfoundland, September 8, 1985

2011–12 TB	81	24	41	65	16
NHL Totals	272	52	98	150	40

Pyatt, Taylor   b. Thunder Bay, Ontario, August 19, 1981

2011–12 PHO	73	9	10	19	23
NHL Totals	755	130	134	264	404

Pyatt, Tom   b. Thunder Bay, Ontario, February 14, 1987

2011–12 TB	74	12	7	19	8
NHL Totals	175	16	15	31	27

Quick, Jonathan   b. Milford, Connecticut, January 21, 1986

2011–12 LA	69	35–21–13	4,099	133	10	1.95
NHL Totals	249	131–87–0–25	14,584	559	24	2.30

Quincey, Kyle   b. Kitchener, Ontario, August 12, 1985

2011–12 COL/DET	72	7	19	26	89
NHL Totals	257	18	77	95	250

• traded by Colorado to Detroit on February 21, 2012, for Steve Downie

Radulov, Alexander   b. Nizhi Tagil, Soviet Union (Russia), July 5, 1986

2011–12 NAS	9	3	4	7	4
NHL Totals	154	47	55	102	74

Rakhshani, Rhett   b. Orange, California, March 6, 1988

2011–12 NYI	5	0	0	0	2
NHL Totals	7	0	0	0	2

Rallo, Greg   b. Gurnee, Illinois, August 26, 1981

2011–12 FLO	1	0	0	0	0
NHL Totals	1	0	0	0	0

Rask, Tuukka   b. Savonlinna, Finland, March 10, 1987

2011–12 BOS	23	11–8–3	1,289	44	3	2.05
NHL Totals	102	47–35–0–11	5,690	209	11	2.20

Rau, Chad   b. Eden Prairie, Minnesota, January 18, 1987

2011–12 MIN	9	2	0	2	0
NHL Totals	9	2	0	2	0

Raycroft, Andrew   b. Belleville, Ontario, May 4, 1980

2011–12 DAL	10	2–8–0	529	31	0	3.52
NHL Totals	280	113–114–10–21	15,192	732	9	2.89

Raymond, Mason   b. Cochrane, Alberta, September 17, 1985

2011–12 VAN	55	10	10	20	18
NHL Totals	328	70	86	156	102

Read, Matt   b. Ilderton, Ontario, June 14, 1986

2011–12 PHI	79	24	23	47	12
NHL Totals	79	24	23	47	12

Reasoner, Marty   b. Honeoye Falls, New York, February 26, 1977

2011–12 NYI	61	1	5	6	34
NHL Totals	767	97	164	261	375

Reaves, Ryan   b. Winnipeg, Manitoba, January 20, 1987

2011–12 STL	60	3	1	4	124
NHL Totals	88	5	3	8	202

Rechlicz, Joel   b. Brookfield, Wisconsin, June 14, 1987

2011–12 WAS	3	0	0	0	10
NHL Totals	26	0	1	1	105

Reese, Dylan   b. Pittsburgh, Pennsylvania, August 29, 1984

2011–12 NYI	28	1	6	7	11
NHL Totals	74	3	14	17	40

Regehr, Robyn b. Recife, Brazil, April 19, 1980

2011–12 BUF	76	1	4	5	56
NHL Totals	902	30	138	168	858

Regin, Peter b. Herning, Denmark, April 16, 1986

2011–12 OTT	10	2	2	4	2
NHL Totals	151	19	33	52	36

Reimer, James b. Winnipeg, Manitoba, March 15, 1988

2011–12 TOR	34	14–14–4	1,879	97	3	3.10
NHL Totals	71	34–24–0–9	3,959	187	6	2.83

Repik, Michal b. Vlasim, Czechoslovakia (Czech Republic), December 31, 1988

2011–12 FLO	17	2	3	5	6
NHL Totals	72	9	11	20	36

Ribeiro, Mike b. Montreal, Quebec, February 10, 1980

2011–12 DAL	74	18	45	63	66
NHL Totals	737	173	387	560	344

Richards, Brad b. Murray Harbour, Prince Edward Island, May 2, 1980

2011–12 NYR	82	25	41	66	22
NHL Totals	854	245	537	782	199

Richards, Mike b. Kenora, Ontario, February 11, 1985

2011–12 LA	74	18	26	44	71
NHL Totals	527	151	242	393	468

Richardson, Brad b. Belleville, Ontario, February 4, 1985

2011–12 LA	59	5	3	8	30
NHL Totals	375	42	57	99	173

Rinaldo, Zac b. Mississauga, Ontario, June 15, 1990

2011–12 PHI	66	2	7	9	232
NHL Totals	66	2	7	9	232

Rinne, Pekka b. Kempele, Finland, November 3, 1982

2011–12 NAS	73	43–18–8	4,169	166	5	2.39
NHL Totals	250	138–72–0–26	14,296	560	25	2.35

Ritola, Mattias b. Borlange, Sweden, March 14, 1987

2011–12 TB	5	0	0	0	6
NHL Totals	43	4	5	9	17

Robak, Colby b. Dauphin, Manitoba, April 24, 1990

2011–12 FLO	3	0	0	0	0		
NHL Totals	3	0	0	0	0		

Robidas, Stephane b. Sherbrooke, Quebec, March 3, 1977

2011–12 DAL	75	5	17	22	48		
NHL Totals	799	50	178	228	603		

Rodney, Bryan b. London, Ontario, April 22, 1984

2011–12 EDM	1	0	0	0	0		
NHL Totals	34	1	12	13	12		

Roloson, Dwayne b. Simcoe, Ontario, October 12, 1969

2011–12 TB	40	13–16–3	2,099	128	1	3.66
NHL Totals	606	227–257–42–51	34,296	1,552	29	2.72

Rolston, Brian b. Flint, Michigan, February 21, 1973

2011–12 NYI/BOS	70	7	17	24	14	
NHL Totals	1,256	342	419	761	472	

• traded by NY Islanders to Boston on February 27, 2012, with Mike Mottau for Yannick Riendeau and Marc Cantin

Rome, Aaron b. Nesbitt, Manitoba, September 27, 1983

2011–12 VAN	43	4	6	10	46	
NHL Totals	174	6	16	22	156	

Rosehill, Jay b. Olds, Alberta, July 16, 1985

2011–12 TOR	31	0	0	0	60	
NHL Totals	72	2	3	5	198	

Roy, Derek b. Ottawa, Ontario, May 4, 1983

2011–12 BUF	80	17	27	44	54	
NHL Totals	549	161	266	427	331	

Rozsival, Michal b. Vlasim, Czechoslovakia (Czech Republic), September 3, 1978

2011–12 PHO	54	1	12	13	34	
NHL Totals	756	64	196	260	589	

Rundblad, David b. Lycksele, Sweden, October 8, 1990

2011–12 OTT/PHO	30	1	6	7	6	
NHL Totals	30	1	6	7	6	

• traded by Ottawa to Phoenix on December 16, 2011, with a 2nd-round draft choice in 2012 for Kyle Turris

Rupp, Mike   b. Cleveland, Ohio, January 13, 1980

2011–12 NYR	60	4	1	5	97
NHL Totals	557	53	41	94	753

Russell, Kris   b. Caroline, Alberta, May 2, 1987

2011–12 CBJ/STL	55	6	6	12	25
NHL Totals	331	22	66	88	136

• traded by Columbus to St. Louis on November 10, 2011 for Nikita Nikitin

Russell, Ryan   b. Caroline, Alberta, May 2, 1987

2011–12 CBJ	41	2	0	2	2
NHL Totals	41	2	0	2	2

Ruutu, Tuomo   b. Vantaa, Finland, February 16, 1983

2011–12 CAR	72	18	16	34	50
NHL Totals	532	129	170	299	508

Ryan, Bobby   b. Cherry Hill, New Jersey, March 17, 1987

2011–12 ANA	82	31	26	57	53
NHL Totals	332	136	123	259	234

Ryder, Michael   b. St. John's, Newfoundland, March 31, 1980

2011–12 DAL	82	35	27	62	46
NHL Totals	631	197	199	396	289

Rynnas, Jussi   b. Pori, Finland, May 22, 1987

2011–12 TOR	2	0–1–0	99	7	0	4.24
NHL Totals	2	0–1–0	99	7	0	4.24

Saad, Brandon   b. Pittsburgh, Pennsylvania, October 27, 1992

2011–12 CHI	2	0	0	0	0
NHL Totals	2	0	0	0	0

Salo, Sami   b. Turku, Finland, September 2, 1974

2011–12 VAN	69	9	16	25	10
NHL Totals	761	93	212	305	252

Salvador, Bryce   b. Brandon, Manitoba, February 11, 1976

2011–12 NJ	82	0	9	9	66
NHL Totals	692	23	79	102	625

Samson, Jerome b. Greenfield Park, Quebec, September 4, 1987

2011–12 CAR	16	2	3	5	8
NHL Totals	46	2	7	9	18

Samuelsson, Mikael b. Mariefred, Sweden, December 23, 1976

2011–12 VAN/FLO	54	14	17	31	20
NHL Totals	669	148	194	342	364

• traded by Vancouver to Florida on October 22, 2011, with Marco Sturm for David Booth, Steve Reinprecht and a 3rd-round draft choice in 2013

Sanford, Curtis b. Owen Sound, Ontario, October 5, 1979

2011–12 CBJ	36	10–18–4	1,983	86	1	2.60
NHL Totals	144	47–55–0–15	7,354	333	6	2.72

Sanguinetti, Bobby b. Trenton, New Jersey, February 29, 1988

2011–12 CAR	3	0	0	0	0
NHL Totals	8	0	0	0	4

Santorelli, Mike b. Vancouver, British Columbia, December 14, 1985

2011–12 FLO	60	9	2	11	18
NHL Totals	174	31	24	55	48

Sarich, Cory b. Saskatoon, Saskatchewan, August 16, 1978

2011–12 CAL	62	1	6	7	66
NHL Totals	887	20	126	146	1,035

Sauer, Mike b. St. Cloud, Minnesota, August 7, 1987

2011–12 NYR	19	1	2	3	21
NHL Totals	98	4	14	18	28

Sauve, Max b. Tours, France, January 30, 1990

2011–12 BOS	1	0	0	0	0
NHL Totals	1	0	0	0	0

Savard, David b. St-Hyacinthe, Quebec, October 22, 1990

2011–12 CBJ	31	2	8	10	16
NHL Totals	31	2	8	10	16

Sbisa, Luca b. Ozieri, Italy, January 30, 1990

2011–12 ANA	80	5	19	24	66
NHL Totals	195	7	35	42	151

Scandella, Marco   b. Montreal, Quebec, February 23, 1990

2011–12 MIN	63	3	9	12	19
NHL Totals	83	3	11	14	21

Scheifele, Mark   b. Kitchener, Ontario, March 15, 1993

2011–12 WIN	7	1	0	1	0
NHL Totals	7	1	0	1	0

Schenn, Brayden   b. Saskatoon, Saskatchewan, August 22, 1991

2011–12 PHI	54	12	6	18	34
NHL Totals	63	12	8	20	34

Schenn, Luke   b. Saskatoon, Saskatchewan, November 2, 1989

2011–12 TOR	79	2	20	22	62
NHL Totals	310	14	61	75	217

Schlemko, David   b. Edmonton, Alberta, May 7, 1987

2011–12 PHO	46	1	10	11	10
NHL Totals	109	6	21	31	42

Schneider, Cory   b. Marblehead, Massachusetts, March 18, 1986

2011–12 VAN	33	20–8–1	1,833	60	3	1.96
NHL Totals	68	38–17–0–4	3,639	136	4	2.24

Schultz, Jeff   b. Calgary, Alberta, February 25, 1986

2011–12 WAS	54	1	5	6	12
NHL Totals	373	11	61	72	121

Schultz, Nick   b. Strasbourg, Saskatchewan, August 25, 1982

2011–12 MIN/EDM	82	1	6	7	40
NHL Totals	763	26	106	132	332

• traded by Minnesota to Edmonton on February 27, 2012, for Tom Gilbert

Schwartz, Jaden   b. Melfort, Saskatchewan, June 25, 1992

2011–12 STL	7	2	1	3	0
NHL Totals	7	2	1	3	0

Scott, John   b. St. Catharines, Ontario, September 26, 1982

2011–12 CHI/NYR	35	0	1	1	53
NHL Totals	146	1	4	5	236

• traded by Chicago to NY Rangers on February 27, 2012, for a 5th-round draft choice in 2012

Scrivens, Ben b. Spruce Grove, Alberta, September 11, 1986

2011–12 TOR	12	4–5–2	359	35	0	3.13
NHL Totals	12	4–5–2	359	35	0	3.13

Scuderi, Rob b. Syosset, New York, December 30, 1978

2011–12 LA	82	1	8	9	16
NHL Totals	537	6	68	74	165

Seabrook, Brent b. Richmond, British Columbia, April 20, 1985

2011–12 CHI	78	9	25	34	22
NHL Totals	552	48	178	226	444

Sedin, Daniel b. Ornskoldsvik, Sweden, September 26, 1980

2011–12 VAN	72	30	37	67	40
NHL Totals	859	279	439	718	364

Sedin, Henrik b. Ornskoldsvik, Sweden, September 26, 1980

2011–12 VAN	82	14	67	81	52
NHL Totals	892	171	576	747	510

Segal, Brandon b. Richmond, British Columbia, July 12, 1983

2011–12 TB	10	0	0	0	4
NHL Totals	102	11	11	22	83

Seguin, Tyler b. Brampton, Ontario, January 31, 1992

2011–12 BOS	81	29	38	67	30
NHL Totals	155	40	49	89	48

Seidenberg, Dennis b. Schwenningen, West Germany (Germany), July 18, 1981

2011–12 BOS	80	5	18	23	39
NHL Totals	535	30	141	171	232

Sekera, Andrej b. Bojnice, Czechoslovakia (Slovakia), June 8, 1986

2011–12 BUF	69	3	10	13	18
NHL Totals	302	15	65	80	98

Selanne, Teemu b. Helsinki, Finland, July 3, 1970

2011–12 ANA	82	26	40	66	50
NHL Totals	1,341	663	743	1,406	620

Semin, Alexander b. Krasjonarsk, Soviet Union (Russia), March 3, 1984

2011–12 WAS	77	21	33	54	56
NHL Totals	469	197	211	408	450

Sestito, Tim b. Rome, New York, August 28, 1984

2011–12 NJ	18	0	0	0	7
NHL Totals	64	0	3	3	18

Sestito, Tom b. Rome, New York, September 28, 1987

2011–12 PHI	14	0	1	1	83
NHL Totals	27	2	3	5	147

Setoguchi, Devin b. Taber, Alberta, January 1, 1987

2011–12 MIN	69	19	17	36	28
NHL Totals	336	103	92	195	117

Shannon, Ryan b. Darien, Connecticut, March 2, 1983

2011–12 TB	45	4	8	12	10
NHL Totals	305	35	64	99	90

Sharp, Patrick b. Thunder Bay, Ontario, December 27, 1981

2011–12 CHI	74	33	36	69	38
NHL Totals	567	193	192	385	377

Shattenkirk, Kevin b. Greenwich, Connecticut, January 29, 1989

2011–12 STL	81	9	34	43	60
NHL Totals	153	18	68	86	96

Shaw, Andrew b. Belleville, Ontario, July 20, 1991

2011–12 CHI	37	12	11	23	50
NHL Totals	37	12	11	23	50

Sheahan, Riley b. St. Catharines, Ontario, December 7, 1991

2011–12 DET	1	0	0	0	4
NHL Totals	1	0	0	0	4

Shelley, Jody b. Thompson, Manitoba, February 7, 1976

2011–12 PHI	30	0	1	1	64
NHL Totals	626	18	36	54	1,538

Silfverberg, Jakob b. Gavle, Sweden, October 13, 1990

2011–12 OTT	0	0	0	0	0
NHL Totals	0	0	0	0	0

• made NHL debut in the playoffs this season

Simmonds, Wayne b. Scarborough (Toronto), Ontario, August 26, 1988

2011–12 PHI	82	28	21	49	114
NHL Totals	322	67	75	142	378

Skille, Jack b. Madison, Wisconsin, May 19, 1987

2011–12 FLO	46	4	6	10	28
NHL Totals	138	17	20	37	62

Skinner, Jeff b. Markham, Ontario, May 16, 1992

2011–12 CAR	64	20	24	44	56
NHL Totals	146	51	56	107	102

Slater, Jim b. Petoskey, Michigan, December 9, 1982

2011–12 WIN	78	13	8	21	42
NHL Totals	449	60	61	121	322

Smid, Ladislav b. Frydlant, Czechoslovakia (Czech Republic), February 1, 1986

2011–12 EDM	78	5	10	15	44
NHL Totals	409	9	50	59	320

Smith, Ben b. Winston-Salem, North Carolina, July 11, 1988

2011–12 CHI	13	2	0	2	0
NHL Totals	19	3	0	3	0

Smith, Brendan b. Toronto, Ontario, February 8, 1989

2011–12 DET	14	1	6	7	13
NHL Totals	14	1	6	7	13

Smith, Craig b. Madison, Wisconsin, September 5, 1989

2011–12 NAS	72	14	22	36	30
NHL Totals	72	14	22	36	30

Smith, Derek b. Belleville, Ontario, October 13, 1984

2011–12 CAL	47	2	9	11	12
NHL Totals	58	2	10	12	12

Smith, Mike b. Kingston, Ontario, March 22, 1982

2011–12 PHO	67	38–18–10	3,903	144	8	2.21
NHL Totals	229	105–84–0–29	13,009	556	19	2.56

Smith, Reilly b. Toronto, Ontario, April 1, 1991

2011–12 DAL	3	0	0	0	2
NHL Totals	3	0	0	0	2

Smith, Trevor b. Ottawa, Ontario, February 8, 1985

2011–12 TB	16	2	3	5	4
NHL Totals	23	3	3	6	4

Smith, Zack b. Medicine Hat, Alberta, April 5, 1988

2011–12 OTT	81	14	12	26	98
NHL Totals	152	20	18	38	232

Smith-Pelly, Devante b. Scarborough (Toronto), Ontario, June 14, 1992

2011–12 ANA	49	7	6	13	16
NHL Totals	49	7	6	13	16

Smithson, Jerred b. Vernon, British Columbia, February 4, 1979

2011–12 NAS/FLO	69	1	5	6	34
NHL Totals	543	36	54	90	342

• traded by Nashville to Florida on February 24, 2012, for a 6th-round draft choice in 2012

Smyth, Ryan b. Banff, Alberta, February 21, 1976

2011–12 EDM	82	19	27	46	82
NHL Totals	1,151	374	432	806	892

Sneep, Carl b. St. Louis Park, Minnesota, November 5, 1987

2011–12 PIT	1	0	1	1	0
NHL Totals	1	0	1	1	0

Sobotka, Vladimir b. Trebic, Czechoslovakia (Czech Republic), July 2, 1987

2011–12 STL	73	5	15	20	42
NHL Totals	272	18	53	71	175

Souray, Sheldon b. Elk Point, Alberta, July 13, 1976

2011–12 DAL	64	6	15	21	73
NHL Totals	714	102	181	283	1,093

Spacek, Jaroslav b. Rokycany, Czechoslovakia (Czech Republic), February 11, 1974

2011–12 MON/CAR	46	5	10	15	8
NHL Totals	880	82	273	355	618

• traded by Montreal to Carolina on December 9, 2011, for Tomas Kaberle

Spaling, Nick b. Palmerston, Ontario, September 19, 1988

2011–12 NAS	77	10	12	22	18
NHL Totals	179	18	21	39	38

Spezza, Jason b. Mississauga, Ontario, June 13, 1983

2011–12 OTT	80	34	50	84	56
NHL Totals	606	226	390	616	386

Spurgeon, Jared b. Edmonton, Alberta, November 29, 1989

2011–12 MIN	70	3	20	23	6
NHL Totals	123	7	28	35	8

Staal, Eric b. Thunder Bay, Ontario, October 29, 1984

2011–12 CAR	82	24	46	70	48
NHL Totals	642	250	324	574	477

Staal, Jordan b. Thunder Bay, Ontario, September 10, 1988

2011–12 PIT	62	25	25	50	34
NHL Totals	431	120	128	248	231

Staal, Marc b. Thunder Bay, Ontario, January 13, 1987

2011–12 NYR	46	2	3	5	16
NHL Totals	367	22	64	86	216

Stafford, Drew b. Milwaukee, Wisconsin, October 30, 1985

2011–12 BUF	80	20	30	50	46
NHL Totals	397	114	132	246	228

Staios, Steve b. Hamilton, Ontario, July 28, 1973

2011–12 NYI	65	0	8	8	53
NHL Totals	1,001	56	164	220	1,322

• retired at season's end

Stajan, Matt b. Mississauga, Ontario, December 19, 1983

2011–12 CAL	61	8	10	18	29
NHL Totals	609	104	184	288	310

Stalberg, Viktor b. Stockholm, Sweden, January 17, 1986

2011–12 CHI	79	22	21	43	34
NHL Totals	196	43	38	81	107

Stamkos, Steve b. Markham, Ontario, February 7, 1960

2011–12 TB	82	60	37	97	66
NHL Totals	325	179	150	329	217

Stapleton, Tim b. LaGrange, Illinois, July 9, 1982

2011–12 WIN	63	11	16	27	10
NHL Totals	118	19	18	37	24

Stastny, Paul b. Quebec City, Quebec, December 27, 1985

2011–12 COL	79	21	32	53	34
NHL Totals	427	126	248	374	228

Staubitz, Brad b. Brights Grove, Ontario, July 28, 1984

2011–12 MIN/MON	62	1	0	1	121
NHL Totals	215	9	10	19	480

• claimed off waivers on February 27, 2012, by Montreal from Minnesota

St. Denis, Frederic b. Greenfield Park, Quebec, January 23, 1986

2011–12 MON	17	1	2	3	10
NHL Totals	17	1	2	3	10

Steckel, David b. Milwaukee, Wisconsin, March 15, 1982

2011–12 TOR	76	8	5	13	10
NHL Totals	385	32	40	72	125

Steen, Alexander b. Winnipeg, Manitoba, March 1, 1984

2011–12 STL	43	15	13	28	28
NHL Totals	497	115	161	276	214

Stempniak, Lee b. Buffalo, New York, February 4, 1983

2011–12 CAL	61	14	14	28	16
NHL Totals	517	129	146	275	189

Stepan, Derek b. Hastings, Minnesota, June 18, 1990

2011–12 NYR	82	17	34	51	22
NHL Totals	164	38	58	96	42

Sterling, Brett b. Los Angeles, California, April 24, 1984

2011–12 STL	4	0	0	0	0
NHL Totals	30	5	4	9	32

Stewart, Anthony b. LaSalle, Quebec, January 5, 1985

2011–12 CAR	77	9	11	20	30
NHL Totals	262	27	44	71	123

Stewart, Chris   b. Toronto, Ontario, October 30, 1987

2011–12 STL	79	15	15	30	109
NHL Totals	271	82	84	166	289

St. Louis, Martin   b. Laval, Quebec, June 18, 1975

2011–12 TB	77	25	49	74	16
NHL Totals	931	323	529	852	266

Stoll, Jarret   b. Melville, Saskatchewan, June 25, 1982

2011–12 LA	78	6	15	21	60
NHL Totals	593	119	198	317	448

Stone, Michael   b. Winnipeg, Manitoba, June 7, 1990

2011–12 PHO	13	1	2	3	2
NHL Totals	13	1	2	3	2

Stoner, Clayton   b. Port McNeill, British Columbia, February 19, 1985

2011–12 MIN	51	1	4	5	62
NHL Totals	116	3	13	16	170

Stortini, Zack   b. Elliot Lake, Ontario, September 11, 1985

2011–12 NAS	1	0	0	0	7
NHL Totals	257	14	27	41	725

Strachan, Tyson   b. Melfort, Saskatchewan, October 30, 1984

2011–12 FLO	15	1	2	3	5
NHL Totals	82	1	8	9	87

Strait, Brian   b. Boston, Massachusetts, January 4, 1988

2011–12 PIT	9	0	1	1	4
NHL Totals	12	0	1	1	4

Stralman, Anton   b. Tibro, Sweden, August 1, 1986

2011–12 NYR	53	2	16	18	20
NHL Totals	265	13	79	92	117

Streit, Mark   b. Bern, Switzerland, December 11, 1977

2011–12 NYI	82	7	40	47	46
NHL Totals	443	59	202	261	226

Stuart, Brad   b. Rocky Mountain House, Alberta, November 6, 1979

2011–12 DET	81	6	15	21	29
NHL Totals	876	74	231	305	489

Stuart, Colin b. Rochester, Minnesota, July 8, 1982

2011–12 BUF	2	0	0	0	0
NHL Totals	56	8	5	13	26

Stuart, Mark b. Rochester, Minnesota, April 27, 1984

2011–12 WIN	80	3	11	14	98
NHL Totals	386	17	38	55	406

Sturm, Marco b. Dingolfing, West Germany (Germany), September 8, 1978

2011–12 VAN/FLO	48	3	2	5	25
NHL Totals	938	242	245	487	446

• traded by Vancouver to Florida on October 22, 2011, with Mikael Samuelsson for David Booth, Steve Reinprecht and a 3rd-round draft choice in 2013

Subban, P.K. b. Toronto, Ontario, May 13, 1989

2011–12 MON	81	7	29	36	119
NHL Totals	160	21	55	76	245

Sullivan, Steve b. Timmins, Ontario, July 6, 1974

2011–12 PIT	79	17	31	48	20
NHL Totals	969	283	447	730	563

Sulzer, Alexander b. Kaufbeuren, West Germany (Germany), May 30, 1984

2011–12 VAN/BUF	27	3	6	9	8
NHL Totals	89	4	12	16	26

• traded by Vancouver to Buffalo on February 27, 2012, with Cody Hodgson for Zack Kassian and Marc-Andre Gragnani

Summers, Chris b. Ann Arbor, Michigan, February 5, 1988

2011–12 PHO	21	0	3	3	11
NHL Totals	23	0	3	3	15

Suter, Ryan b. Madison, Wisconsin, January 21, 1985

2011–12 NAS	79	7	39	46	30
NHL Totals	542	38	200	238	396

Sutter, Brandon b. Huntington, New York, February 14, 1989

2011–12 CAR	82	17	15	32	21
NHL Totals	286	53	54	107	64

Sutter, Brett b. Viking, Alberta, June 2, 1987

2011–12 CAR	15	0	3	3	11
NHL Totals	34	1	4	5	23

Sutton, Andy b. Kingston, Ontario, March 10, 1975

2011–12 EDM	52	3	7	10	80
NHL Totals	676	38	112	150	1,185

Sweatt, Bill b. Elburn, Illinois, September 21, 1988

2011–12 VAN	2	0	0	0	0
NHL Totals	2	0	0	0	0

Sykora, Petr b. Plzen, Czechoslovakia (Czech Republic), November 19, 1976

2011–12 NJ	82	21	23	44	40
NHL Totals	1,017	323	398	721	455

Szczechura, Paul b. Brantford, Ontario, November 30, 1985

2011–12 BUF	9	1	3	4	4
NHL Totals	92	10	10	20	34

Taffe, Jeff b. Hastings, Minnesota, February 19, 1981

2011–12 MIN	5	0	2	2	0
NHL Totals	180	21	25	46	40

Talbot, Maxime b. Lemoyne, Quebec, February 11, 1984

2011–12 PHI	81	19	15	34	59
NHL Totals	469	71	71	142	383

Tallinder, Henrik b. Stockholm, Sweden, January 10, 1979

2011–12 NJ	39	0	6	6	16
NHL Totals	589	25	105	130	334

Tanev, Chris b. Toronto, Ontario, December 20, 1989

2011–12 VAN	25	0	2	2	2
NHL Totals	54	0	3	3	2

Tangradi, Eric b. Philadelphia, Pennsylvania, February 10, 1989

2011–12 PIT	24	0	2	2	16
NHL Totals	40	1	4	5	26

Tanguay, Alex b. Ste-Justine, Quebec, November 21, 1979

2011–12 CAL	64	13	36	49	28
NHL Totals	882	238	497	735	429

Taormina, Matt b. Washington Township, Michigan, October 20, 1986

2011–12 NJ	30	1	6	7	4
NHL Totals	47	4	8	12	6

Tarki, Iiro b. Rauma, Finland, July 1, 1985

2011–12 ANA	1	1–0–0	41	3	0	4.39
NHL Totals	1	1–0–0	41	3	0	4.39

Tavares, John b. Mississauga, Ontario, September 20, 1990

2011–12 NYI	82	31	50	81	26
NHL Totals	243	84	118	202	101

Tedenby, Mattias b. Vetlanda, Sweden, February 21, 1990

2011–12 NJ	43	1	5	6	16
NHL Totals	101	9	19	28	30

Teubert, Colten b. White Rock, British Columbia, March 8, 1990

2011–12 EDM	24	0	1	1	25
NHL Totals	24	0	1	1	25

Thang, Ryan b. Chicago, Illinois, May 11, 1987

2011–12 NAS	1	0	0	0	0
NHL Totals	1	0	0	0	0

Theodore, Jose b. Laval, Quebec, September 13, 1976

2011–12 FLO	53	22–16–11	3,049	125	3	2.46
NHL Totals	633	282–248–30–55	35,840	1,593	33	2.67

Thiessen, Brad b. Aldergrove, British Columbia, March 19, 1986

2011–12 PIT	5	3–1–0	258	16	0	3.72
NHL Totals	5	3–1–0	258	16	0	3.72

Thomas, Bill b. Pittsburgh, Pennsylvania, June 20, 1983

2011–12 FLO	7	1	0	1	0
NHL Totals	87	16	12	28	18

Thomas, Tim b. Flint, Michigan, April 15, 1974

2011–12 BOS	59	35–19–1	3,352	132	5	2.36
NHL Totals	378	196–121–0–45	21,784	899	31	2.48

Thompson, Nate b. Anchorage, Alaska, October 5, 1984

2011–12 TB	68	9	6	15	21
NHL Totals	265	23	31	54	155

Thorburn, Chris b. Sault Ste. Marie, Ontario, June 3, 1983

2011–12 WIN	72	4	7	11	83
NHL Totals	426	32	50	82	521

Thornton, Joe b. London, Ontario, July 2, 1979

2011–12 SJ	82	18	59	77	31	
NHL Totals	1,077	324	754	1,078	963	

Thornton, Shawn b. Oshawa, Ontario, July 23, 1977

2011–12 BOS	81	5	8	13	154	
NHL Totals	450	30	43	73	772	

Timonen, Kimmo b. Kuopio, Finland, March 18, 1975

2011–12 PHI	76	4	39	43	46	
NHL Totals	970	106	401	507	584	

Tlusty, Jiri b. Slany, Czechoslovakia (Czech Republic), March 16, 1988

2011–12 CAR	79	19	19	36	26	
NHL Totals	228	34	40	74	60	

Toews, Jonathan b. Winnipeg, Manitoba, April 29, 1988

2011–12 CHI	59	29	28	57	28	
NHL Totals	361	144	180	324	196	

Tokarski, Dustin b. Humboldt, Saskatchewan, September 16, 1989

2011–12 TB	5	1–3–1	244	14	0	3.44
NHL Totals	7	1–3–0–1	288	17	0	3.54

Tootoo, Jordin b. Churchill, Manitoba, February 2, 1983

2011–12 NAS	77	6	24	30	92	
NHL Totals	486	46	79	125	725	

Torres, Raffi b. Toronto, Ontario, October 8, 1981

2011–12 PHO	79	15	11	26	83	
NHL Totals	591	127	110	237	473	

Tropp, Corey b. Grosse Pointe, Michigan, July 25, 1989

2011–12 BUF	34	3	5	8	20	
NHL Totals	34	3	5	8	20	

Turco, Marty b. Sault Ste. Marie, Ontario, August 13, 1975

2011–12 BOS	5	2–2–0	261	16	0	3.68
NHL Totals	543	275–167–26–43	30,955	1,216	41	2.36

Turnbull, Travis b. St. Louis, Missouri, July 7, 1986

2011–12 BUF	3	1	0	1	5	
NHL Totals	3	1	0	1	5	

Turris, Kyle b. New Westminster, British Columbia, August 14, 1989

2011–12 PHO/OTT	55	12	17	29	31
NHL Totals	186	31	44	75	70

• traded by Phoenix to Ottawa on December 16, 2011, for David Rundblad and a 2nd-round draft choice in 2012

Tyrell, Dana b. Airdrie, Alberta, April 23, 1989

2011–12 TB	26	0	5	5	6
NHL Totals	104	6	14	20	18

Tyutin, Fedor b. Izhevsk, Soviet Union (Russia), July 19, 1983

2011–12 CBJ	66	5	21	26	49
NHL Totals	558	42	143	185	370

Ullstrom, David b. Jonkoping, Sweden, April 22, 1989

2011–12 NYI	29	4	4	8	6
NHL Totals	29	4	4	8	6

Umberger, R.J. b. Pittsburgh, Pennsylvania, May 3, 1982

2011–12 CBJ	77	20	20	40	27
NHL Totals	551	143	171	314	236

Upshall, Scottie b. Fort McMurray, Alberta, October 7, 1983

2011–12 FLO	26	2	3	5	29
NHL Totals	387	88	89	177	354

Urbom, Alexander b. Stockholm, Sweden, December 20, 1990

2011–12 NJ	5	1	0	1	9
NHL Totals	13	2	0	2	9

Van der Gulik, David b. Abbotsford, British Columbia, April 20, 1983

2011–12 COL	25	1	5	6	2
NHL Totals	37	2	9	11	4

Vandermeer, Jim b. Caroline, Alberta, February 21, 1980

2011–12 SJ	25	1	3	4	33
NHL Totals	461	25	80	105	664

VandeVelde, Chris b. Moorhead, Minnesota, March 15, 1987

2011–12 EDM	5	1	0	1	2
NHL Totals	17	1	2	3	14

Vanek, Thomas   b. Vienna, Austria, January 19, 1984

2011–12 BUF	78	26	35	61	52	
NHL Totals	547	230	217	447	338	

van Riemsdyk, James   b. Middletown, New Jersey, May 4, 1989

2011–12 PHI	43	11	13	24	24	
NHL Totals	196	47	52	99	89	

Varlamov, Semyon   b. Kuybyshev, Soviet Union (Russia), April 27, 1988

2011–12 COL	53	26–24–3	3,151	136	4	2.59
NHL Totals	112	56–37–0–15	6,567	272	8	2.48

Veilleux, Stephane   b. Beauceville, Quebec, November 16, 1981

2011–12 NJ/MIN	22	0	2	2	15	
NHL Totals	460	46	55	101	317	

• traded by New Jersey to Minnesota on February 24, 2012, with Nick Palmieri, Kurtis Foster, a 2nd-round draft choice in 2012 and a conditional 3rd-round draft choice in 2013 for Marek Zidlicky

Vermette, Antoine   b. St-Agapit, Quebec, July 20, 1982

2011–12 CBJ/PHO	82	11	26	37	28	
NHL Totals	622	144	185	329	333	

• traded by Columbus to Phoenix on February 22, 2012, for Curtis McElhinney, a 2nd-round draft choice in 2012 and a conditional 5th-round draft choice in 2013

Versteeg, Kris   b. Lethbridge, Alberta, May 13, 1986

2011–12 FLO	71	23	31	54	49	
NHL Totals	321	88	113	201	198	

Vincour, Tomas   b. Brno, Czechoslovakia (Czech Republic), November 19, 1990

2011–12 DAL	47	4	6	10	2	
NHL Totals	71	5	7	12	6	

Visnovsky, Lubomir   b. Topolcany, Czechoslovakia (Slovakia), August 11, 1976

2011–12 ANA	68	6	21	27	47	
NHL Totals	771	117	333	450	335	

Vitale, Joe   b. St. Louis, Missouri, August 20, 1985

2011–12 PIT	68	4	10	14	56	
NHL Totals	77	5	11	16	69	

Vlasic, Marc-Edouard   b. Montreal, Quebec, March 30, 1987

2011–12 SJ	82	4	19	23	40	
NHL Totals	471	22	111	133	175	

Vokoun, Tomas   b. Karlovy Vary, Czechoslovakia (Czech Republic), July 2, 1976

2011–12 WAS	48	25–17–2	2,583	108	4	2.51
NHL Totals	680	287–284–35–57	38,665	1,646	48	2.55

Volchenkov, Anton   b. Moscow, Soviet Union (Russia), February 25, 1982

2011–12 NJ	72	2	9	11	34
NHL Totals	557	18	95	113	367

Volpatti, Aaron   b. Revelstoke, British Columbia, May 30, 1985

2011–12 VAN	23	1	0	1	37
NHL Totals	38	2	1	3	53

Voracek, Jakub   b. Kladno, Czechoslovakia (Czech Republic), August 15, 1989

2011–12 PHI	78	18	31	49	32
NHL Totals	319	57	126	183	128

Voynov, Slava   b. Chelyabinsk, Soviet Union (Russia), January 15, 1990

2011–12 LA	54	8	12	20	12
NHL Totals	54	8	12	20	12

Vrbata, Radim   b. Mlada Boleslav, Czechoslovakia (Czech Republic), June 13, 1981

2011–12 PHO	77	35	27	62	24
NHL Totals	678	183	202	385	194

Walker, Matt   b. Beaverlodge, Alberta, April 7, 1980

2011–12 PHI	4	0	0	0	16
NHL Totals	314	4	26	30	464

Wallace, Tim   b. Anchorage, Alaska, August 6, 1984

2011–12 NYI/TB	49	3	6	9	16
NHL Totals	73	3	8	11	28

• claimed off waivers on February 23, 2012, by Tampa Bay from NY Islanders

Wandell, Tom   b. Sodertalje, Sweden, January 29, 1987

2011–12 DAL	72	6	9	15	16
NHL Totals	211	19	23	42	48

Ward, Cam   b. Sherwood Park, Alberta, February 29, 1984

2011–12 CAR	68	30–23–13	3,988	182	5	2.74
NHL Totals	414	205–149–0–46	23,721	1,083	21	2.74

Ward, Joel   b. Toronto, Ontario, December 2, 1980

2011–12 WAS	73	6	12	18	20
NHL Totals	314	46	71	117	109

Wathier, Francis   b. St. Isidore, Ontario, December 7, 1984

2011–12 DAL	1	0	0	0	0
NHL Totals	9	0	0	0	5

Watkins, Matt   b. Regina, Saskatchewan, November 22, 1986

2011–12 PHO	1	0	0	0	0
NHL Totals	1	0	0	0	0

Weaver, Mike   b. Bramalea, Ontario, May 2, 1978

2011–12 FLO	82	0	16	16	14
NHL Totals	503	6	65	71	182

Weber, Mike   b. Pittsburgh, Pennsylvania, December 16, 1987

2011–12 BUF	51	1	4	5	64
NHL Totals	132	5	20	25	166

Weber, Shea   b. Sicamous, British Columbia, August 14, 1985

2011–12 NAS	78	19	30	49	46
NHL Totals	480	99	164	263	369

Weber, Yannick   b. Morges, Switzerland, September 23, 1988

2011–12 MON	60	4	14	18	30
NHL Totals	109	5	20	25	50

Weise, Dale   b. Winnipeg, Manitoba, August 5, 1988

2011–12 VAN	68	4	4	8	81
NHL Totals	78	4	4	8	100

Weiss, Stephen   b. Toronto, Ontario, April 3, 1983

2011–12 FLO	80	20	37	57	60
NHL Totals	637	144	246	390	288

Wellman, Casey   b. Brentwood, California, October 18, 1987

2011–12 MIN	14	2	5	7	0
NHL Totals	41	4	9	13	4

Wellwood, Eric   b. Windsor, Ontario, March 6, 1990

2011–12 PHI	24	5	4	9	2
NHL Totals	27	5	5	10	4

Wellwood, Kyle b. Windsor, Ontario, May 16, 1983

2011–12 WIN	77	18	29	47	4
NHL Totals	450	86	134	220	34

Welsh, Jeremy b. Bayfield, Ontario, April 30, 1988

2011–12 CAR	1	0	0	0	4
NHL Totals	1	0	0	0	4

Westgarth, Kevin b. Amherstburg, Ontario, February 7, 1984

2011–12 LA	25	1	1	2	39
NHL Totals	90	1	4	5	153

Wheeler, Blake b. Robbinsdale, Minnesota, August 31, 1986

2011–12 WIN	80	17	47	64	55
NHL Totals	324	74	117	191	200

White, Colin b. New Glasgow, Nova Scotia, December 12, 1977

2011–12 SJ	54	1	3	4	21
NHL Totals	797	21	108	129	869

White, Ian b. Winnipeg, Manitoba, June 4, 1984

2011–12 DET	77	7	25	32	22
NHL Totals	478	43	132	175	250

White, Ryan b. Brandon, Manitoba, March 17, 1988

2011–12 MON	20	0	3	3	61
NHL Totals	63	2	8	10	115

Whitfield, Trent b. Estevan, Saskatchewan, June 17, 1977

2011–12 BOS	1	0	0	0	0
NHL Totals	191	11	18	29	104

Whitmore, Derek b. Rochester, New York, December 17, 1984

2011–12 BUF	2	0	0	0	0
NHL Totals	2	0	0	0	0

Whitney, Ray b. Fort Saskatchewan, Alberta, May 8, 1972

2011–12 PHO	82	24	53	77	28
NHL Totals	1,229	365	638	1,003	447

Whitney, Ryan b. Boston, Massachusetts, February 19, 1983

2011–12 EDM	51	3	17	20	16
NHL Totals	440	46	200	246	354

Wideman, Dennis b. Kitchener, Ontario, March 20, 1983

2011–12 WAS	82	11	35	46	46
NHL Totals	535	67	183	250	377

Williams, Jason b. London, Ontario, August 11, 1980

2011–12 PIT	8	1	1	2	4
NHL Totals	455	94	133	227	157

Williams, Justin b. Cobourg, Ontario, October 4, 1981

2011–12 LA	82	22	37	59	44
NHL Totals	707	179	286	465	475

Wilson, Clay b. Sturgeon Lake, Minnesota, April 5, 1983

2011–12 CAL	5	0	0	0	4
NHL Totals	36	4	4	8	12

Wilson, Colin b. Greenwich, Connecticut, October 20, 1989

2011–12 NAS	68	15	20	35	21
NHL Totals	185	39	45	84	45

Wilson, Kyle b. Oakville, Ontario, December 15, 1984

2011–12 NAS	5	0	0	0	0
NHL Totals	39	4	9	13	12

Wilson, Ryan b. Windsor, Ontario, February 3, 1987

2011–12 COL	59	1	20	21	33
NHL Totals	187	7	51	58	137

Winchester, Brad b. Madison, Wisconsin, March 1, 1981

2011–12 SJ	67	6	4	10	88
NHL Totals	390	37	31	68	552

Winchester, Jesse b. Long Sault, Ontario, October 4, 1983

2011–12 OTT	32	2	6	8	22
NHL Totals	233	11	41	52	121

Wingels, Tommy b. Evanston, Illinois, April 12, 1988

2011–12 SJ	33	3	6	9	18
NHL Totals	38	3	6	9	18

Winnik, Daniel   b. Toronto, Ontario, March 6, 1985

2011–12 COL/SJ	84	8	15	23	52
NHL Totals	366	37	64	101	187

• traded by Colorado to San Jose on February 27, 2012, with T.J. Galiardi, and a 7th-round draft choice in 2013 for Jamie McGinn, Mike Connolly and Michael Sgarbossa

Wishart, Ty   b. Belleville, Ontario, May 19, 1988

2011–12 NYI	1	0	0	0	0
NHL Totals	26	1	5	6	10

Wisniewski, James   b. Canton, Michigan, February 21, 1984

2011–12 CBJ	48	6	21	27	37
NHL Totals	377	33	142	175	339

Wolski, Wojtek   b. Zabrze, Poland, February 24, 1986

2011–12 NYR/FLO	31	4	8	12	2
NHL Totals	424	95	163	258	107

• traded by NY Rangers to Florida on February 25, 2012, for Michael Vernace and a 3rd-round draft choice in 2013

Woywitka, Jeff   b. Vermilion, Alberta, September 1, 1983

2011–12 NYR	27	1	5	6	8
NHL Totals	278	9	46	55	149

Wyman, J.T.   b. Edina, Minnesota, February 27, 1986

2011–12 TB	40	2	9	11	8
NHL Totals	43	2	9	11	8

Yandle, Keith   b. Boston, Massachusetts, September 9, 1986

2011–12 PHO	82	11	32	43	51
NHL Totals	365	43	144	187	223

Yip, Brandon   b. Vancouver, British Columbia, April 25, 1985

2011–12 COL/NAS	35	3	4	7	28
NHL Totals	138	26	22	48	104

• claimed off waivers on January 19, 2012, by Nashville from Colorado

Yonkman, Nolan   b. Punnichy, Saskatchewan, April 1, 1981

2011–12 FLO	1	0	0	0	0
NHL Totals	67	1	8	9	129

York, Allen b. Wetaskiwin, Alberta, June 17, 1989

2011–12 CBJ	11	3–2–0	417	16	0	2.30
NHL Totals	11	3–2–0	417	16	0	2.30

Zajac, Travis b. Winnipeg, Manitoba, May 13, 1985

2011–12 NJ	15	2	4	6	4
NHL Totals	423	91	164	255	128

Zalewski, Steven b. Utica, New York, August 20, 1986

2011–12 NJ	7	0	0	0	0
NHL Totals	10	0	0	0	0

Zanon, Greg b. Burnaby, British Columbia, June 5, 1980

2011–12 MIN/BOS	56	3	5	8	18
NHL Totals	449	12	44	56	202

• traded by Minnesota to Boston on February 27, 2012, for Steven Kampfer

Zetterberg, Henrik b. Njurunda, Sweden, October 9, 1980

2011–12 DET	82	22	47	69	47
NHL Totals	668	252	372	624	271

Zharkov, Vladimir b. Elektrostal, Soviet Union (Russia), January 10, 1988

2011–12 NJ	4	0	0	0	0
NHL Totals	82	2	12	14	10

Zibanejad, Mika b. Stockholm, Sweden, April 18, 1993

2011–12 OTT	9	0	1	1	2
NHL Totals	9	0	1	1	2

Zidlicky, Marek b. Most, Czechoslovakia (Czech Republic), February 3, 1977

2011–12 MIN/NJ	63	2	20	22	34
NHL Totals	570	62	244	306	506

• traded by Minnesota to New Jersey on February 24, 2012, for Nick Palmieri, Stephane Veilleux, a 2nd-round draft choice in 2012 and a conditional 3rd-round draft choice in 2013

Zolnierczyk, Harry b. Toronto, Ontario, September 1, 1987

2011–12 PHI	37	3	3	6	35
NHL Totals	37	3	3	6	35

Zubrus, Dainius b. Eelektrenai, Soviet Union (Lithuania), June 16, 1978

2011–12 NJ	82	17	27	44	34
NHL Totals	1,065	206	333	539	671

Zuccarello, Mats   b. Oslo, Norway, September 1, 1987

2011–12 NYR	10	2	1	3	6
NHL Totals	52	8	18	26	10

Zucker, Jason   b. Newport Beach, California, January 16, 1992

2011–12 MIN	6	0	2	2	2
NHL Totals	6	0	2	2	2

COACHES' REGISTER, 2011–12

(OTL are listed in ties column)

	Games	W	L	T
Arniel, Scott b. Kingston, Ontario, September 17, 1962				
2011–12 CBJ	41	11	25	5
NHL Totals	123	45	60	18

• hired by Columbus, June 8, 2010; fired January 9, 2012

Babcock, Mike b. Manitouwadge, Ontario, April 29, 1963				
2011–12 DET	82	48	28	6
NHL Totals	738	421	216	101

• hired July 14, 2005

Boucher, Guy b. Notre-Dame-du-Lac, Quebec, August 3, 1971				
2011–12 TB	82	38	36	8
NHL Totals	164	84	61	19

• hired by Tampa Bay, June 10, 2010

Boudreau, Bruce b. Toronto, Ontario, January 9, 1955				
2011–12 WAS/ANA	80	39	32	9
NHL Totals	387	228	111	48

• hired November 22, 2007; fired by Washington on November 28, 2011; hired by Anaheim on December 1, 2011

Bylsma, Dan b. Grand Haven, Michigan, September 19, 1970				
2011–12 PIT	82	51	25	6
NHL Totals	271	165	81	25

• hired February 15, 2009

Capuano, Jack b. Cranston, Rhode Island, July 7, 1966				
2011–12 NYI	82	34	37	11
NHL Totals	147	60	66	21

• hired November 15, 2010

Carlyle, Randy b. Sudbury, Ontario, April 19, 1956				
2011–12 ANA/TOR	42	13	22	7
NHL Totals	534	279	191	64

• hired August 1, 2005; fired by Anaheim on December 1, 2011; hired by Toronto on March 2, 2012

Cunneyworth, Randy   b. Toronto, Ontario, May 10, 1961

2011–12 MON	50	18	23	9
NHL Totals	50	18	23	9

• hired December 17, 2011

DeBoer, Peter   b. Dunnville, Ontario, June 13, 1968

2011–12 NJ	82	48	28	6
NHL Totals	328	151	135	42

• hired July 19, 2011

Dineen, Kevin   b. Quebec City, Quebec, October 28, 1963

2011–12 FLO	82	38	26	18
NHL Totals	82	38	26	18

• hired June 1, 2011

Gulutzan, Glen   b. The Pas, Manitoba, August 12, 1971

2011–12 DAL	82	42	35	5
NHL Totals	82	42	35	5

• hired June 17, 2011

Hitchcock, Ken   b. Edmonton, Alberta, December 17, 1951

2011–12 STL	69	43	15	11
NHL Totals	1,111	577	365	169

• hired November 7, 2011

Hunter, Dale   b. Petrolia, Ontario, July 31, 1960

2011–12 WAS	60	30	23	7
NHL Totals	60	30	23	7

• hired November 28, 2011

Julien, Claude   b. Orleans, Ontario, April 23, 1960

2011–12 BOS	82	49	29	4
NHL Totals	648	347	218	83

• hired June 21, 2007

Laviolette, Peter   b. Norwood, Massachusetts, December 7, 1964

2011–12 PHI	82	47	26	9
NHL Totals	708	366	257	85

• hired December 4, 2009

MacLean, Paul   b. Grostenquin, France, March 9, 1958

2011–12 OTT	82	41	31	10
NHL Totals	82	41	31	10

• hired by Ottawa on June 13, 2011

Martin, Jacques   b. St. Pascal, Ontario, October 1, 1952

2011–12 MON	32	13	12	7
NHL Totals	1,294	613	481	200

• hired June 1, 2009; fired December 17, 2011

Maurice, Paul   b. Sault Ste. Marie, Ontario, January 30, 1967

2011–12 CAR	25	8	13	4
NHL Totals	1,084	460	457	167

• hired December 3, 2008; fired November 28, 2011

McLellan, Todd   b. Melville, Saskatchewan, October 3, 1967

2011–12 SJ	82	43	29	10
NHL Totals	328	195	92	41

• hired June 12, 2008

Muller, Kirk   b. Kingston, Ontario, February 8, 1966

2011–12 CAR	57	25	20	12
NHL Totals	57	25	20	12

• hired November 28, 2011

Murray, Terry   b. Shawville, Quebec, July 20, 1950

2011–12 LA	29	13	12	4
NHL Totals	1,012	499	383	130

• hired July 17, 2008; fired December 12, 2011

Noel, Claude   b. Kirkland Lake, Ontario, October 31, 1955

2011–12 WIN	82	37	35	10
NHL Totals	106	47	43	16

• hired June 24, 2011

Payne, Davis   b. King City, Ontario, October 24, 1970

2011–12 STL	13	6	7	0
NHL Totals	137	67	55	5

• hired January 2, 2010; fired November 7, 2011

Quenneville, Joel   b. Windsor, Ontario, September 15, 1958

2011–12 CHI	82	45	26	11
NHL Totals	1,163	624	382	157

• hired October 16, 2008

Renney, Tom   b. Cranbrook, British Columbia, March 1, 1955

2011–12 EDM	82	32	40	10
NHL Totals	592	260	255	76

• hired June 22, 2010

Richards, Todd   b. Crystal, Minnesota, October 20, 1966

2011–12 CBJ	41	18	21	2
NHL Totals	41	18	21	2

• hired January 9, 2012

Ruff, Lindy   b. Warburg, Alberta, February 17, 1960

2011–12 BUF	82	39	32	11
NHL Totals	1,148	565	422	161

• hired July 21, 1997

Sacco, Joe   b. Medford, Massachusetts, February 4, 1969

2011–12 COL	82	41	35	6
NHL Totals	246	114	109	23

• hired June 4, 2009

Stevens, John   b. Campbellton, New Brunswick, May 4, 1966

2011–12 LA	4	1	2	1
NHL Totals	267	122	111	34

• hired December 12, 2011, on an interim basis; replaced December 17, 2011

Sutter, Brent   b. Viking, Alberta, June 10, 1962

2011–12 CAL	82	37	29	16
NHL Totals	410	215	146	49

• hired June 23, 2009

Sutter, Darryl   b. Viking, Alberta, August 19, 1958

2011–12 LA	48	25	13	10
NHL Totals	909	434	333	142

• hired December 17, 2011

Tippett, Dave   b. Moosomin, Saskatchewan, August 25, 1961

2011–12 PHO	82	42	27	13
NHL Totals	738	406	234	98

• hired September 24, 2009

Tortorella, John   b. Boston, Massachusetts, June 24, 1958

2011–12 NYR	82	51	24	7
NHL Totals	806	384	322	100

• hired February 23, 2009

Trotz, Barry   b. Winnipeg, Manitoba, July 15, 1962

2011–12 NAS	82	48	26	8
NHL Totals	1,066	503	424	139

• hired August 6, 1997, a year before the Predators played their first NHL game

Vigneault, Alain   b. Quebec City, Quebec, May 14, 1961

2011–12 VAN	82	51	22	9
NHL Totals	758	396	273	89

• hired June 20, 2006

Wilson, Ron   b. Windsor, Ontario, May 28, 1955

2011–12 TOR	64	29	28	7
NHL Totals	1,391	638	561	192

• hired June 10, 2008; fired March 2, 2012

Yeo, Mike   b. North Bay, Ontario, July 31, 1973

2011–12 MIN	82	35	36	11
NHL Totals	82	35	36	11

• hired June 17, 2011

2012 NHL ENTRY DRAFT

Pittsburgh, Pennsylvania, June 22–23, 2012

First Round

1. Edmonton—Nail Yakupov (RUS)
2. Columbus—Ryan Murray (CAN)
3. Montreal—Alex Galchenyuk (USA)
4. NY Islanders—Griffin Reinhart (CAN)
5. Toronto—Morgan Rielly (CAN)
6. Anaheim—Hampus Lindholm (SWE)
7. Minnesota—Matt Dumba (CAN)
8. Pittsburgh—Derrick Pouliot (CAN)
9. Winnipeg—Jacob Trouba (USA)
10. Tampa Bay—Slater Koekkoek (CAN)
11. Washington—Filip Forsberg (SWE)
12. Buffalo—Mikhail Grigorenko (RUS)
13. Dallas—Radek Faksa (CZE)
14. Buffalo—Zemgus Girgensons (LAT)
15. Ottawa—Cody Ceci (CAN)
16. Washington—Thomas Wilson (CAN)
17. San Jose—Tomas Hertl (CZE)
18. Chicago—Teuvo Teravainen (FIN)
19. Tampa Bay—Andrei Vasilevski (RUS)
20. Philadelphia—Scott Laughton (CAN)
21. Calgary—Mark Jankowski (CAN)
22. Pittsburgh—Olli Maatta (FIN)
23. Florida—Michael Matheson (CAN)
24. Boston—Malcolm Subban (CAN)
25. St. Louis—Jordan Schmaltz (USA)
26. Vancouver—Brendan Gaunce (CAN)
27. Phoenix—Henrik Samuelsson (USA)
28. NY Rangers—Brady Skjei (USA)
29. New Jersey—Stefan Matteau (USA)
30. Los Angeles—Tanner Pearson (CAN)

Second Round

31. Columbus—Oscar Dansk (SWE)
32. Edmonton—Mitchell Moroz (CAN)
33. Montreal—Sebastian Collberg (SWE)
34. NY Islanders—Ville Pokka (FIN)
35. Toronto—Matthew Finn (CAN)

36. Anaheim—Nick Kerdiles (USA)
37. Nashville—Pontus Aberg (SWE)
38. Carolina—Phillip Di Giuseppe (CAN)
39. Winnipeg—Lukas Sutter (USA)
40. Tampa Bay—Dylan Blujus (USA)
41. Colorado—Mitchell Heard (CAN)
42. Calgary—Patrick Sieloff (USA)
43. Dallas—Ludwig Bystrom (SWE)
44. Buffalo—Jake McCabe (USA)
45. Philadelphia—Anthony Stolarz (USA)
46. Minnesota—Raphael Bussieres (CAN)
47. Carolina—Brock McGinn (CAN)
48. Chicago—Dillon Fournier (CAN)
49. Detroit—Martin Frk (CZE)
50. Nashville—Colton Sissons (CAN)
51. Montreal—Dalton Thrower (CAN)
52. Pittsburgh—Theodor Blueger (LAT)
53. Tampa Bay—Brian Hart (USA)
54. Dallas—Mike Winther (CAN)
55. San Jose—Chris Tierney (CAN)
56. St. Louis—Samuel Kurker (USA)
57. Vancouver—Alexandre Mallet (CAN)
58. Phoenix—Jordan Martinook (CAN)
59. NY Rangers—Cristoval Nieves (USA)
60. New Jersey—Damon Severson (CAN)
61. Dallas—Devin Shore (CAN)

Third Round
62. Columbus—Joonas Korpisalo (FIN)
63. Edmonton—Jujhar Khaira (CAN)
64. Montreal—Tim Bozon (USA)
65. NY Islanders—Adam Pelech (CAN)
66. Nashville—Jimmy Vesey (USA)
67. St. Louis—Mackenzie MacEachern (USA)
68. Minnesota—John Draeger (USA)
69. Carolina—Daniel Altshuller (CAN)
70. Winnipeg—Scott Kosmachuk (CAN)
71. Tampa Bay—Tanner Richard (CAN)
72. Colorado—Troy Bourke (CAN)
73. Buffalo—Justin Kea (CAN)
74. Dallas—Esa Lindell (FIN)
75. Calgary—Jon Gillies (USA)

76. Ottawa—Chris Driedger (CAN)
77. Washington—Chandler Stephenson (CAN)
78. Philadelphia—Shayne Gostisbehere (USA)
79. Chicago—Chris Calnan (USA)
80. Detroit—Jake Paterson (CAN)
81. Pittsburgh—Oskar Sundqvist (SWE)
82. Ottawa—Jarrod Maidens (CAN)
83. Pittsburgh—Matthew Murray (CAN)
84. Florida—Steven Hodges (CAN)
85. Boston—Matthew Grzelcyk (USA)
86. St. Louis—Colten Parayko (CAN)
87. Anaheim—Frederik Andersen (DEN)
88. Phoenix—James Melindy (CAN)
89. Nashville—Brendan Leipsic (CAN)
90. New Jersey—Ben Johnson (USA)
91. Edmonton—Daniil Zharkov (RUS)

Fourth Round
92. Pittsburgh—Matia Marcantuoni (CAN)
93. Edmonton—Erik Gustafsson (SWE)
94. Montreal—Brady Vail (USA)
95. Columbus—Josh Anderson (CAN)
96. New Jersey—Ben Thomson (CAN)
97. Anaheim—Kevin Roy (CAN)
98. Minnesota—Adam Gilmour (USA)
99. Carolina—Erik Karlsson (SWE)
100. Washington—Thomas Di Pauli (USA)
101. Tampa Bay—Cedric Paquette (CAN)
102. Phoenix—Rhett Holland (CAN)
103. NY Islanders—Loic Leduc (CAN)
104. Dallas—Gemel Smith (CAN)
105. Calgary—Brett Kulak (CAN)
106. Ottawa—Tim Boyle (USA)
107. Washington—Austin Wuthrich (USA)
108. Anaheim—Andrew O'Brien (CAN)
109. San Jose—Christophe Lalancette (CAN)
110. Detroit—Andreas Athanasiou (CAN)
111. Philadelphia—Fredrik Larsson (SWE)
112. Nashville—Zachary Stepan (USA)
113. Pittsburgh—Sean Maguire (CAN)
114. Florida—Alexander Delnov (RUS)
115. Carolina—Trevor Carrick (CAN)

116.   St. Louis—Nicholas Walters (CAN)
117.   Philadelphia—Taylor Leier (CAN)
118.   Nashville—Mikko Vainonen (FIN)
119.   NY Rangers—Calle Andersson (SWE)
120.   Carolina—Jaccob Slavin (USA)
121.   Los Angeles—Nikolai Prokhorkhin (RUS)

Fifth Round
122.   Montreal—Charles Hudon (CAN)
123.   Edmonton—Joey Laleggia (CAN)
124.   Calgary—Ryan Culkin (CAN)
125.   NY Islanders—Doyle Somerby (USA)
126.   Toronto—Dominic Toninato (USA)
127.   Anaheim—Brian Cooper (USA)
128.   Minnesota—Daniel Gunnarsson (SWE)
129.   Carolina—Brendan Woods (CAN)
130.   Winnipeg—Connor Hellebuyck (USA)
131.   Boston—Seth Griffith (CAN)
132.   Colorado—Michael Clarke (CAN)
133.   Buffalo—Logan Nelson (USA)
134.   Dallas—Branden Troock (CAN)
135.   New Jersey—Graham Black (CAN)
136.   Ottawa—Robert Baillargeon (USA)
137.   Washington—Connor Carrick (USA)
138.   San Jose—Daniel O'Regan (GER)
139.   Chicago—Garret Ross (USA)
140.   Detroit—Michael McKee (CAN)
141.   Philadelphia—Reece Willcox (CAN)
142.   NY Rangers—Thomas Spelling (DEN)
143.   Pittsburgh—Clark Seymour (CAN)
144.   Dallas—Henri Kiviaho (FIN)
145.   Boston—Cody Payne (GBR)
146.   St. Louis—Francois Tremblay (CAN)
147.   Vancouver—Ben Hutton (CAN)
148.   Phoenix—Niklas Tikkinen (FIN)
149.   Chicago—Travis Brown (CAN)
150.   New Jersey—Alexander Kerfoot (CAN)
151.   Los Angeles—Colin Miller (CAN)

Sixth Round
152.   Columbus—Daniel Zaar (SWE)
153.   Edmonton—John McCarron (USA)

154. Montreal—Erik Nystrom (SWE)
155. NY Islanders—Jesse Graham (CAN)
156. Toronto—Connor Brown (CAN)
157. Toronto—Ryan Rupert (CAN)
158. Minnesota—Christoph Bertschy (SUI)
159. Carolina—Collin Olson (USA)
160. Winnipeg—Ryan Olsen (CAN)
161. Tampa Bay—Jake Dotchin (CAN)
162. Colorado—Joseph Blandisi (CAN)
163. Buffalo—Linus Ullmark (SWE)
164. Nashville—Simon Fernholm (SWE)
165. Calgary—Coda Gordon (CAN)
166. Ottawa—Francois Brassard (CAN)
167. Washington—Riley Barber (USA)
168. San Jose—Clifford Watson (USA)
169. Chicago—Vincent Hinostroza (USA)
170. Detroit—James De Haas (CAN)
171. Los Angeles—Tomas Hyka (CZE)
172. Nashville—Max Gortz (SWE)
173. Pittsburgh—Anton Zlobin (RUS)
174. Florida—Francis Beauvillier (CAN)
175. Boston—Matthew Benning (CAN)
176. St. Louis—Petteri Lindbohm (FIN)
177. Vancouver—Wesley Myron (CAN)
178. Phoenix—Samuel Fejes (USA)
179. Nashville—Marek Mazanec (CZE)
180. New Jersey—Artur Gavrus (BLR)
181. Los Angeles—Paul Ladue (USA)

Seventh Round
182. Columbus—Gianluca Curcuruto (CAN)
183. Dallas—Dmitri Sinitsyn (RUS)
184. Phoenix—Marek Langhamer (CZE)
185. NY Islanders—Jake Bischoff (USA)
186. Calgary—Matthew Deblouw (USA)
187. Anaheim—Kenton Helgesen (CAN)
188. Minnesota—Lou Nanne (USA)
189. Carolina—Brendan Collier (USA)
190. Winnipeg—Jamie Phillips (CAN)
191. Chicago—Brandon Whitney (CAN)
192. Colorado—Colin Smith (CAN)
193. Buffalo—Brady Austin (CAN)

194.   Florida—Jonatan Nielsen (SWE)
195.   Washington—Christian Djoos (SWE)
196.   Ottawa—Mikael Wikstrand (SWE)
197.   Washington—Jaynen Rissling (CAN)
198.   San Jose—Joakim Ryan (USA)
199.   Chicago—Matt Tomkins (CAN)
200.   Detroit—Rasmus Bodin (SWE)
201.   Philadelphia—Valeri Vasiliev (RUS)
202.   Tampa Bay—Nikita Gusev (RUS)
203.   Washington—Sergei Kostenko (RUS)
204.   Buffalo—Judd Peterson (USA)
205.   Boston—Colton Hargrove (USA)
206.   St. Louis—Tyrel Seaman (CAN)
207.   Vancouver—Matthew Beattie (USA)
208.   Phoenix—Justin Hache (CAN)
209.   Toronto—Viktor Loov (SWE)
210.   Anaheim—Jaycob Megna (USA)
211.   Los Angeles—Nick Ebert (USA)

FATHERS-SONS-GRANDSONS

• Griffin Reinhart, son of former NHLer Paul, drafted 4th overall
• Mark Jankowski, grandson of former NHLer Lou, drafted 21st overall
• Henrik Samuelsson, son of former NHLer Ulf, drafted 27th overall
• Stefan Matteau, son of former NHLer Stephane, drafted 29th overall
• Lukas Sutter, son of former NHLer Rich, drafted 39th overall
• Tim Bozon, son of former NHLer Philippe, drafted 64th overall
• Justin Kea, son of former NHLer Ed, drafted 73rd overall
• Calle Andersson, son of former NHLer Peter, drafted 119th overall
• Erik Nystrom, son of former NHLer Bob, drafted 154th overall
• Lou Nanne, son of former NHLer Lou, drafted 188th overall
• Christian Djoos, son of former NHLer Per, drafted 195th overall

MODERN OUTDOOR GAMES

Date	Dubbed	League	Host City	Venue	Att.	Score
March 5, 1957	none	IIHF WM	Moscow	Lenin Stadium	55,000	Soviet Union 4–Sweden 4
November 8, 1962	none	SEL	Gothenburg	Ullevi Stadium	23,192	Frolunda 3–Djurgarden 2
September 28, 1991	none	NHL	Las Vegas	Caesar's Palace	13,000	Los Angeles Kings 5–New York Rangers 2
October 6, 2001	Cold War	NCAA	East Lansing	Spartan Stadium	74,554	Michigan State University 3–University of Michigan 3
November 22, 2003	Heritage Classic	NHL	Edmonton	Commonwealth Stadium	57,167	Montreal 4–Edmonton 3
February 11, 2006	Frozen Tundra Classic	NCAA	Green Bay	Lambeau Field	40,890	Ohio State 2–Wisconsin 4
January 14, 2007	Tatzen Derby	SUI	Bern	Strade de Suisse	30,076	Langnau 2–Bern 5
January 1, 2008	Winter Classic 1	NHL	Buffalo	Ralph Wilson Stadium	71,217	Pittsburgh 2–Buffalo 1 (SO)
January 10, 2008	All-Star Game	KHL	Moscow	Red Square	3,000	Team Jagr 7–Team Yashin 6
January 1, 2009	Winter Classic 2	NHL	Chicago	Wrigley Field	40,818	Detroit 6–Chicago 4
December 28, 2009	none	SEL	Gothenburg	Ullevi Stadium	31,144	Frolunda 4–Farjestad 1
January 1, 2010	Winter Classic 3	NHL	Boston	Fenway Park	38,112	Boston 2–Philadelphia 1
January 8, 2010	Frozen Fenway	NCAA	Boston	Fenway Park	6,889	New Hampshire 5–Northeastern 3 (women)
January 8, 2010	Frozen Fenway	NCAA	Boston	Fenway Park	38,472	Boston University 3–Boston College 2
January 9, 2010	none	AUT	Klagenfurt	Sportpark	30,500	Klagenfurt 1–Villach 3

Date	Event	League	City	Venue	Attendance	Score
February 6, 2010	Camp Randall Hockey Classic	NCAA	Madison	Camp Randall Stadium	8,263	Wisconsin 6–Bemidji State 1 (women)
February 6, 2010	Camp Randall Hockey Classic	NCAA	Madison	Camp Randall Stadium	55,031	Wisconsin 3–Michigan 2
February 20, 2010	Mirabito Outdoor Classic	AHL	Syracuse	New York State Fairgrounds	21,502	Syracuse 2–Binghamton 1
April 8, 2010	Frozen Four Semi-Finals 1	NCAA	Detroit	Ford Field	34,954	Wisconsin 8–Rochester 1
April 8, 2010	Frozen Four Semi-Finals 2	NCAA	Detroit	Ford Field	34,954	Boston College 7–Miami (Ohio) 1
April 10, 2010	Frozen Four Final	NCAA	Detroit	Ford Field	37,592	Boston College 5–Wisconsin 0
May 7, 2010	none	IIHF WM	Gelsenkirchen	Veltins Arena	77,803	Germany 2–United States 1 (OT)
December 11, 2010	The Big Chill at the Big House	NCAA	Ann Arbour	Michigan Stadium	104,173	Michigan 5–Michigan State 0
December 26, 2010	none	SEL	Karlstad	Löfbergs Lila Utomhusarena	15,274	Farjestad 5–Frolunda 2
January 1, 2011	Winter Classic 4	NHL	Pittsburgh	Heinz Field	68,111	Washington 3–Pittsburgh 1
January 9, 2011	none	IIHF WM20-III	Mexico City	Zocalo Square	3,000	Mexico 8–Bulgaria 0
February 5, 2011	Talviklassikko	FIN	Helsinki	Olympic Stadium	36,644	HIFK 4–Jokerit 3
February 20, 2011	Heritage Classic 2	NHL	Calgary	McMahon Stadium	41,022	Calgary 4–Montreal 0
January 2, 2012	Winter Classic 5	NHL	Philadelphia	Citizens Bank Park	46,967	NY Rangers 3–Philadelphia 2

NHL HISTORY

ALL-TIME LEADERS

MOST GAMES

1,767	Gordie Howe
1,756	Mark Messier
1,731	Ron Francis
1,652	Mark Recchi
1,651	Chris Chelios
1,639	Dave Andreychuk

MOST POINTS, REGULAR SEASON

2,857	Wayne Gretzky
1,887	Mark Messier
1,850	Gordie Howe
1,798	Ron Francis
1,771	Marcel Dionne

MOST GOALS, REGULAR SEASON

894	Wayne Gretzky
801	Gordie Howe
741	Brett Hull
731	Marcel Dionne
717	Phil Esposito

MOST ASSISTS, REGULAR SEASON

1,963	Wayne Gretzky
1,249	Ron Francis
1,193	Mark Messier
1,169	Ray Bourque
1,135	Paul Coffey

MOST PENALTY MINUTES, REGULAR SEASON

3,966	Dave "Tiger" Williams
3,565	Dale Hunter
3,515	Tie Domi
3,381	Marty McSorley
3,300	Bob Probert

MOST GAMES, GOALIE, REGULAR SEASON

1,191	Martin Brodeur*
1,029	Patrick Roy
971	Terry Sawchuk
963	Ed Belfour
943	Curtis Joseph

MOST WINS, GOALIE, REGULAR SEASON

656	Martin Brodeur*
551	Patrick Roy
484	Ed Belfour
454	Curtis Joseph
447	Terry Sawchuk

MOST SHUTOUTS, GOALIE, REGULAR SEASON

119	Martin Brodeur*
103	Terry Sawchuk
94	George Hainsworth
84	Glenn Hall
82	Jacques Plante

* active

YEAR-BY-YEAR STANDINGS AND STANLEY CUP FINALS RESULTS

After playoff scores, goalies who have registered a shutout will appear in square brackets (i.e., [Broda] means Turk Broda registered a shutout). All overtime goals are also recorded.

1917–18

First Half

	GP	W	L	GF	GA	PTS
Canadiens	14	10	4	81	47	20
Arenas	14	8	6	71	75	16
Ottawa	14	5	9	67	79	10
Wanderers*	6	1	5	17	35	2

Second Half

Arenas	8	5	3	37	34	10
Ottawa	8	4	4	35	35	8
Canadiens	8	3	5	34	37	6

* Wanderers' rink burned down on January 2, 1918, and team withdrew from league; Arenas and Canadiens each counted a win for defaulted games with the Wanderers
* winner of first half played winner of second half in a two-game total-goals series for a place in the Stanley Cup finals against the winner of the Pacific Coast Hockey Association and the Western Canada Hockey League; if one team won both halves, it went to the best-of-five Stanley Cup finals automatically.
* from 1917–21, games were played until a winner was decided

NHL Finals

| March 11 | Canadiens 3 at Arenas 7 |
| March 13 | Arenas 3 at Canadiens 4 |

Arenas won two-game total-goals series 10–7

Stanley Cup Finals

March 20	Vancouver 3 at Toronto 5
March 23	Vancouver 6 at Toronto 4
March 26	Vancouver 3 at Toronto 6
March 28	Vancouver 8 at Toronto 1
March 30	Vancouver 1 at Toronto 2

Toronto won best-of-five finals 3–2

1918–19

First Half

	GP	W	L	GF	GA	PTS
Canadiens	10	7	3	57	50	14
Ottawa	10	5	5	39	39	10
Arenas	10	3	7	42	49	6

Second Half

	GP	W	L	GF	GA	PTS
Ottawa	8	7	1	32	14	14
Canadiens	8	3	5	31	28	6
Arenas	8	2	6	22	43	4

- the 1918–19 season was supposed to be, like the ones before and after it, a 24-game schedule; however, when Canadiens and Ottawa clinched first place in both halves early, Arenas manager Charlie Querrie refused to play the remaining games, fearing a lack of fan interest; the league almost sued the Arenas, but instead Canadiens and Ottawa played a best-of-seven, rather than a two-game total-goals series, to create extra home dates for the clubs

NHL Finals

February 22   Ottawa 4 at Canadiens 8
February 27   Canadiens 5 at Ottawa 3
March 1   Ottawa 3 at Canadiens 6
March 3   Canadiens 3 at Ottawa 6
March 6   Ottawa 2 at Canadiens 4
Canadiens won best-of-seven series 4–1

Stanley Cup Finals

March 19   Canadiens 0 at Seattle 7 [Holmes]
March 22   Canadiens 4 at Seattle 2
March 24   Canadiens 2 at Seattle 7
March 26   Canadiens 0 at Seattle 0 (20:00 OT) [Vezina/Holmes]
March 29   Canadiens 4 at Seattle 3 (Jack McDonald 15:57 OT)

Finals cancelled after five games because of Spanish influenza and the death of Canadiens player Joe Hall

1919–20

First Half

	GP	W	L	GP	GA	PTS
Ottawa	12	9	3	59	23	18
Canadiens	12	8	4	62	51	16
St. Pats	12	5	7	52	62	10
Bulldogs	12	2	10	44	81	4

Second Half

	GP	W	L	GP	GA	PTS
Ottawa	12	10	2	62	41	20
St. Pats	12	7	5	67	44	14
Canadiens	12	5	7	67	62	10
Bulldogs	12	2	10	47	96	4

No NHL finals because Ottawa won both halves

Stanley Cup Finals

March 22	Seattle 2 at Ottawa 3
March 24	Seattle 0 at Ottawa 3 [Benedict]
March 27	Seattle 3 at Ottawa 1
March 30	Seattle 5 Ottawa 2*
April 1	Ottawa 6 Seattle 1*

Ottawa won best-of-five finals 3–2

* played in Toronto because of poor ice conditions in Ottawa

1920–21

First Half

	GP	W	L	GP	GA	PTS
Ottawa	10	8	2	49	23	16
St. Pats	10	5	5	39	47	10
Canadiens	10	4	6	37	51	8
Hamilton	10	3	7	34	38	6

Second Half

	GP	W	L	GP	GA	PTS
St. Pats	14	10	4	66	53	20
Canadiens	14	9	5	75	48	18
Ottawa	14	6	8	48	52	12
Hamilton	14	3	11	58	94	6

NHL Finals
    March 10   St. Pats 0 at Ottawa 5 [Benedict]
    March 15   Ottawa 2 at St. Pats 0 [Benedict]
    Ottawa won two-game total-goals series 7–0

Stanley Cup Finals
    March 21   Ottawa 1 at Vancouver 3
    March 24   Ottawa 4 at Vancouver 3
    March 28   Ottawa 3 at Vancouver 2
    March 31   Ottawa 2 at Vancouver 3
    April 4   Ottawa 2 at Vancouver 1
    Ottawa won best-of-five finals 3–2

1921–22

	GP	W	L	T	GF	GA	PTS
Ottawa	24	14	8	2	106	84	30
St. Pats	24	13	10	1	98	97	27
Canadiens	24	12	11	1	88	94	25
Hamilton	24	7	17	0	88	105	14

• overtime limited to 20 minutes (not sudden-death); minor penalties reduced from three to two minutes
• top two teams advance to playoffs; winner met the Pacific Coast Hockey Association–Western Canadian Hockey League champion for the Stanley Cup

NHL Finals
    March 11   Ottawa 4 at St. Pats 5
    March 13   St. Pats 0 at Ottawa 0 [Roach/Benedict]
    St. Pats won two-game total-goals series 5–4

Stanley Cup Finals
    March 17   Vancouver 4 at St. Pats 3
    March 21   Vancouver 1 at St. Pats 2 (Babe Dye 4:50 OT)
    March 23   Vancouver 3 at St. Pats 0 [Lehman]
    March 25   Vancouver 0 at St. Pats 6 [Roach]
    March 28   Vancouver 1 at St. Pats 5
    St. Pats won best-of-five finals 3–2

1922–23

	GP	W	L	T	GF	GA	PTS
Ottawa	24	14	9	1	77	54	29
Canadiens	24	13	9	2	73	61	28
St. Pats	24	13	10	1	82	88	27
Hamilton	24	6	18	0	81	110	12

NHL Finals
March 7   Ottawa 2 at Canadiens 0 [Benedict]
March 9   Canadiens 2 at Ottawa 1
Ottawa won two-game total-goals series 3–2

Stanley Cup Playoffs
March 16   Ottawa 1 at Vancouver 0 [Benedict]
March 19   Ottawa 1 at Vancouver 4
March 23   Ottawa 3 at Vancouver 2
March 26   Ottawa 5 at Vancouver 1
Ottawa won best-of-five semifinals 3–1

Stanley Cup Finals
March 29   Ottawa 2 Edmonton 1 (Cy Denneny 2:08 OT)*
March 31   Ottawa 1 Edmonton 0 [Benedict]*
Ottawa won best-of-three finals 2–0
* games played at Vancouver

1923–24

	GP	W	L	T	GF	GA	PTS
Ottawa	24	16	8	0	74	54	32
Canadiens	24	13	11	0	59	48	26
St. Pats	24	10	14	0	59	85	20
Hamilton	24	9	15	0	63	68	18

NHL Finals
March 8   Ottawa 0 at Canadiens 1 [Vezina]
March 11   Canadiens 4 at Ottawa 2
Canadiens won two-game total-goals series 5–2

Stanley Cup Playoffs
March 18   Vancouver 2 at Canadiens 3
March 20   Vancouver 1 at Canadiens 2
Canadiens won best-of-three semifinals 2–0

Stanley Cup Finals
    March 22   Calgary 1 at Canadiens 6
    March 25   Canadiens 3 Calgary 0 [Vezina]*
    Canadiens won best-of-three finals 2–0
    * played at Ottawa

1924–25

	GP	W	L	T	GF	GA	PTS
Hamilton	30	19	10	1	90	60	39
St. Pats	30	19	11	0	90	84	38
Canadiens	30	17	11	2	93	56	36
Ottawa	30	17	12	1	83	66	35
Maroons	30	9	19	2	45	65	20
Boston	30	6	24	0	49	119	12

• the top two teams (Hamilton and Toronto) were supposed to compete for the NHL championship
  and the right to advance to the Stanley Cup Finals against the WCHL winners; however, the Tigers'
  players demanded more money for these extra games and the NHL simply disqualified the team;
  thus, the St. Pats played the Canadiens.

NHL Finals
    March 13   Canadiens 2 at St. Pats 0
    March 19   St. Pats 2 at Canadiens 3
    Canadiens won two-game total-goals series 5–2

Stanley Cup Finals
    March 21   Canadiens 2 at Victoria 5
    March 23   Canadiens 1 at Victoria 3*
    March 27   Canadiens 4 at Victoria 2
    March 30   Canadiens 1 at Victoria 6
    Victoria won best-of-five finals 3–1
    * played at Vancouver

1925–26

	GP	W	L	T	GF	GA	PTS
Ottawa	36	24	8	4	77	42	52
Maroons	36	20	11	5	91	73	45
Pirates	36	19	16	1	82	70	39
Boston	36	17	15	4	92	85	38
Americans	36	12	20	4	68	89	28
St. Pats	36	12	21	3	92	114	27
Canadiens	36	11	24	1	79	108	23

NHL Finals

March 25   Ottawa 1 at Maroons 1
March 27   Maroons 1 at Ottawa 0 [Benedict]
Maroons win two-game total-goals finals 2–1

Stanley Cup Finals

March 30   Victoria 0 at Maroons 3 [Benedict]
April 1   Victoria 0 at Maroons 3 [Benedict]
April 3   Victoria 3 at Maroons 2
April 6   Victoria 0 at Maroons 2 [Benedict]
Maroons won best-of-five finals 3–1

1926–27

Canadian Division

	GP	W	L	T	GF	GA	PTS
Ottawa	44	30	10	4	86	69	64
Canadiens	44	28	14	2	99	67	58
Maroons	44	20	20	4	71	68	44
Americans	44	17	25	2	82	91	36
Toronto*	44	15	24	5	79	94	35

* on February 14, 1927, the St. Pats changed their name to Maple Leafs

American Division

	GP	W	L	T	GF	GA	PTS
Rangers	44	25	13	6	95	72	56
Boston	44	21	20	3	97	89	45
Chicago	44	19	22	3	115	116	41
Pirates	44	15	26	3	79	108	33
Cougars	44	12	28	4	76	105	28

Stanley Cup Finals

April 7   Ottawa 0 at Boston 0* [Connell/Winkler]
April 9   Ottawa 3 at Boston 1
April 11   Boston 1 at Ottawa 1**
April 13   Boston 1 at Ottawa 3
Ottawa won best-of-five finals 2–0–2

* two 10-minute overtime periods
** one 20-minute overtime period

1927–28

Canadian Division

	GP	W	L	T	GF	GA	PTS
Canadiens	44	26	11	7	116	48	59
Maroons	44	24	14	6	96	77	54
Ottawa	44	20	14	10	78	57	50
Toronto	44	18	18	8	89	88	44
Americans	44	11	27	6	63	128	28

American Division

	GP	W	L	T	GF	GA	PTS
Boston	44	20	13	11	77	70	51
Rangers	44	19	16	9	94	79	47
Pirates	44	19	17	8	67	76	46
Cougars	44	19	19	6	88	79	44
Chicago	44	7	34	3	68	134	17

• overtime limited to 10 minutes of sudden-death; forward passing now allowed in defending zone

Stanley Cup Finals

April 5   Rangers 0 at Maroons 2 [Benedict]
April 7   Rangers 2 at Maroons 1 (Frank Boucher 7:05 OT)
April 10   Rangers 0 at Maroons 2 [Benedict]
April 12   Rangers 1 at Maroons 0 [Miller]
April 14   Rangers 2 at Maroons 1
Rangers won best-of-five finals 3–2

1928–29

Canadian Division

	GP	W	L	T	GF	GA	PTS
Canadiens	44	22	7	15	71	43	59
Americans	44	19	13	12	53	53	50
Toronto	44	21	18	5	85	69	47
Ottawa	44	14	17	13	54	67	41
Maroons	44	15	20	9	67	65	39

American Division

Boston	44	26	13	5	89	52	57
Rangers	44	21	13	10	72	65	52
Cougars	44	19	16	9	72	63	47
Pirates	44	9	27	8	46	80	26
Chicago	44	7	29	8	33	85	22

- overtime set at 10 minutes without sudden-death; passing allowed into, but not within, the offensive zone
- the two division winners played a best-of-five and the two second place teams and third-place teams played two-game total-goals series; those two winners then played to see who would play the winner of the two division champions' series

Stanley Cup Finals

March 28   Rangers 0 at Boston 2 [Thompson]
March 29   Boston 2 at Rangers 1
Boston won best-of-three finals 2–0

1929–30

Canadian Division

	GP	W	L	T	GF	GA	PTS
Maroons	44	23	16	5	141	114	51
Canadiens	44	21	14	9	142	114	51
Ottawa	44	21	15	8	138	118	50
Toronto	44	17	21	6	116	124	40
Americans	44	14	25	5	113	161	33

American Division

Boston	44	38	5	1	179	98	77
Chicago	44	21	18	5	117	111	47
Rangers	44	17	17	10	136	143	44
Falcons	44	14	24	6	117	133	34
Pirates	44	5	36	3	102	185	13

* forward passing allowed in all three zones, producing twice the number of goals this season over last

Stanley Cup Finals

April 1   Canadiens 3 at Boston 0 [Hainsworth]
April 3   Boston 3 at Canadiens 4
Canadiens won best-of-three finals 2–0

1930–31

Canadian Division

	GP	W	L	T	GF	GA	PTS
Canadiens	44	26	10	8	129	89	60
Toronto	44	22	13	9	118	99	53
Maroons	44	20	18	6	105	106	46
Americans	44	18	16	10	76	74	46
Ottawa	44	10	30	4	91	142	24

American Division

	GP	W	L	T	GF	GA	PTS
Boston	44	28	10	6	143	90	62
Chicago	44	24	17	3	108	78	51
Rangers	44	19	16	9	106	87	47
Falcons	44	16	21	7	102	105	39
Quakers	44	4	36	4	76	184	12

Stanley Cup Finals

April 3	Canadiens 2 at Chicago 1
April 5	Canadiens 1 at Chicago 2 (Johnny Gottselig 24:50 OT)
April 9	Chicago 3 at Canadiens 2 (Cy Wentworth 53:50 OT)
April 11	Chicago 2 at Canadiens 4
April 14	Chicago 0 at Canadiens 2 [Hainsworth]

Canadiens won best-of-five finals 3–2

1931–32

Canadian Division

	GP	W	L	T	GF	GA	PTS
Canadiens	48	25	16	7	128	111	57
Toronto	48	23	18	7	155	127	53
Maroons	48	19	22	7	142	139	45
Americans	48	16	24	8	95	142	40

American Division

	GP	W	L	T	GF	GA	PTS
Rangers	48	23	17	8	134	112	54
Chicago	48	18	19	11	86	101	47
Falcons	48	18	20	10	95	108	46
Boston	48	15	21	12	122	117	42

Stanley Cup Finals

April 5	Toronto 6 at Rangers 4
April 7	Toronto 6 at Rangers 2*
April 9	Rangers 4 at Toronto 6

Toronto won best-of-five finals 3–0

* played at Boston because Madison Square Garden unavailable April 7 because of circus; because of the scores in the finals (6–4, 6–2, 6–4) this series has long been dubbed the "Tennis Series"
* all members of this Toronto team were given gold coins by Conn Smythe as lifetime passes to the Gardens

1932–33

Canadian Division

	GP	W	L	T	GF	GA	PTS
Toronto	48	24	18	6	119	111	54
Maroons	48	22	20	6	135	119	50
Canadiens	48	18	25	5	92	115	41
Americans	48	15	22	11	91	118	41
Ottawa	48	11	27	10	88	131	32

American Division

	GP	W	L	T	GF	GA	PTS
Boston	48	25	15	8	124	88	58
Detroit	48	25	15	8	111	93	58
Rangers	48	23	17	8	135	107	54
Chicago	48	16	20	12	88	101	44

Stanley Cup Finals

April 4	Toronto 1 at Rangers 5
April 8	Rangers 3 at Toronto 1
April 11	Rangers 2 at Toronto 3
April 13	Rangers 1 at Toronto 0 (Bill Cook 7:33 OT) [Aitkenhead]

Rangers won best-of-five finals 3–1

1933–34

Canadian Division

	GP	W	L	T	GF	GA	PTS
Toronto	48	26	13	9	174	119	61
Canadiens	48	22	20	6	99	101	50
Maroons	48	19	18	11	117	122	49
Americans	48	15	23	10	104	132	40
Ottawa	48	13	29	6	115	143	32

American Division

Detroit	48	24	14	10	113	98	58
Chicago	48	20	17	11	88	83	51
Rangers	48	21	19	8	120	113	50
Boston	48	18	25	5	111	130	41

Stanley Cup Finals

April 3	Chicago 2 at Detroit 1 (Paul Thompson 21:10 OT)
April 5	Chicago 4 at Detroit 1
April 8	Detroit 5 at Chicago 2
April 10	Detroit 0 at Chicago 1 (Mush March 30:05 OT) [Gardiner]

Chicago won best-of-five finals 3–1

1934–35

Canadian Division

	GP	W	L	T	GF	GA	PTS
Toronto	48	30	14	4	157	111	64
Maroons	48	24	19	5	123	92	53
Canadiens	48	19	23	6	110	145	44
Americans	48	12	27	9	100	142	33
Eagles	48	11	31	6	86	144	28

American Division

Boston	48	26	16	6	129	112	58
Chicago	48	26	17	5	118	88	57
Rangers	48	22	20	6	137	139	50
Detroit	48	19	22	7	127	114	45

Stanley Cup Finals

April 4	Maroons 3 at Toronto 2 (Dave Trottier 5:28 OT)
April 6	Maroons 3 at Toronto 1
April 9	Toronto 1 at Maroons 4

Maroons won best-of-five finals 3–0

1935–36

Canadian Division

	GP	W	L	T	GF	GA	PTS
Maroons	48	22	16	10	114	106	54
Toronto	48	23	19	6	126	106	52
Americans	48	16	25	7	109	122	39
Canadiens	48	11	26	11	82	123	33

American Division

	GP	W	L	T	GF	GA	PTS
Detroit	48	24	16	8	124	103	56
Boston	48	22	20	6	92	83	50
Chicago	48	21	19	8	93	92	50
Rangers	48	19	17	12	91	96	50

Stanley Cup Finals

April 5	Toronto 1 at Detroit 3
April 7	Toronto 4 at Detroit 9
April 9	Detroit 3 at Toronto 4 (Buzz Boll 0:31 OT)
April 11	Detroit 3 at Toronto 2

Detroit won best-of-five finals 3–1

1936–37

Canadian Division

	GP	W	L	T	GF	GA	PTS
Canadiens	48	24	18	6	115	111	54
Maroons	48	22	17	9	126	110	53
Toronto	48	22	21	5	119	115	49
Americans	48	15	29	4	122	161	34

American Division

	GP	W	L	T	GF	GA	PTS
Detroit	48	25	14	9	128	102	59
Boston	48	23	18	7	120	110	53
Rangers	48	19	20	9	117	106	47
Chicago	48	14	27	7	99	131	35

Stanley Cup Finals

April 6	Detroit 1 at Rangers 5
April 8	Rangers 2 at Detroit 4
April 11	Rangers 1 at Detroit 0 [Kerr]

April 13   Rangers 0 at Detroit 1 [Robertson]
April 15   Rangers 0 at Detroit 3 [Robertson]
Detroit won best-of-five finals 3–2

1937–38

Canadian Division

	GP	W	L	T	GF	GA	PTS
Toronto	48	24	15	9	151	127	57
Americans	48	19	18	11	110	111	49
Canadiens	48	18	17	13	123	128	49
Maroons	48	12	30	6	101	149	30

American Division

	GP	W	L	T	GF	GA	PTS
Boston	48	30	11	7	142	89	67
Rangers	48	27	15	6	149	96	60
Chicago	48	14	25	9	97	139	37
Detroit	48	12	25	11	99	133	35

Stanley Cup Finals

April 5   Chicago 3 at Toronto 1
April 7   Chicago 1 at Toronto 5
April 10   Toronto 1 at Chicago 2
April 12   Toronto 1 at Chicago 4
Chicago won best-of-five finals 3–1

1938–39

	GP	W	L	T	GF	GA	PTS
Boston	48	36	10	2	156	76	74
Rangers	48	26	16	6	149	105	58
Toronto	48	19	20	9	114	107	47
Americans	48	17	21	10	119	157	44
Detroit	48	18	24	6	107	128	42
Canadiens	48	15	24	9	115	146	39
Chicago	48	12	28	8	91	132	32

• only the last-place team did not qualify for the playoffs under the new one-division, seven-team format; the first- and second-place team played a best-of-seven to advance to the finals; the second played third and fourth played fifth in best-of-three, the two winners playing another best-of-three to advance to the finals

Stanley Cup Finals

April 6	Toronto 1 at Boston 2
April 9	Toronto 3 at Boston 2 (Doc Romnes 10:38 OT)
April 11	Boston 3 at Toronto 1
April 13	Boston 2 at Toronto 0 [Brimsek]
April 16	Toronto 1 at Boston 3

Boston won best-of-seven finals 4–1

1939–40

	GP	W	L	T	GF	GA	PTS
Boston	48	31	12	5	170	98	67
Rangers	48	27	11	10	136	77	64
Toronto	48	25	17	6	134	110	56
Chicago	48	23	19	6	112	120	52
Detroit	48	16	26	6	90	126	38
Americans	48	15	29	4	106	140	34
Canadiens	48	10	33	5	90	167	25

Stanley Cup Finals

April 2	Toronto 1 at Rangers 2 (Alf Pike 15:30 OT)
April 3	Toronto 2 at Rangers 6
April 6	Rangers 1 at Toronto 2
April 9	Rangers 0 at Toronto 3 [Broda]
April 11	Rangers 2 at Toronto 1 (Muzz Patrick 31:43 OT)*
April 13	Rangers 3 at Toronto 2 (Bryan Hextall 2:07 OT)

Rangers won best-of-seven finals 4–2

* game could not be played at Madison Square Garden as it was previously booked for the circus

1940–41

	GP	W	L	T	GF	GA	PTS
Boston	48	27	8	13	168	102	67
Toronto	48	28	14	6	145	99	62
Detroit	48	21	16	11	112	102	53
Rangers	48	21	19	8	143	125	50
Chicago	48	16	25	7	112	139	39
Canadiens	48	16	26	6	121	147	38
Americans	48	8	29	11	99	186	27

Stanley Cup Finals

April 6	Detroit 2 at Boston 3
April 8	Detroit 1 at Boston 2
April 10	Boston 4 at Detroit 2
April 12	Boston 3 at Detroit 1

Boston won best-of-seven finals 4–0

1941–42

	GP	W	L	T	GF	GA	PTS
Rangers	48	29	17	2	177	143	60
Toronto	48	27	18	3	158	136	57
Boston	48	25	17	6	160	118	56
Chicago	48	22	23	3	145	155	47
Detroit	48	19	25	4	140	147	42
Canadiens	48	18	27	3	134	173	39
Brooklyn	48	16	29	3	133	175	35

Stanley Cup Finals

April 4	Detroit 3 at Toronto 2
April 7	Detroit 4 at Toronto 2
April 9	Toronto 2 at Detroit 5
April 12	Toronto 4 at Detroit 3
April 14	Detroit 3 at Toronto 9
April 16	Toronto 3 at Detroit 0 [Broda]
April 18	Detroit 1 at Toronto 3

Toronto won best-of-seven finals 4–3

* only time in NHL history that a team has trailed 3–0 in the finals and won the Stanley Cup

1942–43

	GP	W	L	T	GF	GA	PTS
Detroit	50	25	14	11	169	124	61
Boston	50	24	17	9	195	176	57
Toronto	50	22	19	9	198	159	53
Canadiens	50	19	19	12	181	191	50
Chicago	50	17	18	15	179	180	49
Rangers	50	11	31	8	161	253	30

• because of wartime restrictions on train schedules, overtime was eliminated as of November 21, 1942

• the top four teams qualified for the playoffs in the six-team league, and both rounds were best-of-seven

Stanley Cup Finals

April 1	Boston 2 at Detroit 6
April 4	Boston 3 at Detroit 4
April 7	Detroit 4 at Boston 0 [Mowers]
April 8	Detroit 2 at Boston 0 [Mowers]

Detroit won best-of-seven finals 4–0

1943–44

	GP	W	L	T	GF	GA	PTS
Canadiens	50	38	5	7	234	109	83
Detroit	50	26	18	6	214	177	58
Toronto	50	23	23	4	214	174	50
Chicago	50	22	23	5	178	187	49
Boston	50	19	26	5	223	268	43
Rangers	50	6	39	5	162	310	17

Stanley Cup Finals

April 4	Chicago 1 at Canadiens 5
April 6	Canadiens 3 at Chicago 1
April 9	Canadiens 3 at Chicago 2
April 13	Chicago 4 at Canadiens 5 (Toe Blake 9:12 OT)

Canadiens won best-of-seven finals 4–0

1944–45

	GP	W	L	T	GF	GA	PTS
Canadiens	50	38	8	4	228	121	80
Detroit	50	31	14	5	218	161	67
Toronto	50	24	22	4	183	161	52
Boston	50	16	30	4	179	219	36
Chicago	50	13	30	7	141	194	33
Rangers	50	11	29	10	154	247	32

Stanley Cup Finals

April 6	Toronto 1 at Detroit 0 [McCool]
April 8	Toronto 2 at Detroit 0 [McCool]
April 12	Detroit 0 at Toronto 1 [McCool]
April 14	Detroit 5 at Toronto 3
April 19	Toronto 0 at Detroit 2 [Lumley]
April 21	Detroit 1 at Toronto 0 (Ed Bruneteau 14:16 OT) [Lumley]
April 22	Toronto 2 at Detroit 1

Toronto won best-of-seven finals 4–3

1945–46

	GP	W	L	T	GF	GA	PTS
Canadiens	50	28	17	5	172	134	61
Boston	50	24	18	8	167	156	56
Chicago	50	23	20	7	200	178	53
Detroit	50	20	20	10	146	159	50
Toronto	50	19	24	7	174	185	45
Rangers	50	13	28	9	144	191	35

Stanley Cup Finals

March 30   Boston 3 at Canadiens 4 (Maurice Richard 9:08 OT)
April 2   Boston 2 at Canadiens 3 (Jimmy Peters 16:55 OT)
April 4   Canadiens 4 at Boston 2
April 7   Canadiens 2 at Boston 3 (Terry Reardon 15:13 OT)
April 9   Boston 3 at Canadiens 6
Canadiens won best-of-seven finals 4–1

1946–47

	GP	W	L	T	GF	GA	PTS
Canadiens	60	34	16	10	189	138	78
Toronto	60	31	19	10	209	172	72
Boston	60	26	23	11	190	175	63
Detroit	60	22	27	11	190	193	55
Rangers	60	22	32	6	167	186	50
Chicago	60	19	37	4	193	274	42

Stanley Cup Finals

April 8   Toronto 0 at Canadiens 6 [Durnan]
April 10   Toronto 4 at Canadiens 0 [Broda]
April 12   Canadiens 2 at Toronto 4
April 15   Canadiens 1 at Toronto 2 (Syl Apps 16:36 OT)
April 17   Toronto 1 at Canadiens 3
April 19   Canadiens 1 at Toronto 2
Toronto won best-of-seven finals 4–2

1947–48

	GP	W	L	T	GF	GA	PTS
Toronto	60	32	15	13	182	143	77
Detroit	60	30	18	12	187	148	72
Boston	60	23	24	13	167	168	59
Rangers	60	21	26	13	176	201	55
Canadiens	60	20	29	11	147	169	51
Chicago	60	20	34	6	195	225	46

Stanley Cup Finals
April 7   Detroit 3 at Toronto 5
April 10   Detroit 2 at Toronto 4
April 11   Toronto 2 at Detroit 0 [Broda]
April 14   Toronto 7 at Detroit 2
Toronto won best-of-seven finals 4–0

1948–49

	GP	W	L	T	GF	GA	PTS
Detroit	60	34	19	7	195	145	75
Boston	60	29	23	8	178	163	66
Canadiens	60	28	23	9	152	126	65
Toronto	60	22	25	13	147	161	57
Chicago	60	21	31	8	173	211	50
Rangers	60	18	31	11	133	172	47

Stanley Cup Finals
April 8   Toronto 3 at Detroit 2 (Joe Klukay 17:31 OT)
April 10   Toronto 3 at Detroit 1
April 13   Detroit 1 at Toronto 3
April 16   Detroit 1 at Toronto 3
Toronto won best-of-seven finals 4–0

1949–50

	GP	W	L	T	GF	GA	PTS
Detroit	70	37	19	14	229	164	88
Canadiens	70	29	22	19	172	150	77
Toronto	70	31	27	12	176	173	74
Rangers	70	28	31	11	170	189	67
Boston	70	22	32	16	198	228	60
Chicago	70	22	38	10	203	244	54

Stanley Cup Finals

April 11	Rangers 1 at Detroit 4
April 13	Detroit 1 Rangers 3*
April 15	Detroit 4 Rangers 0*[Lumley]
April 18	Rangers 4 at Detroit 3 (Don Raleigh 8:34 OT)
April 20	Rangers 2 at Detroit 1 (Don Raleigh 1:38 OT)
April 22	Rangers 4 at Detroit 5
April 23	Rangers 3 at Detroit 4 (Pete Babando 28:31 OT)**

Detroit won best-of-seven finals 4–3

* played at Toronto because Madison Square Garden was previously booked for the circus; games 6 and 7 played in Detroit because league by-laws stipulated a Stanley Cup–winning game could not be played on neutral ice

** first time in history the Cup was won on an OT goal in game 7

1950–51

	GP	W	L	T	GF	GA	PTS
Detroit	70	44	13	13	236	139	101
Toronto	70	41	16	13	212	138	95
Canadiens	70	25	30	15	173	184	65
Boston	70	22	30	18	178	197	62
Rangers	70	20	29	21	169	201	61
Chicago	70	13	47	10	171	280	36

Stanley Cup Finals

April 11	Canadiens 2 at Toronto 3 (Sid Smith 5:51 OT)
April 14	Canadiens 3 at Toronto 2 (Maurice Richard 2:55 OT)
April 17	Toronto 2 at Canadiens 1 (Ted Kennedy 4:47 OT)
April 19	Toronto 3 at Canadiens 2 (Harry Watson 5:15 OT)
April 21	Canadiens 2 at Toronto 3 (Bill Barilko 2:53 OT)

Toronto won best-of-seven finals 4–1

1951–52

	GP	W	L	T	GF	GA	PTS
Detroit	70	44	14	12	215	133	100
Canadiens	70	34	26	10	195	164	78
Toronto	70	29	25	16	168	157	74
Boston	70	25	29	16	162	176	66
Rangers	70	23	34	13	192	219	59
Chicago	70	17	44	9	158	241	43

Stanley Cup Finals

April 10	Detroit 3 at Canadiens 1
April 12	Detroit 2 at Canadiens 1
April 13	Canadiens 0 at Detroit 3 [Sawchuk]
April 15	Canadiens 0 at Detroit 3 [Sawchuk]

Detroit won best-of-seven finals 4–0

1952–53

	GP	W	L	T	GF	GA	PTS
Detroit	70	36	16	18	222	133	90
Canadiens	70	28	23	19	155	148	75
Boston	70	28	29	13	152	172	69
Chicago	70	27	28	15	169	175	69
Toronto	70	27	30	13	156	167	67
Rangers	70	17	37	16	152	211	50

Stanley Cup Finals

April 9	Boston 2 at Canadiens 4
April 11	Boston 4 at Canadiens 1
April 12	Canadiens 3 at Boston 0 [McNeil]
April 14	Canadiens 7 at Boston 3
April 16	Boston 0 at Canadiens 1 (Elmer Lach 1:22 OT) [McNeil]

Canadiens won best-of-seven finals 4–1

1953–54

	GP	W	L	T	GF	GA	PTS
Detroit	70	37	19	14	191	132	88
Canadiens	70	35	24	11	195	141	81
Toronto	70	32	24	14	152	131	78
Boston	70	32	28	10	177	181	74
Rangers	70	29	31	10	161	182	68
Chicago	70	12	51	7	133	242	31

Stanley Cup Finals

April 4	Canadiens 1 at Detroit 3
April 6	Canadiens 3 at Detroit 1
April 8	Detroit 5 at Canadiens 2
April 10	Detroit 2 at Canadiens 0 [Sawchuk]
April 11	Canadiens 1 at Detroit 0 (Ken Mosdell 5:45 OT) [McNeil]
April 13	Detroit 1 at Canadiens 4
April 16	Canadiens 1 at Detroit 2 (Tony Leswick 4:29 OT)

Detroit won best-of-seven finals 4–3

1954–55

	GP	W	L	T	GF	GA	PTS
Detroit	70	42	17	11	204	134	95
Canadiens	70	41	18	11	228	157	93
Toronto	70	24	24	22	147	135	70
Boston	70	23	26	21	169	188	67
Rangers	70	17	35	18	150	210	52
Chicago	70	13	40	17	161	235	43

Stanley Cup Finals

April 3	Canadiens 2 at Detroit 4
April 5	Canadiens 1 at Detroit 7
April 7	Detroit 2 at Canadiens 4
April 9	Detroit 3 at Canadiens 5
April 10	Canadiens 1 at Detroit 5
April 12	Detroit 3 at Canadiens 6
April 14	Canadiens 1 at Detroit 3

Detroit won best-of-seven finals 4–3

1955–56

	GP	W	L	T	GF	GA	PTS
Canadiens	70	45	15	10	222	131	100
Detroit	70	30	24	16	183	148	76
Rangers	70	32	28	10	204	203	74
Toronto	70	24	33	13	153	181	61
Boston	70	23	34	13	147	185	59
Chicago	70	19	39	12	155	216	50

Stanley Cup Finals

March 31	Detroit 4 at Canadiens 6
April 3	Detroit 1 at Canadiens 5
April 5	Canadiens 1 at Detroit 3
April 8	Canadiens 3 at Detroit 0 [Plante]
April 10	Detroit 1 at Canadiens 3

Canadiens won best-of-seven finals 4–1

1956–57

	GP	W	L	T	GF	GA	PTS
Detroit	70	38	20	12	198	157	88
Canadiens	70	35	23	12	210	155	82
Boston	70	34	24	12	195	174	80
Rangers	70	26	30	14	184	227	66
Toronto	70	21	34	15	174	192	57
Chicago	70	16	39	15	169	225	47

• penalized player allowed to return to the ice after a power-play goal has been scored by the opposition

Stanley Cup Finals

April 6   Boston 1 at Canadiens 5
April 9   Boston 0 at Canadiens 1 [Plante]
April 11   Canadiens 4 at Boston 2
April 14   Canadiens 0 at Boston 2 [Simmons]
April 16   Boston 1 at Canadiens 5
Canadiens won best-of-seven finals 4–1

1957–58

	GP	W	L	T	GF	GA	PTS
Canadiens	70	43	17	10	250	158	96
Rangers	70	32	25	13	195	188	77
Detroit	70	29	29	12	176	207	70
Boston	70	27	28	15	199	194	69
Chicago	70	24	39	7	163	202	55
Toronto	70	21	38	11	192	226	53

Stanley Cup Finals

April 8   Boston 1 at Canadiens 2
April 10   Boston 5 at Canadiens 2
April 13   Canadiens 3 at Boston 0 [Plante]
April 15   Canadiens 1 at Boston 3
April 17   Boston 2 at Canadiens 3 (Maurice Richard 5:45 OT)
April 20   Canadiens 5 at Boston 3
Canadiens won best-of-seven finals 4–2

1958–59

	GP	W	L	T	GF	GA	PTS
Canadiens	70	39	18	13	258	158	91
Boston	70	32	29	9	205	215	73
Chicago	70	28	29	13	197	208	69
Toronto	70	27	32	11	189	201	65
Rangers	70	26	32	12	201	217	64
Detroit	70	25	37	8	167	218	58

Stanley Cup Finals

April 9	Toronto 3 at Canadiens 5
April 11	Toronto 1 at Canadiens 3
April 14	Canadiens 2 at Toronto 3 (Dick Duff 10:06 OT)
April 16	Canadiens 3 at Toronto 2
April 18	Toronto 3 at Canadiens 5

Canadiens won best-of-seven finals 4–1

1959–60

	GP	W	L	T	GF	GA	PTS
Canadiens	70	40	18	12	255	178	92
Toronto	70	35	26	9	199	195	79
Chicago	70	28	29	13	191	180	69
Detroit	70	26	29	15	186	197	67
Boston	70	28	34	8	220	241	64
Rangers	70	17	38	15	187	247	49

Stanley Cup Finals

April 7	Toronto 2 at Canadiens 4
April 9	Toronto 1 at Canadiens 2
April 12	Canadiens 5 at Toronto 2
April 14	Canadiens 4 at Toronto 0 [Plante]

Canadiens won best-of-seven finals 4–0

1960–61

	GP	W	L	T	GF	GA	PTS
Canadiens	70	41	19	10	254	188	92
Toronto	70	39	19	12	234	176	90
Chicago	70	29	24	17	198	180	75
Detroit	70	25	29	16	195	215	66
Rangers	70	22	38	10	204	248	54
Boston	70	15	42	13	176	254	43

Stanley Cup Finals

April 6	Detroit 2 at Chicago 3
April 8	Chicago 1 at Detroit 3
April 10	Detroit 1 at Chicago 3
April 12	Chicago 1 at Detroit 2
April 14	Detroit 3 at Chicago 6
April 16	Chicago 5 at Detroit 1

Chicago won best-of-seven finals 4–2

1961–62

	GP	W	L	T	GF	GA	PTS
Canadiens	70	42	14	14	259	166	98
Toronto	70	37	22	11	232	180	85
Chicago	70	31	26	13	217	186	75
Rangers	70	26	32	12	195	207	64
Detroit	70	23	33	14	184	219	60
Boston	70	15	47	8	177	306	38

Stanley Cup Finals

April 10	Chicago 1 at Toronto 4
April 12	Chicago 2 at Toronto 3
April 15	Toronto 0 at Chicago 3 [Hall]
April 17	Toronto 1 at Chicago 4
April 19	Chicago 4 at Toronto 8
April 22	Toronto 2 at Chicago 1

Toronto won best-of-seven finals 4–2

1962–63

	GP	W	L	T	GF	GA	PTS
Toronto	70	35	23	12	221	180	82
Chicago	70	32	21	17	194	178	81
Canadiens	70	28	19	23	225	183	79
Detroit	70	32	25	13	200	194	77
Rangers	70	22	36	12	211	233	56
Boston	70	14	39	17	198	281	45

Stanley Cup Finals

April 9	Detroit 2 at Toronto 4
April 11	Detroit 2 at Toronto 4
April 14	Toronto 2 at Detroit 3
April 16	Toronto 4 at Detroit 2
April 18	Detroit 1 at Toronto 3

Toronto won best-of-seven finals 4–1

1963–64

	GP	W	L	T	GF	GA	PTS
Canadiens	70	36	21	13	209	167	85
Chicago	70	36	22	12	218	169	84
Toronto	70	33	25	12	192	172	78
Detroit	70	30	29	11	191	204	71
Rangers	70	22	38	10	186	242	54
Boston	70	18	40	12	170	212	48

Stanley Cup Finals

April 11	Detroit 2 at Toronto 3
April 14	Detroit 4 at Toronto 3 (Larry Jeffrey 7:52 OT)
April 16	Toronto 3 at Detroit 4
April 18	Toronto 4 at Detroit 2
April 21	Detroit 2 at Toronto 1
April 23	Toronto 4 at Detroit 3 (Bobby Baun 1:43 OT)
April 25	Detroit 0 at Toronto 4 [Bower]

Toronto won best-of-seven finals 4–3

1964–65

	GP	W	L	T	GF	GA	PTS
Detroit	70	40	23	7	224	175	87
Canadiens	70	36	23	11	211	185	83
Chicago	70	34	28	8	224	176	76
Toronto	70	30	26	14	204	173	74
Rangers	70	20	38	12	179	246	52
Boston	70	21	43	6	166	253	48

Stanley Cup Finals

April 17	Chicago 2 at Canadiens 3
April 20	Chicago 0 at Canadiens 2 [Worsley]
April 22	Canadiens 1 at Chicago 3
April 25	Canadiens 1 at Chicago 5
April 27	Chicago 0 at Canadiens 6 [Hodge]
April 29	Canadiens 1 at Chicago 2
May 1	Chicago 0 at Canadiens 4 [Worsley]

Canadiens won best-of-seven finals 4–3

1965–66

	GP	W	L	T	GF	GA	PTS
Canadiens	70	41	21	8	239	173	90
Chicago	70	37	25	8	240	187	82
Toronto	70	34	25	11	208	187	79
Detroit	70	31	27	12	221	194	74
Boston	70	21	43	6	174	275	48
Rangers	70	18	41	11	195	261	47

Stanley Cup Finals

April 24	Detroit 3 at Canadiens 2
April 26	Detroit 5 at Canadiens 2
April 28	Canadiens 4 at Detroit 2
May 1	Canadiens 2 at Detroit 1
May 3	Detroit 1 at Canadiens 5
May 5	Canadiens 3 at Detroit 2 (Henri Richard 2:20 OT)

Canadiens won best-of-seven finals 4–2

1966–67

	GP	W	L	T	GF	GA	PTS
Chicago	70	41	17	12	264	170	94
Canadiens	70	32	25	13	202	188	77
Toronto	70	32	27	11	204	211	75
Rangers	70	30	28	12	188	189	72
Detroit	70	27	39	4	212	241	58
Boston	70	17	43	10	182	253	44

Stanley Cup Finals

April 20	Toronto 2 at Canadiens 6
April 22	Toronto 3 at Canadiens 0 [Bower]
April 25	Canadiens 2 at Toronto 3 (Bob Pulford 28:26 OT)
April 27	Canadiens 6 at Toronto 2
April 29	Toronto 4 at Canadiens 1
May 2	Canadiens 1 at Toronto 3

Toronto won best-of-seven finals 4–2

1967–68

East Division

	GP	W	L	T	GF	GA	PTS
Canadiens	74	42	22	10	236	167	94
Rangers	74	39	23	12	226	183	90
Boston	74	37	27	10	259	216	84
Chicago	74	32	26	16	212	222	80
Toronto	74	33	31	10	209	176	76
Detroit	74	27	35	12	245	257	66

West Division

	GP	W	L	T	GF	GA	PTS
Philadelphia	74	31	32	11	173	179	73
Los Angeles	74	31	33	10	200	224	72
St. Louis	74	27	31	16	177	191	70
North Stars	74	27	32	15	191	226	69
Pittsburgh	74	27	34	13	195	216	67
Oakland	74	15	42	17	153	219	47

• top four teams in each division qualified for the playoffs

Stanley Cup Finals

May 5	Canadiens 3 at St. Louis 2 (Jacques Lemaire 1:41 OT)
May 7	Canadiens 1 at St. Louis 0 [Worsley]

May 9   St. Louis 3 at Canadiens 4 (Bobby Rousseau 1:13 OT)
May 11   St. Louis 2 at Canadiens 3
Canadiens won best-of-seven finals 4–0

1968–69

East Division

	GP	W	L	T	GF	GA	PTS
Canadiens	76	46	19	11	271	202	103
Boston	76	42	18	16	303	221	100
Rangers	76	41	26	9	231	196	91
Toronto	76	35	26	15	234	217	85
Detroit	76	33	31	12	239	221	78
Chicago	76	34	33	9	280	246	77

West Division

	GP	W	L	T	GF	GA	PTS
St. Louis	76	37	25	14	204	157	88
Oakland	76	29	36	11	219	251	69
Philadelphia	76	20	35	21	174	225	61
Los Angeles	76	24	42	10	185	260	58
Pittsburgh	76	20	45	11	189	252	51
North Stars	76	18	43	15	189	270	51

Stanley Cup Finals

April 27   St. Louis 1 at Canadiens 3
April 29   St. Louis 1 at Canadiens 3
May 1   Canadiens 4 at St. Louis 0 [Vachon]
May 4   Canadiens 2 at St. Louis 1
Canadiens won best-of-seven finals 4–0

1969–70

East Division

	GP	W	L	T	GF	GA	PTS
Chicago	76	45	22	9	250	170	99
Boston	76	40	17	19	277	216	99
Detroit	76	40	21	15	246	199	95
Rangers	76	38	22	16	246	189	92
Canadiens	76	38	22	16	244	201	92
Toronto	76	29	34	13	222	242	71

West Division

St. Louis	76	37	27	12	224	179	86
Pittsburgh	76	26	38	12	182	238	64
North Stars	76	19	35	22	224	257	60
Oakland	76	22	40	14	169	243	58
Philadelphia	76	17	35	24	197	225	58
Los Angeles	76	14	52	10	168	290	38

Stanley Cup Finals

May 3	Boston 6 at St. Louis 1
May 5	Boston 6 at St. Louis 2
May 7	St. Louis 1 at Boston 4
May 10	St. Louis 3 at Boston 4 (Bobby Orr 0:40 OT)

Boston won best-of-seven finals 4–0

1970–71

East Division

	GP	W	L	T	GF	GA	PTS
Boston	78	57	14	7	399	207	121
Rangers	78	49	18	11	259	177	109
Canadiens	78	42	23	13	291	216	97
Toronto	78	37	33	8	248	211	82
Buffalo	78	24	39	15	217	291	63
Vancouver	78	24	46	8	229	296	56
Detroit	78	22	45	11	209	308	55

West Division

	GP	W	L	T	GF	GA	PTS
Chicago	78	49	20	9	277	184	107
St. Louis	78	34	25	19	223	208	87
Philadelphia	78	28	33	17	207	225	73
North Stars	78	28	34	16	191	223	72
Los Angeles	78	25	40	13	239	303	63
Pittsburgh	78	21	37	20	221	240	62
California	78	20	53	5	199	320	45

Stanley Cup Finals

May 4	Canadiens 1 at Chicago 2 (Jim Pappin 21:11 OT)
May 6	Canadiens 3 at Chicago 5
May 9	Chicago 2 at Canadiens 4
May 11	Chicago 2 at Canadiens 5
May 13	Canadiens 0 at Chicago 2 [Esposito]

May 16	Chicago 3 at Canadiens 4	
May 18	Canadiens 3 at Chicago 2	

Canadiens won best-of-seven finals 4–3

1971–72

East Division

	GP	W	L	T	GF	GA	PTS
Boston	78	54	13	11	330	204	119
Rangers	78	48	17	13	317	192	109
Canadiens	78	46	16	16	307	205	108
Toronto	78	33	31	14	209	208	80
Detroit	78	33	35	10	261	262	76
Buffalo	78	16	43	19	203	289	51
Vancouver	78	20	50	8	203	297	48

West Division

	GP	W	L	T	GF	GA	PTS
Chicago	78	46	17	15	256	166	107
North Stars	78	37	29	12	212	191	86
St. Louis	78	28	39	11	208	247	67
Pittsburgh	78	26	38	14	220	258	66
Philadelphia	78	26	38	14	200	236	66
California	78	21	39	18	216	288	60
Los Angeles	78	20	49	9	206	305	49

Stanley Cup Finals

April 30	Rangers 5 at Boston 6	
May 2	Rangers 1 at Boston 2	
May 4	Boston 2 at Rangers 5	
May 7	Boston 3 at Rangers 2	
May 9	Rangers 3 at Boston 2	
May 11	Boston 3 at Rangers 0 [Johnston]	

Boston won best-of-seven finals 4–2

1972–73

East Division

	GP	W	L	T	GF	GA	PIM	PTS
Canadiens	78	52	10	16	329	184	783	120
Boston	78	51	22	5	330	235	1097	107
Rangers	78	47	23	8	297	208	765	102
Buffalo	78	37	27	14	257	219	940	88
Detroit	78	37	29	12	265	243	893	86
Toronto	78	27	41	10	247	279	716	64
Vancouver	78	22	47	9	233	339	943	53
Islanders	78	12	60	6	170	347	881	30

West Division

	GP	W	L	T	GF	GA	PIM	PTS
Chicago	78	42	27	9	284	225	864	93
Philadelphia	78	37	30	11	296	256	1756	85
North Stars	78	37	30	11	254	230	881	85
St. Louis	78	32	34	12	233	251	1195	76
Pittsburgh	78	32	37	9	257	265	866	73
Los Angeles	78	31	36	11	232	245	888	73
Flames	78	25	38	15	191	239	852	65
California	78	16	46	16	213	323	840	48

Stanley Cup Finals

April 29	Chicago 3 at Canadiens 8
May 1	Chicago 1 at Canadiens 4
May 3	Canadiens 4 at Chicago 7
May 6	Canadiens 4 at Chicago 0 [Dryden]
May 8	Chicago 8 at Canadiens 7
May 10	Canadiens 6 at Chicago 4

Canadiens won best-of-seven finals 4–2

1973–74

East Division

	GP	W	L	T	GF	GA	PTS
Boston	78	52	17	9	349	221	113
Canadiens	78	45	24	9	293	240	99
Rangers	78	40	24	14	300	251	94
Toronto	78	35	27	16	274	230	86
Buffalo	78	32	34	12	242	250	76
Detroit	78	29	39	10	255	319	68
Vancouver	78	24	43	11	224	296	59
Islanders	78	19	41	18	182	247	56

West Division

	GP	W	L	T	GF	GA	PTS
Philadelphia	78	50	16	12	273	164	112
Chicago	78	41	14	23	272	164	105
Los Angeles	78	33	33	12	233	231	78
Flames	78	30	34	14	214	238	74
Pittsburgh	78	28	41	9	242	273	65
St. Louis	78	26	40	12	206	248	64
North Stars	78	23	38	17	235	275	63
California	78	13	55	10	195	342	36

Stanley Cup Finals

May 7	Philadelphia 2 at Boston 3
May 9	Philadelphia 3 at Boston 2 (Bobby Clarke 12:01 OT)
May 12	Boston 1 at Philadelphia 4
May 14	Boston 2 at Philadelphia 4
May 16	Philadelphia 1 at Boston 5
May 19	Boston 0 at Philadelphia 1 [Parent]

Philadelphia won best-of-seven finals 4–2

1974–75

PRINCE OF WALES CONFERENCE
Adams Division

	GP	W	L	T	GF	GA	PTS
Buffalo	80	49	16	15	354	240	113
Boston	80	40	26	14	345	245	94
Toronto	80	31	33	16	280	309	78
California	80	19	48	13	212	316	51

Norris Division

	GP	W	L	T	GF	GA	PTS
Canadiens	80	47	14	19	374	225	113
Los Angeles	80	42	17	21	269	185	105
Pittsburgh	80	37	28	15	326	289	89
Detroit	80	23	45	12	259	335	58
Washington	80	8	67	5	181	446	21

CLARENCE CAMPBELL CONFERENCE
Patrick Division

	GP	W	L	T	GF	GA	PTS
Philadelphia	80	51	18	11	293	181	113
Rangers	80	37	29	14	319	276	88
Islanders	80	33	25	22	264	221	88
Flames	80	34	31	15	243	233	83

Smythe Division

	GP	W	L	T	GF	GA	PTS
Vancouver	80	38	32	10	271	254	86
St. Louis	80	35	31	14	269	267	84
Chicago	80	37	35	8	268	241	82
North Stars	80	23	50	7	221	341	53
Kansas City	80	15	54	11	184	328	41

• the top three teams in each division qualified for the playoffs; the four division champions received byes to the second round and all second- and third-place clubs were seeded 1–8 by points, #1 playing #8, #2 and #7, etc.; the first round was best-of-three, the subsequent rounds best-of-seven

Stanley Cup Finals

May 15	Buffalo 1 at Philadelphia 4
May 18	Buffalo 1 at Philadelphia 2
May 20	Philadelphia 4 at Buffalo 5 (Rene Robert 18:29 OT)
May 22	Philadelphia 2 at Buffalo 4
May 25	Buffalo 1 at Philadelphia 5
May 27	Philadelphia 2 at Buffalo 0 [Parent]

Philadelphia won best-of-seven finals 4–2

1975–76

PRINCE OF WALES CONFERENCE

Adams Division

	GP	W	L	T	GF	GA	PTS
Boston	80	48	15	17	313	237	113
Buffalo	80	46	21	13	339	240	105
Toronto	80	34	31	15	294	276	83
California	80	27	42	11	250	278	65

Norris Division

	GP	W	L	T	GF	GA	PTS
Canadiens	80	58	11	11	337	174	127
Los Angeles	80	38	33	9	263	265	85
Pittsburgh	80	35	33	12	339	303	82
Detroit	80	26	44	10	226	300	62
Washington	80	11	59	10	224	394	32

CLARENCE CAMPBELL CONFERENCE

Patrick Division

	GP	W	L	T	GF	GA	PTS
Philadelphia	80	51	13	16	348	209	118
Islanders	80	42	21	17	297	190	101
Flames	80	35	33	12	262	237	82
Rangers	80	29	42	9	262	333	67

Smythe Division

	GP	W	L	T	GF	GA	PTS
Chicago	80	32	30	18	254	261	82
Vancouver	80	33	32	15	271	272	81
St. Louis	80	29	37	14	249	290	72
North Stars	80	20	53	7	195	303	47
Kansas City	80	12	56	12	190	351	36

Stanley Cup Finals

May 9	Philadelphia 3 at Canadiens 4
May 11	Philadelphia 1 at Canadiens 2
May 13	Canadiens 3 at Philadelphia 2
May 16	Canadiens 5 at Philadelphia 3

Canadiens won best-of-seven finals 4–0

1976–77

PRINCE OF WALES CONFERENCE

Adams Division

	GP	W	L	T	GF	GA	PTS
Boston	80	49	23	8	312	240	106
Buffalo	80	48	24	8	301	220	104
Toronto	80	33	32	15	301	285	81
Cleveland	80	25	42	13	240	292	63

Norris Division

Canadiens	80	60	8	12	387	171	132
Los Angeles	80	34	31	15	271	241	83
Pittsburgh	80	34	33	13	240	252	81
Washington	80	24	42	14	221	307	62
Detroit	80	16	55	9	183	309	41

CLARENCE CAMPBELL CONFERENCE

Patrick Division

Philadelphia	80	48	16	16	323	213	112
Islanders	80	47	21	12	288	193	106
Flames	80	34	34	12	264	265	80
Rangers	80	29	37	14	272	310	64

Smythe Division

St. Louis	80	32	39	9	239	276	73
North Stars	80	23	39	18	240	310	64
Chicago	80	26	43	11	240	298	63
Vancouver	80	25	42	13	235	294	63
Rockies	80	20	46	14	226	307	54

Stanley Cup Finals

May 7	Boston 3 at Canadiens 7
May 10	Boston 0 at Canadiens 3 [Dryden]
May 12	Canadiens 4 at Boston 2
May 14	Canadiens 2 at Boston 1 (Jacques Lemaire 4:32 OT)

Canadiens won best-of-seven finals 4–0

1977–78

PRINCE OF WALES CONFERENCE

Adams Division

	GP	W	L	T	GF	GA	PTS
Boston	80	51	18	11	333	218	113
Buffalo	80	44	19	17	288	215	105
Toronto	80	41	29	10	271	237	92
Cleveland	80	22	45	13	230	325	57

Norris Division

	GP	W	L	T	GF	GA	PTS
Canadiens	80	59	10	11	359	183	129
Detroit	80	32	34	14	252	266	78
Los Angeles	80	31	34	15	243	245	77
Pittsburgh	80	25	37	18	254	321	68
Washington	80	17	49	14	195	321	48

CLARENCE CAMPBELL CONFERENCE

Patrick Division

	GP	W	L	T	GF	GA	PTS
Islanders	80	48	17	15	334	210	111
Philadelphia	80	45	20	15	296	200	105
Flames	80	34	27	19	274	252	87
Rangers	80	30	37	13	279	280	73

Smythe Division

	GP	W	L	T	GF	GA	PTS
Chicago	80	32	29	19	230	220	83
Rockies	80	19	40	21	257	305	59
Vancouver	80	20	43	17	239	320	57
St. Louis	80	20	47	13	195	304	53
North Stars	80	18	53	9	218	325	45

- all 1st- and 2nd-place teams qualified for playoffs and the next best four regardless of division also qualified

Stanley Cup Finals

May 13	Boston 1 at Canadiens 4
May 16	Boston 2 at Canadiens 3 (Guy Lafleur 13:09 OT)
May 18	Canadiens 0 at Boston 4 [Cheevers]
May 21	Canadiens 3 at Boston 4 (Bobby Schmautz 6:22 OT)
May 23	Boston 1 at Canadiens 4
May 25	Canadiens 4 at Boston 1

Canadiens won best-of-seven finals 4–2

1978–79

PRINCE OF WALES CONFERENCE

Adams Division

	GP	W	L	T	GF	GA	PTS
Boston	80	43	23	14	316	270	100
Buffalo	80	36	28	16	280	263	88
Toronto	80	34	33	13	267	252	81
North Stars	80	28	40	12	257	289	68

Norris Division

	GP	W	L	T	GF	GA	PTS
Canadiens	80	52	17	11	337	204	115
Pittsburgh	80	36	31	13	281	279	85
Los Angeles	80	34	34	12	292	286	80
Washington	80	24	41	15	273	338	63
Detroit	80	23	41	16	252	295	62

CLARENCE CAMPBELL CONFERENCE

Patrick Division

	GP	W	L	T	GF	GA	PTS
Islanders	80	51	15	14	358	214	116
Philadelphia	80	40	25	15	281	248	95
Rangers	80	40	29	11	316	292	91
Flames	80	41	31	8	327	280	90

Smythe Division

	GP	W	L	T	GF	GA	PTS
Chicago	80	29	36	15	244	277	73
Vancouver	80	25	42	13	217	291	63
St. Louis	80	18	50	12	249	348	48
Rockies	80	15	53	12	210	331	42

Stanley Cup Finals

May 13	Rangers 4 at Canadiens 1
May 15	Rangers 2 at Canadiens 6
May 17	Canadiens 4 at Rangers 1
May 19	Canadiens 4 at Rangers 3 (Serge Savard 7:25 OT)
May 21	Rangers 1 at Canadiens 4

Canadiens won best-of-seven finals 4–1

1979–80

PRINCE OF WALES CONFERENCE
Adams Division

	GP	W	L	T	GF	GA	PTS
Buffalo	80	47	17	16	318	201	110
Boston	80	46	21	13	310	234	105
North Stars	80	36	28	16	311	253	88
Toronto	80	35	40	5	304	327	75
Quebec	80	25	44	11	248	313	61

Norris Division

	GP	W	L	T	GF	GA	PTS
Canadiens	80	47	20	13	328	240	107
Los Angeles	80	30	36	14	290	313	74
Pittsburgh	80	30	37	13	251	303	73
Hartford	80	27	34	19	303	312	73
Detroit	80	26	43	11	268	306	63

CLARENCE CAMPBELL CONFERENCE
Patrick Division

	GP	W	L	T	GF	GA	PTS
Philadelphia	80	48	12	20	327	254	116
Islanders	80	39	28	13	281	247	91
Rangers	80	38	32	10	308	284	86
Flames	80	35	32	13	282	269	83
Washington	80	27	40	13	261	293	67

Smythe Division

	GP	W	L	T	GF	GA	PTS
Chicago	80	34	27	19	241	250	87
St. Louis	80	34	34	12	266	278	80
Vancouver	80	27	37	16	256	281	70
Edmonton	80	28	39	13	301	322	69
Winnipeg	80	20	49	11	214	314	51
Rockies	80	19	48	13	234	308	51

• top four teams in each division qualified for the playoffs

Stanley Cup Finals

May 13	Islanders 4 at Philadelphia 3 (Denis Potvin 4:07 OT)
May 15	Islanders 3 at Philadelphia 8
May 17	Philadelphia 2 at Islanders 6
May 19	Philadelphia 2 at Islanders 5
May 22	Islanders 3 at Philadelphia 6
May 24	Philadelphia 4 at Islanders 5 (Bob Nystrom 7:11 OT)

Islanders won best-of-seven finals 4–2

1980–81

PRINCE OF WALES CONFERENCE

Adams Division

	GP	W	L	T	GF	GA	PTS
Buffalo	80	39	20	21	327	250	99
Boston	80	37	30	13	316	272	87
North Stars	80	35	28	17	291	263	87
Quebec	80	30	32	18	314	318	78
Toronto	80	28	37	15	322	367	71

Norris Division

	GP	W	L	T	GF	GA	PTS
Canadiens	80	45	22	13	332	232	103
Los Angeles	80	43	24	13	337	290	99
Pittsburgh	80	30	37	13	302	345	73
Hartford	80	21	41	18	292	372	60
Detroit	80	19	43	18	252	339	56

CLARENCE CAMPBELL CONFERENCE

Patrick Division

	GP	W	L	T	GF	GA	PTS
Islanders	80	48	18	14	355	260	110
Philadelphia	80	41	24	15	313	249	97
Calgary	80	39	27	14	329	298	92
Rangers	80	30	36	14	312	317	74
Washington	80	26	36	18	286	317	70

Smythe Division

	GP	W	L	T	GF	GA	PTS
St. Louis	80	45	18	17	352	281	107
Chicago	80	31	33	16	304	315	78
Vancouver	80	28	32	20	289	301	76
Edmonton	80	29	35	16	328	327	74
Rockies	80	22	45	13	258	344	57
Winnipeg	80	9	57	14	246	400	32

Stanley Cup Finals

May 12	North Stars 3 at Islanders 6
May 14	North Stars 3 at Islanders 6
May 17	Islanders 7 at North Stars 5
May 19	Islanders 2 at North Stars 4
May 21	North Stars 1 at Islanders 5

Islanders won best-of-seven finals 4–1

1981–82

CLARENCE CAMPBELL CONFERENCE

Norris Division

	GP	W	L	T	GF	GA	PTS
North Stars	80	37	23	20	346	288	94
Winnipeg	80	33	33	14	319	332	80
St. Louis	80	32	40	8	315	349	72
Chicago	80	30	38	12	332	363	72
Toronto	80	20	44	16	298	380	56
Detroit	80	21	47	12	270	351	54

Smythe Division

	GP	W	L	T	GF	GA	PTS
Edmonton	80	48	17	15	417	295	111
Vancouver	80	30	33	17	290	286	77
Calgary	80	29	34	17	334	345	75
Los Angeles	80	24	41	15	314	369	63
Rockies	80	18	49	13	241	362	49

PRINCE OF WALES CONFERENCE

Adams Division

	GP	W	L	T	GF	GA	PTS
Canadiens	80	46	17	17	360	223	109
Boston	80	43	27	10	323	285	96
Buffalo	80	39	26	15	307	273	93
Quebec	80	33	31	16	356	345	82
Hartford	80	21	41	18	264	351	60

Patrick Division

	GP	W	L	T	GF	GA	PTS
Islanders	80	54	16	10	385	250	118
Rangers	80	39	27	14	316	306	92
Philadelphia	80	38	31	11	325	313	87
Pittsburgh	80	31	36	13	310	337	75
Washington	80	26	41	13	319	338	65

Stanley Cup Finals

May 8	Vancouver 5 at Islanders 6 (Mike Bossy 19:58 OT)
May 11	Vancouver 4 at Islanders 6
May 13	Islanders 3 at Vancouver 0 [Smith]
May 16	Islanders 3 at Vancouver 1

Islanders won best-of-seven finals 4–0

1982–83

CLARENCE CAMPBELL CONFERENCE

Norris Division

	GP	W	L	T	GF	GA	PTS
Chicago	80	47	23	10	338	268	104
North Stars	80	40	24	16	321	290	96
Toronto	80	28	40	12	293	330	68
St. Louis	80	25	40	15	285	316	65
Detroit	80	21	44	15	263	344	57

Smythe Division

	GP	W	L	T	GF	GA	PTS
Edmonton	80	47	21	12	424	315	106
Calgary	80	32	34	14	321	317	78
Vancouver	80	30	35	15	303	309	75
Winnipeg	80	33	39	8	311	333	74
Los Angeles	80	27	41	12	308	365	66

PRINCE OF WALES CONFERENCE

Adams Division

	GP	W	L	T	GF	GA	PTS
Boston	80	50	20	10	327	228	110
Canadiens	80	42	24	14	350	286	98
Buffalo	80	38	29	13	318	285	89
Quebec	80	34	34	12	343	336	80
Hartford	80	19	54	7	261	403	45

Patrick Division

	GP	W	L	T	GF	GA	PTS
Philadelphia	80	49	23	8	326	240	106
Islanders	80	42	26	12	302	226	96
Washington	80	39	25	16	306	283	94
Rangers	80	35	35	10	306	287	80
New Jersey	80	17	49	14	230	338	48
Pittsburgh	80	18	53	9	257	394	45

Stanley Cup Finals

May 10	Islanders 2 at Edmonton 0 [Smith]
May 12	Islanders 6 at Edmonton 3
May 14	Edmonton 1 at Islanders 5
May 17	Edmonton 2 at Islanders 4

Islanders won best-of-seven finals 4–0

1983–84

CLARENCE CAMPBELL CONFERENCE

Norris Division

	GP	W	L	T	GF	GA	PTS
North Stars	80	39	31	10	345	344	88
St. Louis	80	32	41	7	293	316	71
Detroit	80	31	42	7	298	323	69
Chicago	80	30	42	8	277	311	68
Toronto	80	26	45	9	303	387	61

Smythe Division

	GP	W	L	T	GF	GA	PTS
Edmonton	80	57	18	5	446	314	119
Calgary	80	34	32	14	311	314	82
Vancouver	80	32	39	9	306	328	73
Winnipeg	80	31	38	11	340	374	73
Los Angeles	80	23	44	13	309	376	59

PRINCE OF WALES CONFERENCE

Adams Division

	GP	W	L	T	GF	GA	PTS
Boston	80	49	25	6	336	261	104
Buffalo	80	48	25	7	315	257	103
Quebec	80	42	28	10	360	278	94
Canadiens	80	35	40	5	286	295	75
Hartford	80	28	42	10	288	320	66

Patrick Division

	GP	W	L	T	GF	GA	PTS
Islanders	80	50	26	4	357	269	104
Washington	80	48	27	5	308	226	101
Philadelphia	80	44	26	10	350	290	98
Rangers	80	42	29	9	314	304	93
New Jersey	80	17	56	7	231	350	41
Pittsburgh	80	16	58	6	254	390	38

• five-minute sudden-death overtime introduced for regular-season games

Stanley Cup Finals

May 10	Edmonton 1 at Islanders 0 [Fuhr]
May 12	Edmonton 1 at Islanders 6
May 15	Islanders 2 at Edmonton 7
May 17	Islanders 2 at Edmonton 7
May 19	Islanders 2 at Edmonton 5

Edmonton won best-of-seven finals 4–1

1984–85

CLARENCE CAMPBELL CONFERENCE
Norris Division

	GP	W	L	T	GF	GA	PTS
St. Louis	80	37	31	12	299	288	86
Chicago	80	38	35	7	309	299	83
Detroit	80	27	41	12	313	357	66
North Stars	80	25	43	12	268	321	62
Toronto	80	20	52	8	253	358	48

Smythe Division

	GP	W	L	T	GF	GA	PTS
Edmonton	80	49	20	11	401	298	109
Winnipeg	80	43	27	10	358	332	96
Calgary	80	41	27	12	363	302	94
Los Angeles	80	34	32	14	339	326	82
Vancouver	80	25	46	9	284	401	59

PRINCE OF WALES CONFERENCE
Adams Division

	GP	W	L	T	GF	GA	PTS
Canadiens	80	41	27	12	309	262	94
Quebec	80	41	30	9	323	275	91
Buffalo	80	38	28	14	290	237	90
Boston	80	36	34	10	303	287	82
Hartford	80	30	41	9	268	318	69

Patrick Division

	GP	W	L	T	GF	GA	PTS
Philadelphia	80	53	20	7	348	241	113
Washington	80	46	25	9	322	240	101
Islanders	80	40	34	6	345	312	86
Rangers	80	26	44	10	295	345	62
New Jersey	80	22	48	10	264	346	54
Pittsburgh	80	24	51	5	276	385	53

Stanley Cup Finals

May 21	Edmonton 1 at Philadelphia 4
May 23	Edmonton 3 at Philadelphia 1
May 25	Philadelphia 3 at Edmonton 4
May 28	Philadelphia 3 at Edmonton 5
May 30	Philadelphia 3 at Edmonton 8

Edmonton won best-of-seven finals 4–1

1985–86

CLARENCE CAMPBELL CONFERENCE
Norris Division

	GP	W	L	T	GF	GA	PTS
Chicago	80	39	33	8	351	349	86
North Stars	80	38	33	9	327	305	85
St. Louis	80	37	34	9	302	291	83
Toronto	80	25	48	7	311	386	57
Detroit	80	17	57	6	266	415	40

Smythe Division

	GP	W	L	T	GF	GA	PTS
Edmonton	80	56	17	7	426	310	119
Calgary	80	40	31	9	354	315	89
Winnipeg	80	26	47	7	295	372	59
Vancouver	80	23	44	13	282	333	59
Los Angeles	80	23	49	8	284	389	54

PRINCE OF WALES CONFERENCE
Adams Division

	GP	W	L	T	GF	GA	PTS
Quebec	80	43	31	6	330	289	92
Canadiens	80	40	33	7	330	280	87
Boston	80	37	31	12	311	288	86
Hartford	80	40	36	4	332	302	84
Buffalo	80	37	37	6	296	291	80

Patrick Division

	GP	W	L	T	GF	GA	PTS
Philadelphia	80	53	23	4	335	241	110
Washington	80	50	23	7	315	272	107
Islanders	80	39	29	12	327	284	90
Rangers	80	36	38	6	280	276	78
Pittsburgh	80	34	38	8	313	305	76
New Jersey	80	28	49	3	300	374	59

Stanley Cup Finals
May 16	Canadiens 2 at Calgary 5
May 18	Canadiens 3 at Calgary 2 (Brian Skrudland 0:09 OT)
May 20	Calgary 3 at Canadiens 5
May 22	Calgary 0 at Canadiens 1 [Roy]
May 24	Canadiens 4 at Calgary 3

Canadiens won best-of-seven finals 4–1

1986–87

CLARENCE CAMPBELL CONFERENCE
Norris Division

	GP	W	L	T	GF	G	PTS
St. Louis	80	32	33	15	281	293	79
Detroit	80	34	36	10	260	274	78
Chicago*	80	29	37	14	290	310	72
Toronto	80	32	42	6	286	319	70
North Stars	80	30	40	10	296	314	70

* Chicago changed spelling of nickname from Black Hawks to Blackhawks at start of season

Smythe Division

Edmonton	80	50	24	6	372	284	106
Calgary	80	46	31	3	318	289	95
Winnipeg	80	40	32	8	279	271	88
Los Angeles	80	31	41	8	318	341	70
Vancouver	80	29	43	8	282	314	66

PRINCE OF WALES CONFERENCE
Adams Division

Hartford	80	43	30	7	287	270	93
Canadiens	80	41	29	10	277	241	92
Boston	80	39	34	7	301	276	85
Quebec	80	31	39	10	267	276	72
Buffalo	80	28	44	8	280	308	64

Patrick Division

Philadelphia	80	46	26	8	310	245	100
Washington	80	38	32	10	285	278	86
Islanders	80	35	33	12	279	281	82
Rangers	80	34	38	8	307	323	76
Pittsburgh	80	30	38	12	297	290	72
New Jersey	80	29	45	6	293	368	64

Stanley Cup Finals

May 17	Philadelphia 2 at Edmonton 4
May 20	Philadelphia 2 at Edmonton 3 (Jari Kurri 6:50 OT)
May 22	Edmonton 3 at Philadelphia 5
May 24	Edmonton 4 at Philadelphia 1
May 26	Philadelphia 4 at Edmonton 3
May 28	Edmonton 2 at Philadelphia 3
May 31	Philadelphia 1 at Edmonton 3

Edmonton won best-of-seven finals 4–3

1987–88

CLARENCE CAMPBELL CONFERENCE

Norris Division

	GP	W	L	T	GF	GA	PTS
Detroit	80	41	28	11	322	269	93
St. Louis	80	34	38	8	278	294	76
Chicago	80	30	41	9	284	326	69
Toronto	80	21	49	10	273	345	52
North Stars	80	19	48	13	242	349	51

Smythe Division

	GP	W	L	T	GF	GA	PTS
Calgary	80	48	23	9	397	305	105
Edmonton	80	44	25	11	363	288	99
Winnipeg	80	33	36	11	292	310	77
Los Angeles	80	30	42	8	318	359	68
Vancouver	80	25	46	9	272	320	59

PRINCE OF WALES CONFERENCE

Adams Division

	GP	W	L	T	GF	GA	PTS
Canadiens	80	45	22	13	298	238	103
Boston	80	44	30	6	300	251	94
Buffalo	80	37	32	11	283	305	85
Hartford	80	35	38	7	249	267	77
Quebec	80	32	43	5	271	306	69

Patrick Division

	GP	W	L	T	GF	GA	PTS
Islanders	80	39	31	10	308	267	88
Washington	80	38	33	9	281	249	85
Philadelphia	80	38	33	9	292	282	85
New Jersey	80	38	36	6	295	296	82
Rangers	80	36	34	10	300	283	82
Pittsburgh	80	36	35	9	319	316	81

Stanley Cup Finals

May 18	Boston 1 at Edmonton 2
May 20	Boston 2 at Edmonton 4
May 22	Edmonton 6 at Boston 3
May 24	Edmonton 3 at Boston 3*
May 26	Boston 3 at Edmonton 6

Edmonton won best-of-seven finals 4–0

* game suspended because of power failure but statistics counted (if necessary, this game would have been made up at the end of the series)

1988–89

CLARENCE CAMPBELL CONFERENCE

Norris Division

	GP	W	L	T	GF	GA	PTS
Detroit	80	34	34	12	313	316	80
St. Louis	80	33	35	12	275	285	78
North Stars	80	27	37	16	258	278	70
Chicago	80	27	41	12	297	335	66
Toronto	80	28	46	6	259	342	62

Smythe Division

	GP	W	L	T	GF	GA	PTS
Calgary	80	54	17	9	354	226	117
Los Angeles	80	42	31	7	376	335	91
Edmonton	80	38	34	8	325	306	84
Vancouver	80	33	39	8	251	253	74
Winnipeg	80	26	42	12	300	355	64

PRINCE OF WALES CONFERENCE

Adams Division

	GP	W	L	T	GF	GA	PTS
Canadiens	80	53	18	9	315	218	115
Boston	80	37	29	14	289	256	88
Buffalo	80	38	35	7	291	299	83
Hartford	80	37	38	5	299	290	79
Quebec	80	27	46	7	269	342	61

Patrick Division

	GP	W	L	T	GF	GA	PTS
Washington	80	41	29	10	305	259	92
Pittsburgh	80	40	33	7	347	349	87
Rangers	80	37	35	8	310	307	82
Philadelphia	80	36	36	8	307	285	80
New Jersey	80	27	41	12	281	325	66
Islanders	80	28	47	5	265	325	61

Stanley Cup Finals

May 14	Canadiens 2 at Calgary 3
May 17	Canadiens 4 at Calgary 2
May 19	Calgary 3 at Canadiens 4 (Ryan Walter 38:08 OT)
May 21	Calgary 4 at Canadiens 2
May 23	Canadiens 2 at Calgary 3
May 25	Calgary 4 at Canadiens 2

Calgary won best-of-seven finals 4–2

1989–90

CLARENCE CAMPBELL CONFERENCE

Norris Division

	GP	W	L	T	GF	GA	PTS
Chicago	80	41	33	6	316	294	88
St. Louis	80	37	34	9	295	279	83
Toronto	80	38	38	4	337	358	80
North Stars	80	36	40	4	284	291	76
Detroit	80	28	38	14	288	323	70

Smythe Division

	GP	W	L	T	GF	GA	PTS
Calgary	80	42	23	15	348	265	99
Edmonton	80	38	28	14	315	283	90
Winnipeg	80	37	32	11	298	290	85
Los Angeles	80	34	39	7	338	337	75
Vancouver	80	25	41	14	245	306	64

PRINCE OF WALES CONFERENCE

Adams Division

	GP	W	L	T	GF	GA	PTS
Boston	80	46	25	9	289	232	101
Buffalo	80	45	27	8	286	248	98
Canadiens	80	41	28	11	288	234	93
Hartford	80	38	33	9	275	268	85
Quebec	80	12	61	7	240	407	31

Patrick Division

	GP	W	L	T	GF	GA	PTS
Rangers	80	36	31	13	279	267	85
New Jersey	80	37	34	9	295	288	83
Washington	80	36	38	6	284	275	78
Islanders	80	31	38	11	281	288	73
Pittsburgh	80	32	40	8	318	359	72
Philadelphia	80	30	39	11	290	297	71

Stanley Cup Finals

May 15	Edmonton 3 at Boston 2 (Petr Klima 55:13 OT)
May 18	Edmonton 7 at Boston 2
May 20	Boston 2 at Edmonton 1
May 22	Boston 1 at Edmonton 5
May 24	Edmonton 4 at Boston 1

Edmonton won best-of-seven finals 4–1

1990–91

CLARENCE CAMPBELL CONFERENCE
Norris Division

	GP	W	L	T	GF	GA	PTS
Chicago	80	49	23	8	284	211	106
St. Louis	80	47	22	11	310	250	105
Detroit	80	34	38	8	273	298	76
North Stars	80	27	39	14	256	266	68
Toronto	80	23	46	11	241	318	57

Smythe Division

	GP	W	L	T	GF	GA	PTS
Los Angeles	80	46	24	10	340	254	102
Calgary	80	46	26	8	344	263	100
Edmonton	80	37	37	6	272	272	80
Vancouver	80	28	43	9	243	315	65
Winnipeg	80	26	43	11	260	288	63

PRINCE OF WALES CONFERENCE
Adams Division

	GP	W	L	T	GF	GA	PTS
Boston	80	44	24	12	299	264	100
Canadiens	80	39	30	11	273	249	89
Buffalo	80	31	30	19	292	278	81
Hartford	80	31	38	11	238	276	73
Quebec	80	16	50	14	236	354	46

Patrick Division

	GP	W	L	T	GF	GA	PTS
Pittsburgh	80	41	33	6	342	305	88
Rangers	80	36	31	13	297	265	85
Washington	80	37	36	7	258	258	81
New Jersey	80	32	33	15	272	264	79
Philadelphia	80	33	37	10	252	267	76
Islanders	80	25	45	10	223	290	60

Stanley Cup Finals
May 15	Minnesota 5 at Pittsburgh 4
May 17	Minnesota 1 at Pittsburgh 4
May 19	Pittsburgh 1 at Minnesota 3
May 21	Pittsburgh 5 at Minnesota 3
May 23	Minnesota 4 at Pittsburgh 6
May 25	Pittsburgh 8 at Minnesota 0 [Barrasso]

Pittsburgh won best-of-seven finals 4–2

1991–92

CLARENCE CAMPBELL CONFERENCE

Norris Division

	GP	W	L	T	GF	GA	PTS
Detroit	80	43	25	12	320	256	98
Chicago	80	36	29	15	257	236	87
St. Louis	80	36	33	11	279	266	83
North Stars	80	32	42	6	246	278	70
Toronto	80	30	43	7	234	294	67

Smythe Division

	GP	W	L	T	GF	GA	PTS
Vancouver	80	42	26	12	285	250	96
Los Angeles	80	35	31	14	287	296	84
Edmonton	80	36	34	10	295	297	82
Winnipeg	80	33	32	15	251	244	81
Calgary	80	31	37	12	296	305	74
San Jose	80	17	58	5	219	359	39

PRINCE OF WALES CONFERENCE

Adams Division

	GP	W	L	T	GF	GA	PTS
Canadiens	80	41	28	11	267	207	93
Boston	80	36	32	12	270	275	84
Buffalo	80	31	37	12	289	299	74
Hartford	80	26	41	13	247	283	65
Quebec	80	20	48	12	255	318	52

Patrick Division

	GP	W	L	T	GF	GA	PTS
Rangers	80	50	25	5	321	246	105
Washington	80	45	27	8	330	275	98
Pittsburgh	80	39	32	9	343	308	87
New Jersey	80	38	31	11	289	259	87
Islanders	80	34	35	11	291	299	79
Philadelphia	80	32	37	11	252	273	75

Stanley Cup Finals

May 26	Chicago 4 at Pittsburgh 5
May 28	Chicago 1 at Pittsburgh 3
May 30	Pittsburgh 1 at Chicago 0 [Barrasso]
June 1	Pittsburgh 6 at Chicago 5

Pittsburgh won best-of-seven finals 4–0

1992–93

CLARENCE CAMPBELL CONFERENCE

Norris Division

	GP	W	L	T	GF	GA	PTS
Chicago	84	47	25	12	279	230	106
Detroit	84	47	28	9	369	280	103
Toronto	84	44	29	11	288	241	99
St. Louis	84	37	36	11	282	278	85
North Stars	84	36	38	10	272	293	82
Tampa Bay	84	23	54	7	245	332	53

Smythe Division

	GP	W	L	T	GF	GA	PTS
Vancouver	84	46	29	9	346	278	101
Calgary	84	43	30	11	322	282	97
Los Angeles	84	39	35	10	338	340	88
Winnipeg	84	40	37	7	322	320	87
Edmonton	84	26	50	8	242	337	60
San Jose	84	11	71	2	218	414	24

PRINCE OF WALES CONFERENCE

Adams Division

	GP	W	L	T	GF	GA	PTS
Boston	84	51	26	7	332	268	109
Quebec	84	47	27	10	351	300	104
Canadiens	84	48	30	6	326	280	102
Buffalo	84	38	36	10	335	297	86
Hartford	84	26	52	6	284	369	58
Ottawa	84	10	70	4	202	395	24

Patrick Division

	GP	W	L	T	GF	GA	PTS
Pittsburgh	84	56	21	7	367	268	119
Washington	84	43	34	7	325	286	93
Islanders	84	40	37	7	335	297	87
New Jersey	84	40	37	7	308	299	87
Philadelphia	84	36	37	11	319	319	83
Rangers	84	34	39	11	304	308	79

Stanley Cup Finals

June 1	Los Angeles 4 at Canadiens 1
June 3	Los Angeles 2 at Canadiens 3 (Eric Desjardins 0:51 OT)
June 5	Canadiens 4 at Los Angeles 3 (John LeClair 0:34 OT)
June 7	Canadiens 3 at Los Angeles 2 (John LeClair 14:37 OT)
June 9	Los Angeles 1 at Canadiens 4

Canadiens won best-of-seven finals 4–1

1993–94

WESTERN CONFERENCE
Central Division

	GP	W	L	T	GF	GA	PTS
Detroit	84	46	30	8	356	275	100
Toronto	84	43	29	12	280	243	98
Dallas	84	42	29	13	286	265	97
St. Louis	84	40	33	11	270	283	91
Chicago	84	39	36	9	254	240	87
Winnipeg	84	24	51	9	245	344	57

Pacific Division

	GP	W	L	T	GF	GA	PTS
Calgary	84	42	29	13	302	256	97
Vancouver	84	41	40	3	279	276	85
San Jose	84	33	35	16	252	265	82
Anaheim	84	33	46	5	229	251	71
Los Angeles	84	27	45	12	294	322	66
Edmonton	84	25	45	14	261	305	64

EASTERN CONFERENCE
Northeast Division

	GP	W	L	T	GF	GA	PTS
Pittsburgh	84	44	27	13	299	285	101
Boston	84	42	29	13	289	252	97
Canadiens	84	41	29	14	283	248	96
Buffalo	84	43	32	9	282	218	95
Quebec	84	34	42	8	277	292	76
Hartford	84	27	48	9	227	288	63
Ottawa	84	14	61	9	201	397	37

Atlantic Division

	GP	W	L	T	GF	GA	PTS
Rangers	84	52	24	8	299	231	112
New Jersey	84	47	25	12	306	220	106
Washington	84	39	35	10	277	263	88
Islanders	84	36	36	12	282	264	84
Florida	84	33	34	17	233	233	83
Philadelphia	84	35	39	10	294	314	80
Tampa Bay	84	30	43	11	224	251	71

• the top eight teams in each conference qualified for the playoffs

Stanley Cup Finals

May 31	Vancouver 3 at Rangers 2 (Greg Adams 19:26 OT)
June 2	Vancouver 1 at Rangers 3
June 4	Rangers 5 at Vancouver 1
June 7	Rangers 4 at Vancouver 2
June 9	Vancouver 6 at Rangers 3
June 11	Rangers 1 at Vancouver 4
June 14	Vancouver 2 at Rangers 3

Rangers won best-of-seven finals 4–3

1994–95

WESTERN CONFERENCE

Central Division

	GP	W	L	T	GF	GA	PTS
Detroit	48	33	11	4	180	117	70
St. Louis	48	28	15	5	178	135	61
Chicago	48	24	19	5	156	115	53
Toronto	48	21	19	8	135	146	50
Dallas	48	17	23	8	136	135	42
Winnipeg	48	16	25	7	157	177	39

Pacific Division

	GP	W	L	T	GF	GA	PTS
Calgary	48	24	17	7	163	135	55
Vancouver	48	18	18	12	153	148	48
San Jose	48	19	25	4	129	161	42
Los Angeles	48	16	23	9	142	174	41
Edmonton	48	17	27	4	136	183	38
Anaheim	48	16	27	5	125	164	37

EASTERN CONFERENCE

Northeast Division

Quebec	48	30	13	5	185	134	65
Pittsburgh	48	29	16	3	181	158	61
Boston	48	27	18	3	150	127	57
Buffalo	48	22	19	7	130	119	51
Hartford	48	19	24	5	127	141	43
Canadiens	48	18	23	7	125	148	43
Ottawa	48	9	34	5	116	174	23

Atlantic Division

Philadelphia	48	28	16	4	150	132	60
New Jersey	48	22	18	8	136	121	52
Washington	48	22	18	8	136	120	52
Rangers	48	22	23	3	139	134	47
Florida	48	20	22	6	115	127	46
Tampa Bay	48	17	28	3	120	144	37
Islanders	48	15	28	5	126	158	35

Stanley Cup Finals

June 17	New Jersey 2 at Detroit 1
June 20	New Jersey 4 at Detroit 2
June 22	Detroit 2 at New Jersey 5
June 24	Detroit 2 at New Jersey 5

New Jersey won best-of-seven finals 4–0

1995–96

WESTERN CONFERENCE

Central Division

	GP	W	L	T	GF	GA	PTS
Detroit	82	62	13	7	325	181	131
Chicago	82	40	28	14	273	220	94
Toronto	82	34	36	12	247	252	80
St. Louis	82	32	34	16	219	248	80
Winnipeg	82	36	40	6	275	291	78
Dallas	82	26	42	14	227	280	66

Pacific Division

Colorado	82	47	25	10	326	240	104
Calgary	82	34	37	11	241	240	79
Vancouver	82	32	35	15	278	278	79
Anaheim	82	35	39	8	234	247	78
Edmonton	82	30	44	8	240	304	68
Los Angeles	82	24	40	18	256	302	66
San Jose	82	20	55	7	252	357	47

EASTERN CONFERENCE

Northeast Division

Pittsburgh	82	49	29	4	362	284	102
Boston	82	40	31	11	282	269	91
Canadiens	82	40	32	10	265	248	90
Hartford	82	34	39	9	237	259	77
Buffalo	82	33	42	7	247	262	73
Ottawa	82	18	59	5	191	291	41

Atlantic Division

Philadelphia	82	45	24	13	282	208	103
Rangers	82	41	27	14	272	237	96
Florida	82	41	31	10	254	234	92
Washington	82	39	32	11	234	204	89
Tampa Bay	82	38	32	12	238	248	88
New Jersey	82	37	33	12	215	202	86
Islanders	82	22	50	10	229	315	54

Stanley Cup Finals

June 4	Florida 1 at Colorado 3
June 6	Florida 1 at Colorado 8
June 8	Colorado 3 at Florida 2
June 10	Colorado 1 at Florida 0 (Uwe Krupp 44:31 OT) [Roy]

Colorado won best-of seven finals 4–0

1996–97

WESTERN CONFERENCE

Central Division

	GP	W	L	T	GF	GA	PTS
Dallas	82	48	26	8	252	198	104
Detroit	82	38	26	18	253	197	94
Phoenix	82	38	37	7	240	243	83
St. Louis	82	36	35	11	236	239	83
Chicago	82	34	35	13	223	210	81
Toronto	82	30	44	8	230	273	68

Pacific Division

	GP	W	L	T	GF	GA	PTS
Colorado	82	49	24	9	277	205	107
Anaheim	82	36	33	13	245	233	85
Edmonton	82	36	37	9	252	247	81
Vancouver	82	35	40	7	257	273	77
Calgary	82	32	41	9	214	239	73
Los Angeles	82	28	43	11	214	268	67
San Jose	82	27	47	8	211	278	62

EASTERN CONFERENCE

Northeast Division

	GP	W	L	T	GF	GA	PTS
Buffalo	82	40	30	12	237	208	92
Pittsburgh	82	38	36	8	285	280	84
Ottawa	82	31	36	15	226	234	77
Canadiens	82	31	36	15	249	276	77
Hartford	82	32	39	11	226	256	75
Boston	82	26	47	9	234	300	61

Atlantic Division

	GP	W	L	T	GF	GA	PTS
New Jersey	82	45	23	14	231	182	104
Philadelphia	82	45	24	13	274	217	103
Florida	82	35	28	19	221	201	89
Rangers	82	38	34	10	258	231	86
Washington	82	33	40	9	214	231	75
Tampa Bay	82	32	40	10	217	247	74
Islanders	82	29	41	12	240	250	70

Stanley Cup Finals

May 31	Detroit 4 at Philadelphia 2
June 3	Detroit 4 at Philadelphia 2
June 5	Philadelphia 1 at Detroit 6
June 7	Philadelphia 1 at Detroit 2

Detroit won best-of-seven finals 4–0

1997–98

WESTERN CONFERENCE

Central Division

	GP	W	L	T	GF	GA	PTS
Dallas	82	49	22	11	242	167	109
Detroit	82	44	23	15	250	196	103
St. Louis	82	45	29	8	256	204	98
Phoenix	82	35	35	12	224	227	82
Chicago	82	30	39	13	192	199	73
Toronto	82	30	43	9	194	237	69

Pacific Division

	GP	W	L	T	GF	GA	PTS
Colorado	82	39	26	17	231	205	95
Los Angeles	82	38	33	11	227	225	87
Edmonton	82	35	37	10	215	224	80
San Jose	82	34	38	10	210	216	78
Calgary	82	26	41	15	217	252	67
Anaheim	82	26	43	13	205	261	65
Vancouver	82	25	43	14	224	273	64

EASTERN CONFERENCE

Northeast Division

	GP	W	L	T	GF	GA	PTS
Pittsburgh	82	40	24	18	228	188	98
Boston	82	39	30	13	221	194	91
Buffalo	82	36	29	17	211	187	89
Canadiens	82	37	32	13	235	208	87
Ottawa	82	34	33	15	193	20	83
Carolina	82	33	41	8	200	219	74

Atlantic Division

New Jersey	82	48	23	11	225	166	107
Philadelphia	82	42	29	11	242	193	95
Washington	82	40	30	12	219	202	92
Islanders	82	30	41	11	212	225	71
Rangers	82	25	39	18	197	231	68
Florida	82	24	43	15	203	256	63
Tampa Bay	82	17	55	10	151	269	44

Stanley Cup Finals

June 9	Washington 1 at Detroit 2
June 11	Washington 4 at Detroit 5 (Kris Draper 15:24 OT)
June 13	Detroit 2 at Washington 1
June 16	Detroit 4 at Washington 1

Detroit won best-of-seven finals 4–0

1998–99

EASTERN CONFERENCE

Northeast Division

	GP	W	L	T	GF	GA	PTS
Ottawa	82	44	23	15	239	179	103
Toronto	82	45	30	7	268	231	97
Boston	82	39	30	13	214	181	91
Buffalo	82	37	28	17	207	175	91
Canadiens	82	32	39	11	184	209	75

Atlantic Division

New Jersey	82	47	24	11	248	196	105
Philadelphia	82	37	26	19	231	196	93
Pittsburgh	82	38	30	14	242	225	90
Rangers	82	33	38	11	217	227	77
Islanders	82	24	48	10	194	244	58

Southeast Division

Carolina	82	34	30	18	210	202	86
Florida	82	30	34	18	210	228	78
Washington	82	31	45	6	200	218	68
Tampa Bay	82	19	54	9	179	292	47

WESTERN CONFERENCE

Central Division

Detroit	82	43	32	7	245	202	93
St. Louis	82	37	32	13	237	209	87
Chicago	82	29	41	12	202	248	70
Nashville	82	28	47	7	190	261	63

Pacific Division

Dallas	82	51	19	12	236	168	114
Phoenix	82	39	31	12	205	197	90
Anaheim	82	35	34	13	215	206	83
San Jose	82	31	33	18	196	191	80
Los Angeles	82	32	45	5	189	222	69

Northwest Division

Colorado	82	44	28	10	239	205	98
Edmonton	82	33	37	12	230	226	78
Calgary	82	30	40	12	211	234	72
Vancouver	82	23	47	12	192	258	58

Stanley Cup Finals

June 8	Buffalo 3 at Dallas 2 (Jason Woolley 15:30 OT)
June 10	Buffalo 2 at Dallas 4
June 12	Dallas 2 at Buffalo 1
June 15	Dallas 1 at Buffalo 2
June 17	Buffalo 0 at Dallas 2 [Belfour]
June 19	Dallas 2 at Buffalo 1 (Brett Hull 54:51 OT)

Dallas won best-of-seven finals 4–2

1999–2000

EASTERN CONFERENCE

Northeast Division

	GP	W	L	T	OTL	GF	GA	PTS
Toronto	82	45	30	7	3	246	222	100
Ottawa	82	41	30	11	2	244	210	95
Buffalo	82	35	36	11	4	213	204	85
Canadiens	82	35	38	9	4	196	194	83
Boston	82	24	39	19	6	210	248	73

Atlantic Division

Philadelphia	82	45	25	12	3	237	179	105
New Jersey	82	45	29	8	5	251	203	103
Pittsburgh	82	37	37	8	6	241	236	88
Rangers	82	29	42	12	3	218	246	73
Islanders	82	24	49	9	1	194	275	58

Southeast Division

Washington	82	44	26	12	2	227	194	102
Florida	82	43	33	6	6	244	209	98
Carolina	82	37	35	10	0	217	216	84
Tampa Bay	82	19	54	9	7	204	309	54
Atlanta	82	14	61	7	4	170	313	39

WESTERN CONFERENCE

Central Division

St. Louis	82	51	20	11	1	248	165	114
Detroit	82	48	24	10	2	278	210	108
Chicago	82	33	39	10	2	242	245	78
Nashville	82	28	47	7	7	199	240	70

Northwest Division

Colorado	82	42	29	11	1	233	201	96
Edmonton	82	32	34	16	8	226	212	88
Vancouver	82	30	37	15	8	227	237	83
Calgary	82	31	41	10	5	211	256	77

Pacific Division

Dallas	82	43	29	10	6	211	184	102
Los Angeles	82	39	31	12	4	245	228	94
Phoenix	82	39	35	8	4	232	228	90
San Jose	82	35	37	10	7	225	214	87
Anaheim	82	34	36	12	3	217	227	83

Stanley Cup Finals

May 30	Dallas 3 at New Jersey 7
June 1	Dallas 2 at New Jersey 1
June 3	New Jersey 2 at Dallas 1
June 5	New Jersey 3 at Dallas 1
June 8	Dallas 1 at New Jersey 0 (Mike Modano 46:21 OT) [Belfour]
June 10	New Jersey 2 at Dallas 1 (Jason Arnott 28:20 OT)

New Jersey won best-of-seven finals 4–2

2000–01

EASTERN CONFERENCE
Northeast Division

	GP	W	L	T	OTL	GF	GA	PTS
Ottawa	82	48	21	9	4	274	205	109
Buffalo	82	46	30	5	1	218	184	98
Toronto	82	37	29	11	5	232	207	90
Boston	82	36	30	8	8	227	249	88
Montreal	82	28	40	8	6	206	232	70

Atlantic Division

	GP	W	L	T	OTL	GF	GA	PTS
New Jersey	82	48	19	12	3	295	195	111
Philadelphia	82	43	25	11	3	240	207	100
Pittsburgh	82	42	28	9	3	281	256	96
Rangers	82	33	43	5	1	250	290	72
Islanders	82	21	51	7	3	185	268	52

Southeast Division

	GP	W	L	T	OTL	GF	GA	PTS
Washington	82	41	27	10	4	233	211	96
Carolina	82	38	32	9	3	212	225	88
Florida	82	22	38	13	9	200	246	66
Atlanta	82	23	45	12	2	211	289	60
Tampa Bay	82	24	47	6	5	201	280	59

WESTERN CONFERENCE
Central Division

	GP	W	L	T	OTL	GF	GA	PTS
Detroit	82	49	20	9	4	253	202	111
St. Louis	82	43	22	12	5	249	195	103
Nashville	82	34	36	9	3	186	200	80
Chicago	82	29	40	8	5	210	246	71
Columbus	82	28	39	9	6	190	233	71

Northwest Division

	GP	W	L	T	OTL	GF	GA	PTS
Colorado	82	52	16	10	4	270	192	118
Edmonton	82	39	28	12	3	243	222	93
Vancouver	82	36	28	11	7	239	238	90
Calgary	82	27	36	15	4	197	236	73
Minnesota	82	25	39	13	5	168	210	68

Pacific Division

Dallas	82	48	24	8	2	241	187	106
San Jose	82	40	27	12	3	217	192	95
Los Angeles	82	38	28	13	3	252	228	92
Phoenix	82	35	27	17	3	214	212	90
Anaheim	82	25	41	11	5	188	245	66

Stanley Cup Finals

May 26	New Jersey 0 at Colorado 5 [Roy]
May 29	New Jersey 2 at Colorado 1
May 31	Colorado 3 at New Jersey 1
June 2	Colorado 2 at New Jersey 3
June 4	New Jersey 4 at Colorado 1
June 7	Colorado 4 at New Jersey 0 [Roy]
June 9	New Jersey 1 at Colorado 3

Colorado won best-of-seven finals 4–3

2001–02

EASTERN CONFERENCE

Northeast Division

	GP	W	L	T	OTL	GF	GA	PTS
Boston	82	43	24	6	9	236	201	101
Toronto	82	43	25	10	4	249	207	100
Ottawa	82	39	27	9	7	243	208	94
Montreal	82	36	31	12	3	207	209	87
Buffalo	82	35	35	11	1	213	200	82

Atlantic Division

Philadelphia	82	42	27	10	3	234	192	97
Islanders	82	42	28	8	4	239	220	96
New Jersey	82	41	28	9	4	205	187	95
Rangers	82	36	38	4	4	227	258	80
Pittsburgh	82	28	41	8	5	198	249	69

Southeast Division

Carolina	82	35	26	16	5	217	217	91
Washington	82	36	33	11	2	228	240	85
Tampa Bay	82	27	40	11	4	178	219	69
Florida	82	22	44	10	6	180	250	60
Atlanta	82	19	47	11	5	187	288	54

WESTERN CONFERENCE

Central Division

Detroit	82	51	17	10	4	251	187	116
St. Louis	82	43	27	8	4	227	188	98
Chicago	82	41	27	13	1	216	207	96
Nashville	82	28	41	13	0	196	230	69
Columbus	82	22	47	8	5	164	255	57

Pacific Division

San Jose	82	44	27	8	3	248	199	99
Phoenix	82	40	27	9	6	228	210	95
Los Angeles	82	40	27	11	4	214	190	95
Dallas	82	36	28	13	5	215	213	90
Anaheim	82	29	42	8	3	175	198	69

Northwest Division

Colorado	82	42	28	8	1	212	169	99
Vancouver	82	42	30	7	3	254	211	94
Edmonton	82	38	28	12	4	205	182	92
Calgary	82	32	35	12	3	201	220	79
Minnesota	82	26	35	12	9	195	238	73

Stanley Cup Finals

June 4	Carolina 3 at Detroit 2 (Ron Francis 0:58 OT)
June 6	Carolina 1 at Detroit 3
June 8	Detroit 3 at Carolina 2 (Igor Larionov 54:47 OT)
June 10	Detroit 3 at Carolina 0
June 13	Carolina 1 at Detroit 3

Detroit won best-of-seven finals 4–1

2002–03

EASTERN CONFERENCE

Northeast Division

	GP	W	L	T	OTL	GF	GA	PTS
Ottawa	82	52	21	8	1	263	182	113
Toronto	82	44	28	7	3	236	208	98
Boston	82	36	31	11	4	245	237	87
Montreal	82	30	35	8	9	206	234	77
Buffalo	82	27	37	10	8	190	219	72

Atlantic Division

New Jersey	82	46	20	10	6	216	166	108
Philadelphia	82	45	20	13	4	211	166	107
Islanders	82	35	34	11	2	224	231	83
Rangers	82	32	36	10	4	210	231	78
Pittsburgh	82	27	44	6	5	189	255	65

Southeast Division

Tampa Bay	82	36	25	16	5	219	210	93
Washington	82	39	29	8	6	224	220	92
Atlanta	82	31	39	7	5	226	284	74
Florida	82	24	36	13	9	176	237	70
Carolina	82	22	43	11	6	171	240	61

WESTERN CONFERENCE

Central Division

Detroit	82	48	20	10	4	269	203	110
St. Louis	82	41	24	11	6	253	222	99
Chicago	82	30	33	13	6	207	226	79
Nashville	82	27	35	13	7	183	206	74
Columbus	82	29	42	8	3	213	263	69

Pacific Division

Dallas	82	46	17	15	4	245	169	111
Anaheim	82	40	27	9	6	203	193	95
Los Angeles	82	33	37	6	6	203	221	78
Phoenix	82	31	35	11	5	204	230	78
San Jose	82	28	37	9	8	214	239	73

Northwest Division

Colorado	82	42	19	13	8	251	194	105
Vancouver	82	45	23	13	1	264	208	104
Minnesota	82	42	29	10	1	198	178	95
Edmonton	82	36	26	11	9	231	230	92
Calgary	82	29	36	13	4	186	228	75

Stanley Cup Finals

May 27	Anaheim 0 at New Jersey 3 [Brodeur]
May 29	Anaheim 0 at New Jersey 3 [Brodeur]
May 31	New Jersey 2 at Anaheim 3 (Ruslan Salei 6:59 OT)
June 2	New Jersey 0 at Anaheim 1 (Steve Thomas 0:39 OT) [Giguere]
June 5	Anaheim 3 at New Jersey 6
June 7	New Jersey 2 at Anaheim 5
June 9	Anaheim 0 at New Jersey 3 [Brodeur]

New Jersey won best-of-seven finals 4–3

2003–04

EASTERN CONFERENCE

Atlantic Division

	GP	W	L	T	OTL	PTS	GF	GA
Philadelphia	82	40	21	15	6	101	229	186
New Jersey	82	43	25	12	2	100	213	164
Islanders	82	38	29	11	4	91	237	210
Rangers	82	27	40	7	8	69	206	250
Pittsburgh	82	23	47	8	4	58	190	303

Northeast Division

	GP	W	L	T	OTL	PTS	GF	GA
Boston	82	41	19	15	7	104	209	188
Toronto	82	45	24	10	3	103	242	204
Ottawa	82	43	23	10	6	102	262	189
Montreal	82	41	30	7	4	93	208	192
Buffalo	82	37	34	7	4	85	220	221

Southeast Division

	GP	W	L	T	OTL	PTS	GF	GA
Tampa Bay	82	46	22	8	6	106	245	192
Atlanta	82	33	37	8	4	78	214	243
Carolina	82	28	34	14	6	76	172	209
Florida	82	28	35	15	4	75	188	221
Washington	82	23	46	10	3	59	186	253

WESTERN CONFERENCE

Central Division

Detroit	82	48	21	11	2	109	255	189
St. Louis	82	39	30	11	2	91	191	198
Nashville	82	38	29	11	4	91	216	217
Columbus	82	25	45	8	4	62	177	238
Chicago	82	20	43	11	8	59	188	259

Northwest Division

Vancouver	82	43	24	10	5	101	235	194
Colorado	82	40	22	13	7	100	236	198
Calgary	82	42	30	7	3	94	200	176
Edmonton	82	36	29	12	5	89	221	208
Minnesota	82	30	29	20	3	83	188	183

Pacific Division

San Jose	82	43	21	12	6	104	219	183
Dallas	82	41	26	13	2	97	194	175
Los Angeles	82	28	29	16	9	81	205	217
Anaheim	82	29	35	10	8	76	184	213
Phoenix	82	22	36	18	6	68	188	245

Note: overtime losses (OTL) are worth one point in the standings and are not included in the loss column (L)

Stanley Cup Finals

May 25	Calgary 4 at Tampa Bay 1
May 27	Calgary 1 at Tampa Bay 4
May 29	Tampa Bay 0 at Calgary 3 [Kiprusoff]
May 31	Tampa Bay 1 at Calgary 0 [Khabibulin]
June 3	Calgary 3 at Tampa Bay 2 (Oleg Saprykin 14:40 OT)
June 5	Tampa Bay 3 at Calgary 2 (Martin St. Louis 20:33 OT)
June 7	Calgary 1 at Tampa Bay 2

Tampa Bay won best-of-seven finals 4–3

Note: 2004–05 no season

2005–06

EASTERN CONFERENCE

Northeast Division

	GP	W	L	OTL	SOL	GF	GA	P
Ottawa	82	52	21	3	6	314	211	113
Buffalo	82	52	24	1	5	281	239	110
Canadiens	82	42	31	6	3	243	247	93
Toronto	82	41	33	1	7	257	270	90
Boston	82	29	37	8	8	230	266	74

Atlantic Division

	GP	W	L	OTL	SOL	GF	GA	P
New Jersey	82	46	27	5	4	242	229	101
Philadelphia	82	45	26	5	6	267	259	101
Rangers	82	44	26	8	4	257	215	100
Islanders	82	36	40	3	3	230	278	78
Pittsburgh	82	22	46	8	6	244	316	58

Southeast Division

	GP	W	L	OTL	SOL	GF	GA	P
Carolina	82	52	22	6	2	294	260	112
Tampa Bay	82	43	33	2	4	252	260	92
Atlanta	82	41	33	3	5	281	275	90
Florida	82	37	34	6	5	240	257	85
Washington	82	29	41	6	6	237	306	70

WESTERN CONFERENCE

Central Division

	GP	W	L	OTL	SOL	GF	GA	P
Detroit	82	58	16	5	3	305	209	124
Nashville	82	49	25	5	3	259	227	106
Columbus	82	35	43	1	3	223	279	74
Chicago	82	26	43	7	6	211	285	65
St. Louis	82	21	46	6	9	197	292	57

Northwest Division

	GP	W	L	OTL	SOL	GF	GA	P
Calgary	82	46	25	4	7	218	200	103
Colorado	82	43	30	3	6	283	257	95
Edmonton	82	41	28	4	9	256	251	95
Vancouver	82	42	32	4	4	256	255	92
Minnesota	82	38	36	5	3	231	215	84

Pacific Division

Dallas	82	53	23	5	1	265	218	112
San Jose	82	44	27	4	7	266	242	99
Anaheim	82	43	27	5	7	254	229	98
Los Angeles	82	42	35	4	1	249	270	89
Phoenix	82	38	39	2	3	246	271	81

Stanley Cup Finals

June 5	Edmonton 4 at Carolina 5
June 7	Edmonton 0 at Carolina 5 [Ward]
June 10	Carolina 1 at Edmonton 2
June 12	Carolina 2 at Edmonton 1
June 14	Edmonton 4 at Carolina 3 (Fernando Pisani 3:31 OT)
June 17	Carolina 0 at Edmonton 4 [Ward]
June 19	Edmonton 1 at Carolina 3

Carolina won best-of-seven finals 4–3

2006–07

EASTERN CONFERENCE

Atlantic Division

	GP	W	L	OT	GF	GA	P
New Jersey	82	49	24	9	216	201	107
Pittsburgh	82	47	24	11	277	246	105
Rangers	82	42	30	10	242	216	94
Islanders	82	40	30	12	248	240	92
Philadelphia	82	22	48	12	214	303	56

Northeast Division

Buffalo	82	53	22	7	308	242	113
Ottawa	82	48	25	9	288	222	105
Toronto	82	40	31	11	258	269	91
Canadiens	82	42	34	6	245	256	90
Boston	82	35	41	6	219	289	76

Southeast Division

Atlanta	82	43	28	11	246	245	97
Tampa Bay	82	44	33	5	253	261	93
Carolina	82	40	34	8	241	253	88
Florida	82	35	31	16	247	257	86
Washington	82	28	40	14	235	286	70

WESTERN CONFERENCE

Central Division

Detroit	82	50	19	13	254	199	113
Nashville	82	51	23	8	272	212	110
St. Louis	82	34	35	13	214	254	81
Columbus	82	33	42	7	201	249	73
Chicago	82	31	42	9	201	258	71

Northwest Division

Vancouver	82	49	26	7	222	201	105
Minnesota	82	48	26	8	235	191	104
Calgary	82	43	29	10	258	226	96
Colorado	82	44	31	7	272	251	95
Edmonton	82	32	43	7	195	248	71

Pacific Division

Anaheim	82	48	20	14	258	208	110
San Jose	82	51	26	5	258	199	107
Dallas	82	50	25	7	226	197	107
Los Angeles	82	27	41	14	227	283	68
Phoenix	82	31	46	5	216	284	67

Stanley Cup Finals

May 28	Ottawa 2 at Anaheim 3
May 30	Ottawa 0 at Anaheim 1 [Giguere]
June 2	Anaheim 3 at Ottawa 5
June 4	Anaheim 3 at Ottawa 2
June 6	Ottawa 2 at Anaheim 6

Anaheim won best-of-seven 4–1

2007–08

EASTERN CONFERENCE

Northeast Division

	GP	W	L	OT	GF	GA	P
Canadiens	82	47	25	10	262	222	104
Ottawa	82	43	31	8	261	247	94
Boston	82	41	29	12	212	222	94
Buffalo	82	39	31	12	255	242	90
Toronto	82	36	35	11	231	260	83

Atlantic Division

Pittsburgh	82	47	27	8	247	216	102
New Jersey	82	46	29	7	206	197	99
Rangers	82	42	27	13	213	199	97
Philadelphia	82	42	29	11	248	233	95
Islanders	82	35	38	9	194	243	79

Southeast Division

Washington	82	43	31	8	242	231	94
Carolina	82	43	33	6	252	249	92
Florida	82	38	35	9	216	226	85
Atlanta	82	34	40	8	216	272	76
Tampa Bay	82	31	42	9	223	267	71

WESTERN CONFERENCE

Central Division

Detroit	82	54	21	7	257	184	115
Nashville	82	41	32	9	230	229	91
Chicago	82	40	34	8	239	235	88
Columbus	82	34	36	12	193	218	80
St. Louis	82	33	36	13	205	237	79

Northwest Division

Minnesota	82	44	28	10	223	218	98
Colorado	82	44	31	7	231	219	95
Calgary	82	42	30	10	229	227	94
Edmonton	82	41	35	6	235	251	88
Vancouver	82	39	33	10	213	215	88

Pacific Division

San Jose	82	49	23	10	222	193	108
Anaheim	82	47	27	8	205	191	102
Dallas	82	45	30	7	242	207	97
Phoenix	82	38	37	7	214	231	83
Los Angeles	82	32	43	7	231	266	71

Stanley Cup Finals

May 24	Pittsburgh 0 at Detroit 4 [Osgood]
May 26	Pittsburgh 0 at Detroit 3 [Osgood]
May 28	Detroit 2 at Pittsburgh 3
May 31	Detroit 2 at Pittsburgh 1

June 2   Pittsburgh 4 at Detroit 3 (Petr Sykora 49:57 OT)
June 4   Detroit 3 at Pittsburgh 2
Detroit won best of seven 4–2

2008–09

EASTERN CONFERENCE
Northeast Division

	GP	W	L	OT	GF	GA	Pts
Boston	82	53	19	10	274	196	116
Montreal	82	41	30	11	249	247	93
Buffalo	82	41	32	9	250	234	91
Ottawa	82	36	35	11	217	237	83
Toronto	82	34	35	13	250	293	81

Southeast Division

	GP	W	L	OT	GF	GA	Pts
Washington	82	50	24	8	272	245	108
Carolina	82	45	30	7	239	226	97
Florida	82	41	30	11	234	231	93
Atlanta	82	35	41	6	257	280	76
Tampa Bay	82	24	40	18	210	279	66

Atlantic Division

	GP	W	L	OT	GF	GA	Pts
New Jersey	82	51	27	4	244	209	106
Pittsburgh	82	45	28	9	264	239	99
Philadelphia	82	44	27	11	264	238	99
NY Rangers	82	43	30	9	210	218	95
NY Islanders	82	26	47	9	201	279	61

WESTERN CONFERENCE
Central Division

	GP	W	L	OT	GF	GA	Pts
Detroit	82	51	21	10	295	244	112
Chicago	82	46	24	12	264	216	104
St. Louis	82	41	31	10	233	233	92
Columbus	82	41	31	10	226	230	92
Nashville	82	40	34	8	213	233	88

Northwest Division

	GP	W	L	OT	GF	GA	Pts
Vancouver	82	45	27	10	246	220	100
Calgary	82	46	30	6	254	248	98
Minnesota	82	40	33	9	219	200	89
Edmonton	82	38	35	9	234	248	85
Colorado	82	32	45	5	199	257	69

Pacific Division

San Jose	82	53	18	11	257	204	117
Anaheim	82	42	33	7	245	238	91
Dallas	82	36	35	11	230	257	83
Phoenix	82	36	39	7	208	252	79
Los Angeles	82	34	37	11	207	234	79

Stanley Cup Finals

May 30	Pittsburgh 1 at Detroit 3
May 31	Pittsburgh 1 at Detroit 3
June 2	Detroit 2 at Pittsburgh 4
June 4	Detroit 2 at Pittsburgh 4
June 6	Pittsburgh 0 at Detroit 5 [Osgood]
June 9	Detroit 1 at Pittsburgh 2
June 12	Pittsburgh 2 at Detroit 1

Pittsburgh won best-of-seven finals 4–3

2009–10

EASTERN CONFERENCE
Northeast Division

	GP	W	L	OT	GF	GA	Pts
Buffalo	82	45	27	10	235	207	100
Ottawa	82	44	32	6	225	238	94
Boston	82	39	30	13	206	200	91
Montreal	82	39	33	10	217	223	88
Toronto	82	30	38	14	214	267	74

Southeast Division

Washington	82	54	15	13	318	233	121
Atlanta	82	35	34	13	234	256	83
Carolina	82	35	37	10	230	256	80
Tampa Bay	82	34	36	12	217	260	80
Florida	82	32	37	13	208	244	77

Atlantic Division

New Jersey	82	48	27	7	222	191	103
Pittsburgh	82	47	28	7	257	237	101
Philadelphia	82	41	35	6	236	225	88
NY Rangers	82	38	33	11	222	218	87
NY Islanders	82	34	37	11	222	264	79

WESTERN CONFERENCE
Central Division

Chicago	82	52	22	8	271	209	112
Detroit	82	44	24	14	229	216	102
Nashville	82	47	29	6	225	225	100
St. Louis	82	40	32	10	225	223	90
Columbus	82	32	35	15	216	259	79

Northwest Division

Vancouver	82	49	28	5	272	222	103
Colorado	82	43	30	9	244	233	95
Calgary	82	40	32	10	204	210	90
Minnesota	82	38	36	8	219	246	84
Edmonton	82	27	47	8	214	284	62

Pacific Division

San Jose	82	51	20	11	264	215	113
Phoenix	82	50	25	7	225	202	107
Los Angeles	82	46	27	9	241	219	101
Anaheim	82	39	32	11	238	251	89
Dallas	82	37	31	14	237	254	88

Stanley Cup Finals

May 29	Philadelphia 5 at Chicago 6
May 31	Philadelphia 1 at Chicago 2
June 2	Chicago 3 at Philadelphia 4 [Claude Giroux 5:59 OT]
June 4	Chicago 3 at Philadelphia 5
June 6	Philadelphia 4 at Chicago 7
June 9	Chicago 4 at Philadelphia 3 [Patrick Kane 4:06 OT]

Chicago won best-of-seven finals 4–2

2010–11

EASTERN CONFERENCE
Atlantic Division

	GP	W	L	OT	GF	GA	Pts
Philadelphia	82	47	23	12	259	223	106
Pittsburgh	82	49	25	8	238	199	106
NY Rangers	82	44	33	5	233	198	93
New Jersey	82	38	39	5	174	209	81
NY Islanders	82	30	39	13	229	264	73

Northeast Division

Boston	82	46	25	11	246	195	103
Montreal	82	44	30	8	216	209	96
Buffalo	82	43	29	10	245	229	96
Toronto	82	37	34	11	218	251	85
Ottawa	82	32	40	10	192	250	74

Southeast Division

Washington	82	48	23	11	224	197	107
Tampa Bay	82	46	25	11	247	240	103
Carolina	82	40	31	11	236	239	91
Atlanta	82	34	36	12	223	269	80
Florida	82	30	40	12	195	229	72

WESTERN CONFERENCE

Central Division

	GP	W	L	OT	GF	GA	Pts
Detroit	82	47	25	10	261	241	104
Nashville	82	44	27	11	219	194	99
Chicago	82	44	29	9	258	225	97
St. Louis	82	38	33	11	240	234	87
Columbus	82	34	35	13	215	258	81

Northwest Division

Vancouver	82	54	19	9	262	185	117
Calgary	82	41	29	12	250	237	94
Minnesota	82	39	35	8	206	233	86
Colorado	82	30	44	8	227	288	68
Edmonton	82	25	45	12	193	269	62

Pacific Division

San Jose	82	48	25	9	248	213	105
Anaheim	82	47	30	5	239	235	99
Phoenix	82	43	26	13	231	226	99
Los Angeles	82	46	30	6	219	198	98
Dallas	82	42	29	11	227	233	95

Stanley Cup Finals

June 1	Boston 0 at Vancouver 1 [Luongo]
June 4	Boston 2 at Vancouver 3 (Alexandre Burrows 0:11 OT)
June 6	Vancouver 1 at Boston 8
June 8	Vancouver 0 at Boston 4 [Thomas]
June 10	Boston 0 at Vancouver 1 [Luongo]
June 13	Vancouver 2 at Boston 5
June 15	Boston 4 at Vancouver 0 [Thomas]

STANLEY CUP CHAMPIONS

1892–93	Montreal AAA
1893–94	Montreal AAA
1894–95	Montreal Victorias
1895–96	Winnipeg Victorias, Montreal Victorias
1896–97	Montreal Victorias
1897–98	Montreal Victorias
1898–99	Montreal Victorias, Montreal Shamrocks
1899–00	Montreal Shamrocks
1900–01	Winnipeg Victorias
1901–02	Montreal AAA, Winnipeg Victorias
1902–03	Montreal AAA, Ottawa Silver Seven
1903–04	Ottawa Silver Seven
1904–05	Ottawa Silver Seven
1905–06	Ottawa Silver Seven, Montreal Wanderers
1906–07	Kenora Thistles, Montreal Wanderers
1907–08	Montreal Wanderers
1908–09	Ottawa Senators
1909–10	Ottawa Senators, Montreal Wanderers
1910–11	Ottawa Senators
1911–12	Quebec Bulldogs
1912–13	Quebec Bulldogs
1913–14	Toronto Blueshirts
1914–15	Vancouver Millionaires
1915–16	Montreal Canadiens
1916–17	Seattle Metropolitans
1917–18	Toronto Arenas
1918–19	*No winner—flu pandemic*
1919–20	Ottawa Senators
1920–21	Ottawa Senators
1921–22	Toronto St. Pats
1922–23	Ottawa Senators
1923–24	Montreal Canadiens
1924–25	Victoria Cougars
1925–26	Montreal Maroons
1926–27	Ottawa Senators
1927–28	New York Rangers
1928–29	Boston Bruins
1929–30	Montreal Canadiens
1930–31	Montreal Canadiens
1931–32	Toronto Maple Leafs

1932–33	New York Rangers
1933–34	Chicago Black Hawks
1934–35	Montreal Maroons
1935–36	Detroit Red Wings
1936–37	Detroit Red Wings
1937–38	Chicago Black Hawks
1938–39	Boston Bruins
1939–40	New York Rangers
1940–41	Boston Bruins
1941–42	Toronto Maple Leafs
1942–43	Detroit Red Wings
1943–44	Montreal Canadiens
1944–45	Toronto Maple Leafs
1945–46	Montreal Canadiens
1946–47	Toronto Maple Leafs
1947–48	Toronto Maple Leafs
1948–49	Toronto Maple Leafs
1949–50	Detroit Red Wings
1950–51	Toronto Maple Leafs
1951–52	Detroit Red Wings
1952–53	Montreal Canadiens
1953–54	Detroit Red Wings
1954–55	Detroit Red Wings
1955–56	Montreal Canadiens
1956–57	Montreal Canadiens
1957–58	Montreal Canadiens
1958–59	Montreal Canadiens
1959–60	Montreal Canadiens
1960–61	Chicago Black Hawks
1961–62	Toronto Maple Leafs
1962–63	Toronto Maple Leafs
1963–64	Toronto Maple Leafs
1964–65	Montreal Canadiens
1965–66	Montreal Canadiens
1966–67	Toronto Maple Leafs
1967–68	Montreal Canadiens
1968–69	Montreal Canadiens
1969–70	Boston Bruins
1970–71	Montreal Canadiens
1971–72	Boston Bruins
1972–73	Montreal Canadiens
1973–74	Philadelphia Flyers

1974–75	Philadelphia Flyers
1975–76	Montreal Canadiens
1976–77	Montreal Canadiens
1977–78	Montreal Canadiens
1978–79	Montreal Canadiens
1979–80	New York Islanders
1980–81	New York Islanders
1981–82	New York Islanders
1982–83	New York Islanders
1983–84	Edmonton Oilers
1984–85	Edmonton Oilers
1985–86	Montreal Canadiens
1986–87	Edmonton Oilers
1987–88	Edmonton Oilers
1988–89	Calgary Flames
1989–90	Edmonton Oilers
1990–91	Pittsburgh Penguins
1991–92	Pittsburgh Penguins
1992–93	Montreal Canadiens
1993–94	New York Rangers
1994–95	New Jersey Devils
1995–96	Colorado Avalanche
1996–97	Detroit Red Wings
1997–98	Detroit Red Wings
1998–99	Dallas Stars
1999–00	New Jersey Devils
2000–01	Detroit Red Wings
2001–02	Colorado Avalanche
2002–03	New Jersey Devils
2003–04	Tampa Bay Lightning
2004–05	*No winner—lockout*
2005–06	Carolina Hurricanes
2006–07	Anaheim Ducks
2007–08	Detroit Red Wings
2008–09	Pittsburgh Penguins
2009–10	Chicago Blackhawks
2010–11	Boston Bruins
2011–12	Los Angeles Kings

NHL AWARDS

ART ROSS TROPHY

Awarded to the player with the most points (goals plus assists) in the regular season

1917–18	Joe Malone	Montreal Canadiens (48 points)
1918–19	Newsy Lalonde	Montreal Canadiens (32 points)
1919–20	Joe Malone	Quebec Bulldogs (49 points)
1920–21	Newsy Lalonde	Montreal Canadiens (43 points)
1921–22	Punch Broadbent	Ottawa Senators (46 points)
1922–23	Babe Dye	Toronto St. Pats (37 points)
1923–24	Cy Denneny	Ottawa Senators (24 points)
1924–25	Babe Dye	Toronto St. Pats (46 points)
1925–26	Nels Stewart	Montreal Maroons (42 points)
1926–27	Bill Cook	New York Rangers (37 points)
1927–28	Howie Morenz	Montreal Canadiens (51 points)
1928–29	Ace Bailey	Toronto Maple Leafs (32 points)
1929–30	Cooney Weiland	Boston Bruins (73 points)
1930–31	Howie Morenz	Montreal Canadiens (51 points)
1931–32	Busher Jackson	Toronto Maple Leafs (53 points)
1932–33	Bill Cook	New York Rangers (50 points)
1933–34	Charlie Conacher	Toronto Maple Leafs (52 points)
1934–35	Charlie Conacher	Toronto Maple Leafs (57 points)
1935–36	Sweeney Schriner	New York Americans (45 points)
1936–37	Sweeney Schriner	New York Americans (46 points)
1937–38	Gordie Drillon	Toronto Maple Leafs (52 points)
1938–39	Toe Blake	Montreal Canadiens (47 points)
1939–40	Milt Schmidt	Boston Bruins (52 points)
1940–41	Bill Cowley	Boston Bruins (62 points)
1941–42	Bryan Hextall	New York Rangers (56 points)
1942–43	Doug Bentley	Chicago Black Hawks (73 points)
1943–44	Herb Cain	Boston Bruins (82 points)
1944–45	Elmer Lach	Montreal Canadiens (80 points)
1945–46	Max Bentley	Chicago Black Hawks (61 points)
1947–48	Elmer Lach	Montreal Canadiens (61 points)
1948–49	Roy Conacher	Chicago Black Hawks (68 points)
1949–50	Ted Lindsay	Detroit Red Wings (78 points)
1950–51	Gordie Howe	Detroit Red Wings (86 points)
1951–52	Gordie Howe	Detroit Red Wings (86 points)
1952–53	Gordie Howe	Detroit Red Wings (95 points)
1953–54	Gordie Howe	Detroit Red Wings (81 points)
1954–55	Bernie Geoffrion	Montreal Canadiens (75 points)

1955–56	Jean Beliveau	Montreal Canadiens (88 points)
1956–57	Gordie Howe	Detroit Red Wings (89 points)
1957–58	Dickie Moore	Montreal Canadiens (84 points)
1958–59	Dickie Moore	Montreal Canadiens (96 points)
1959–60	Bobby Hull	Chicago Black Hawks (81 points)
1960–61	Bernie Geoffrion	Montreal Canadiens (95 points)
1961–62	Bobby Hull	Chicago Black Hawks (84 points)
1962–63	Gordie Howe	Detroit Red Wings (86 points)
1963–64	Stan Mikita	Chicago Black Hawks (89 points)
1964–65	Stan Mikita	Chicago Black Hawks (87 points)
1965–66	Bobby Hull	Chicago Black Hawks (97 points)
1966–67	Stan Mikita	Chicago Black Hawks (97 points)
1967–68	Stan Mikita	Chicago Black Hawks (87 points)
1968–69	Phil Esposito	Boston Bruins (126 points)
1969–70	Bobby Orr	Boston Bruins (120 points)
1970–71	Phil Esposito	Boston Bruins (152 points)
1971–72	Phil Esposito	Boston Bruins (133 points)
1972–73	Phil Esposito	Boston Bruins (130 points)
1973–74	Phil Esposito	Boston Bruins (145 points)
1974–75	Bobby Orr	Boston Bruins (135 points)
1975–76	Guy Lafleur	Montreal Canadiens (125 points)
1976–77	Guy Lafleur	Montreal Canadiens (136 points)
1977–78	Guy Lafleur	Montreal Canadiens (132 points)
1978–79	Bryan Trottier	New York Islanders (134 points)
1979–80	Marcel Dionne	Los Angeles Kings (137 points)
1980–81	Wayne Gretzky	Edmonton Oilers (164 points)
1981–82	Wayne Gretzky	Edmonton Oilers (212 points)
1982–83	Wayne Gretzky	Edmonton Oilers (196 points)
1983–84	Wayne Gretzky	Edmonton Oilers (205 points)
1984–85	Wayne Gretzky	Edmonton Oilers (208 points)
1985–86	Wayne Gretzky	Edmonton Oilers (215 points)
1986–87	Wayne Gretzky	Edmonton Oilers (183 points)
1987–88	Mario Lemieux	Pittsburgh Penguins (168 points)
1988–89	Mario Lemieux	Pittsburgh Penguins (199 points)
1989–90	Wayne Gretzky	Los Angeles Kings (142 points)
1990–91	Wayne Gretzky	Los Angeles Kings (163 points)
1991–92	Mario Lemieux	Pittsburgh Penguins (131 points)
1992–93	Mario Lemieux	Pittsburgh Penguins (160 points)
1993–94	Wayne Gretzky	Los Angeles Kings (130 points)
1994–95	Jaromir Jagr	Pittsburgh Penguins (70 points)
1995–96	Mario Lemieux	Pittsburgh Penguins (161 points)
1996–97	Mario Lemieux	Pittsburgh Penguins (122 points)

1997–98	Jaromir Jagr	Pittsburgh Penguins (102 points)
1998–99	Jaromir Jagr	Pittsburgh Penguins (127 points)
1999–00	Jaromir Jagr	Pittsburgh Penguins (96 points)
2000–01	Jaromir Jagr	Pittsburgh Penguins (121 points)
2001–02	Jarome Iginla	Calgary Flames (96 points)
2002–03	Peter Forsberg	Colorado Avalanche (106 points)
2003–04	Martin St. Louis	Tampa Bay Lightning (94 points)
2004–05	no winner	
2005–06	Joe Thornton	Boston Bruins/San Jose Sharks (125 points)
2006–07	Sidney Crosby	Pittsburgh Penguins (120 points)
2007–08	Alexander Ovechkin	Washington Capitals (112 points)
2008–09	Evgeni Malkin	Pittsburgh Penguins (113 points)
2009–10	Henrik Sedin	Vancouver Canucks (112 points)
2010–11	Daniel Sedin	Vancouver Canucks (104 points)
2011–12	Evgeni Malkin	Pittsburgh Penguins (109 points)

HART TROPHY

Awarded to the league's most valuable player as voted by members of the Professional Hockey Writers' Association

1923–24	Frank Nighbor	Ottawa Senators
1924–25	Billy Burch	Hamilton Tigers
1925–26	Nels Stewart	Montreal Maroons
1926–27	Herb Gardiner	Montreal Canadiens
1927–28	Howie Morenz	Montreal Canadiens
1928–29	Roy Worters	New York Americans
1929–30	Nels Stewart	Montreal Maroons
1930–31	Howie Morenz	Montreal Canadiens
1931–32	Howie Morenz	Montreal Canadiens
1932–33	Eddie Shore	Boston Bruins
1933–34	Aurel Joliat	Montreal Canadiens
1934–35	Eddie Shore	Boston Bruins
1935–36	Eddie Shore	Boston Bruins
1936–37	Babe Siebert	Montreal Canadiens
1937–38	Eddie Shore	Boston Bruins
1938–39	Toe Blake	Montreal Canadiens
1939–40	Ebbie Goodfellow	Detroit Red Wings
1940–41	Bill Cowley	Boston Bruins
1941–42	Tom Anderson	Brooklyn Americans
1942–43	Bill Cowley	Boston Bruins
1943–44	Babe Pratt	Toronto Maple Leafs
1944–45	Elmer Lach	Montreal Canadiens

1945–46	Max Bentley	Chicago Black Hawks
1946–47	Maurice Richard	Montreal Canadiens
1947–48	Buddy O'Connor	New York Rangers
1948–49	Sid Abel	Detroit Red Wings
1949–50	Chuck Rayner	New York Rangers
1950–51	Milt Schmidt	Boston Bruins
1951–52	Gordie Howe	Detroit Red Wings
1952–53	Gordie Howe	Detroit Red Wings
1953–54	Al Rollins	Chicago Black Hawks
1954–55	Ted Kennedy	Toronto Maple Leafs
1955–56	Jean Beliveau	Montreal Canadiens
1956–57	Gordie Howe	Detroit Red Wings
1957–58	Gordie Howe	Detroit Red Wings
1958–59	Andy Bathgate	New York Rangers
1959–60	Gordie Howe	Detroit Red Wings
1960–61	Bernie Geoffrion	Montreal Canadiens
1961–62	Jacques Plante	Montreal Canadiens
1962–63	Gordie Howe	Detroit Red Wings
1963–64	Jean Beliveau	Montreal Canadiens
1964–65	Bobby Hull	Chicago Black Hawks
1965–66	Bobby Hull	Chicago Black Hawks
1966–67	Stan Mikita	Chicago Black Hawks
1967–68	Stan Mikita	Chicago Black Hawks
1968–69	Phil Esposito	Boston Bruins
1969–70	Bobby Orr	Boston Bruins
1970–71	Bobby Orr	Boston Bruins
1971–72	Bobby Orr	Boston Bruins
1972–73	Bobby Clarke	Philadelphia Flyers
1973–74	Phil Esposito	Boston Bruins
1974–75	Bobby Clarke	Philadelphia Flyers
1975–76	Bobby Clarke	Philadelphia Flyers
1976–77	Guy Lafleur	Montreal Canadiens
1977–78	Guy Lafleur	Montreal Canadiens
1978–79	Bryan Trottier	New York Islanders
1979–80	Wayne Gretzky	Edmonton Oilers
1980–81	Wayne Gretzky	Edmonton Oilers
1981–82	Wayne Gretzky	Edmonton Oilers
1982–83	Wayne Gretzky	Edmonton Oilers
1983–84	Wayne Gretzky	Edmonton Oilers
1984–85	Wayne Gretzky	Edmonton Oilers
1985–86	Wayne Gretzky	Edmonton Oilers
1986–87	Wayne Gretzky	Edmonton Oilers

1987–88	Mario Lemieux	Pittsburgh Penguins
1988–89	Wayne Gretzky	Edmonton Oilers
1989–90	Mark Messier	Edmonton Oilers
1990–91	Brett Hull	St. Louis Blues
1991–92	Mark Messier	New York Rangers
1992–93	Mario Lemieux	Pittsburgh Penguins
1993–94	Sergei Fedorov	Detroit Red Wings
1994–95	Eric Lindros	Philadelphia Flyers
1995–96	Mario Lemieux	Pittsburgh Penguins
1996–97	Dominik Hasek	Buffalo Sabres
1997–98	Dominik Hasek	Buffalo Sabres
1998–99	Jaromir Jagr	Pittsburgh Penguins
1999–00	Chris Pronger	St. Louis Blues
2000–01	Joe Sakic	Colorado Avalanche
2001–02	Jose Theodore	Montreal Canadiens
2002–03	Peter Forsberg	Colorado Avalanche
2003–04	Martin St. Louis	Tampa Bay Lightning
2004–05	no winner	
2005–06	Joe Thornton	Boston Bruins/San Jose Sharks
2006–07	Sidney Crosby	Pittsburgh Penguins
2007–08	Alexander Ovechkin	Washington Capitals
2008–09	Alexander Ovechkin	Washington Capitals
2009–10	Henrik Sedin	Vancouver Canucks
2010–11	Corey Perry	Anaheim Ducks
2011–12	Evgeni Malkin	Pittsburgh Penguins

LADY BYNG TROPHY

Awarded to the player who best displays gentlemanly play

1924–25	Frank Nighbor	Ottawa Senators
1925–26	Frank Nighbor	Ottawa Senators
1926–27	Billy Burch	New York Americans
1927–28	Frank Boucher	New York Rangers
1928–29	Frank Boucher	New York Rangers
1929–30	Frank Boucher	New York Rangers
1930–31	Frank Boucher	New York Rangers
1931–32	Joe Primeau	Toronto Maple Leafs
1932–33	Frank Boucher	New York Rangers
1933–34	Frank Boucher	New York Rangers
1934–35	Frank Boucher	New York Rangers
1935–36	Doc Romnes	Chicago Black Hawks
1936–37	Marty Barry	Detroit Red Wings

1937–38	Gordie Drillon	Toronto Maple Leafs
1938–39	Clint Smith	New York Rangers
1939–40	Bobby Bauer	Boston Bruins
1940–41	Bobby Bauer	Boston Bruins
1941–42	Syl Apps	Toronto Maple Leafs
1942–43	Max Bentley	Chicago Black Hawks
1943–44	Clint Smith	Chicago Black Hawks
1944–45	Bill Mosienko	Chicago Black Hawks
1945–46	Toe Blake	Montreal Canadiens
1946–47	Bobby Bauer	Boston Bruins
1947–48	Buddy O'Connor	New York Rangers
1948–49	Bill Quackenbush	Detroit Red Wings
1949–50	Edgar Laprade	New York Rangers
1950–51	Red Kelly	Detroit Red Wings
1951–52	Sid Smith	Toronto Maple Leafs
1952–53	Red Kelly	Detroit Red Wings
1953–54	Red Kelly	Detroit Red Wings
1954–55	Sid Smith	Toronto Maple Leafs
1955–56	Dutch Reibel	Detroit Red Wings
1956–57	Andy Hebenton	New York Rangers
1957–58	Camille Henry	New York Rangers
1958–59	Alex Delvecchio	Detroit Red Wings
1959–60	Don McKenney	Boston Bruins
1960–61	Red Kelly	Toronto Maple Leafs
1961–62	Dave Keon	Toronto Maple Leafs
1962–63	Dave Keon	Toronto Maple Leafs
1963–64	Kenny Wharram	Chicago Black Hawks
1964–65	Bobby Hull	Chicago Black Hawks
1965–66	Alex Delvecchio	Detroit Red Wings
1966–67	Stan Mikita	Chicago Black Hawks
1967–68	Stan Mikita	Chicago Black Hawks
1968–69	Alex Delvecchio	Detroit Red Wings
1969–70	Phil Goyette	St. Louis Blues
1970–71	John Bucyk	Boston Bruins
1971–72	Jean Ratelle	New York Rangers
1972–73	Gilbert Perreault	Buffalo Sabres
1973–74	John Bucyk	Boston Bruins
1974–75	Marcel Dionne	Detroit Red Wings
1975–76	Jean Ratelle	New York Rangers/Boston Bruins
1976–77	Marcel Dionne	Los Angeles Kings
1977–78	Butch Goring	Los Angeles Kings
1978–79	Bob MacMillan	Atlanta Flames

1979–80	Wayne Gretzky	Edmonton Oilers
1980–81	Rick Kehoe	Pittsburgh Penguins
1981–82	Rick Middleton	Boston Bruins
1982–83	Mike Bossy	New York Islanders
1983–84	Mike Bossy	New York Islanders
1984–85	Jari Kurri	Edmonton Oilers
1985–86	Mike Bossy	New York Islanders
1986–87	Joe Mullen	Calgary Flames
1987–88	Mats Naslund	Montreal Canadiens
1988–89	Joe Mullen	Calgary Flames
1989–90	Brett Hull	St. Louis Blues
1990–91	Wayne Gretzky	Los Angeles Kings
1991–92	Wayne Gretzky	Los Angeles Kings
1992–93	Pierre Turgeon	New York Islanders
1993–94	Wayne Gretzky	Los Angeles Kings
1994–95	Ron Francis	Pittsburgh Penguins
1995–96	Paul Kariya	Mighty Ducks of Anaheim
1996–97	Paul Kariya	Mighty Ducks of Anaheim
1997–98	Ron Francis	Pittsburgh Penguins
1998–99	Wayne Gretzky	New York Rangers
1999–00	Pavol Demitra	St. Louis Blues
2000–01	Joe Sakic	Colorado Avalanche
2001–02	Ron Francis	Carolina Hurricanes
2002–03	Alexander Mogilny	Toronto Maple Leafs
2003–04	Brad Richards	Tampa Bay Lightning
2004–05	no winner	
2005–06	Pavel Datsyuk	Detroit Red Wings
2006–07	Pavel Datsyuk	Detroit Red Wings
2007–08	Pavel Datsyuk	Detroit Red Wings
2008–09	Pavel Datsyuk	Detroit Red Wings
2009–10	Martin St. Louis	Tampa Bay Lightning
2010–11	Martin St. Louis	Tampa Bay Lightning
2011–12	Brian Campbell	Florida Panthers

VEZINA TROPHY

Awarded to the best goalie as voted on by the league's 30 general managers

1926–27	George Hainsworth	Montreal Canadiens (1.47 GAA)
1927–28	George Hainsworth	Montreal Canadiens (1.05 GAA)
1928–29	George Hainsworth	Montreal Canadiens (0.92 GAA)
1929–30	Tiny Thompson	Boston Bruins (2.19 GAA)
1930–31	Roy Worters	New York Americans (1.61 GAA)

1931–32	Charlie Gardiner	Chicago Black Hawks (1.85 GAA)
1932–33	Tiny Thompson	Boston Bruins (1.76 GAA)
1933–34	Charlie Gardiner	Chicago Black Hawks (1.63 GAA)
1934–35	Lorne Chabot	Chicago Black Hawks (1.80 GAA)
1935–36	Tiny Thompson	Boston Bruins (1.68 GAA)
1936–37	Normie Smith	Detroit Red Wings (2.05 GAA)
1937–38	Tiny Thompson	Boston Bruins (1.80 GAA)
1938–39	Frank Brimsek	Boston Bruins (1.56 GAA)
1939–40	Dave Kerr	New York Rangers (1.54 GAA)
1940–41	Turk Broda	Toronto Maple Leafs (2.00 GAA)
1941–42	Frank Brimsek	Boston Bruins (2.35 GAA)
1942–43	Johnny Mowers	Detroit Red Wings (2.47 GAA)
1943–44	Bill Durnan	Montreal Canadiens (2.18 GAA)
1944–45	Bill Durnan	Montreal Canadiens (2.42 GAA)
1945–46	Bill Durnan	Montreal Canadiens (2.60 GAA)
1946–47	Bill Durnan	Montreal Canadiens (2.30 GAA)
1947–48	Turk Broda	Toronto Maple Leafs (2.38 GAA)
1948–49	Bill Durnan	Montreal Canadiens (2.10 GAA)
1949–50	Bill Durnan	Montreal Canadiens (2.20 GAA)
1950–51	Al Rollins	Toronto Maple Leafs (1.77 GAA)
1951–52	Terry Sawchuk	Detroit Red Wings (1.90 GAA)
1952–53	Terry Sawchuk	Detroit Red Wings (1.90 GAA)
1953–54	Harry Lumley	Toronto Maple Leafs (1.86 GAA)
1954–55	Terry Sawchuk	Detroit Red Wings (1.96 GAA)
1955–56	Jacques Plante	Montreal Canadiens (1.86 GAA)
1956–57	Jacques Plante	Montreal Canadiens (2.00 GAA)
1957–58	Jacques Plante	Montreal Canadiens (2.11 GAA)
1958–59	Jacques Plante	Montreal Canadiens (2.16 GAA)
1959–60	Jacques Plante	Montreal Canadiens (2.54 GAA)
1960–61	Johnny Bower	Toronto Maple Leafs (2.50 GAA)
1961–62	Jacques Plante	Montreal Canadiens (2.37 GAA)
1962–63	Glenn Hall	Chicago Black Hawks (2.47 GAA)
1963–64	Charlie Hodge	Montreal Canadiens (2.26 GAA)
1964–65	Terry Sawchuk	Toronto Maple Leafs (2.56 GAA)
	Johnny Bower	Toronto Maple Leafs (2.38 GAA)
1965–66	Gump Worsley	Montreal Canadiens (2.36 GAA)
	Charlie Hodge	Montreal Canadiens (2.58 GAA)
1966–67	Glenn Hall	Chicago Black Hawks (2.38 GAA)
	Denis DeJordy	Chicago Black Hawks (2.46 GAA)
1967–68	Gump Worsley	Montreal Canadiens (1.98 GAA)
	Rogie Vachon	Montreal Canadiens (2.48 GAA)

1968–69	Jacques Plante	St. Louis Blues (1.96 GAA)
	Glenn Hall	St. Louis Blues (2.17 GAA)
1969–70	Tony Esposito	Chicago Black Hawks (2.17 GAA)
1970–71	Ed Giacomin	New York Rangers (2.16 GAA)
	Gilles Villemure	New York Rangers (2.30 GAA)
1971–72	Tony Esposito	Chicago Black Hawks (1.77 GAA)
	Gary Smith	Chicago Black Hawks (2.42 GAA)
1972–73	Ken Dryden	Montreal Canadiens (2.26 GAA)
1973–74	Bernie Parent	Philadelphia Flyers (1.89 GAA)
	Tony Esposito	Chicago Black Hawks (2.04 GAA)
1974–75	Bernie Parent	Philadelphia Flyers (2.03 GAA)
1975–76	Ken Dryden	Montreal Canadiens (2.03 GAA)
1976–77	Ken Dryden	Montreal Canadiens (2.14 GAA)
	Michel Larocque	Montreal Canadiens (2.09 GAA)
1977–78	Ken Dryden	Montreal Canadiens (2.05 GAA)
	Michel Larocque	Montreal Canadiens (2.67 GAA)
1978–79	Ken Dryden	Montreal Canadiens (2.30 GAA)
	Michel Larocque	Montreal Canadiens (2.84 GAA)
1979–80	Bob Sauve	Buffalo Sabres (2.36 GAA)
	Don Edwards	Buffalo Sabres (2.57 GAA)
1980–81	Richard Sevigny	Montreal Canadiens (2.40 GAA)
	Denis Herron	Montreal Canadiens (3.50 GAA)
	Michel Larocque	Montreal Canadiens (3.03 GAA)
1981–82	Billy Smith	New York Islanders (2.97 GAA)
1982–83	Pete Peeters	Boston Bruins (2.36 GAA)
1983–84	Tom Barrasso	Buffalo Sabres (2.84 GAA)
1984–85	Pelle Lindbergh	Philadelphia Flyers (3.02 GAA)
1985–86	John Vanbiesbrouck	New York Rangers (3.32 GAA)
1986–87	Ron Hextall	Philadelphia Flyers (3.00 GAA)
1987–88	Grant Fuhr	Edmonton Oilers (3.43 GAA)
1988–89	Patrick Roy	Montreal Canadiens (2.47 GAA)
1989–90	Patrick Roy	Montreal Canadiens (2.53 GAA)
1990–91	Ed Belfour	Chicago Blackhawks (2.47 GAA)
1991–92	Patrick Roy	Montreal Canadiens (2.36 GAA)
1992–93	Ed Belfour	Chicago Blackhawks (2.59 GAA)
1993–94	Dominik Hasek	Buffalo Sabres (1.95 GAA)
1994–95	Dominik Hasek	Buffalo Sabres (2.11 GAA)
1995–96	Jim Carey	Washington Capitals (2.26 GAA)
1996–97	Dominik Hasek	Buffalo Sabres (2.27 GAA)
1997–98	Dominik Hasek	Buffalo Sabres (2.09 GAA)
1998–99	Dominik Hasek	Buffalo Sabres (1.87 GAA)
1999–00	Olaf Kolzig	Washington Capitals (2.24 GAA)

2000–01	Dominik Hasek	Buffalo Sabres (2.11 GAA)
2001–02	Jose Theodore	Montreal Canadiens (2.11 GAA)
2002–03	Martin Brodeur	New Jersey Devils (2.02 GAA)
2003–04	Martin Brodeur	New Jersey Devils (2.62 GAA)
2004–05	no winner	
2005–06	Miikka Kiprusoff	Calgary Flames (2.07 GAA)
2006–07	Martin Brodeur	New Jersey Devils (2.18 GAA)
2007–08	Martin Brodeur	New Jersey Devils (2.17 GAA)
2008–09	Tim Thomas	Boston Bruins (2.10 GAA)
2009–10	Ryan Miller	Buffalo Sabres (2.22 GAA)
2010–11	Tim Thomas	Boston Bruins (2.00 GAA)
2011–12	Henrik Lundqvist	New York Rangers (1.97 GAA)

CALDER MEMORIAL TROPHY

Awarded to the best rookie in the league

1932–33	Carl Voss	Detroit Red Wings
1933–34	Russ Blinco	Montreal Maroons
1934–35	Sweeney Schriner	New York Americans
1935–36	Mike Karakas	Chicago Black Hawks
1936–37	Syl Apps	Toronto Maple Leafs
1937–38	Cully Dahlstrom	Chicago Black Hawks
1938–39	Frank Brimsek	Boston Bruins
1939–40	Kilby MacDonald	New York Rangers
1940–41	John Quilty	Montreal Canadiens
1941–42	Grant Warwick	New York Rangers
1942–43	Gaye Stewart	Toronto Maple Leafs
1943–44	Gus Bodnar	Toronto Maple Leafs
1944–45	Frank McCool	Toronto Maple Leafs
1945–46	Edgar Laprade	New York Rangers
1946–47	Howie Meeker	Toronto Maple Leafs
1947–48	Jim McFadden	Detroit Red Wings
1948–49	Pentti Lund	New York Rangers
1949–50	Jack Gelineau	Boston Bruins
1950–51	Terry Sawchuk	Detroit Red Wings
1951–52	Bernie Geoffrion	Montreal Canadiens
1952–53	Gump Worsley	New York Rangers
1953–54	Camille Henry	New York Rangers
1954–55	Ed Litzenberger	Chicago Black Hawks
1955–56	Glenn Hall	Detroit Red Wings
1956–57	Larry Regan	Boston Bruins
1957–58	Frank Mahovlich	Toronto Maple Leafs

1958–59	Ralph Backstrom	Montreal Canadiens
1959–60	Bill Hay	Chicago Black Hawks
1960–61	Dave Keon	Toronto Maple Leafs
1961–62	Bobby Rousseau	Montreal Canadiens
1962–63	Kent Douglas	Toronto Maple Leafs
1963–64	Jacques Laperriere	Montreal Canadiens
1964–65	Roger Crozier	Detroit Red Wings
1965–66	Brit Selby	Toronto Maple Leafs
1966–67	Bobby Orr	Boston Bruins
1967–68	Derek Sanderson	Boston Bruins
1968–69	Danny Grant	Minnesota North Stars
1969–70	Tony Esposito	Chicago Black Hawks
1970–71	Gilbert Perreault	Buffalo Sabres
1971–72	Ken Dryden	Montreal Canadiens
1972–73	Steve Vickers	New York Rangers
1973–74	Denis Potvin	New York Islanders
1974–75	Eric Vail	Atlanta Flames
1975–76	Bryan Trottier	New York Islanders
1976–77	Willi Plett	Atlanta Flames
1977–78	Mike Bossy	New York Islanders
1978–79	Bobby Smith	Minnesota North Stars
1979–80	Raymond Bourque	Boston Bruins
1980–81	Peter Stastny	Quebec Nordiques
1981–82	Dale Hawerchuk	Winnipeg Jets
1982–83	Steve Larmer	Chicago Black Hawks
1983–84	Tom Barrasso	Buffalo Sabres
1984–85	Mario Lemieux	Pittsburgh Penguins
1985–86	Gary Suter	Calgary Flames
1986–87	Luc Robitaille	Los Angeles Kings
1987–88	Joe Nieuwendyk	Calgary Flames
1988–89	Brian Leetch	New York Rangers
1989–90	Sergei Makarov	Calgary Flames
1990–91	Ed Belfour	Chicago Blackhawks
1991–92	Pavel Bure	Vancouver Canucks
1992–93	Teemu Selanne	Winnipeg Jets
1993–94	Martin Brodeur	New Jersey Devils
1994–95	Peter Forsberg	Quebec Nordiques
1995–96	Daniel Alfredsson	Ottawa Senators
1996–97	Bryan Berard	New York Islanders
1997–98	Sergei Samsonov	Boston Bruins
1998–99	Chris Drury	Colorado Avalanche
1999–00	Scott Gomez	New Jersey Devils

2000–01	Evgeni Nabokov	San Jose Sharks
2001–02	Danny Heatley	Atlanta Thrashers
2002–03	Barret Jackman	St. Louis Blues
2003–04	Andrew Raycroft	Boston Bruins
2004–05	no winner	
2005–06	Alexander Ovechkin	Washington Capitals
2006–07	Evgeni Malkin	Pittsburgh Penguins
2007–08	Patrick Kane	Chicago Blackhawks
2008–09	Steve Mason	Columbus Blue Jackets
2009–10	Tyler Myers	Buffalo Sabres
2010–11	Jeff Skinner	Carolina Hurricanes
2011–12	Gabriel Landeskog	Colorado Avalanche

JAMES NORRIS TROPHY

Awarded to the best defenceman during the regular season

1953–54	Red Kelly	Detroit Red Wings
1954–55	Doug Harvey	Montreal Canadiens
1955–56	Doug Harvey	Montreal Canadiens
1956–57	Doug Harvey	Montreal Canadiens
1957–58	Doug Harvey	Montreal Canadiens
1958–59	Tom Johnson	Montreal Canadiens
1959–60	Doug Harvey	Montreal Canadiens
1960–61	Doug Harvey	Montreal Canadiens
1961–62	Doug Harvey	Montreal Canadiens
1962–63	Pierre Pilote	Chicago Black Hawks
1963–64	Pierre Pilote	Chicago Black Hawks
1964–65	Pierre Pilote	Chicago Black Hawks
1965–66	Jacques Laperriere	Montreal Canadiens
1966–67	Harry Howell	New York Rangers
1967–68	Bobby Orr	Boston Bruins
1968–69	Bobby Orr	Boston Bruins
1969–70	Bobby Orr	Boston Bruins
1970–71	Bobby Orr	Boston Bruins
1971–72	Bobby Orr	Boston Bruins
1972–73	Bobby Orr	Boston Bruins
1973–74	Bobby Orr	Boston Bruins
1974–75	Bobby Orr	Boston Bruins
1975–76	Denis Potvin	New York Islanders
1976–77	Larry Robinson	Montreal Canadiens
1977–78	Denis Potvin	New York Islanders
1978–79	Denis Potvin	New York Islanders

1979–80	Larry Robinson	Montreal Canadiens
1980–81	Randy Carlyle	Pittsburgh Penguins
1981–82	Doug Wilson	Chicago Black Hawks
1982–83	Rod Langway	Washington Capitals
1983–84	Rod Langway	Washington Capitals
1984–85	Paul Coffey	Edmonton Oilers
1985–86	Paul Coffey	Edmonton Oilers
1986–87	Raymond Bourque	Boston Bruins
1987–88	Raymond Bourque	Boston Bruins
1988–89	Chris Chelios	Montreal Canadiens
1989–90	Raymond Bourque	Boston Bruins
1990–91	Raymond Bourque	Boston Bruins
1991–92	Brian Leetch	New York Rangers
1992–93	Chris Chelios	Chicago Blackhawks
1993–94	Raymond Bourque	Boston Bruins
1994–95	Paul Coffey	Detroit Red Wings
1995–96	Chris Chelios	Chicago Blackhawks
1996–97	Brian Leetch	New York Rangers
1997–98	Rob Blake	Los Angeles Kings
1998–99	Al MacInnis	St. Louis Blues
1999–00	Chris Pronger	St. Louis Blues
2000–01	Nicklas Lidstrom	Detroit Red Wings
2001–02	Nicklas Lidstrom	Detroit Red Wings
2002–03	Nicklas Lidstrom	Detroit Red Wings
2003–04	Scott Niedermayer	New Jersey Devils
2004–05	no winner	
2005–06	Nicklas Lidstrom	Detroit Red Wings
2006–07	Nicklas Lidstrom	Detroit Red Wings
2007–08	Nicklas Lidstrom	Detroit Red Wings
2008–09	Zdeno Chara	Boston Bruins
2009–10	Duncan Keith	Chicago Blackhawks
2010–11	Nicklas Lidstrom	Detroit Red Wings
2011–12	Erik Karlsson	Ottawa Senators

LESTER PATRICK TROPHY

Awarded for contributions to hockey in the United States

1965–66	Jack Adams
1966–67	Gordie Howe
	Charles F. Adams
	James Norris, Sr.

1967–68	Tommy Lockhart
	Walter A. Brown
	Gen. John R. Kilpatrick
1968–69	Bobby Hull
	Ed Jeremiah
1969–70	Eddie Shore
	Jim Hendy
1970–71	Bill Jennings
	John B. Sollenberger
	Terry Sawchuk
1971–72	Clarence Campbell
	John A. Kelly
	Cooney Weiland
	James D. Norris
1972–73	Walter Bush, Jr.
1973–74	Alex Delvecchio
	Murray Murdoch
	Weston W. Adams Sr.
	Charles L. Crovat
1974–75	Donald M. Clark
	Bill Chadwick
	Tommy Ivan
1975–76	Stan Mikita
	George Leader
	Bruce A. Norris
1976–77	Johnny Bucyk
	Murray Armstrong
	John Mariucci
1977–78	Phil Esposito
	Tom Fitzgerald
	William T. Tutt
	Bill Wirtz
1978–79	Bobby Orr
1979–80	Bobby Clarke
	Ed Snider
	Fred Shero
	1980 U.S. Olympic Hockey Team
1980–81	Charles M. Schulz
1981–82	Emile Francis
1982–83	Bill Torrey
1983–84	John A. Ziegler Jr.
	Art Ross

1984–85	Jack Butterfield
	Arthur M. Wirtz
1985–86	John MacInnes
	Jack Riley
1986–87	Hobey Baker
	Frank Mathers
1987–88	Keith Allen
	Fred Cusick
	Bob Johnson
1988–89	Dan Kelly
	Lou Nanne
	Lynn Patrick
	Bud Poile
1989–90	Len Ceglarski
1990–91	Rod Gilbert
	Mike Ilitch
1991–92	Al Arbour
	Art Berglund
	Lou Lamoriello
1992–93	Frank Boucher
	Red Dutton
	Bruce McNall
	Gil Stein
1993–94	Wayne Gretzky
	Robert Ridder
1994–95	Joe Mullen
	Brian Mullen
	Bob Fleming
1995–96	George Gund
	Ken Morrow
	Milt Schmidt
1996–97	Seymour H. Knox III
	Bill Cleary
	Pat LaFontaine
1997–98	Peter Karmanos
	Neal Broten
	John Mayasich
	Max McNab
1998–99	Harry Sinden
	1998 U.S. Olympic Women's Hockey Team

1999–00	Mario Lemieux
	Craig Patrick
	Lou Vairo
2000–01	Scotty Bowman
	David Poile
	Gary Bettman
2001–02	1960 U.S. Olympic Team
	Herb Brooks
	Larry Pleau
2002–03	Ray Bourque
	Ron DeGregorio
	Willie O'Ree
2003–04	Mike Emrick
	John Davidson
	Ray Miron
2004–05	none
2005–06	Red Berenson
	Marcel Dionne
	Reed Larson
	Glen Sonmor
	Steve Yzerman
2006–07	Brian Leetch
	Cammi Granato
	John Halligan
	Stan Fischler
2007–08	Brian Burke
	Ted Lindsay
	Phil Housley
	Bob Naegele, Jr.
2008–09	Mark Messier
	Mike Richter
	Jimmy Devellano
2009–10	Dave Andrews
	Cam Neely
	Jack Parker
	Jerry York
2010–11	Mark Johnson
	Bob Pulford
	Tony Rossi
	Jeff Sauer

CONN SMYTHE TROPHY

Awarded to the most valuable player in the playoffs
* indicates played for losing team

1964–65	Jean Beliveau	Montreal Canadiens
1965–66	Roger Crozier*	Detroit Red Wings
1966–67	Dave Keon	Toronto Maple Leafs
1967–68	Glenn Hall*	St. Louis Blues
1968–69	Serge Savard	Montreal Canadiens
1969–70	Bobby Orr	Boston Bruins
1970–71	Ken Dryden	Montreal Canadiens
1971–72	Bobby Orr	Boston Bruins
1972–73	Yvan Cournoyer	Montreal Canadiens
1973–74	Bernie Parent	Philadelphia Flyers
1974–75	Bernie Parent	Philadelphia Flyers
1975–76	Reggie Leach*	Philadelphia Flyers
1976–77	Guy Lafleur	Montreal Canadiens
1977–78	Larry Robinson	Montreal Canadiens
1978–79	Bob Gainey	Montreal Canadiens
1979–80	Bryan Trottier	New York Islanders
1980–81	Butch Goring	New York Islanders
1981–82	Mike Bossy	New York Islanders
1982–83	Billy Smith	New York Islanders
1983–84	Mark Messier	Edmonton Oilers
1984–85	Wayne Gretzky	Edmonton Oilers
1985–86	Patrick Roy	Montreal Canadiens
1986–87	Ron Hextall	Philadelphia Flyers
1987–88	Wayne Gretzky	Edmonton Oilers
1988–89	Al MacInnis	Calgary Flames
1989–90	Bill Ranford	Edmonton Oilers
1990–91	Mario Lemieux	Pittsburgh Penguins
1991–92	Mario Lemieux	Pittsburgh Penguins
1992–93	Patrick Roy	Montreal Canadiens
1993–94	Brian Leetch	New York Rangers
1994–95	Claude Lemieux	New Jersey Devils
1995–96	Joe Sakic	Colorado Avalanche
1996–97	Mike Vernon	Detroit Red Wings
1997–98	Steve Yzerman	Detroit Red Wings
1998–99	Joe Nieuwendyk	Dallas Stars
1999–00	Scott Stevens	New Jersey Devils
2000–01	Patrick Roy	Colorado Avalanche
2001–02	Nicklas Lidstrom	Detroit Red Wings

2002–03	J-S Giguere*	Mighty Ducks of Anaheim
2003–04	Brad Richards	Tampa Bay Lightning
2004–05	no winner	
2005–06	Cam Ward	Carolina Hurricanes
2006–07	Scott Niedermayer	Anaheim Ducks
2007–08	Henrik Zetterberg	Detroit Red Wings
2008–09	Evgeni Malkin	Pittsburgh Penguins
2009–10	Jonathan Toews	Chicago Blackhawks
2010–11	Tim Thomas	Boston Bruins
2011–12	Jonathan Quick	Los Angeles Kings

BILL MASTERTON MEMORIAL TROPHY

Awarded to the player who best displays perseverance, sportsmanship and dedication to the game

1967–68	Claude Provost	Montreal Canadiens
1968–69	Ted Hampson	Oakland Seals
1969–70	Pit Martin	Chicago Black Hawks
1970–71	Jean Ratelle	New York Rangers
1971–72	Bobby Clarke	Philadelphia Flyers
1972–73	Lowell MacDonald	Pittsburgh Penguins
1973–74	Henri Richard	Montreal Canadiens
1974–75	Don Luce	Buffalo Sabres
1975–76	Rod Gilbert	New York Rangers
1976–77	Ed Westfall	New York Islanders
1977–78	Butch Goring	Los Angeles Kings
1978–79	Serge Savard	Montreal Canadiens
1979–80	Al MacAdam	Minnesota North Stars
1980–81	Blake Dunlop	St. Louis Blues
1981–82	Glenn Resch	Colorado Rockies
1982–83	Lanny McDonald	Calgary Flames
1983–84	Brad Park	Detroit Red Wings
1984–85	Anders Hedberg	New York Rangers
1985–86	Charlie Simmer	Boston Bruins
1986–87	Doug Jarvis	Hartford Whalers
1987–88	Bob Bourne	Los Angeles Kings
1988–89	Tim Kerr	Philadelphia Flyers
1989–90	Gord Kluzak	Boston Bruins
1990–91	Dave Taylor	Los Angeles Kings
1991–92	Mark Fitzpatrick	New York Islanders
1992–93	Mario Lemieux	Pittsburgh Penguins
1993–94	Cam Neely	Boston Bruins

1994–95	Pat LaFontaine	Buffalo Sabres
1995–96	Gary Roberts	Calgary Flames
1996–97	Tony Granato	San Jose Sharks
1997–98	Jamie McLennan	St. Louis Blues
1998–99	John Cullen	Tampa Bay Lightning
1999–00	Ken Daneyko	New Jersey Devils
2000–01	Adam Graves	New York Rangers
2001–02	Saku Koivu	Montreal Canadiens
2002–03	Steve Yzerman	Detroit Red Wings
2003–04	Bryan Berard	Chicago Blackhawks
2004–05	no winner	
2005–06	Teemu Selanne	Mighty Ducks of Anaheim
2006–07	Phil Kessel	Boston Bruins
2007–08	Jason Blake	Toronto Maple Leafs
2008–09	Steve Sullivan	Nashville Predators
2009–10	Jose Theodore	Washington Capitals
2010–11	Ian Laperriere	Philadelphia Flyers
2011–12	Max Pacioretty	Montreal Canadiens

JACK ADAMS AWARD

Awarded to the coach of the year

1973–74	Fred Shero	Philadelphia Flyers
1974–75	Bob Pulford	Los Angeles Kings
1975–76	Don Cherry	Boston Bruins
1976–77	Scotty Bowman	Montreal Canadiens
1977–78	Bobby Kromm	Detroit Red Wings
1978–79	Al Arbour	New York Islanders
1979–80	Pat Quinn	Philadelphia Flyers
1980–81	Red Berenson	St. Louis Blues
1981–82	Tom Watt	Winnipeg Jets
1982–83	Orval Tessier	Chicago Black Hawks
1983–84	Bryan Murray	Washington Capitals
1984–85	Mike Keenan	Philadelphia Flyers
1985–86	Glen Sather	Edmonton Oilers
1986–87	Jacques Demers	Detroit Red Wings
1987–88	Jacques Demers	Detroit Red Wings
1988–89	Pat Burns	Montreal Canadiens
1989–90	Bob Murdoch	Winnipeg Jets
1990–91	Brian Sutter	St. Louis Blues
1991–92	Pat Quinn	Vancouver Canucks
1992–93	Pat Burns	Toronto Maple Leafs

1993–94	Jacques Lemaire	New Jersey Devils
1994–95	Marc Crawford	Quebec Nordiques
1995–96	Scotty Bowman	Detroit Red Wings
1996–97	Ted Nolan	Buffalo Sabres
1997–98	Pat Burns	Boston Bruins
1998–99	Jacques Martin	Ottawa Senators
1999–00	Joel Quenneville	St. Louis Blues
2000–01	Bill Barber	Philadelphia Flyers
2001–02	Bob Francis	Phoenix Coyotes
2002–03	Jacques Lemaire	Minnesota Wild
2003–04	John Tortorella	Tampa Bay Lightning
2004–05	no winner	
2005–06	Lindy Ruff	Buffalo Sabres
2006–07	Alain Vigneault	Vancouver Canucks
2007–08	Bruce Boudreau	Washington Capitals
2008–09	Claude Julien	Boston Bruins
2009–10	Dave Tippett	Phoenix Coyotes
2010–11	Dan Bylsma	Pittsburgh Penguins
2011–12	Ken Hitchcock	St. Louis Blues

LESTER B. PEARSON AWARD

Awarded to the league's most valuable player as voted on by the players

1970–71	Phil Esposito	Boston Bruins
1971–72	Jean Ratelle	New York Rangers
1972–73	Bobby Clarke	Philadelphia Flyers
1973–74	Phil Esposito	Boston Bruins
1974–75	Bobby Orr	Boston Bruins
1975–76	Guy Lafleur	Montreal Canadiens
1976–77	Guy Lafleur	Montreal Canadiens
1977–78	Guy Lafleur	Montreal Canadiens
1978–79	Marcel Dionne	Los Angeles Kings
1979–80	Marcel Dionne	Los Angeles Kings
1980–81	Mike Liut	St. Louis Blues
1981–82	Wayne Gretzky	Edmonton Oilers
1982–83	Wayne Gretzky	Edmonton Oilers
1983–84	Wayne Gretzky	Edmonton Oilers
1984–85	Wayne Gretzky	Edmonton Oilers
1985–86	Mario Lemieux	Pittsburgh Penguins
1986–87	Wayne Gretzky	Edmonton Oilers
1987–88	Mario Lemieux	Pittsburgh Penguins
1988–89	Steve Yzerman	Detroit Red Wings

1989–90	Mark Messier	Edmonton Oilers
1990–91	Brett Hull	St. Louis Blues
1991–92	Mark Messier	New York Rangers
1992–93	Mario Lemieux	Pittsburgh Penguins
1993–94	Sergei Fedorov	Detroit Red Wings
1994–95	Eric Lindros	Philadelphia Flyers
1995–96	Mario Lemieux	Pittsburgh Penguins
1996–97	Dominik Hasek	Buffalo Sabres
1997–98	Dominik Hasek	Buffalo Sabres
1998–99	Jaromir Jagr	Pittsburgh Penguins
1999–00	Jaromir Jagr	Pittsburgh Penguins
2000–01	Joe Sakic	Colorado Avalanche
2001–02	Jarome Iginla	Calgary Flames
2002–03	Markus Naslund	Vancouver Canucks
2003–04	Martin St. Louis	Tampa Bay Lightning
2004–05	no winner	
2005–06	Jaromir Jagr	New York Rangers
2006–07	Sidney Crosby	Pittsburgh Penguins
2007–08	Alexander Ovechkin	Washington Capitals
2008–09	Alexander Ovechkin	Washington Capitals

TED LINDSAY AWARD

(Formerly Lester B. Pearson Award)

2009–10	Alexander Ovechkin	Washington Capitals
2010–11	Daniel Sedin	Vancouver Canucks
2011–12	Evgeni Malkin	Pittsburgh Penguins

FRANK J. SELKE TROPHY

Awarded to the forward who best displays defensive skills

1977–78	Bob Gainey	Montreal Canadiens
1978–79	Bob Gainey	Montreal Canadiens
1979–80	Bob Gainey	Montreal Canadiens
1980–81	Bob Gainey	Montreal Canadiens
1981–82	Steve Kasper	Boston Bruins
1982–83	Bobby Clarke	Pittsburgh Penguins
1983–84	Doug Jarvis	Washington Capitals
1984–85	Craig Ramsay	Buffalo Sabres
1985–86	Troy Murray	Chicago Black Hawks
1986–87	Dave Poulin	Philadelphia Flyers
1987–88	Guy Carbonneau	Montreal Canadiens

1988–89	Guy Carbonneau	Montreal Canadiens
1989–90	Rick Meagher	St. Louis Blues
1990–91	Dirk Graham	Chicago Blackhawks
1991–92	Guy Carbonneau	Montreal Canadiens
1992–93	Doug Gilmour	Toronto Maple Leafs
1993–94	Sergei Fedorov	Detroit Red Wings
1994–95	Ron Francis	Pittsburgh Penguins
1995–96	Sergei Fedorov	Detroit Red Wings
1996–97	Michael Peca	Buffalo Sabres
1997–98	Jere Lehtinen	Dallas Stars
1998–99	Jere Lehtinen	Dallas Stars
1999–00	Steve Yzerman	Detroit Red Wings
2000–01	John Madden	New Jersey Devils
2001–02	Michael Peca	New York Islanders
2002–03	Jere Lehtinen	Dallas Stars
2003–04	Kris Draper	Detroit Red Wings
2004–05	no winner	
2005–06	Rod Brind'Amour	Carolina Hurricanes
2006–07	Rod Brind'Amour	Carolina Hurricanes
2007–08	Pavel Datsyuk	Detroit Red Wings
2008–09	Pavel Datsyuk	Detroit Red Wings
2009–10	Pavel Datsyuk	Detroit Red Wings
2010–11	Ryan Kesler	Vancouver Canucks
2011–12	Patrice Bergeron	Boston Bruins

WILLIAM M. JENNINGS TROPHY

Awarded to the goalie(s) with the best goals-against average in the regular season

1981–82	Rick Wamsley & Denis Herron	Montreal Canadiens
1982–83	Rollie Melanson & Billy Smith	New York Islanders
1983–84	Al Jensen & Pat Riggin	Washington Capitals
1984–85	Tom Barrasso & Bob Sauve	Buffalo Sabres
1985–86	Bob Froese & Darren Jensen	Philadelphia Flyers
1986–87	Patrick Roy & Brian Hayward	Montreal Canadiens
1987–88	Patrick Roy & Brian Hayward	Montreal Canadiens
1988–89	Patrick Roy & Brian Hayward	Montreal Canadiens
1989–90	Andy Moog & Reggie Lemelin	Boston Bruins
1990–91	Ed Belfour	Chicago Blackhawks
1991–92	Patrick Roy	Montreal Canadiens
1992–93	Ed Belfour	Chicago Blackhawks
1993–94	Dominik Hasek & Grant Fuhr	Buffalo Sabres
1994–95	Ed Belfour	Chicago Blackhawks

1995–96	Chris Osgood & Mike Vernon	Detroit Red Wings
1996–97	Martin Brodeur & Mike Dunham	New Jersey Devils
1997–98	Martin Brodeur	New Jersey Devils
1998–99	Ed Belfour & Roman Turek	Dallas Stars
1999–00	Roman Turek	St. Louis Blues
2000–01	Dominik Hasek	Buffalo Sabres
2001–02	Patrick Roy	Colorado Avalanche
2002–03	Martin Brodeur	New Jersey Devils
	Roman Cechmanek	Philadelphia Flyers
	Robert Esche	Philadelphia Flyers
2003–04	Martin Brodeur	New Jersey Devils
2004–05	no winner	
2005–06	Miikka Kiprusoff	Calgary Flames
2006–07	Manny Fernandez & Niklas Backstrom	Minnesota Wild
2007–08	Chris Osgood & Dominik Hasek	Detroit Red Wings
2008–09	Tim Thomas & Manny Fernandez	Boston Bruins
2009–10	Martin Brodeur	New Jersey Devils
2010–11	Roberto Luongo & Corey Schneider	Vancouver Canucks
2011–12	Jaroslav Halak & Brian Elliot	St. Louis Blues

KING CLANCY MEMORIAL TROPHY

Awarded to the player who best displays leadership both on and off the ice

1987–88	Lanny McDonald	Calgary Flames
1988–89	Bryan Trottier	New York Islanders
1989–90	Kevin Lowe	Edmonton Oilers
1990–91	Dave Taylor	Los Angeles Kings
1991–92	Raymond Bourque	Boston Bruins
1992–93	Dave Poulin	Boston Bruins
1993–94	Adam Graves	New York Rangers
1994–95	Joe Nieuwendyk	Calgary Flames
1995–96	Kris King	Winnipeg Jets
1996–97	Trevor Linden	Vancouver Canucks
1997–98	Kelly Chase	St. Louis Blues
1998–99	Rob Ray	Buffalo Sabres
1999–00	Curtis Joseph	Toronto Maple Leafs
2000–01	Shjon Podein	Colorado Avalanche
2001–02	Ron Francis	Carolina Hurricanes
2002–03	Brendan Shanahan	Detroit Red Wings
2003–04	Jarome Iginla	Calgary Flames
2004–05	no winner	
2005–06	Olaf Kolzig	Washington Capitals

2006–07	Saku Koivu	Montreal Canadiens
2007–08	Vincent Lecavalier	Tampa Bay Lightning
2008–09	Ethan Moreau	Edmonton Oilers
2009–10	Shane Doan	Phoenix Coyotes
2010–11	Doug Weight	New York Islanders
2011–12	Daniel Alfredsson	Ottawa Senators

ROCKET RICHARD TROPHY

Awarded to the player(s) who leads the regular season in goals scored

1998–99	Teemu Selanne	Mighty Ducks of Anaheim (47 goals)
1999–00	Pavel Bure	Florida Panthers (58 goals)
2000–01	Pavel Bure	Florida Panthers (59 goals)
2001–02	Jarome Iginla	Calgary Flames (52 goals)
2002–03	Milan Hejduk	Colorado Avalanche (50 goals)
2003–04	Rick Nash	Columbus Blue Jackets (41 goals)
	Jarome Iginla	Calgary Flames (41 goals)
	Ilya Kovalchuk	Atlanta Thrashers (41 goals)
2004–05	no winner	
2005–06	Jonathan Cheechoo	San Jose Sharks (56 goals)
2006–07	Vincent Lacavalier	Tampa Bay Lightning (52 goals)
2007–08	Alexander Ovechkin	Washington Capitals (65 goals)
2008–09	Alexander Ovechkin	Washington Capitals (56 goals)
2009–10	Sidney Crosby	Pittsburgh Penguins (51 goals)
	Steve Stamkos	Tampa Bay Lightning (51 goals)
2010–11	Corey Perry	Anaheim Ducks (50 goals)
2011–12	Steve Stamkos	Tampa Bay Lightning (60 goals)

2012 HOCKEY HALL OF FAME INDUCTEES

Selection Committee Meeting: June 26, 2012
Induction Ceremony: November 12, 2012

PLAYER INDUCTEES

Pavel Bure

Bure was a star in the NHL for 12 seasons before a knee injury forced him into early retirement in 2003, but he was nicknamed the "Russian Rocket" in honour of his heritage and in homage to Rocket Richard, the great Canadiens scoring star who was both a goal-scoring wizard and a tremendous skater. The name was apt, though, because Bure could put the puck in the net like few others. He scored at least 50 goals five times, and two of those seasons were 60-goal gems with Vancouver. He brought people out of their seats with his tremendous speed and puck handling, but he never won the Stanley Cup. Bure first came to prominence in international hockey at the 1989 World Junior Championship. He, Alexander Mogilny and Sergei Fedorov stole the show in Alaska, as this troika of Soviets clearly defined themselves as the next generation of stars. They all ended up leaving for the NHL, but before he did, Bure won a gold and two silvers at the U20. He later won a silver and bronze at the Olympics and a gold at the World Championship.

Adam Oates

At first blush, Oates might seem like the surprise member of the Class of 2012, yet his credentials are impressive all the same. Perhaps the most astounding fact about his induction and sensational career is that he was never drafted. He signed as a free agent with Detroit in 1985 and played his first four NHL seasons with the Red Wings. He later played two and a half years with St. Louis, centring Brett Hull, but played the majority of his career with Boston and Washington. Known as a passer much more than a scorer, he had 1,040 assists and 1,420 points in 1,337 regular-season games. The closest he came to winning the Cup was in 1998, when the Capitals went to the finals, only to be swept aside by Detroit. Oates never played for Team Canada at any level.

Joe Sakic

Joe Sakic is, quite simply, one of the finest players ever to skate on a sheet of ice. The 12th member of the Triple Gold Club, he was brilliant in the NHL and for Team Canada. In 20 NHL seasons, he won the Stanley Cup twice, in 1996 and 2001 with Colorado, the franchise for which he played his entire career. He had 1,641 points in 1,378 regular-season games, and another 188 points in 172 playoff games. He captained the Avs for 18 years, and only Fetisov and Igor Larionov are TGC members as well as Hall of Famers. For Canada, Sakic won gold at all levels, starting with the 1988 junior team. He won gold at the 1994 World Championship, and then Olympic gold in 2002. He also played for Canada's victorious World Cup team in 2004. Known for his quick snapshot, sportsmanlike play and tremendous leadership, Sakic represented the game with an integrity and dedication worthy of his Hockey Hall of Fame honour.

Mats Sundin
The first European drafted first overall, by Quebec in 1989, Sundin played 18 seasons in the NHL and achieved every statistical milestone expected of a Hall of Fame forward. In all, he finished with 564 goals and 1,349 career points in 1,346 regular-season games. He was captain of the Maple Leafs for 12 years, but the one blemish on his otherwise sensational record is that he wasn't able to win a Stanley Cup. His play with Tre Kronor was another story. Sundin captained Sweden to Olympic gold in 2006, and at the 1991 World Championship he scored what is considered the greatest goal in that tournament's history, making an end-to-end rush that included a perfect deke on Vyacheslav Fetisov and scoring to give Sweden a 2–1 over Russia and the gold medal. In all, he won seven WM medals (three gold) and also played in the 1991 Canada Cup and 1996 and 2004 World Cups, being quite possibly the best player in 1996. When he donned the Three Crowns sweater of his native Sweden, he elevated his game accordingly.

Other Notable Names Eligible but Not Inducted

Men
Curtis Joseph, Olaf Kolzig, Martin Gelinas, Bobby Holik, Darius Kasparaitis, Claude Lemieux, Teppo Numminen, Gary Roberts, Jeremy Roenick, Brendan Shanahan, Viktor Tikhonov, Pat Burns, Eric Lindros, Dave Andreychuk, Phil Housley, Sergei Makarov, Mike Vernon, Tom Barrasso, Arturs Irbe, Tommy Salo, Peter Bondra

Women
Fran Rider, Shirley Cameron, Cassie Campbell, Danielle Goyette, Geraldine Heaney, Nancy Drolet, France St. Louis, Ben Smith, Vicky Sunohara, Krissy Wendell, Lady Isobel Constance Mary Stanley

Selection Committee: Jim Gregory, Pat Quinn, Scotty Bowman, David Branch, Brian Burke, Colin Campbell, John Davidson, Eric Duhatschek, Mike Emrick, Michael Farber, Marc de Foy, Mike Gartner, Anders Hedberg, Igor Larionov, Lanny McDonald, Serge Savard, Peter Stastny, Bill Torrey

HOCKEY HALL OF FAME HONOURED MEMBERS

(member—category, year inducted)

Sid Abel—Player, 1969
Charles Adams—Builder, 1960
Jack Adams—Player, 1959
Weston Adams—Builder, 1972
Frank Ahearn—Builder, 1962

Bunny Ahearne—Builder, 1977
Sir Montagu Allan—Builder, 1945
Keith Allen—Builder, 1992
Glenn Anderson—Player, 2008
Syl Apps—Player, 1961

Al Arbour—Builder, 1996

George Armstrong—Player, 1975

Neil Armstrong—Official, 1991

John Ashley—Official, 1981

Ace Bailey—Player, 1975

Dan Bain—Player, 1945

Hobey Baker—Player, 1945

Harold Ballard—Builder, 1977

Bill Barber—Player, 1990

Marty Barry—Player, 1965

Andy Bathgate—Player, 1978

Bobby Bauer—Player, 1996

Father David Bauer—Builder, 1989

Jean Beliveau—Player, 1972

Ed Belfour—Player, 2011

Clint Benedict—Player, 1965

Doug Bentley—Player, 1964

Max Bentley—Player, 1966

Jack Bickell—Builder, 1978

Toe Blake—Player, 1966

Leo Boivin—Player, 1986

Dickie Boon—Player, 1952

Mike Bossy—Player, 1991

Butch Bouchard—Player, 1966

Frank Boucher—Player, 1958

George Boucher—Player, 1960

Ray Bourque—Player, 2004

Johnny Bower—Player, 1976

Russell Bowie—Player, 1945

Scotty Bowman—Builder, 1991

Frank Brimsek—Player, 1966

Punch Broadbent—Player, 1962

Turk Broda—Player, 1967

Herb Brooks—Builder, 2006

George Brown—Builder, 1961

Walter Brown—Builder, 1962

Frank Buckland—Builder, 1975

Johnny Bucyk—Player, 1981

Billy Burch—Player, 1974

Pavel Dure—Player, 2012

Walter Bush—Builder, 2000

Jack Butterfield—Builder, 1980

Frank Calder—Builder, 1947

Harry Cameron—Player, 1962

Angus Campbell—Builder, 1964

Clarence Campbell—Builder, 1966

Joe Cattarinich—Builder, 1977

Bill Chadwick—Official, 1964

Gerry Cheevers—Player, 1985

Ed Chynoweth—Builder, 2008

King Clancy—Player, 1958

Dino Ciccarelli—Player, 2010

Dit Clapper—Player, 1947

Bobby Clarke—Player, 1987

Sprague Cleghorn—Player, 1958

Paul Coffey—Player, 2004

Neil Colville—Player, 1967

Charlie Conacher—Player, 1961

Lionel Conacher—Player, 1994

Roy Conacher—Player, 1998

Alex Connell—Player, 1958

Bill Cook—Player, 1952

Bun Cook—Player, 1995

Murray Costello—Builder, 2005

Art Coulter—Player, 1974

Yvan Cournoyer—Player, 1982

Bill Cowley—Player, 1968

Rusty Crawford—Player, 1962

John D'Amico—Official, 1993

Leo Dandurand—Builder, 1963

Jack Darragh—Player, 1962

Scotty Davidson—Player, 1950

Hap Day—Player, 1961

Alex Delvecchio—Player, 1977

Cy Denneny—Player, 1959

Frank Dilio—Builder, 1964

Jimmy Devellano—Builder, 2010

Marcel Dionne—Player, 1992

Gord Drillon—Player, 1975

Graham Drinkwater—Player, 1950

Ken Dryden—Player, 1983

George Dudley—Builder, 1958

Dick Duff—Player, 2006

Woody Dumart—Player, 1992

Tommy Dunderdale—Player, 1974

James Dunn—Builder, 1968

Bill Durnan—Player, 1964
Red Dutton—Player, 1958
Babe Dye—Player, 1970
Chaucer Elliott—Official, 1961
Tony Esposito—Player, 1988
Phil Esposito—Player, 1984
Art Farrell—Player, 1965
Bernie Federko—Player, 2002
Slava Fetisov—Player, 2001
Fern Flaman—Player, 1990
Cliff Fletcher—Builder, 2004
Frank Foyston—Player, 1958
Emile Francis—Builder, 1982
Ron Francis—Player, 2007
Frank Fredrickson—Player, 1958
Grant Fuhr—Player, 2003
Bill Gadsby—Player, 1970
Bob Gainey—Player, 1992
Chuck Gardiner—Player, 1945
Herb Gardiner—Player, 1958
Jimmy Gardner—Player, 1962
Mike Gartner—Player, 2001
Bernie Geoffrion—Player, 1972
Eddie Gerard—Player, 1945
Ed Giacomin—Player, 1987
Dr. Jack Gibson—Builder, 1976
Rod Gilbert—Player, 1982
Clark Gillies—Player, 2002
Billy Gilmour—Player, 1962
Doug Gilmour—Player, 2011
Moose Goheen—Player, 1952
Ebbie Goodfellow—Player, 1963
Tommy Gorman—Builder, 1963
Michel Goulet—Player, 1998
Cammi Granato—Women, 2010
Mike Grant—Player, 1950
Shorty Green—Player, 1962
Jim Gregory—Builder, 2007
Wayne Gretzky—Player, 1999
Si Griffis—Player, 1950
Frank Griffiths—Builder, 1993
George Hainsworth—Player, 1961
Glenn Hall—Player, 1975

Joe Hall—Player, 1961
William Hanley—Builder, 1986
Doug Harvey—Player, 1973
Dale Hawerchuk—Player, 2001
Charles Hay—Builder, 1974
George Hay—Player, 1958
George Hayes—Official, 1988
Jim Hendy—Builder, 1968
Riley Hern—Player, 1962
Bobby Hewitson—Official, 1963
Foster Hewitt—Builder, 1965
William Hewitt—Builder, 1947
Bryan Hextall—Player, 1969
Harry Holmes—Player, 1972
Tom Hooper—Player, 1962
Red Horner—Player, 1965
Tim Horton—Player, 1977
Harley Hotchkiss—Builder, 2006
Gordie Howe—Player, 1972
Mark Howe—Player, 2011
Syd Howe—Player, 1965
Harry Howell—Player, 1979
Bobby Hull—Player, 1983
Brett Hull—Player, 2009
Fred Hume—Builder, 1962
Bouse Hutton—Player, 1962
Harry Hyland—Player, 1962
Mike Ilitch—Builder, 2003
Punch Imlach—Builder, 1984
Mickey Ion—Official, 1961
Dick Irvin—Player, 1958
Tommy Ivan—Builder, 1974
Harvey Jackson—Player, 1971
Angela James—Women, 2010
William Jennings—Builder, 1975
Bob Johnson—Builder, 1992
Moose Johnson—Player, 1952
Ching Johnson—Player, 1958
Tom Johnson—Player, 1970
Aurel Joliat—Player, 1947
Gordon Juckes—Builder, 1979
Duke Keats—Player, 1958
Red Kelly—Player, 1969

Ted Kennedy—Player, 1966
Dave Keon—Player, 1986
Valeri Kharlamov—Player, 2005
Gen. John Reed Kilpatrick—Builder, 1960
Brian Kilrea—Builder, 2003
Seymour Knox—Builder, 1993
Jari Kurri—Player, 2001
Elmer Lach—Player, 1966
Guy Lafleur—Player, 1988
Pat LaFontaine—Player, 2003
Newsy Lalonde—Player, 1950
Rod Langway—Player, 2002
Lou Lamoriello—Builder, 2009
Jacques Laperriere—Player, 1987
Guy Lapointe—Player, 1993
Edgar Laprade—Player, 1993
Igor Larionov—Player, 2008
Jack Laviolette—Player, 1962
George Leader—Builder, 1969
Robert LeBel—Builder, 1970
Brian Leetch—Player, 2009
Hugh Lehman—Player, 1958
Jacques Lemaire—Player, 1984
Mario Lemieux—Player, 1997
Percy LeSueur—Player, 1961
Herbie Lewis—Player, 1989
Ted Lindsay—Player, 1966
Tommy Lockhart—Builder, 1965
Paul Loicq—Builder, 1961
Harry Lumley—Player, 1980
Al MacInnis—Player, 2007
Mickey MacKay—Player, 1952
Frank Mahovlich—Player, 1981
Joe Malone—Player, 1950
Sylvio Mantha—Player, 1960
John Mariucci—Builder, 1985
Jack Marshall—Player, 1965
Frank Mathers—Builder, 1992
Steamer Maxwell—Player, 1962
Lanny McDonald—Player, 1992
Frank McGee—Player, 1945
Billy McGimsie—Player, 1962
Major Frederic McLaughlin—Builder, 1963

George McNamara—Player, 1958
Mark Messier—Player, 2007
Stan Mikita—Player, 1983
Jake Milford—Builder, 1984
Hon. Hartland Molson—
    Builder, 1973
Dickie Moore—Player, 1974
Paddy Moran—Player, 1958
Howie Morenz—Player, 1945
Scotty Morrison—Builder, 1999
Bill Mosienko—Player, 1965
Joe Mullen—Player, 2000
Larry Murphy—Player, 2004
Monsignor Athol Murray—Builder, 1998
Cam Neely—Player, 2005
Roger Neilson—Builder, 2002
Francis Nelson—Builder, 1947
Joe Nieuwendyk—Player, 2011
Frank Nighbor—Player, 1947
Reg Noble—Player, 1962
Bruce A. Norris—Builder, 1969
James Norris Jr.—Builder, 1962
James Norris Sr.—Builder, 1958
William Northey—Builder, 1947
Adam Oates—Player, 2012
Ambrose O'Brien—Builder, 1962
Buddy O'Connor—Player, 1988
Harry Oliver—Player, 1967
Bert Olmstead—Player, 1985
Brian O'Neill—Builder, 1994
Bobby Orr—Player, 1979
Fred Page—Builder, 1993
Bernie Parent—Player, 1984
Brad Park—Player, 1988
Craig Patrick—Builder, 2001
Frank Patrick—Builder, 1958
Lester Patrick—Player, 1947
Lynn Patrick—Player, 1980
Matt Pavelich—Official, 1987
Gilbert Perreault—Player, 1990
Tommy Phillips—Player, 1945
Allan Pickard—Builder, 1958
Pierre Pilote—Player, 1975

Rudy Pilous—Builder, 1985
Didier Pitre—Player, 1962
Jacques Plante—Player, 1978
Bud Poile—Builder, 1990
Sam Pollock—Builder, 1978
Denis Potvin—Player, 1991
Babe Pratt—Player, 1966
Joe Primeau—Player, 1963
Marcel Pronovost—Player, 1978
Bob Pulford—Player, 1991
Harvey Pulford—Player, 1945
Bill Quackenbush—Player, 1976
Frank Rankin—Player, 1961
Jean Ratelle—Player, 1985
Sen. Donat Raymond—Builder, 1958
Chuck Rayner—Player, 1973
Ken Reardon—Player, 1966
Henri Richard—Player, 1979
Maurice Richard—Player, 1961
George Richardson—Player, 1950
Gordon Roberts—Player, 1971
John Ross Robertson—Builder, 1947
Claude Robinson—Builder, 1947
Larry Robinson—Player, 1995
Luc Robitaille—Player, 2009
Mike Rodden—Official, 1962
Art Ross—Player, 1945
Philip D. Ross—Builder, 1976
Patrick Roy—Player, 2006
Blair Russel—Player, 1965
Ernie Russell—Player, 1965
Jack Ruttan—Player, 1962
Dr. Gunther Sabetzki—Builder, 1995
Joe Sakic—Player, 2012
Borje Salming—Player, 1996
Glen Sather—Builder, 1997
Denis Savard—Player, 2000
Serge Savard—Player, 1986
Terry Sawchuk—Player, 1971
Fred Scanlan—Player, 1965
Ray Scapinello—Official, 2008
Milt Schmidt—Player, 1961
Sweeney Schriner—Player, 1962

Daryl "Doc" Seaman—Builder, 2010
Earl Seibert—Player, 1963
Oliver Seibert—Player, 1961
Frank Selke—Builder, 1960
Eddie Shore—Player, 1947
Steve Shutt—Player, 1993
Babe Siebert—Player, 1964
Joe Simpson—Player, 1962
Harry Sinden—Builder, 1983
Darryl Sittler—Player, 1989
Cooper Smeaton—Official, 1961
Alf Smith—Player, 1962
Billy Smith—Player, 1993
Clint Smith—Player, 1991
Frank Smith—Builder, 1962
Hooley Smith—Player, 1972
Tommy Smith—Player, 1973
Conn Smythe—Builder, 1958
Ed Snider—Builder, 1988
Allan Stanley—Player, 1981
Barney Stanley—Player, 1962
Peter Stastny—Player, 1998
Scott Stevens—Player, 2007
Jack Stewart—Player, 1964
Lord Stanley of Preston—Builder, 1945
Nels Stewart—Player, 1962
Red Storey—Official, 1967
Bruce Stuart—Player, 1961
Hod Stuart—Player, 1945
Mats Sundin—Player, 2012
Capt. James T. Sutherland—Builder, 1947
Anatoli Tarasov—Builder, 1974
Cyclone Taylor—Player, 1947
Tiny Thompson—Player, 1959
Bill Torrey—Builder, 1995
Vladislav Tretiak—Player, 1989
Harry Trihey—Player, 1950
Bryan Trottier—Player, 1997
Lloyd Turner—Builder, 1958
William Tutt—Builder, 1978
Frank Udvari—Official, 1973
Norm Ullman—Player, 1982
Andy Van Hellemond—Official, 1999

Georges Vezina—Player, 1945
Carl Voss—Builder, 1974
Fred Waghorne—Builder, 1961
Jack Walker—Player, 1960
Marty Walsh—Player, 1962
Harry E. Watson—Player, 1962
Harry Watson—Player, 1994
Cooney Weiland—Player, 1971
Harry Westwick—Player, 1962

Fred Whitcroft—Player, 1962
Phat Wilson—Player, 1962
Arthur Wirtz—Builder, 1971
Bill Wirtz—Builder, 1976
Gump Worsley—Player, 1980
Roy Worters—Player, 1969
Steve Yzerman—Player, 2009
John Ziegler—Builder, 1987

IIHF HALL OF FAME

(name, nationality, year inducted)
° denotes Referee; * denotes Builder; all others are Players

Quido Adamec (Czech Republic), 2005°
John "Bunny" Ahearne (Great Britain), 1997*
Veniamin Alexandrov (Russia), 2007
Ernest Aljancic, Sr. (Slovenia), 2002*
Helmut Balderis (Latvia), 1998
Rudi Ball (Germany), 2004
Father David Bauer (Canada), 1997*
Art Berglund (United States), 2008
Curt Berglund (Sweden), 2003*
Sven Bergqvist (Sweden), 1999
Lars Bjorn (Sweden), 1998
Vsevolod Bobrov (Russia), 1997
Vladimir Bouzek (Czech Republic), 2007
Roger Bourbonnais (Canada), 1999
Philippe Bozon (France), 2008
Herb Brooks (United States), 1999*
Walter Brown (United States), 1997*
Vlastimil Bubnik (Czech Republic), 1997
Mike Buckna (Canada), 2004*
Ludek Bukac (Czech Republic), 2007*
Pavel Bure (Russia), 2012
Walter Bush, Jr. (United States), 2009
Karen Bye (-Dietz) (United States), 2011
Enrico Calcaterra (Italy), 1999*
Ferdinand Cattini (Switzerland), 1998

Hans Cattini (Switzerland), 1998
Josef Cerny (Czech Republic), 2007
Arkady Chernyshev (Russia), 1999*
Bill Christian (United States), 1998
Bill Cleary (United States), 1997
Gerry Cosby (United States), 1997
Jim Craig (United States), 1999
Mike Curran (United States), 1999
Ove Dahlberg (Sweden), 2004°
Vitali Davydov (Russia), 2004
Igor Dimitriev (Russia), 2007
Hans Dobida (Austria), 2007
Jaroslav Drobny (Czechoslovakia), 1997
Vladimir Dzurilla (Slovakia), 1998
Rudolf Eklow (Sweden), 1999*
Carl Erhardt (Great Britain), 1998
Rickard Fagerlund (Sweden), 2010*
Slava Fetisov (Russia), 2005
Anatoli Firsov (Russia), 1998
Josef Golonka (Slovakia), 1998
Cammi Granato (United States), 2008
Wayne Gretzky (Canada), 2000
Arne Grunander (Sweden), 1997*
Henryk Gruth (Poland), 2006
Bengt-Ake Gustafsson (Sweden), 2003*
Karel Gut (Czech Republic), 1998
Geraldine Heaney (Canada), 2008

Anders Hedberg (Sweden), 1997
Dieter Hegen (Germany), 2010
Raimo Helminen (Finland), 2012
Heinz Henschel (Germany), 2003*
William Hewitt (Canada), 1998
Rudi Hiti (Slovenia), 2009
Ivan Hlinka (Czech Republic), 2002
Jiri Holecek (Czech Republic), 1998
Jiri Holik (Czech Republic), 1999
Derek Holmes (Canada), 1999*
Leif Holmqvist (Sweden), 1999
Ladislav Horsky (Slovakia), 2004*
Phil Housley (United States), 2012
Fran Huck (Canada), 1999
Jorgen Hviid (Denmark), 2005*
Arturs Irbe (Latvia), 2010
Gustav Jaenecke (Germany), 1998
Angela James (Canada), 2008
Tore Johannessen (Norway), 1999*
Mark Johnson (United States), 1999
Marshall Johnston (Canada), 1998
Tomas Jonsson (Sweden), 2000
Gord Juckes (Canada), 1997
Timo Jutila (Finland), 2003
Yuri Karandin (Russia), 2004°
Alexei Kasatonov (Russia), 2009
Tsutomu Kawabuchi (Japan), 2004*
Matti Keinonen (Finland), 2002
Valeri Kharlamov (Russia), 1998
Anatoli Khorozov (Ukraine), 2006*
Udo Kiessling (Germany), 2000
Dave King (Canada), 2001*
Jakob Kolliker (Switzerland), 2007
Josef Kompalla (Germany), 2003°
Viktor Konovalenko (Russia), 2007
Vladimir Kostka (Czech Republic), 1997*
Vladimir Krutov (Russia), 2010
Erich Kuhnhackl (Germany), 1997
Jari Kurri (Finland), 2000
Viktor Kuzkin (Russia), 2005
Jacques Lacarriere (France), 1998
Igor Larionov (Russia), 2008

Bob Lebel (Canada), 1997*
Mario Lemieux (Canada), 2008
Harry Lindblad (Finland), 1999*
Vic Lindquist (Canada), 1997
Paul Loicq (Belgium), 1997*
Konstantin Loktev (Russia), 2007
Hakan Loob (Sweden), 1998
Tord Lundstrom (Sweden), 2011
Cesar Luthi (Switzerland), 1998*
Oldrich Machac (Czech Republic), 1999
Barry MacKenzie (Canada), 1999
Sergei Makarov (Russia), 2001
Josef Malecek (Czech Republic), 2003
Alexander Maltsev (Russia), 1999
Louis Magnus (France), 1997*
Pekka Marjamaki (Finland), 1998
Seth Martin (Canada), 1997
Vladimir Martinec (Czech Republic), 2001
John Mayasich (United States), 1997
Boris Mayorov (Russia), 1999
Jack McCartan (United States), 1998
Jack McLeod (Canada), 1999
Boris Mikhailov (Russia), 2000
Bohumil Modry (Czech Republic), 2011
Andy Murray (Canada), 2012
Lou Nanne (United States), 2004
Mats Naslund (Sweden), 2005
Vaclav Nedomansky (Czech Republic), 1997
Riikka Nieminen-Valila (Finland), 2010
Kent Nilsson (Sweden), 2006
Nisse Nilsson (Sweden), 2002
Milan Novy (Czech Republic), 2012
Kalevi Numminen (Finland), 2011*
Lasse Oksanen (Finland), 1999
Terry O'Malley (Canada), 1998
Eduard Pana (Romania), 1998
Gyorgy Pasztor (Hungary), 2001*
Peter Patton (Great Britain), 2002*
Esa Peltonen (Finland), 2007
Vladimir Petrov (Russia), 2006
Ronald Pettersson (Sweden), 2004

Frantisek Pospisil (Czech Republic), 1999
Sepp Puschnig (Austria), 1999
Alexander Ragulin (Russia), 1997
Hans Rampf (Germany), 2001
Gord Renwick (Canada), 2002*
Bob Ridder (United States), 1998*
Jack Riley (United States), 1998*
Thomas Rundquist (Sweden), 2007
Gunther Sabetzki (Germany), 1997*
Borje Salming (Sweden), 1998
Laszlo Schell (Hungary), 2009
Alois Schloder (Germany), 2005
Harry Sinden (Canada), 1997
Nikolai Sologubov (Russia), 2004
Andrei Starovoitov (Russia), 1997*
Vyacheslav Starshinov (Russia), 2007
Jan Starsi (Slovakia), 1999*
Peter Stastny (Slovakia), 2000
Ulf Sterner (Sweden), 2001
Roland Stoltz (Sweden), 1999
Arne Stromberg (Sweden), 1998*
Goran Stubb (Finland), 2000*
Miroslav Subrt (Czech Republic), 2004*
Jan Suchy (Czech Republic), 2009
Anatoli Tarasov (Russia), 1997*
Frantisek Tikal (Czech Republic), 2004

Viktor Tikhonov (Russia), 1998*
Shoichi Tomita (Japan), 2006*
Richard "Bibi" Torriani (Switzerland), 1997
Vladislav Tretiak (Russia), 1997
Ladislav Trojak (Czech Republic), 2011
Hal Trumble (United States), 1999*
Yoshiaki Tsutsumi (Japan), 1999*
Sven Tumba (Sweden), 1997
Doru Tureanu (Romania), 2011
Thayer Tutt (United States), 2002*
Xaver Unsinn (Germany), 1998*
Lou Vairo (United States), 2010*
Jorma Valtonen (Finland), 1999
Valeri Vasiliev (Russia), 1998
Juhani Wahlsten (Finland), 2006
Walter Wasservogel (Austria), 1997*
Harry Watson (Canada), 1998
Unto Wiitala (Finland), 2003°
Alexander Yakushev (Russia), 2003
Urpo Ylonen (Finland), 1997
Vldimir Yurzinov (Russia), 2002*
Vladimir Zabrodsky (Czech Republic), 1997
Joachim Ziesche (Germany), 1999

INTERNATIONAL HOCKEY

TRIPLE GOLD CLUB

These 25 players and one coach form the unique group that has won the IIHF World Championship, the Olympic ice hockey tournament and the Stanley Cup. To be credited with each of these honours, the player or coach must have participated in at least one game of the event.

Players are entered chronologically by the date when they achieved the final championship of the triple. If two or more players completed their triple on the same date, priority is given to the player who was the first to win his first of the three titles. If two or more players have identical accomplishments, priority is given to the player who completes the triple at the younger age.

Legend: OG=Olympic Games; SC=Stanley Cup; WM=World Championship

1. **Tomas Jonsson** b. Falun, Sweden, April 12, 1960
    SC 1982, 1983 (New York Islanders)
    WM 1991 (Sweden)
    OG 1994 (Sweden)
    TGC member as of February 27, 1994 (Olympic final win vs. Canada)

2. **Mats Naslund** b. Timra, Sweden, October 31, 1959
    SC 1986 (Montreal Canadiens)
    WM 1991 (Sweden)
    OG 1994 (Sweden)
    TGC member as of February 27, 1994 (Olympic final win vs. Canada)

3. **Hakan Loob** b. Roma, Sweden, July 3, 1960
    WM 1987, 1991 (Sweden)
    SC 1989 (Calgary Flames)
    OG 1994 (Sweden)
    TGC member as of February 27, 1994 (Olympic final win vs. Canada)

4. **Valeri Kamensky** b. Voskresensk, Soviet Union (Russia), April 18, 1966
    WM 1986, 1989, 1990 (Soviet Union)
    OG 1988 (Soviet Union)
    SC 1996 (Colorado Avalanche)
    TGC member as of June 10, 1996 (Stanley Cup win vs. Florida)

5. **Alexei Gusarov** b. Leningrad (St. Petersburg), Soviet Union (Russia), July 8, 1964
    WM 1986, 1989, 1990 (Soviet Union)
    OG 1988 (Soviet Union)
    SC 1996 (Colorado Avalanche)
    TGC member as of June 10, 1996 (Stanley Cup win vs. Florida)

6. Peter Forsberg b. Ornskoldsvik, Sweden, July 20, 1973
  WM 1992, 1998 (Sweden)
  OG 1994, 2006 (Sweden)
  SC 1996, 2001 (Colorado Avalanche)
  TGC member as of June 10, 1996 (Stanley Cup win vs. Florida)

7. Vyacheslav Fetisov b. Moscow, Soviet Union (Russia), April 20, 1958
  WM 1978, 1981, 1982, 1983, 1986, 1989, 1990 (Soviet Union)
  OG 1984, 1988 (Soviet Union)
  SC 1997, 1998 (Detroit Red Wings)
  TGC member as of June 7, 1997 (Stanley Cup win vs. Philadelphia)

8. Igor Larionov (b. Voskresensk, Soviet Union (Russia), December 3, 1960)
  WM 1982, 1983, 1986, 1989 (Soviet Union)
  OG 1984, 1988 (Soviet Union)
  SC 1997, 1998, 2002 (Detroit Red Wings)
  TGC member as of June 7, 1997 (Stanley Cup win vs. Philadelphia)

9. Alexander Mogilny b. Khabarovsk, Soviet Union (Russia), February 18, 1969
  OG 1988 (Soviet Union)
  WM 1989 (Soviet Union)
  SC 2000 (New Jersey Devils)
  TGC member as of June 10, 2000 (Stanley Cup win vs. Dallas)

10. Vladimir Malakhov b. Ekaterinburg, Soviet Union (Russia), August 30, 1968
  WM 1990 (Soviet Union)
  OG 1992 (Russia)
  SC 2000 (New Jersey Devils)
  TGC member as of June 10, 2000 (Stanley Cup win vs. Dallas)

11. Rob Blake b. Simcoe, Ontario, Canada, December 10, 1969
  WM 1994, 1997 (Canada)
  SC 2001 (Colorado Avalanche)
  OG 2002 (Canada)
  TGC member as of February 24, 2002 (Olympic final win vs. United States)

12. Joe Sakic b. Burnaby, British Columbia, Canada, July 7, 1969
  WM 1994 (Canada)
  SC 1996, 2001 (Colorado Avalanche)
  OG 2002 (Canada)
  TGC member as of February 24, 2002 (Olympic final win vs. United States)

13. **Brendan Shanahan**   b. Mimico, Ontario, Canada, January 23, 1969
    WM 1994 (Canada)
    SC 1997, 1998, 2002 (Detroit Red Wings)
    OG 2002 (Canada)
    TGC member as of February 24, 2002 (Olympic final win vs. United States)

14. **Scott Niedermayer**   b. Edmonton, Alberta, Canada, August 31, 1973
    SC 1995, 2000, 2003 (New Jersey Devils), 2007 (Anaheim Ducks)
    OG 2002, 2010 (Canada)
    WM 2004 (Canada)
    TGC member as of May 9, 2004 (World Championship final win vs. Sweden)

15. **Jaromir Jagr**   b. Kladno, Czechoslovakia (Czech Republic), February 15, 1972
    SC 1991, 1992 (Pittsburgh Penguins)
    OG 1998 (Czech Republic)
    WM 2005, 2010 (Czech Republic)
    TGC member as of May 15, 2005 (World Championship final win vs. Canada)

16. **Jiri Slegr**   b. Jihlava, Czechoslovakia (Czech Republic), May 30, 1971
    OG 1998 (Czech Republic)
    SC 2002 (Detroit Red Wings)
    WM 2005 (Czech Republic)
    TGC member as of May 15, 2005 (World Championship final win vs. Canada)

17. **Nicklas Lidstrom**   b. Vasteras, Sweden, April 28, 1970
    WM 1991 (Sweden)
    SC 1997, 1998, 2002 (Detroit Red Wings)
    OG 2006 (Sweden)
    TGC member as of February 26, 2006 (Olympic final win vs. Finland)

18. **Fredrik Modin**   b. Sundsvall, Sweden, October 8, 1974
    WM 1998 (Sweden)
    SC 2004 (Tampa Bay Lightning)
    OG 2006 (Sweden)
    TGC member as of February 26, 2006 (Olympic final win vs. Finland)

19. **Chris Pronger**   b. Dryden, Ontario, Canada, October 10, 1974
    WM 1997 (Canada)
    OG 2002, 2010 (Canada)
    SC 2007 (Anaheim Ducks)
    TGC member as of June 6, 2007 (Stanley Cup win vs. Ottawa)

20. **Niklas Kronwall**   b. Stockholm, Sweden, January 12, 1981
    OG 2006 (Sweden)
    WM 2006 (Sweden)
    SC 2008 (Detroit Red Wings)
    TGC member as of June 4, 2008 (Stanley Cup win vs. Pittsburgh)

21. **Henrik Zetterberg**   b. Njurunda, Sweden, October 9, 1980
    OG 2006 (Sweden)
    WM 2006 (Sweden)
    SC 2008 (Detroit Red Wings)
    TGC member as of June 4, 2008 (Stanley Cup win vs. Pittsburgh)

22. **Mikael Samuelsson**   b. Mariefred, Sweden, December 23, 1976
    OG 2006 (Sweden)
    WM 2006 (Sweden)
    SC 2008 (Detroit Red Wings)
    TGC member as of June 4, 2008 (Stanley Cup win vs. Pittsburgh)

23. **Eric Staal**   b. Thunder Bay, Ontario, Canada, October 29, 1984
    SC 2006 (Carolina Hurricanes)
    WM 2007 (Canada)
    OG 2010 (Canada)
    TGC member as of February 28, 2010 (Olympic final win vs. United States)

24. **Jonathan Toews**   b. Winnipeg, Manitoba, Canada, April 29, 1988
    WM 2007 (Canada)
    OG 2010 (Canada)
    SC 2010 (Chicago Blackhawks)
    TGC member as of June 9, 2010 (Stanley Cup win vs. Philadelphia)

25. **Patrice Bergeron**   b. L'Ancienne-Lorette, Quebec, Canada, July 24, 1985
    WM 2004 (Canada)
    OG 2010 (Canada)
    SC 2011 (Boston Bruins)
    TGC member as of June 15, 2011 (Stanley Cup win vs. Vancouver)

TRIPLE GOLD CLUB COACH

1. **Mike Babcock**   (b. Saskatoon, Saskatchewan, Canada, April 29, 1963)
    WM 2004 (Canada)
    SC 2008 (Detroit Red Wings)
    OG 2010 (Canada)
    TGC member as of February 28, 2010 (Olympic final win vs. United States)

2013 WOMEN'S WORLD CHAMPIONSHIP SCHEDULE

OTTAWA, CANADA, April 2–9, 2013

Group A: Canada, Finland, Switzerland, United States
Group B: Czech Republic, Germany, Russia, Sweden

SCHEDULE

All times local (Eastern Daylight Time)

1	April 2	Preliminary	Germany–Russia	12:00 p.m.	Nepean
2	April 2	Preliminary	Switzerland–Finland	3:30 p.m.	Ottawa
3	April 2	Preliminary	Czech Republic–Sweden	4:00 p.m.	Nepean
4	April 2	Preliminary	United States–Canada	7:30 p.m.	Ottawa
5	April 3	Preliminary	Czech Republic–Russia	12:00 p.m.	Nepean
6	April 3	Preliminary	Finland–United States	3:30 p.m.	Nepean
7	April 3	Preliminary	Sweden–Germany	4:00 p.m.	Nepean
8	April 3	Preliminary	Canada–Switzerland	7:30 p.m.	Ottawa
9	April 5	Preliminary	Germany–Czech Republic	12:00 p.m.	Nepean
10	April 5	Preliminary	Switzerland–United States	3:30 p.m.	Ottawa
11	April 5	Preliminary	Russia–Sweden	4:00 p.m.	Nepean
12	April 5	Preliminary	Finland–Canada	7:30 p.m.	Ottawa
13	April 6	Quarter–final	TBD	3:30 p.m.	Ottawa
14	April 6	Relegation	4B vs. 3B	4:00 p.m.	Nepean
15	April 6	Quarter–final	TBD	7:30 p.m.	Ottawa
16	April 8	Fifth-Place	L13 vs. L15	11:30 a.m.	Ottawa
17	April 8	Relegation	3B vs. 4B	12:00 p.m.	Nepean
18	April 8	Semifinal	TBD	3:30 p.m.	Ottawa
19	April 8	Semifinal	TBD	7:30 p.m.	Ottawa
20	April 9	Bronze	L18 vs. L19	3:30 p.m.	Ottawa
21	April 9	Relegation	4B vs. 3B	4:00 p.m.	Nepean*
22	April 9	Gold	W18 vs. W19	7:30 p.m.	Ottawa

* if necessary

2012 WORLD CHAMPIONSHIP, MEN

HELSINKI, FINLAND/STOCKHOLM, SWEDEN, May 4–20, 2012

Final Placings

GOLD MEDAL	Russia
SILVER MEDAL	Slovakia
BRONZE MEDAL	Czech Republic
Fourth Place	Finland
Fifth Place	Canada
Sixth Place	Sweden
Seventh Place	United States
Eighth Place	Norway
Ninth Place	France
Tenth Place	Latvia
Eleventh Place	Switzerland
Twelfth Place	Germany
Thirteenth Place	Denmark
Fourteenth Place	Belarus
Fifteenth Place	Italy*
Sixteenth Place	Kazakhstan*

* promoted from Division I in 2011/demoted to Division I for 2013

Tournament Format

A new format was adopted at the same time as a new hosting structure was used. Finland and Sweden acted as co-hosts through the quarterfinals, after which the games were played only in Helsinki.

The 16 teams were divided into two groups of eight, and each group played a round-robin preliminary round. The last-place team in each group was demoted to Division I, and only the top four from each group advanced to the playoffs. The bottom four teams didn't play again, the relegation round having been abolished. The top team played the fourth (and second played third) within each group in the quarterfinals, while the semifinals saw teams cross over.

RESULTS & STANDINGS

Preliminary Round

Group H (Helsinki)

	GP	W	OTW	OTL	L	GF	GA	P
Canada	7	6	0	1	0	35	15	19
United States	7	4	2	0	1	32	17	16
Finland	7	5	0	0	2	21	14	15
Slovakia	7	5	0	0	2	21	13	15
France	7	3	0	0	4	21	32	9

Switzerland	7	2	0	0	5	16	21	6
Belarus	7	1	0	0	6	11	23	3
Kazakhstan	7	0	0	1	6	11	33	1

May 4	United States 7/France 2
May 4	Canada 3/Slovakia 2
May 4	Finland 1/Belarus 0
May 5	Switzerland 5/Kazakhstan 1
May 5	United States 5/Canada 4 (Jack Johnson 1:47 OT)
May 6	France 6/Kazakhstan 3
May 6	Finland 1/Slovakia 0
May 6	Switzerland 3/Belarus 2
May 7	Canada 7/France 2
May 7	Slovakia 4/United States 2
May 8	Belarus 3/Kazakhstan 2
May 8	Finland 5/Switzerland 2
May 9	Slovakia 4/Kazakhstan 2
May 9	Canada 3/Switzerland 2
May 10	United States 5/Belarus 3
May 10	Finland 7/France 1
May 11	United States 3/Kazakhstan 2 (Justin Faulk 4:38 OT)
May 11	Canada 5/Finland 3
May 12	Slovakia 5/Belarus 1
May 12	France 4/Switzerland 2
May 12	Canada 8/Kazakhstan 0
May 13	United States 5/Finland 0
May 13	Slovakia 1/Switzerland 0
May 14	France 2/Belarus 1
May 14	Finland 4/Kazakhstan 1
May 15	Canada 5/Belarus 1
May 15	Slovakia 5/France 4
May 15	United States 5/Switzerland 1

Group S (Stockholm)

	GP	W	OTW	OTL	L	GF	GA	P
Russia	7	7	0	0	0	27	8	21
Sweden	7	6	0	0	1	29	15	18
Czech Republic	7	4	1	0	2	24	11	14
Norway	7	4	0	1	2	33	19	13
Latvia	7	2	0	0	5	11	19	6
Germany	7	2	0	0	5	14	31	6
Denmark	7	1	0	1	5	13	23	4
Italy	7	0	1	0	6	6	31	2

May 4	Germany 3/Italy 0
May 4	Czech Republic 2/Denmark 0
May 4	Sweden 3/Norway 1
May 5	Russia 5/Latvia 2
May 5	Sweden 4/Czech Republic 1
May 6	Italy 4/Denmark 3 (Giulio Scandella 0:52 OT)
May 6	Russia 4/Norway 2
May 6	Latvia 3/Germany 2
May 7	Czech Republic 4/Norway 3 (5:00 OT/Ales Hemsky GWS)
May 7	Sweden 6/Denmark 4
May 8	Latvia 5/Italy 0
May 8	Russia 2/Germany 0
May 9	Norway 6/Italy 2
May 9	Sweden 5/Germany 2
May 10	Russia 3/Denmark 1
May 10	Czech Republic 3/Latvia 1
May 11	Czech Republic 6/Italy 0
May 11	Russia 7/Sweden 3
May 12	Norway 3/Latvia 0
May 12	Germany 2/Denmark 1
May 12	Sweden 4/Italy 0
May 13	Russia 2/Czech Republic 0
May 13	Norway 12/Germany 4
May 14	Denmark 2/Latvia 0
May 14	Russia 4/Italy 0
May 15	Norway 6/Denmark 2
May 15	Czech Republic 8/Germany 1
May 15	Sweden 4/Latvia 0

PLAYOFFS

Quarterfinals

May 17	Helsinki	Slovakia 4/Canada 3
May 17	Stockholm	Russia 5/Norway 2
May 17	Helsinki	Finland 3/United States 2
May 17	Stockholm	Czech Republic 4/Sweden 3

Semifinals (Helsinki)

May 19	Russia 6/Finland 2
May 19	Slovakia 3/Czech Republic 1

Bronze Medal Game (Helsinki)

May 20	Czech Republic 3/Finland 2

Gold Medal Game (Helsinki)
   May 20   Russia 5   Slovakia 2

TEAM CANADA STATISTICS
   Brent Sutter, coach

	GP	G	A	P	PIM
Duncan Keith	8	1	10	11	0
John Tavares	8	4	5	9	12
Ryan Getzlaf	8	2	7	9	27
Jordan Eberle	8	4	4	8	0
Patrick Sharp	8	1	7	8	2
Evander Kane	8	4	3	7	2
Corey Perry	8	3	4	7	8
Ryan Nugent-Hopkins	8	4	2	6	4
Jamie Benn	8	3	2	5	4
Jeff Skinner	8	3	2	5	4
Andrew Ladd	8	1	4	5	2
Ryan O'Reilly	7	2	2	4	4
Alex Burrows	5	3	0	3	2
Kris Russell	4	0	3	3	2
Dion Phaneuf	8	2	0	2	4
Teddy Purcell	8	1	1	2	0
Marc Methot	6	0	2	2	25
Jay Bouwmeester	8	0	2	2	0
Luke Schenn	8	0	1	1	25
Cam Ward	8	0	1	1	0
Devan Dubnyk	2	0	0	0	0
Marc-Edouard Vlasic	2	0	0	0	0
Ryan Murray	6	0	0	0	0
Kyle Quincey	6	0	0	0	4

In Goal	GP	W-L	Mins	GA	SO	GAA
Cam Ward	6	4–2	360:32	17	0	2.83
Devan Dubnyk	2	2–0	120:00	2	1	1.00

2012 WORLD U20 (JUNIOR) CHAMPIONSHIP

CALGARY & EDMONTON, CANADA, December 26, 2011–January 5, 2012

Final Placings

GOLD MEDAL	Sweden
SILVER MEDAL	Russia
BRONZE MEDAL	Canada
Fourth Place	Finland
Fifth Place	Czech Republic
Sixth Place	Slovakia
Seventh Place	United States
Eighth Place	Switzerland
Ninth Place	Latvia*
Tenth Place	Denmark*

* promoted from Division I in 2011

Tournament Format

There were two divisions of five teams, and each group played a preliminary round-robin series. The top team from each division advanced to the semifinals, and the second- and third-place teams played for the other two spots. The second-place team from one division played the third-place team from the other, and vice versa. The two semifinal winners played for gold, and the losers played for bronze.

RESULTS & STANDINGS

Preliminary Round

Group A (Calgary)

	GP	W	OTW	OTL	L	GF	GA	P
Sweden	4	2	2	0	0	26	11	10
Russia	4	3	0	1	0	23	5	10
Slovakia	4	2	0	0	2	11	17	6
Switzerland	4	1	0	1	2	12	16	4
Latvia	4	0	0	0	4	8	31	0

December 26	Sweden 9/Latvia 4
December 26	Russia 3/Switzerland 0
December 27	Slovakia 3/Latvia 1
December 28	Sweden 4/Switzerland 3 (5:00 OT/GWS—Sebastian Collberg)
December 28	Russia 3/Slovakia 1
December 29	Russia 14/Latvia 0
December 30	Sweden 9/Slovakia 1

December 30   Switzerland 5/Latvia 3
December 31   Slovakia 6/Switzerland 4
December 31   Sweden 4/Russia 3 (Joakim Nordstrom 2:44 OT)

Group B (Edmonton)

	GP	W	OTW	OTL	L	GF	GA	P
Canada	4	4	0	0	0	26	5	12
Finland	4	3	0	0	1	19	10	9
Czech Republic	4	2	0	0	2	12	11	6
United States	4	1	0	0	3	16	15	3
Denmark	4	0	0	0	4	6	38	0

December 26   Canada 8/Finland 1
December 26   United States 11/Denmark 3
December 27   Czech Republic 7/Denmark 0
December 28   Finland 4/United States 1
December 28   Canada 5/Czech Republic 0
December 29   Canada 10/Denmark 2
December 30   Czech Republic 5/United States 2
December 30   Finland 10/Denmark 1
December 31   Finland 4/Czech Republic 0
December 31   Canada 3/United States 2

RELEGATION ROUND (CALGARY)

	GP	W	OTW	OTL	L	GF	GA	P
United States	3	3	0	0	0	25	6	9
Switzerland	3	1	1	0	1	10	8	5
Latvia	3	0	1	0	2	7	18	2
Denmark	3	0	0	2	1	7	17	2

January 2   Switzerland 4/Denmark 3 (Tanner Richard 3:27 OT)
January 3   United States 12/Latvia 2
January 4   Latvia 2/Denmark 1 (Nikita Jevpalovs 1:43 OT)
January 4   United States 2/Switzerland 1

PLAYOFFS (CALGARY)

Quarterfinals

January 2   Finland 8/Slovakia 5
January 2   Russia 2/Czech Republic 1

Semifinals

January 3   Sweden 3/Finland 2 (10:00 OT/GWS—Max Friberg)
January 3   Russia 6/Canada 5

Fifth-Place Game

  January 4   Czech Republic 5/Slovakia 2

Bronze Medal Game

  January 5   Canada 4/Finland 0

Gold Medal Game

  January 5   Sweden 1/Russia 0 (Mika Zibanejad 10:09 OT)

TEAM CANADA STATISTICS

  Don Hay, coach

	GP	G	A	P	PIM
Mark Stone	6	7	3	10	2
Ryan Strome	6	3	6	9	8
Jonathan Huberdeau	6	1	8	9	16
Freddie Hamilton	6	1	6	7	2
Brett Connolly	6	5	1	6	4
Brendan Gallagher	6	3	3	6	12
Brandon Gormley	6	3	3	6	2
Quinton Howden	6	3	3	6	2
Mark Scheifele	6	3	3	6	0
Dougie Hamilton	6	2	4	6	6
Tanner Pearson	6	1	5	6	6
Jaden Schwartz	6	2	3	5	4
Scott Harrington	5	1	3	4	0
Ryan Murray	6	0	3	3	0
Boone Jenner	5	0	2	2	29
Scott Wedgewood	3	0	1	1	0
Nathan Beaulieu	6	0	1	1	16
Michael Bournival	6	0	1	1	0
Devante Smith-Pelly	1	0	0	0	0
Mark Visentin	4	0	0	0	0
Jamie Oleksiak	6	0	0	0	2
Mark Pysyk	6	0	0	0	2

In Goal	GP	W-L	Mins	GA	SO	GAA
Mark Visentin	4	3–1	210:08	5	1	1.43
Scott Wedgewood	3	2–0	148:48	6	1	2.42

2012 WORLD CHAMPIONSHIP, WOMEN

BURLINGTON, VERMONT, USA, April 7–14, 2012

Final Placings

GOLD MEDAL	Canada
SILVER MEDAL	United States
BRONZE MEDAL	Switzerland
Fourth Place	Finland
Fifth Place	Sweden
Sixth Place	Russia
Seventh Place	Germany*
Eighth Place	Slovakia†

* promoted from Division I in 2011
† demoted to Division I for 2013

Tournament Format

Eight teams were placed in two groups and each group played a round-robin preliminary round. For the first time, the groups were arranged vertically, not horizontally, so the top-ranked teams played in Group A and the lower-ranked in Group B. All teams from Group A advanced to the playoffs. The top two went directly to the semifinals, while the bottom two played a crossover quarterfinal round with the top two from Group B. The bottom two in Group B played a best-of-three series in the relegation round.

RESULTS & STANDINGS

Group A

	GP	W	OTW	OTL	L	GF	GA	P
United States	3	3	0	0	0	29	2	9
Canada	3	2	0	0	1	19	12	6
Finland	3	1	0	0	2	7	18	3
Russia	3	0	0	0	3	5	28	0

April 7	Finland 5/Russia 4
April 7	United States 9/Canada 2
April 8	Canada 3/Finland 2
April 8	United States 9/Russia 0
April 10	Canada 14/Russia 1
April 10	United States 11/Finland 0

Group B

	GP	W	OTW	OTL	L	GF	GA	P
Switzerland	3	2	0	0	1	7	6	6
Sweden	3	1	1	0	1	9	5	5
Germany	3	1	0	1	1	6	8	4
Slovakia	3	1	0	0	2	6	9	3

April 7	Sweden 5/Slovakia 1
April 7	Germany 3/Switzerland 2
April 8	Sweden 2/Germany 1 (Elin Holmlov 0:24 OT)
April 8	Switzerland 2/Slovakia 1
April 10	Switzerland 3/Sweden 2
April 10	Slovakia 4/Germany 2

Relegation Round

	GP	W	OTW	OTL	L	GF	GA	P
Germany	2	1	1	0	0	5	2	5
Slovakia	2	0	0	1	1	2	5	1

April 11	Germany 2/Slovakia 1 (5:00 OT/GWS—Manuela Anwander)
April 13	Germany 3/Slovakia 1

PLAYOFFS

Quarterfinals
April 11	Switzerland 5/Russia 2
April 11	Finland 2/Sweden 1

Semifinals
April 13	Canada 5/Finland 1
April 13	United States 10/Switzerland 0

Fifth-Place Game
April 13	Sweden 2/Russia 1

Bronze Medal Game
April 14	Switzerland 6/Finland 2

Gold Medal Game
April 14	Canada 5/United States 4 (Caroline Ouellette 1:50 OT)

TEAM CANADA STATISTICS
Ben Church, coach

	GP	G	A	P	PIM
Hayley Wickenheiser	5	3	7	10	4
Caroline Ouellette	5	4	5	9	6
Jayna Hefford	5	3	6	9	4
Meghan Agosta	5	4	4	8	8
Marie-Philip Poulin	5	3	4	7	6
Rebecca Johnston	5	1	6	7	0
Natalie Spooner	5	4	2	6	4
Meaghan Mikkelson	5	0	5	5	2
Gillian Apps	5	2	2	4	10
Laura Fortino	5	2	2	4	6
Lauriane Rougeau	5	1	1	2	2
Catherine Ward	5	0	2	2	4
Jennifer Wakefield	5	1	0	1	8
Courtney Birchard	5	1	0	1	2
Jocelyne Larocque	5	0	1	1	6
Bailey Bram	5	0	1	1	4
Tessa Bonhomme	5	0	1	1	2
Vicki Bendus	5	0	1	1	0
Brianne Jenner	5	0	1	1	0
Haley Irwin	1	0	0	0	0
Charline Labonte	2	0	0	0	0
Shannon Szabados	4	0	0	0	0

In Goal	GP	W-L	Mins	GA	SO	GAA
Shannon Szabados	4	3–0	198:18	9	0	2.72
Charline Labonte	2	1–1	103:32	8	0	4.64

2012 WORLD U18 CHAMPIONSHIP, MEN

BRNO/ZNOJMO/BRECLAV, CZECH REPUBLIC, April 12–22, 2012

FINAL PLACINGS

GOLD MEDAL	United States
SILVER MEDAL	Sweden
BRONZE MEDAL	Canada
Fourth Place	Finland
Fifth Place	Russia
Sixth Place	Germany
Seventh Place	Switzerland
Eighth Place	Czech Republic
Ninth Place	Latvia[†]
Tenth Place	Denmark*

[†] promoted from Division I in 2011

* demoted to Division I for 2013

Tournament Format

The 10 teams were divided into two groups of five and each group played a round-robin preliminary round. The top team in each group advanced to the semifinals, while the second- and third-place teams played a crossover quarterfinal round. The bottom two teams played a four-team relegation round, the bottom two being demoted to Division I for 2012.

RESULTS & STANDINGS

Preliminary Round

Group A

	GP	W	OTW	OTL	L	GF	GA	P
United States	4	4	0	0	0	18	3	12
Finland	4	3	0	0	1	15	9	9
Canada	4	2	0	0	2	17	12	6
Czech Republic	4	1	0	0	3	12	21	3
Denmark	4	0	0	0	4	6	23	0

April 12	Brno	Canada 6/Denmark 1
April 12	Brno	United States 4/Finland 0
April 13	Znojmo	Czech Republic 8/Denmark 4
April 14	Breclav	United States 5/Czech Republic 0
April 14	Breclav	Finland 4/Canada 2
April 15	Brno	United States 4/Denmark 0

April 16	Brno	Canada 6/Czech Republic 2
April 16	Brno	Finland 5/Denmark 1
April 17	Brno	Finland 6/Czech Republic 2
April 17	Brno	United States 5/Canada 3

Group B (Znojmo)

	GP	W	OTW	OTL	L	GF	GA	P
Sweden	4	4	0	0	0	20	4	12
Russia	4	2	0	0	2	14	7	6
Germany	4	2	0	0	2	15	17	6
Latvia	4	2	0	0	2	11	15	6
Switzerland	4	0	0	0	4	6	23	0

April 12	Russia 6/Latvia 1
April 12	Sweden 8/Germany 1
April 13	Latvia 4/Switzerland 2
April 14	Germany 4/Russia 2
April 14	Sweden 7/Switzerland 2
April 15	Sweden 3/Latvia 1
April 16	Latvia 5/Germany 4
April 16	Russia 6/Switzerland 0
April 17	Sweden 2/Russia 0
April 17	Germany 6/Switzerland 2

Relegation Round (Znojmo)

	GP	W	OTW	OTL	L	GF	GA	P
Switzerland	3	2	0	0	1	8	7	6
Czech Republic	3	2	0	0	1	17	12	6
Latvia	3	1	0	1	1	11	13	4
Denmark	3	0	1	0	2	9	13	2

April 19	Switzerland 4/Czech Republic 2
April 19	Denmark 4/Latvia 3 (Kristoffer Lauridsen 4:04 OT)
April 20	Czech Republic 7/Latvia 4
April 20	Switzerland 2/Denmark 1

PLAYOFFS

Quarterfinals (Breclav)

| April 21 | Finland 8/Germany 0 |
| April 21 | Canada 4/Russia 2 |

Semifinals (Brno)

| April 20 | Sweden 7/Finland 3 |
| April 20 | United States 2/Canada 1 |

Fifth-Place Game (Brno)

| April 21 | Russia 4/Germany 1 |

Bronze Medal Game (Brno)

| April 22 | Canada 5/Finland 4 (Hunter Shinkaruk 2:05 OT) |

Gold Medal Game (Brno)

| April 22 | United States 7/Sweden 0 |

Team Canada Statistics

Jesse Wallin, coach

	GP	G	A	P	PIM
Matt Dumba	7	5	7	12	20
Kerby Rychel	7	5	3	8	12
Hunter Shinkaruk	6	4	4	8	6
Scott Laughton	7	2	5	7	4
Troy Bourke	7	0	7	7	2
Sam Reinhart	7	2	4	6	0
Gemel Smith	7	2	3	5	2
Brendan Gaunce	7	3	1	4	8
Josh Morrissey	7	0	3	3	25
Mike Winther	7	1	1	2	4
Ryan Pulock	6	1	1	2	0
Damon Severson	7	0	2	2	8
Branden Troock	7	0	1	1	10
Felix Girard	5	1	0	1	6
Tony Mantha	7	1	0	1	0
Darnell Nurse	7	0	0	0	14
Adam Pelech	7	0	0	0	8
Scott Kosmachuk	7	0	0	0	4
Warren Steele	7	0	0	0	4
William Carrier	7	0	0	0	0
Matt Murray	7	0	0	0	0

In Goal	GP	W-L	Mins	GA	SO	GAA
Matt Murray	7	4–3	419:51	19	0	2.72

2012 WORLD U18 CHAMPIONSHIP, WOMEN

ZLIN/PREROV, CZECH REPUBLIC, December 31, 2011–January 7, 2012

FINAL PLACINGS

GOLD MEDAL	Canada
SILVER MEDAL	United States
BRONZE MEDAL	Sweden
Fourth Place	Germany
Fifth Place	Finland
Sixth Place	Czech Republic
Seventh Place	Russia*
Eighth Place	Switzerland†

* promoted from Division I in 2011

† demoted to Division I for 2013

Tournament Format

The eight teams were divided into two groups of four, and each group played a round-robin preliminary round. The top two teams in each group advanced to the playoffs, where they played a crossover semifinal round, while the bottom two teams in each group played a series of placement games.

RESULTS & STANDINGS

Preliminary Round

Group A (Zlin)

	GP	W	OTW	OTL	L	GF	GA	P
United States	3	3	0	0	0	28	1	9
Sweden	3	2	0	0	1	10	10	6
Czech Republic	3	1	0	0	2	4	17	3
Russia	3	0	0	0	3	2	16	0

December 31	Sweden 4/Czech Republic 1
December 31	United States 8/Russia 0
January 1	Czech Republic 2/Russia 0
January 1	United States 7/Sweden 0
January 3	Sweden 6/Russia 2
January 3	United States 13/Czech Republic 1

Group B (Prerov)

	GP	W	OTW	OTL	L	GF	GA	P
Canada	3	3	0	0	0	26	1	9
Germany	3	1	0	0	2	6	10	3
Finland	3	1	0	0	2	6	12	3
Switzerland	3	1	0	0	2	7	22	3

December 31	Canada 13/Switzerland 1
December 31	Finland 3/Germany 0
January 1	Switzerland 5/Finland 3
January 1	Canada 6/Germany 0
January 3	Germany 6/Switzerland 1
January 3	Canada 7/Finland 0

Relegation Round (Prerov)

	GP	W	OTW	OTL	L	GF	GA	P
Russia	3	1	1	0	1	10	9	5
Switzerland	3	1	0	1	1	9	10	4

January 4	Switzerland 4/Russia 2
January 6	Russia 5/Switzerland 3
January 7	Russia 3/Switzerland 2 (Valeria Pavlova 1:44 OT)

Playoffs (Zlin)

Quarterfinals

| January 4 | Sweden 2/Finland 1 (Matildah Andersson 7:27 OT) |
| January 4 | Germany 2/Czech Republic 1 |

Semifinals

| January 6 | United States 7/Germany 1 |
| January 6 | Canada 7/Sweden 0 |

Fifth-Place Game

| January 6 | Prerov | Finland 5/Czech Republic 3 |

Bronze Medal Game

| January 7 | Sweden 4/Germany 1 |

Gold Medal Game

| January 7 | Canada 3/United States 0 |

TEAM CANADA STATISTICS

Pierre Alain, coach

	GP	G	A	P	PIM
Laura Stacey	5	4	3	7	4
Cayley Mercer	5	4	3	7	0
Sarah Lefort	5	3	4	7	4
Taylor Woods	5	3	3	6	0
Nicole Connery	5	2	4	6	6
Catherine Dubois	5	4	1	5	6
Cydney Roesler	5	4	1	5	4
Rebecca Kohler	5	3	2	5	4
Alexis Crossley	5	2	3	5	4
Erin Ambrose	5	2	3	5	0
Meghan Dufault	5	1	4	5	4
Emily Clark	5	2	2	4	2
Shannon MacAulay	5	0	3	3	0
Kristyn Capizzano	5	1	1	2	2
Erika Sowchuk	5	1	1	2	0
Halli Krzyzaniak	5	0	1	1	8
Morgan Richardson	5	0	1	1	2
Ashleigh Brykaliuk	5	0	1	1	0
Abbey Frazer	5	0	0	0	2
Jordan Krause	5	0	0	0	0
Emerance Maschmeyer	3	0	0	0	0
Elaine Chuli	2	0	0	0	0

In Goal	GP	W-L	Mins	GA	SO	GAA
Elaine Chuli	2	2–0	120:00	0	2	0.00
Emerance Maschmeyer	3	3–0	180:00	1	2	0.33

OLYMPICS, MEN, 1920–2010

THE GAMES OF THE VII OLYMPIAD

ANTWERP, BELGIUM, April 23–September 12, 1920
(hockey games played April 23–29, 1920)

FINAL PLACINGS
GOLD MEDAL	Canada
SILVER MEDAL	United States
BRONZE MEDAL	Czechoslovakia
Fourth Place	Sweden
Fifth Place	Switzerland
	France
	Belgium

THE FIRST OLYMPIC WINTER GAMES

CHAMONIX, FRANCE, January 28–February 3, 1924

FINAL PLACINGS
GOLD MEDAL	Canada
SILVER MEDAL	United States
BRONZE MEDAL	Great Britain
Fourth Place	Sweden
Fifth Place	Czechoslovakia
	France
Seventh Place	Belgium
	Switzerland

THE SECOND OLYMPIC WINTER GAMES

ST. MORITZ, SWITZERLAND, February 11–19, 1928

FINAL PLACINGS
GOLD MEDAL	Canada
SILVER MEDAL	Sweden
BRONZE MEDAL	Switzerland
Fourth Place	Great Britain
Fifth Place	France
	Czechoslovakia
	Austria

Eighth Place	Belgium
	Poland
	Germany
Eleventh Place	Hungary

THE THIRD OLYMPIC WINTER GAMES

LAKE PLACID, UNITED STATES, February 4–13, 1932

FINAL PLACINGS

GOLD MEDAL	Canada
SILVER MEDAL	United States
BRONZE MEDAL	Germany
Fourth Place	Poland

THE FOURTH OLYMPIC WINTER GAMES

GARMISCH-PARTENKIRCHEN, GERMANY, February 6–16, 1936

FINAL PLACINGS

GOLD MEDAL	Great Britain
SILVER MEDAL	Canada
BRONZE MEDAL	United States
Fourth Place	Czechoslovakia
Fifth Place	Germany
	Sweden
Seventh Place	Austria
	Hungary
Ninth Place	Italy
	France
	Japan
	Poland
Thirteenth Place	Belgium
	Latvia
	Switzerland

THE FIFTH OLYMPIC WINTER GAMES

ST. MORITZ, SWITZERLAND, January 30–February 8, 1948

FINAL PLACINGS

| GOLD MEDAL | Canada |
| SILVER MEDAL | Czechoslovakia |

BRONZE MEDAL	Switzerland
Fourth Place	Sweden
Fifth Place	Great Britain
Sixth Place	Poland
Seventh Place	Austria
Eighth Place	Italy
Disqualified	United States

THE SIXTH OLYMPIC WINTER GAMES

OSLO, NORWAY, February 15–25, 1952

FINAL PLACINGS

GOLD MEDAL	Canada
SILVER MEDAL	United States
BRONZE MEDAL	Sweden
Fourth Place	Czechoslovakia
Fifth Place	Switzerland
Sixth Place	Poland
Seventh Place	Finland
Eighth Place	West Germany
Ninth Place	Norway

THE SEVENTH OLYMPIC WINTER GAMES

CORTINA d'AMPEZZO, ITALY, January 26–February 4, 1956

FINAL PLACINGS

GOLD MEDAL	Soviet Union
SILVER MEDAL	United States
BRONZE MEDAL	Canada
Fourth Place	Sweden
Fifth Place	Czechoslovakia
Sixth Place	Germany
Seventh Place	Italy
Eighth Place	Poland
Ninth Place	Switzerland
Tenth Place	Austria

THE EIGHTH OLYMPIC WINTER GAMES

SQUAW VALLEY, UNITED STATES, February 19–28, 1960

FINAL PLACINGS

GOLD MEDAL	United States
SILVER MEDAL	Canada
BRONZE MEDAL	Soviet Union
Fourth Place	Czechoslovakia
Fifth Place	Sweden
Sixth Place	Germany
Seventh Place	Finland
Eighth Place	Japan
Ninth Place	Australia

THE NINTH OLYMPIC WINTER GAMES

INNSBRUCK, AUSTRIA, January 29–February 9, 1964

FINAL PLACINGS

GOLD MEDAL	Soviet Union
SILVER MEDAL	Sweden
BRONZE MEDAL	Czechoslovakia
Fourth Place	Canada
Fifth Place	United States
Sixth Place	Finland
Seventh Place	Germany
Eighth Place	Switzerland
Ninth Place	Poland
Tenth Place	Norway
Eleventh Place	Japan
Twelfth Place	Romania
Thirteenth Place	Austria
Fourteenth Place	Yugoslavia
Fifteenth Place	Italy
Sixteenth Place	Hungary

THE TENTH OLYMPIC WINTER GAMES

GRENOBLE, FRANCE, February 6–17, 1968

FINAL PLACINGS

GOLD MEDAL	Soviet Union
SILVER MEDAL	Czechoslovakia

BRONZE MEDAL	Canada
Fourth Place	Sweden
Fifth Place	Finland
Sixth Place	United States
Seventh Place	West Germany
Eighth Place	East Germany
Ninth Place	Yugoslavia
Tenth Place	Japan
Eleventh Place	Norway
Twelfth Place	Romania
Thirteenth Place	Austria
Fourteenth Place	France

THE ELEVENTH OLYMPIC WINTER GAMES

SAPPORO, JAPAN, February 5–12, 1972

FINAL PLACINGS

GOLD MEDAL	Soviet Union
SILVER MEDAL	United States
BRONZE MEDAL	Czechoslovakia
Fourth Place	Sweden
Fifth Place	Finland
Sixth Place	Poland
Seventh Place	West Germany
Eighth Place	Norway
Ninth Place	Japan
Tenth Place	Switzerland
Eleventh Place	Yugoslavia

THE TWELFTH OLYMPIC WINTER GAMES

INNSBRUCK, AUSTRIA, February 2–13, 1976

FINAL PLACINGS

GOLD MEDAL	Soviet Union
SILVER MEDAL	Czechoslovakia
BRONZE MEDAL	West Germany
Fourth Place	Finland
Fifth Place	United States
Sixth Place	Poland
Seventh Place	Romania

Eighth Place	Austria
Ninth Place	Japan
Tenth Place	Yugoslavia
Eleventh Place	Switzerland
	Norway
Thirteenth Place	Bulgaria

THE THIRTEENTH OLYMPIC WINTER GAMES

LAKE PLACID, UNITED STATES, February 12–24, 1980

FINAL PLACINGS

GOLD MEDAL	United States
SILVER MEDAL	Soviet Union
BRONZE MEDAL	Sweden
Fourth Place	Finland
Fifth Place	Czechoslovakia
Sixth Place	Canada
Seventh Place	Poland
	Romania
Ninth Place	Netherlands
	West Germany
Eleventh Place	Japan
	Norway

THE FOURTEENTH OLYMPIC WINTER GAMES

SARAJEVO, YUGOSLAVIA, February 7–19, 1984

FINAL PLACINGS

GOLD MEDAL	Soviet Union
SILVER MEDAL	Czechoslovakia
BRONZE MEDAL	Sweden
Fourth Place	Canada
Fifth Place	West Germany
Sixth Place	Finland
Seventh Place	United States
Eighth Place	Poland
Ninth Place	Italy
	Austria
Eleventh Place	Norway
	Yugoslavia

THE FIFTEENTH OLYMPIC WINTER GAMES

CALGARY, CANADA, February 13–28, 1988

FINAL PLACINGS

GOLD MEDAL	Soviet Union
SILVER MEDAL	Finland
BRONZE MEDAL	Sweden
Fourth Place	Canada
Fifth Place	West Germany
Sixth Place	Czechoslovakia
Seventh Place	United States
Eighth Place	Switzerland
Ninth Place	Austria
Tenth Place	Poland
Eleventh Place	France
Twelfth Place	Norway

THE SIXTEENTH OLYMPIC WINTER GAMES

ALBERTVILLE, FRANCE, February 8–23, 1992

FINAL PLACINGS

GOLD MEDAL	Unified Team
SILVER MEDAL	Canada
BRONZE MEDAL	Czechoslovakia
Fourth Place	United States
Fifth Place	Sweden
Sixth Place	Germany
Seventh Place	Finland
Eighth Place	France
Ninth Place	Norway
Tenth Place	Switzerland
Eleventh Place	Poland
Twelfth Place	Italy

THE SEVENTEENTH OLYMPIC WINTER GAMES

LILLEHAMMER, NORWAY, February 12–27, 1994

FINAL PLACINGS

GOLD MEDAL	Sweden
SILVER MEDAL	Canada
BRONZE MEDAL	Finland
Fourth Place	Russia
Fifth Place	Czech Republic
Sixth Place	Slovakia
Seventh Place	Germany
Eighth Place	United States
Ninth Place	Italy
Tenth Place	France
Eleventh Place	Norway
Twelfth Place	Austria

THE EIGHTEENTH OLYMPIC WINTER GAMES

NAGANO, JAPAN, February 7–22, 1998

FINAL PLACINGS

GOLD MEDAL	Czech Republic
SILVER MEDAL	Russia
BRONZE MEDAL	Finland
Fourth Place	Canada
Fifth Place	Sweden
	United States
	Belarus
	Kazakhstan
Ninth Place	Germany
Tenth Place	Slovakia
Eleventh Place	France
Twelfth Place	Italy
Thirteenth Place	Japan
Fourteenth Place	Austria

THE NINETEENTH OLYMPIC WINTER GAMES

SALT LAKE CITY, UNITED STATES, February 9–24, 2002

FINAL PLACINGS

GOLD MEDAL	Canada
SILVER MEDAL	United States
BRONZE MEDAL	Russia
Fourth Place	Belarus
Fifth Place	Sweden
	Finland
	Czech Republic
	Germany
Ninth Place	Latvia
Tenth Place	Ukraine
Eleventh Place	Switzerland
Twelfth Place	Austria
Thirteenth Place	Slovakia
Fourteenth Place	France

THE TWENTIETH OLYMPIC WINTER GAMES

TURIN, ITALY, February 15–26, 2006

FINAL PLACINGS

GOLD MEDAL	Sweden
SILVER MEDAL	Finland
BRONZE MEDAL	Czech Republic
Fourth Place	Russia
Fifth Place	Slovakia
Sixth Place	Switzerland
Seventh Place	Canada
Eighth Place	United States
Ninth Place	Kazakhstan
Tenth Place	Germany
Eleventh Place	Italy
Twelfth Place	Latvia

THE TWENTY-FIRST OLYMPIC WINTER GAMES

VANCOUVER, CANADA, February 13–28, 2010

FINAL PLACINGS

GOLD MEDAL	Canada
SILVER MEDAL	United States
BRONZE MEDAL	Finland
Fourth Place	Slovakia
Fifth Place	Sweden
Sixth Place	Russia
Seventh Place	Czech Republic
Eighth Place	Switzerland
Ninth Place	Belarus
Tenth Place	Norway
Eleventh Place	Germany
Twelfth Place	Latvia

OLYMPICS, WOMEN, 1998–2010

THE EIGHTEENTH OLYMPIC WINTER GAMES

NAGANO, JAPAN, February 8–17, 1998

FINAL PLACINGS

GOLD MEDAL	United States
SILVER MEDAL	Canada
BRONZE MEDAL	Finland
Fourth Place	China
Fifth Place	Sweden
Sixth Place	Japan

THE NINETEENTH OLYMPIC WINTER GAMES

SALT LAKE CITY, UNITED STATES, February 11–21, 2002

FINAL PLACINGS

GOLD MEDAL	Canada
SILVER MEDAL	United States
BRONZE MEDAL	Sweden
Fourth Place	Finland
Fifth Place	Russia
Sixth Place	Germany
Seventh Place	China
Eighth Place	Kazakhstan

THE TWENTIETH OLYMPIC WINTER GAMES

TURIN, ITALY, February 11–20, 2006

FINAL PLACINGS

GOLD MEDAL	Canada
SILVER MEDAL	Sweden
BRONZE MEDAL	United States
Fourth Place	Finland
Fifth Place	Germany
Sixth Place	Russia
Seventh Place	Switzerland
Eighth Place	Italy

THE TWENTY-FIRST OLYMPIC WINTER GAMES

VANCOUVER, CANADA, February 13–25, 2010

FINAL PLACINGS

GOLD MEDAL	Canada
SILVER MEDAL	United States
BRONZE MEDAL	Finland
Fourth Place	Sweden
Fifth Place	Switzerland
Sixth Place	Russia
Seventh Place	China
Eighth Place	Slovakia

WORLD CHAMPIONSHIPS, MEN, 1930–2011

1930 WORLD CHAMPIONSHIP, MEN

CHAMONIX, FRANCE/BERLIN, GERMANY/VIENNA, AUSTRIA,
January 31–February 10, 1930

Final Placings
GOLD MEDAL	Canada
SILVER MEDAL	Germany
BRONZE MEDAL	Switzerland
Fourth Place	Austria
Fifth Place	Poland
Sixth Place	Czechoslovakia
	France
	Hungary
	Japan
Tenth Place	Belgium
	Great Britain
	Italy

1931 WORLD CHAMPIONSHIP, MEN

KRYNICA, POLAND, March 1–8, 1931

Final Placings
GOLD MEDAL	Canada
SILVER MEDAL	United States
BRONZE MEDAL	Austria
Fourth Place	Poland
Fifth Place	Czechoslovakia
Sixth Place	Sweden
Seventh Place	Hungary
Eighth Place	Great Britain
Ninth Place	France
Tenth Place	Romania

1933 WORLD CHAMPIONSHIP, MEN

PRAGUE, CZECHOSLOVAKIA, February 18–26, 1933

Final Placings

GOLD MEDAL	United States
SILVER MEDAL	Canada
BRONZE MEDAL	Czechoslovakia
Fourth Place	Austria
Fifth Place	Germany
	Switzerland
Seventh Place	Hungary
	Poland
Ninth Place	Romania
Tenth Place	Latvia
Eleventh Place	Italy
Twelfth Place	Belgium

1934 WORLD CHAMPIONSHIP, MEN

MILAN, ITALY, February 3–11, 1934

Final Placings

GOLD MEDAL	Canada
SILVER MEDAL	United States
BRONZE MEDAL	Germany
Fourth Place	Switzerland
Fifth Place	Czechoslovakia
Sixth Place	Hungary
Seventh Place	Austria
Eighth Place	Great Britain
Ninth Place	Italy
Tenth Place	Romania
Eleventh Place	France
Twelfth Place	Belgium

1935 WORLD CHAMPIONSHIP, MEN

DAVOS, SWITZERLAND, January 19–27, 1935

Final Placings

GOLD MEDAL	Canada
SILVER MEDAL	Switzerland
BRONZE MEDAL	Great Britain
Fourth Place	Czechoslovakia
Fifth Place	Sweden
Sixth Place	Austria
Seventh Place	France
Eighth Place	Italy
Ninth Place	Germany
Tenth Place	Poland
Eleventh Place	Hungary
	Romania
Thirteenth Place	Latvia
Fourteenth Place	Belgium
	Netherlands

1937 WORLD CHAMPIONSHIP, MEN

LONDON, GREAT BRITAIN, February 17–27, 1937

Final Placings

GOLD MEDAL	Canada
SILVER MEDAL	Great Britain
BRONZE MEDAL	Switzerland
Fourth Place	Germany
Fifth Place	Hungary
Sixth Place	Czechoslovakia
Seventh Place	France
Eighth Place	Poland
Ninth Place	Norway
	Romania
	Sweden

1938 WORLD CHAMPIONSHIP, MEN

PRAGUE, CZECHOSLOVAKIA, February 11–20, 1938

Final Placings

GOLD MEDAL	Canada
SILVER MEDAL	Great Britain
BRONZE MEDAL	Czechoslovakia
Fourth Place	Germany
Fifth Place	Sweden
Sixth Place	Switzerland
Seventh Place	Hungary
	Poland
	United States
Tenth Place	Austria
	Latvia
	Lithuania
Thirteenth Place	Norway
	Romania

1939 WORLD CHAMPIONSHIP, MEN

BASEL/ZURICH, SWITZERLAND, February 3–12, 1939

Final Placings

GOLD MEDAL	Canada
SILVER MEDAL	United States
BRONZE MEDAL	Switzerland
Fourth Place	Czechoslovakia
Fifth Place	Germany
Sixth Place	Poland
Seventh Place	Hungary
Eighth Place	Great Britain
Ninth Place	Italy
Tenth Place	Latvia
Eleventh Place	Belgium
	Netherlands
Thirteenth Place	Finland
	Yugoslavia

1947 WORLD CHAMPIONSHIP, MEN

PRAGUE, CZECHOSLOVAKIA, February 15–23, 1947

Final Placings
GOLD MEDAL	Czechoslovakia
SILVER MEDAL	Sweden
BRONZE MEDAL	Austria
Fourth Place	Switzerland
Fifth Place	United States
Sixth Place	Poland
Seventh Place	Romania
Eighth Place	Belgium

1949 WORLD CHAMPIONSHIP, MEN

STOCKHOLM, SWEDEN, February 12–20, 1949

Final Placings
GOLD MEDAL	Czechoslovakia
SILVER MEDAL	Canada
BRONZE MEDAL	United States
Fourth Place	Sweden
Fifth Place	Switzerland
Sixth Place	Austria
Seventh Place	Finland
Eighth Place	Norway
Ninth Place	Belgium
Tenth Place	Denmark

1950 WORLD CHAMPIONSHIP, MEN

LONDON, GREAT BRITAIN, March 13–22, 1950

Final Placings
GOLD MEDAL	Canada
SILVER MEDAL	United States
BRONZE MEDAL	Switzerland
Fourth Place	Great Britain
Fifth Place	Sweden
Sixth Place	Norway
Seventh Place	Belgium
Eighth Place	Netherlands
Ninth Place	France

1951 WORLD CHAMPIONSHIP, MEN

PARIS, FRANCE, March 9–17, 1951

Final Placings

GOLD MEDAL	Canada
SILVER MEDAL	Sweden
BRONZE MEDAL	Switzerland
Fourth Place	Norway
Fifth Place	Great Britain
Sixth Place	United States
Seventh Place	Finland

1953 WORLD CHAMPIONSHIP, MEN

ZURICH/BASEL, SWITZERLAND, March 6–15, 1953

Final Placings

GOLD MEDAL	Sweden
SILVER MEDAL	West Germany
BRONZE MEDAL	Switzerland
Fourth Place	Czechoslovakia

1954 WORLD CHAMPIONSHIP, MEN

STOCKHOLM, SWEDEN, February 26–March 7, 1954

Final Placings

GOLD MEDAL	Soviet Union
SILVER MEDAL	Canada
BRONZE MEDAL	Sweden
Fourth Place	Czechoslovakia
Fifth Place	West Germany
Sixth Place	Finland
Seventh Place	Switzerland
Eighth Place	Norway

1955 WORLD CHAMPIONSHIP, MEN

DÜSSELDORF, WEST GERMANY, February 25–March 6, 1955

Final Placings

GOLD MEDAL	Canada
SILVER MEDAL	Soviet Union
BRONZE MEDAL	Czechoslovakia
Fourth Place	United States
Fifth Place	Sweden
Sixth Place	West Germany
Seventh Place	Poland
Eighth Place	Switzerland
Ninth Place	Finland

1957 WORLD CHAMPIONSHIP, MEN

MOSCOW, SOVIET UNION, February 24–March 5, 1957

Final Placings

GOLD MEDAL	Sweden
SILVER MEDAL	Soviet Union
BRONZE MEDAL	Czechoslovakia
Fourth Place	Finland
Fifth Place	West Germany
Sixth Place	Poland
Seventh Place	Austria
Eighth Place	Japan

- To protest the suppression of the Hungarian revolution by Soviet forces, Canadian Prime Minister Louis St. Laurent refused to allow a Canadian team to travel to Moscow to play at the World Championships.

1958 WORLD CHAMPIONSHIP, MEN

OSLO, NORWAY, February 25–March 9, 1958

Final Placings

GOLD MEDAL	Canada
SILVER MEDAL	Soviet Union
BRONZE MEDAL	Sweden
Fourth Place	Czechoslovakia
Fifth Place	United States
Sixth Place	Finland

Seventh Place   Norway
Eighth Place   Poland

1959 WORLD CHAMPIONSHIP, MEN

PRAGUE, CZECHOSLOVAKIA, March 9–15, 1959

Final Placings
GOLD MEDAL   Canada
SILVER MEDAL   Soviet Union
BRONZE MEDAL   Czechoslovakia
Fourth Place   United States
Fifth Place   Sweden
Sixth Place   Finland
Seventh Place   West Germany
Eighth Place   Norway
Ninth Place   East Germany
Tenth Place   Italy
Eleventh Place   Poland
Twelfth Place   Switzerland
Thirteenth Place   Romania
Fourteenth Place   Hungary
Fifteenth Place   Austria

1961 WORLD CHAMPIONSHIP, MEN

GENEVA/LAUSANNE, SWITZERLAND, March 1–12, 1961

Final Placings
GOLD MEDAL   Canada
SIVER MEDAL   Czechoslovakia
BRONZE MEDAL   Soviet Union
Fourth Place   Sweden
Fifth Place   East Germany
Sixth Place   United States
Seventh Place   Finland
Eighth Place   West Germany

1962 WORLD CHAMPIONSHIP, MEN

COLORADO SPRINGS, UNITED STATES, May 8–18, 1962

Final Placings
GOLD MEDAL	Sweden
SILVER MEDAL	Canada
BRONZE MEDAL	United States
Fourth Place	Finland
Fifth Place	Norway
Sixth Place	West Germany
Seventh Place	Switzerland
Eighth Place	Great Britain

1963 WORLD CHAMPIONSHIP, MEN

STOCKHOLM, SWEDEN, March 7–17, 1963

Final Placings
GOLD MEDAL	Soviet Union
SILVER MEDAL	Sweden
BRONZE MEDAL	Czechoslovakia
Fourth Place	Canada
Fifth Place	Finland
Sixth Place	East Germany
Seventh Place	West Germany
Eighth Place	United States

1965 WORLD CHAMPIONSHIP, MEN

TAMPERE, FINLAND, March 3–14, 1965

Final Placings
GOLD MEDAL	Soviet Union
SILVER MEDAL	Czechoslovakia
BRONZE MEDAL	Sweden
Fourth Place	Canada
Fifth Place	East Germany
Sixth Place	United States
Seventh Place	Finland
Eighth Place	Norway

1966 WORLD CHAMPIONSHIP, MEN

LJUBLJANA, YUGOSLAVIA, March 3–14, 1966

Final Placings

GOLD MEDAL	Soviet Union
SILVER MEDAL	Czechoslovakia
BRONZE MEDAL	Canada
Fourth Place	Sweden
Fifth Place	East Germany
Sixth Place	United States
Seventh Place	Finland
Eighth Place	Poland

1967 WORLD CHAMPIONSHIP, MEN

VIENNA, AUSTRIA, March 18–29, 1967

Final Placings

GOLD MEDAL	Soviet Union
SILVER MEDAL	Sweden
BRONZE MEDAL	Canada
Fourth Place	Czechoslovakia
Fifth Place	United States
Sixth Place	Finland
Seventh Place	West Germany
Eighth Place	East Germany

1969 WORLD CHAMPIONSHIP, MEN

STOCKHOLM, SWEDEN, March 15–30, 1969

Final Placings

GOLD MEDAL	Soviet Union
SILVER MEDAL	Sweden
BRONZE MEDAL	Czechoslovakia
Fourth Place	Canada
Fifth Place	Finland
Sixth Place	United States

• To protest the ineligibility of professionals from the World Championships according to IIHF rules, Canada did not compete in IIHF-sanctioned tournaments from 1970 through 1976.

1970 WORLD CHAMPIONSHIP, MEN

STOCKHOLM, SWEDEN, March 14–30, 1970

Final Placings
GOLD MEDAL	Soviet Union
SILVER MEDAL	Sweden
BRONZE MEDAL	Czechoslovakia
Fourth Place	Finland
Fifth Place	East Germany
Sixth Place	Poland

1971 WORLD CHAMPIONSHIP, MEN

BERN/GENEVA, SWITZERLAND, March 19–April 3, 1971

Final Placings
GOLD MEDAL	Soviet Union
SILVER MEDAL	Czechoslovakia
BRONZE MEDAL	Sweden
Fourth Place	Finland
Fifth Place	East Germany
Sixth Place	United States

1972 WORLD CHAMPIONSHIP, MEN

PRAGUE, CZECHOSLOVAKIA, April 7–22, 1972

Final Placings
GOLD MEDAL	Czechoslovakia
SILVER MEDAL	Soviet Union
BRONZE MEDAL	Sweden
Fourth Place	Finland
Fifth Place	East Germany
Sixth Place	Switzerland

1973 WORLD CHAMPIONSHIP, MEN

MOSCOW, SOVIET UNION, March 31–April 15, 1973

Final Placings
GOLD MEDAL	Soviet Union
SILVER MEDAL	Sweden

BRONZE MEDAL   Czechoslovakia
Fourth Place   Finland
Fifth Place   Poland
Sixth Place   East Germany

1974 WORLD CHAMPIONSHIP, MEN

HELSINKI, FINLAND, April 5–20, 1974

Final Placings
GOLD MEDAL   Soviet Union
SILVER MEDAL   Czechoslovakia
BRONZE MEDAL   Sweden
Fourth Place   Finland
Fifth Place   Poland
Sixth Place   East Germany

1975 WORLD CHAMPIONSHIP, MEN

MUNICH/DÜSSELDORF, WEST GERMANY, April 3–19, 1975

Final Placings
GOLD MEDAL   Soviet Union
SILVER MEDAL   Czechoslovakia
BRONZE MEDAL   Sweden
Fourth Place   Finland
Fifth Place   Poland
Sixth Place   United States

1976 WORLD CHAMPIONSHIP, MEN

KATOWICE, POLAND, April 8–25, 1976

Final Placings
GOLD MEDAL   Czechoslovakia
SILVER MEDAL   Soviet Union
BRONZE MEDAL   Sweden
Fourth Place   United States
Fifth Place   Finland
Sixth Place   West Germany
Seventh Place   Poland
Eighth Place   East Germany

1977 WORLD CHAMPIONSHIP, MEN

VIENNA, AUSTRIA, April 21–May 8, 1977

Final Placings

GOLD MEDAL	Czechoslovakia
SILVER MEDAL	Sweden
BRONZE MEDAL	Soviet Union
Fourth Place	Canada
Fifth Place	Finland
Sixth Place	United States
Seventh Place	West Germany
Eighth Place	Romania

1978 WORLD CHAMPIONSHIP, MEN

PRAGUE, CZECHOSLOVAKIA, April 25–May 8, 1978

Final Placings

GOLD MEDAL	Soviet Union
SILVER MEDAL	Czechoslovakia
BRONZE MEDAL	Canada
Fourth Place	Sweden
Fifth Place	West Germany
Sixth Place	United States
Seventh Place	Finland
Eighth Place	East Germany

1979 WORLD CHAMPIONSHIP, MEN

MOSCOW, SOVIET UNION, April 14–27, 1979

Final Placings

GOLD MEDAL	Soviet Union
SILVER MEDAL	Czechoslovakia
BRONZE MEDAL	Sweden
Fourth Place	Canada
Fifth Place	Finland
Sixth Place	West Germany
Seventh Place	United States
Eighth Place	Poland

1981 WORLD CHAMPIONSHIP, MEN

GOTHENBURG/STOCKHOLM, Sweden, April 12–26, 1981

Final Placings
GOLD MEDAL	Soviet Union
SILVER MEDAL	Sweden
BRONZE MEDAL	Czechoslovakia
Fourth Place	Canada
Fifth Place	United States
Sixth Place	Finland
Seventh Place	West Germany
Eighth Place	Netherlands

1982 WORLD CHAMPIONSHIP, MEN

HELSINKI/TAMPERE, FINLAND, April 15–29, 1982

Final Placings
GOLD MEDAL	Soviet Union
SILVER MEDAL	Czechoslovakia
BRONZE MEDAL	Canada
Fourth Place	Sweden
Fifth Place	Finland
Sixth Place	West Germany
Seventh Place	Italy
Eighth Place	United States

1983 WORLD CHAMPIONSHIP, MEN

DORTMUND/DÜSSELDORF/MUNICH, WEST GERMANY, April 16–May 2, 1983

Final Placings
GOLD MEDAL	Soviet Union
SILVER MEDAL	Czechoslovakia
BRONZE MEDAL	Canada
Fourth Place	Sweden
Fifth Place	East Germany
Sixth Place	West Germany
Seventh Place	Finland
Eighth Place	Italy

1985 WORLD CHAMPIONSHIP, MEN

PRAGUE, CZECHOSLOVAKIA, April 17–May 3, 1985

Final Placings
GOLD MEDAL	Czechoslovakia
SILVER MEDAL	Canada
BRONZE MEDAL	Soviet Union
Fourth Place	United States
Fifth Place	Finland
Sixth Place	Sweden
Seventh Place	East Germany
Eighth Place	West Germany

1986 WORLD CHAMPIONSHIP, MEN

MOSCOW, SOVIET UNION, April 12–28, 1986

Final Placings
GOLD MEDAL	Soviet Union
SILVER MEDAL	Sweden
BRONZE MEDAL	Canada
Fourth Place	Finland
Fifth Place	Czechoslovakia
Sixth Place	United States
Seventh Place	East Germany
Eighth Place	Poland

1987 WORLD CHAMPIONSHIP, MEN

VIENNA, AUSTRIA, April 17–May 3, 1987

Final Placings
GOLD MEDAL	Sweden
SILVER MEDAL	Soviet Union
BRONZE MEDAL	Czechoslovakia
Fourth Place	Canada
Fifth Place	Finland
Sixth Place	West Germany
Seventh Place	United States
Eighth Place	Switzerland

1989 WORLD CHAMPIONSHIP, MEN

STOCKHOLM, SWEDEN, April 15–May 1, 1989

Final Placings

GOLD MEDAL	Soviet Union
SILVER MEDAL	Canada
BRONZE MEDAL	Czechoslovakia
Fourth Place	Sweden
Fifth Place	Finland
Sixth Place	United States
Seventh Place	West Germany
Eighth Place	Poland

1990 WORLD CHAMPIONSHIP, MEN

BERNE, SWITZERLAND, April 16–May 2, 1990

Final Placings

GOLD MEDAL	Soviet Union
SILVER MEDAL	Sweden
BRONZE MEDAL	Czechoslovakia
Fourth Place	Canada
Fifth Place	United States
Sixth Place	Finland
Seventh Place	West Germany
Eighth Place	Norway

1991 WORLD CHAMPIONSHIP, MEN

HELSINKI, FINLAND, April 14–May 5, 1991

Final Placings

GOLD MEDAL	Sweden
SILVER MEDAL	Canada
BRONZE MEDAL	Soviet Union
Fourth Place	United States
Fifth Place	Finland
Sixth Place	Czechoslovakia
Seventh Place	Switzerland
Eight Place	Germany

1992 WORLD CHAMPIONSHIP, MEN

PRAGUE/BRATISLAVA, CZECHOSLOVAKIA, April 28–May 10, 1992

Final Placings

GOLD MEDAL	Sweden
SILVER MEDAL	Finland
BRONZE MEDAL	Czechoslovakia
Fourth Place	Switzerland
Fifth Place	Russia
Sixth Place	Germany
Seventh Place	United States
Eighth Place	Canada
Ninth Place	Italy
Tenth Place	Norway
Eleventh Place	France
Twelfth Place	Poland

1993 WORLD CHAMPIONSHIP, MEN

MUNICH, GERMANY, April 18–May 2, 1993

Final Placings

GOLD MEDAL	Russia
SILVER MEDAL	Sweden
BRONZE MEDAL	Czech Republic
Fourth Place	Canada
Fifth Place	Germany
Sixth Place	United States
Seventh Place	Finland
Eighth Place	Italy
Ninth Place	Austria
Tenth Place	France
Eleventh Place	Norway
Twelfth Place	Switzerland

1994 WORLD CHAMPIONSHIP, MEN

BOLZANO, ITALY, April 25–May 8, 1994

Final Placings

GOLD MEDAL	Canada
SILVER MEDAL	Finland

BRONZE MEDAL	Sweden
Fourth Place	United States
Fifth Place	Russia
Sixth Place	Italy
Seventh Place	Czech Republic
Eighth Place	Austria
Ninth Place	Germany
Tenth Place	France
Eleventh Place	Norway
Twelfth Place	Great Britain

1995 WORLD CHAMPIONSHIP, MEN

STOCKHOLM/GAVLE, SWEDEN, April 23–May 7, 1995

Final Placings

GOLD MEDAL	Finland
SILVER MEDAL	Sweden
BRONZE MEDAL	Canada
Fourth Place	Czech Republic
Fifth Place	Russia
Sixth Place	United States
Seventh Place	Italy
Eighth Place	France
Ninth Place	Germany
Tenth Place	Norway
Eleventh Place	Austria
Twelfth Place	Switzerland

1996 WORLD CHAMPIONSHIP, MEN

VIENNA, AUSTRIA, April 21–May 5, 1996

Final Placings

GOLD MEDAL	Czech Republic
SILVER MEDAL	Canada
BRONZE MEDAL	United States
Fourth Place	Russia
Fifth Place	Finland
Sixth Place	Sweden
Seventh Place	Italy
Eighth Place	Germany

Ninth Place	Norway
Tenth Place	Slovakia
Eleventh Place	France
Twelfth Place	Austria

1997 WORLD CHAMPIONSHIP, MEN

HELSINKI/TAMPERE/TURKU, FINLAND, April 26–May 14, 1997

Final Placings

GOLD MEDAL	Canada
SILVER MEDAL	Sweden
BRONZE MEDAL	Czech Republic
Fourth Place	Russia
Fifth Place	Finland
Sixth Place	United States
Seventh Place	Latvia
Eighth Place	Italy
Ninth Place	Slovakia
Tenth Place	France
Eleventh Place	Germany
Twelfth Place	Norway

1998 WORLD CHAMPIONSHIP, MEN

ZURICH, SWITZERLAND, May 1–17, 1998

Final Placings

GOLD MEDAL	Sweden
SILVER MEDAL	Finland
BRONZE MEDAL	Czech Republic
Fourth Place	Switzerland
Fifth Place	Russia
Sixth Place	Canada
Seventh Place	Slovakia
Eighth Place	Belarus
Ninth Place	Latvia
Tenth Place	Italy
Eleventh Place	Germany
Twelfth Place	United States

1999 WORLD CHAMPIONSHIP, MEN

OSLO/HAMAR/LILLEHAMMER, NORWAY, May 1–16, 1999

Final Placings

GOLD MEDAL	Czech Republic
SILVER MEDAL	Finland
BRONZE MEDAL	Sweden
Fourth Place	Canada
Fifth Place	Russia
Sixth Place	United States
Seventh Place	Slovakia
Eighth Place	Switzerland
Ninth Place	Belarus
Tenth Place	Austria
Eleventh Place	Latvia
Twelfth Place	Norway
Thirteenth Place	Italy
Fourteenth Place	Ukraine
Fifteenth Place	France
Sixteenth Place	Japan

2000 WORLD CHAMPIONSHIP, MEN

ST. PETERSBURG, RUSSIA, April 29–May 14, 2000

Final Placings

GOLD MEDAL	Czech Republic
SILVER MEDAL	Slovakia
BRONZE MEDAL	Finland
Fourth Place	Canada
Fifth Place	United States
Sixth Place	Switzerland
Seventh Place	Sweden
Eighth Place	Latvia
Ninth Place	Belarus
Tenth Place	Norway
Eleventh Place	Russia
Twelfth Place	Italy
Thirteenth Place	Austria
Fourteenth Place	Ukraine
Fifteenth Place	France
Sixteenth Place	Japan

2001 WORLD CHAMPIONSHIP, MEN

HANOVER/COLOGNE/NUREMBERG, GERMANY, April 28–May 13, 2001

Final Placings

GOLD MEDAL	Czech Republic
SILVER MEDAL	Finland
BRONZE MEDAL	Sweden
Fourth Place	United States
Fifth Place	Canada
Sixth Place	Russia
Seventh Place	Slovakia
Eighth Place	Germany
Ninth Place	Switzerland
Tenth Place	Ukraine
Eleventh Place	Austria
Twelfth Place	Italy
Thirteenth Place	Latvia
Fourteenth Place	Belarus
Fifteenth Place	Norway
Sixteenth Place	Japan

2002 WORLD CHAMPIONSHIP, MEN

GOTHENBURG/KARLSTAD/JONKOPING, SWEDEN, April 26–May 11, 2002

Final Placings

GOLD MEDAL	Slovakia
SILVER MEDAL	Russia
BRONZE MEDAL	Sweden
Fourth Place	Finland
Fifth Place	Czech Republic
Sixth Place	Canada
Seventh Place	United States
Eighth Place	Germany
Ninth Place	Ukraine
Tenth Place	Switzerland
Eleventh Place	Latvia
Tweflth Place	Austria
Thirteenth Place	Slovenia
Fourteenth Place	Poland
Fifteenth Place	Italy
Sixteenth Place	Japan

2003 WORLD CHAMPIONSHIP, MEN

HELSINKI/TAMPERE/TURKU, FINLAND, April 27–May 11, 2003

Final Placings

GOLD MEDAL	Canada
SILVER MEDAL	Sweden
BRONZE MEDAL	Slovakia
Fourth Place	Czech Republic
Fifth Place	Finland
Sixth Place	Germany
Seventh Place	Russia
Eighth Place	Switzerland
Ninth Place	Latvia
Tenth Place	Austria
Eleventh Place	Denmark
Twelfth Place	Ukraine
Thirteenth Place	United States
Fourteenth Place	Belarus
Fifteenth Place	Slovenia
Sixteenth Place	Japan

2004 WORLD CHAMPIONSHIP, MEN

PRAGUE/OSTRAVA, CZECH REPUBLIC, April 24–May 9, 2004

Final Placings

GOLD MEDAL	Canada
SILVER MEDAL	Sweden
BRONZE MEDAL	United States
Fourth Place	Slovakia
Fifth Place	Czech Republic
Sixth Place	Finland
Seventh Place	Latvia
Eighth Place	Switzerland
Ninth Place	Germany
Tenth Place	Russia
Eleventh Place	Austria
Twelfth Place	Denmark
Thirteenth Place	Kazakhstan
Fourteenth Place	Ukraine
Fifteenth Place	Japan
Sixteenth Place	France

2005 WORLD CHAMPIONSHIP, MEN

VIENNA/INNSBRUCK, AUSTRIA, April 30–May 15, 2005

Final Placings

GOLD MEDAL	Czech Republic
SILVER MEDAL	Canada
BRONZE MEDAL	Russia
Fourth Place	Sweden
Fifth Place	Slovakia
Sixth Place	United States
Seventh Place	Finland
Eighth Place	Switzerland
Ninth Place	Latvia
Tenth Place	Belarus
Eleventh Place	Ukraine
Twelfth Place	Kazakhstan
Thirteenth Place	Slovenia
Fourteenth Place	Denmark
Fifteenth Place	Germany
Sixteenth Place	Austria

2006 WORLD CHAMPIONSHIP, MEN

RIGA, LATVIA, May 5–May 21, 2006

Final Placings

GOLD MEDAL	Sweden
SILVER MEDAL	Czech Republic
BRONZE MEDAL	Finland
Fourth Place	Canada
Fifth Place	Russia
Sixth Place	Belarus
Seventh Place	United States
Eighth Place	Slovakia
Ninth Place	Switzerland
Tenth Place	Latvia
Eleventh Place	Norway
Twelfth Place	Ukraine
Thirteenth Place	Denmark
Fourteenth Place	Italy
Fifteenth Place	Kazakhstan
Sixteenth Place	Slovenia

2007 WORLD CHAMPIONSHIP, MEN

MOSCOW/MYTISCHI, RUSSIA, April 24–May 10, 2007

Final Placings

GOLD MEDAL	Canada
SILVER MEDAL	Finland
BRONZE MEDAL	Russia
Fourth Place	Sweden
Fifth Place	United States
Sixth Place	Slovakia
Seventh Place	Czech Republic
Eighth Place	Switzerland
Ninth Place	Germany
Tenth Place	Denmark
Eleventh Place	Belarus
Twelfth Place	Italy
Thirteenth Place	Latvia
Fourteenth Place	Norway
Fifteenth Place	Austria
Sixteenth Place	Ukraine

2008 WORLD CHAMPIONSHIP, MEN

HALIFAX/QUEBEC CITY, CANADA, May 2–May 18, 2008

Final Placings

GOLD MEDAL	Russia
SILVER MEDAL	Canada
BRONZE MEDAL	Finland
Fourth Place	Sweden
Fifth Place	Czech Republic
Sixth Place	United States
Seventh Place	Switzerland
Eighth Place	Norway
Ninth Place	Belarus
Tenth Place	Germany
Eleventh Place	Latvia
Twelfth Place	Denmark
Thirteenth Place	Slovakia
Fourteenth Place	France
Fifteenth Place	Slovenia
Sixteenth Place	Italy

2009 WORLD CHAMPIONSHIP, MEN

ZURICH/BERNE, SWITZERLAND, April 24–May 10, 2009

Final Placings

GOLD MEDAL	Russia
SILVER MEDAL	Canada
BRONZE MEDAL	Sweden
Fourth Place	United States
Fifth Place	Finland
Sixth Place	Czech Republic
Seventh Place	Latvia
Eighth Place	Belarus
Ninth Place	Switzerland
Tenth Place	Slovakia
Eleventh Place	Norway
Twelfth Place	France
Thirteenth Place	Denmark
Fourteenth Place	Austria
Fifteenth Place	Germany
Sixteenth Place	Hungary

2010 WORLD CHAMPIONSHIP, MEN

GELSENKIRCHEN/MANNHEIM/COLOGNE, GERMANY, May 7–23, 2010

Final Placings

GOLD MEDAL	Czech Republic
SILVER MEDAL	Russia
BRONZE MEDAL	Sweden
Fourth Place	Germany
Fifth Place	Switzerland
Sixth Place	Finland
Seventh Place	Canada
Eighth Place	Denmark
Ninth Place	Norway
Tenth Place	Belarus
Eleventh Place	Latvia
Twelfth Place	Slovakia
Thirteenth Place	United States
Fourteenth Place	France
Fifteenth Place	Italy
Sixteenth Place	Kazakhstan

2011 WORLD CHAMPIONSHIP, MEN

BRATISLAVA/KOSICE, SLOVAKIA, April 29–May 15, 2011

Final Placings

GOLD MEDAL	Finland
SILVER MEDAL	Sweden
BRONZE MEDAL	Czech Republic
Fourth Place	Russia
Fifth Place	Canada
Sixth Place	Norway
Seventh Place	Germany
Eighth Place	United States
Ninth Place	Switzerland
Tenth Place	Slovakia
Eleventh Place	Denmark
Twelfth Place	France
Thirteenth Place	Latvia
Fourteenth Place	Belarus
Fifteenth Place	Austria
Sixteenth PLace	Slovenia

WORLD CHAMPIONSHIPS, WOMEN, 1990–2011

1990 WORLD CHAMPIONSHIP, WOMEN

CANADA, March 19–25, 1990

FINAL PLACINGS

GOLD MEDAL	Canada
SILVER MEDAL	United States
BRONZE MEDAL	Finland
Fourth Place	Sweden
Fifth Place	Switzerland
Sixth Place	Norway
Seventh Place	Germany
Eighth Place	Japan

1992 WORLD CHAMPIONSHIP, WOMEN

FINLAND, April 20–26, 1992

FINAL PLACINGS

GOLD MEDAL	Canada
SILVER MEDAL	United States
BRONZE MEDAL	Finland
Fourth Place	Sweden
Fifth Place	China
Sixth Place	Norway
Seventh Place	Denmark
Eighth Place	Switzerland

DIRECTORATE AWARDS

BEST GOALIE	Annica Ahlen (Sweden)
BEST DEFENCEMAN	Geraldine Heaney (Canada)
BEST FORWARD	Cammi Granato (United States)

1994 WORLD CHAMPIONSHIP, WOMEN

UNITED STATES, April 11–17, 1994

FINAL PLACINGS

GOLD MEDAL	Canada
SILVER MEDAL	United States

BRONZE MEDAL	Finland
Fourth Place	China
Fifth Place	Sweden
Sixth Place	Norway
Seventh Place	Switzerland
Eighth Place	Germany

DIRECTORATE AWARDS

BEST GOALIE	Erin Whitten (United States)
BEST DEFENCEMAN	Geraldine Heaney (Canada)
BEST FORWARD	Riikka Nieminen (Finland)

1997 WORLD CHAMPIONSHIP, WOMEN

CANADA, March 31–April 6, 1997

FINAL PLACINGS

GOLD MEDAL	Canada
SILVER MEDAL	United States
BRONZE MEDAL	Finland
Fourth Place	China
Fifth Place	Sweden
Sixth Place	Russia
Seventh Place	Switzerland
Eighth Place	Norway

DIRECTORATE AWARDS

None awarded

1999 WORLD CHAMPIONSHIP, WOMEN

FINLAND, March 8–14, 1999

FINAL PLACINGS

GOLD MEDAL	Canada
SILVER MEDAL	United States
BRONZE MEDAL	Finland
Fourth Place	Sweden
Fifth Place	China
Sixth Place	Russia
Seventh Place	Germany
Eighth Place	Switzerland

DIRECTORATE AWARDS

BEST GOALIE	Sami Jo Small (Canada)
BEST DEFENCEMAN	Kirsi Hanninen (Finland)
BEST FORWARD	Jenny Schmidgall (United States)

2000 WORLD CHAMPIONSHIP, WOMEN

CANADA, April 3–9, 2000

FINAL PLACINGS

GOLD MEDAL	Canada
SILVER MEDAL	United States
BRONZE MEDAL	Finland
Fourth Place	Sweden
Fifth Place	Russia
Sixth Place	China
Seventh Place	Germany
Eighth Place	Japan

DIRECTORATE AWARDS

BEST GOALIE	Sami Jo Small (Canada)
BEST DEFENCEMAN	Angela Ruggiero (United States)
BEST FORWARD	Katja Riipi (Finland)

2001 WORLD CHAMPIONSHIP, WOMEN

UNITED STATES, April 2–8, 2001

FINAL PLACINGS

GOLD MEDAL	Canada
SILVER MEDAL	United States
BRONZE MEDAL	Russia
Fourth Place	Finland
Fifth Place	Sweden
Sixth Place	Germany
Seventh Place	China
Eighth Place	Kazakhstan

DIRECTORATE AWARDS

BEST GOALIE	Kim St. Pierre (Canada)
BEST DEFENCEMAN	Karyn Bye (United States)
BEST FORWARD	Jennifer Botterill (Canada)
MVP	Jennifer Botterill (Canada)

2003 WORLD CHAMPIONSHIP, WOMEN

CHINA, April 3–9, 2003

CANCELLED DUE TO SARS OUTBREAK

2004 WORLD CHAMPIONSHIP, WOMEN

CANADA, March 30–April 6, 2004

FINAL PLACINGS
GOLD MEDAL	Canada
SILVER MEDAL	United States
BRONZE MEDAL	Finland
Fourth Place	Sweden
Fifth Place	Russia
Sixth Place	Germany
Seventh Place	China
Eighth Place	Switzerland
Ninth Place	Japan

DIRECTORATE AWARDS
BEST GOALIE	Kim St. Pierre (Canada)
BEST DEFENCEMAN	Angela Ruggiero (United States)
BEST FORWARD	Jayna Hefford (Canada)
MVP	Jennifer Botterill (Canada)

ALL-STAR TEAM
Goal	Pam Dreyer (United States)
Defence	Gunilla Andersson (Sweden)
	Angela Ruggiero (United States)
Forward	Jayna Hefford (Canada)
	Jennifer Botterill (Canada)
	Natalie Darwitz (United States)

2005 WORLD CHAMPIONSHIP, WOMEN

SWEDEN, April 2–9, 2005

FINAL PLACINGS
GOLD MEDAL	United States
SILVER MEDAL	Canada
BRONZE MEDAL	Sweden

Fourth Place	Finland
Fifth Place	Germany
Sixth Place	China
Seventh Place	Kazakhstan
Eighth Place	Russia

DIRECTORATE AWARDS

BEST GOALIE	Chanda Gunn (United States)
BEST DEFENCEMAN	Angela Ruggiero (United States)
BEST FORWARD	Jayna Hefford (Canada)
MVP	Krissy Wendell (United States)

ALL-STAR TEAM

Goalie	Natalya Turnova (Kazakhstan)
Defence	Cheryl Pounder (Canada)
	Angela Ruggiero (United States)
Forward	Hayley Wickenheiser (Canada)
	Maria Rooth (Sweden)
	Krissy Wendell (United States)

2007 WORLD CHAMPIONSHIP, WOMEN

CANADA, April 3–10, 2007

FINAL PLACINGS

GOLD MEDAL	Canada
SILVER MEDAL	United States
BRONZE MEDAL	Sweden
Fourth Place	Finland
Fifth Place	Switzerland
Sixth Place	China
Seventh Place	Russia
Eighth Place	Germany
Ninth Place	Kazakhstan

DIRECTORATE AWARDS

BEST GOALIE	Noora Raty (Finland)
BEST DEFENCEMAN	Molly Engstrom (United States)
BEST FORWARD	Hayley Wickenheiser (Canada)
MVP	Hayley Wickenheiser (Canada)

ALL-STAR TEAM

Goalie	Kim St. Pierre (Canada)
Defence	Delaney Collins (Canada)
	Angela Ruggiero (United States)
Forward	Natalie Darwitz (United States)
	Krissy Wendell (United States)
	Hayley Wickenheiser (Canada)

2008 WORLD CHAMPIONSHIP, WOMEN

CHINA, April 4–12, 2008

FINAL PLACINGS

GOLD	United States
SILVER	Canada
BRONZE	Finland
Fourth Place	Switzerland
Fifth Place	Sweden
Sixth Place	Russia
Seventh Place	Japan
Eighth Place	China
Ninth Place	Germany

ALL-STAR TEAM

Goalie	Noora Raty (Finland)
Defence	Emma Laaksonen (Finland)
	Julie Chu (United States)
Forward	Hayley Wickenheiser (Canada)
	Natalie Darwitz (United States)
	Jayne Hefford (Canada)

DIRECTORATE AWARDS

BEST GOALIE	Noora Raty (Finland)
BEST DEFENCEMAN	Angela Ruggiero (United States)
BEST FORWARD	Natalie Darwitz (United States)
MVP	Noora Raty (Finland)

2009 WORLD CHAMPIONSHIP, WOMEN

FINLAND, April 4–12, 2009

FINAL PLACINGS

GOLD	United States
SILVER	Canada
BRONZE	Finland
Fourth Place	Sweden
Fifth Place	Russia
Sixth Place	Kazakhstan
Seventh Place	Switzerland
Eighth Place	Japan
Ninth Place	China

ALL-STAR TEAM

Goalie	Jesse Vetter (USA)
Defence	Carla MacLeod (Canada)
	Angela Ruggiero (USA)
Forward	Michelle Karvinen (Finland)
	Julie Chu (USA)
	Natalie Darwitz (USA)

DIRECTORATE AWARDS

BEST GOALIE	Charline Labonte (Canada)
BEST DEFENCEMAN	Jenni Hiirikoski (Finland)
BEST FORWARD	Hayley Wickenheiser (Canada)
MVP	Carla MacLeod (Canada)

2011 WORLD CHAMPIONSHIP, WOMEN

SWITZERLAND, April 16–25, 2011

FINAL PLACINGS

GOLD MEDAL	United States
SILVER MEDAL	Canada
BRONZE MEDAL	Finland
Fourth Place	Russia
Fifth Place	Sweden
Sixth Place	Switzerland
Seventh Place	Slovakia
Eighth Place	Kazakhstan

ALL-STAR TEAM

Goalie	Zuzana Tomcikova (Slovakia)
Defence	Meaghan Mikkelson (Canada)
	Caitlin Cahow (USA)
Forward	Hilary Knight (USA)
	Michelle Karvinen (Finland)
	Hayley Wickenheiser (Canada)

DIRECTORATE AWARDS

BEST GOALIE	Noora Raty (Finland)
BEST DEFENCEMAN	Meaghan Mikkelson (Canada)
BEST FORWARD	Monique Lamoureux-Kolls (USA)
MVP	Zuzana Tomcikova (Slovakia)

WORLD U20 (JUNIOR) CHAMPIONSHIPS, 1977–2011

ALL MEDAL WINNERS BY CUMULATIVE STANDINGS (1977–2012)

Country	Gold	Silver	Bronze	Total
Canada	15	8	5	28
Russia	5	7	5	17
Sweden	2	8	5	15
Soviet Union	8	3	2	13
Finland	2	4	6	12
Czechoslovakia	0	5	6	11
United States	2	1	4	7
Czech Republic	2	0	1	3
Slovakia	0	0	1	1
Switzerland	0	0	1	1

1977 WORLD JUNIOR CHAMPIONSHIP

CZECHOSLOVAKIA, December 22, 1976–January 2, 1977

FINAL PLACINGS

GOLD MEDAL	Soviet Union
SILVER MEDAL	Canada
BRONZE MEDAL	Czechoslovakia
Fourth Place	Finland
Fifth Place	Sweden
Sixth Place	West Germany
Seventh Place	United States
Eighth Place	Poland*

* relegated to 'B' pool for 1978

ALL-STAR TEAM

Goal	Alexander Tyznych (Soviet Union)
Defence	Risto Siltanen (Finland)
	Lubos Oslizlo (Czechoslovakia)
Forward	Dale McCourt (Canada)
	Bengt-Ake Gustafsson (Sweden)
	Igor Romasin (Soviet Union)

DIRECTORATE AWARDS
BEST GOALIE	Jan Hrabak (Czechoslovakia)
BEST DEFENCEMAN	Vyacheslav Fetisov (Soviet Union)
BEST FORWARD	Dale McCourt (Canada)

1978 WORLD JUNIOR CHAMPIONSHIP

CANADA, December 22, 1977–January 3, 1978

FINAL PLACINGS
GOLD MEDAL	Soviet Union
SILVER MEDAL	Sweden
BRONZE MEDAL	Canada
Fourth Place	Czechoslovakia
Fifth Place	United States
Sixth Place	Finland
Seventh Place	West Germany
Eighth Place	Switzerland*

* promoted from 'B' pool in 1977; relegated to 'B' pool for 1979

ALL-STAR TEAM
Goal	Alexander Tyznych (Soviet Union)
Defence	Risto Siltanen (Finland)
	Vyacheslav Fetisov (Soviet Union)
Forward	Wayne Gretzky (Canada)
	Mats Naslund (Sweden)
	Anton Stastny (Czechoslovakia)

DIRECTORATE AWARDS
BEST GOALIE	Alexander Tyzhnych (Soviet Union)
BEST DEFENCEMAN	Vyacheslav Fetisov (Soviet Union)
BEST FORWARD	Wayne Gretzky (Canada)

1979 WORLD JUNIOR CHAMPIONSHIP

SWEDEN, December 27, 1978–January 3, 1979

FINAL PLACINGS
GOLD MEDAL	Soviet Union
SILVER MEDAL	Czechoslovakia
BRONZE MEDAL	Sweden
Fourth Place	Finland

Fifth Place	Canada
Sixth Place	United States
Seventh Place	West Germany
Eighth Place	Norway*

* promoted from 'B' pool in 1978; relegated to 'B' pool for 1980

ALL-STAR TEAM

Goal	Pelle Lindbergh (Sweden)
Defence	Ivan Cerny (Czechoslovakia)
	Alexei Kasatonov (Soviet Union)
Forward	Anatoli Tarasov (Soviet Union)
	Thomas Steen (Sweden)
	Vladimir Krutov (Soviet Union)

DIRECTORATE AWARDS

BEST GOALIE	Pelle Lindbergh (Sweden)
BEST DEFENCEMAN	Alexei Kasatonov (Soviet Union)
BEST FORWARD	Vladimir Krutov (Soviet Union)

1980 WORLD JUNIOR CHAMPIONSHIP

FINLAND, December 27, 1979–January 2, 1980

FINAL PLACINGS

GOLD MEDAL	Soviet Union
SILVER MEDAL	Finland
BRONZE MEDAL	Sweden
Fourth Place	Czechoslovakia
Fifth Place	Canada
Sixth Place	West Germany
Seventh Place	United States
Eighth Place	Switzerland*

* promoted from 'B' pool in 1979; relegated to 'B' pool for 1981

ALL-STAR TEAM

Goal	Jari Paavola (Finland)
Defence	Reijo Ruotsalainen (Finland)
	Tomas Jonsson (Sweden)
Forward	Hakan Loob (Sweden)
	Igor Larionov (Soviet Union)
	Vladimir Krutov (Soviet Union)

DIRECTORATE AWARDS

BEST GOALIE	Jari Paavola (Finland)
BEST DEFENCEMAN	Reijo Ruotsalainen (Finland)
BEST FORWARD	Vladimir Krutov (Soviet Union)

1981 WORLD JUNIOR CHAMPIONSHIP

WEST GERMANY, December 27, 1980–January 2, 1981

FINAL PLACINGS

GOLD MEDAL	Sweden
SILVER MEDAL	Finland
BRONZE MEDAL	Soviet Union
Fourth Place	Czechoslovakia
Fifth Place	West Germany
Sixth Place	United States
Seventh Place	Canada
Eighth Place	Austria*

* promoted from 'B' pool in 1980; relegated to 'B' pool for 1982

ALL-STAR TEAM

Goal	Lars Eriksson (Sweden)
Defence	Miloslav Horava (Czechoslovakia)
	Hakan Nordin (Sweden)
Forward	Ari Lahteenmaki (Finland)
	Patrik Sundstrom (Sweden)
	Jan Erixon (Sweden)

DIRECTORATE AWARDS

BEST GOALIE	Lars Eriksson (Sweden)
BEST DEFENCEMAN	Miloslav Horava (Czechoslovakia)
BEST FORWARD	Patrik Sundstrom (Sweden)

1982 WORLD JUNIOR CHAMPIONSHIP

UNITED STATES, December 22, 1981–January 2, 1982
(some games played in Canada)

FINAL PLACINGS

GOLD MEDAL	Canada
SILVER MEDAL	Czechoslovakia
BRONZE MEDAL	Finland
Fourth Place	Soviet Union

Fifth Place	Sweden
Sixth Place	United States
Seventh Place	West Germany
Eighth Place	Switzerland*

* promoted from 'B' pool in 1981; relegated to 'B' pool for 1983

ALL-STAR TEAM
Goal	Mike Moffat (Canada)
Defence	Gord Kluzak (Canada)
	Ilya Biakin (Soviet Union)
Forward	Mike Moller (Canada)
	Petri Skriko (Finland)
	Vladimir Ruzicka (Czechoslovakia)

DIRECTORATE AWARDS
BEST GOALIE	Mike Moffat (Canada)
BEST DEFENCEMAN	Gord Kluzak (Canada)
BEST FORWARD	Petri Skriko (Finland)

1983 WORLD JUNIOR CHAMPIONSHIP

SOVIET UNION, December 26, 1982–January 4, 1983

FINAL PLACINGS
GOLD MEDAL	Soviet Union
SILVER MEDAL	Czechoslovakia
BRONZE MEDAL	Canada
Fourth Place	Sweden
Fifth Place	United States
Sixth Place	Finland
Seventh Place	West Germany
Eighth Place	Norway*

* promoted from 'B' pool in 1982; relegated to 'B' pool for 1984

ALL-STAR TEAM
Goal	Matti Rautiainen (Finland)
Defence	Ilya Biakin (Soviet Union)
	Simo Saarinen (Finland)
Forward	Tomas Sandstrom (Sweden)
	Vladimir Ruzicka (Czechoslovakia)
	German Volgin (Soviet Union)

DIRECTORATE AWARDS

BEST GOALIE   Dominik Hasek (Czechoslovakia)
BEST DEFENCEMAN Ilya Biakin (Soviet Union)
BEST FORWARD Tomas Sandstrom (Sweden)

1984 WORLD JUNIOR CHAMPIONSHIP

SWEDEN, December 25, 1983–January 3, 1984

FINAL PLACINGS

GOLD MEDAL	Soviet Union
SILVER MEDAL	Finland
BRONZE MEDAL	Czechoslovakia
Fourth Place	Canada
Fifth Place	Sweden
Sixth Place	United States
Seventh Place	West Germany
Eighth Place	Switzerland*

* promoted from 'B' pool in 1983; relegated to 'B' pool for 1985

ALL-STAR TEAM

Goal	Evgeny Belosheikin (Soviet Union)
Defence	Alexei Gusarov (Soviet Union)
	Frantisek Musil (Czechoslovakia)
Forward	Petr Rosol (Czechoslovakia)
	Raimo Helminen (Finland)
	Nikolai Borschevsky (Soviet Union)

DIRECTORATE AWARDS

BEST GOALIE	Alan Perry (United States)
BEST DEFENCEMAN	Alexei Gusarov (Soviet Union)
BEST FORWARD	Raimo Helminen (Finland)

1985 WORLD JUNIOR CHAMPIONSHIP

FINLAND, December 23, 1984–January 1, 1985

FINAL PLACINGS

GOLD MEDAL	Canada
SILVER MEDAL	Czechoslovakia
BRONZE MEDAL	Soviet Union
Fourth Place	Finland
Fifth Place	Sweden

Sixth Place	United States
Seventh Place	West Germany
Eighth Place	Poland*

* promoted from 'B' pool in 1984; relegated to 'B' pool for 1986

ALL-STAR TEAM
Goal	Timo Lehkonen (Finland)
Defence	Bobby Dollas (Canada)
	Mikhail Tatarinov (Soviet Union)
Forward	Mikko Makela (Finland)
	Michal Pivonka (Czechoslovakia)
	Esa Tikkanen (Finland)

DIRECTORATE AWARDS
BEST GOALIE	Craig Billington (Canada)
BEST DEFENCEMAN	Vesa Salo (Finland)
BEST FORWARD	Michal Pivonka (Czechoslovakia)

1986 WORLD JUNIOR CHAMPIONSHIP

CANADA, December 26, 1985–January 4, 1986

FINAL PLACINGS
GOLD MEDAL	Soviet Union
SILVER MEDAL	Canada
BRONZE MEDAL	United States
Fourth Place	Czechoslovakia
Fifth Place	Sweden
Sixth Place	Finland
Seventh Place	Switzerland*
Eighth Place	West Germany**

* promoted from 'B' pool in 1985
** relegated to 'B' pool for 1987

ALL-STAR TEAM
Goal	Evgeny Belosheikin (Soviet Union)
Defence	Sylvain Cote (Canada)
	Mikhail Tatarinov (Soviet Union)
Forward	Shayne Corson (Canada)
	Igor Viazmikin (Soviet Union)
	Michal Pivonka (Czechoslovakia)

DIRECTORATE AWARDS
BEST GOALIE	Evgeny Belosheikin (Soviet Union)
BEST DEFENCEMAN	Mikhail Tatarinov (Soviet Union)
BEST FORWARD	Jim Sandlak (Canada)

1987 WORLD JUNIOR CHAMPIONSHIP

CZECHOSLOVAKIA, December 26, 1986–January 4, 1987

FINAL PLACINGS
GOLD MEDAL	Finland
SILVER MEDAL	Czechoslovakia
BRONZE MEDAL	Sweden
Fourth Place	United States
Fifth Place	Poland*
Sixth Place	Switzerland**

Canada and the Soviet Union were disqualified

* promoted from 'B' pool in 1986
** relegated to 'B' pool for 1988

ALL-STAR TEAM
Goal	Sam Lindstahl (Sweden)
Defence	Jiri Latal (Czechoslovakia)
	Brian Leetch (United States)
Forward	Ulf Dahlen (Sweden)
	Juraj Jurik (Czechoslovakia)
	Scott Young (United States)

DIRECTORATE AWARDS
BEST GOALIE	Markus Ketterer (Finland)
BEST DEFENCEMAN	Calle Johansson (Sweden)
BEST FORWARD	Robert Kron (Czechoslovakia)

1988 WORLD JUNIOR CHAMPIONSHIP

RUSSIA, December 26, 1987–January 4, 1988

FINAL PLACINGS
GOLD MEDAL	Canada
SILVER MEDAL	Soviet Union
BRONZE MEDAL	Finland
Fourth Place	Czechosloavkia
Fifth Place	Sweden

Sixth Place   United States
Seventh Place   West Germany*
Eighth Place   Poland**

* promoted from 'B' pool in 1987
** relegated to 'B' pool for 1989

ALL-STAR TEAM

Goal	Jimmy Waite (Canada)
Defence	Greg Hawgood (Canada)
	Teppo Numminen (Finland)
Forward	Theoren Fleury (Canada)
	Alexander Mogilny (Soviet Union)
	Petr Hrbek (Czechoslovakia)

DIRECTORATE AWARDS

BEST GOALIE	Jimmy Waite (Canada)
BEST DEFENCEMAN	Teppo Numminen (Finland)
BEST FORWARD	Alexander Mogilny (Soviet Union)

1989 WORLD JUNIOR CHAMPIONSHIP

UNITED STATES, December 26, 1988–January 4, 1989

FINAL PLACINGS

GOLD MEDAL	Soviet Union
SILVER MEDAL	Sweden
BRONZE MEDAL	Czechoslovakia
Fourth Place	Canada
Fifth Place	United States
Sixth Place	Finland
Seventh Place	Norway*
Eighth Place	West Germany**

* promoted from 'B' pool in 1988
** relegated to 'B' pool for 1990

ALL-STAR TEAM

Goal	Alexei Ivashkin (Soviet Union)
Defence	Rickard Persson (Sweden)
	Milan Tichy (Czechoslovakia)
Forward	Niklas Eriksson (Sweden)
	Pavel Bure (Soviet Union)
	Jeremy Roenick (United States)

DIRECTORATE AWARDS

BEST GOALIE	Alexei Ivashkin (Soviet Union)
BEST DEFENCEMAN	Rickard Persson (Sweden)
BEST FORWARD	Pavel Bure (Soviet Union)

1990 WORLD JUNIOR CHAMPIONSHIP

FINLAND, December 26, 1989–January 4, 1990

FINAL PLACINGS

GOLD MEDAL	Canada
SILVER MEDAL	Soviet Union
BRONZE MEDAL	Czechoslovakia
Fourth Place	Finland
Fifth Place	Sweden
Sixth Place	Norway
Seventh Place	United States
Eighth Place	Poland*

* promoted from 'B' pool in 1989; relegated to 'B' pool for 1991

ALL-STAR TEAM

Goal	Stephane Fiset (Canada)
Defence	Alexander Godynyuk (Soviet Union)
	Jiri Slegr (Czechoslovakia)
Forward	Dave Chyzowski (Canada)
	Jaromir Jagr (Czechoslovakia)
	Robert Reichel (Czechoslovakia)

DIRECTORATE AWARDS

BEST GOALIE	Stephane Fiset (Canada)
BEST DEFENCEMAN	Alexander Godynyuk (Soviet Union)
BEST FORWARD	Robert Reichel (Czechoslovakia)

1991 WORLD JUNIOR CHAMPIONSHIP

CANADA, December 26, 1990–January 4, 1991

FINAL PLACINGS

GOLD MEDAL	Canada
SILVER MEDAL	Soviet Union
BRONZE MEDAL	Czechoslovakia
Fourth Place	United States

Fifth Place	Finland
Sixth Place	Sweden
Seventh Place	Switzerland*
Eighth Place	Norway**

* promoted from 'B' pool in 1990
** relegated to 'B' pool for 1992

ALL-STAR TEAM
Goal	Pauli Jaks (Switzerland)
Defence	Dmitri Yushkevich (Soviet Union)
	Scott Lachance (United States)
Forward	Mike Craig (Canada)
	Eric Lindros (Canada)
	Martin Rucinsky (Czechoslovakia)

DIRECTORATE AWARDS
BEST GOALIE	Pauli Jaks (Switzerland)
BEST DEFENCEMAN	Jiri Slegr (Czechoslovakia)
BEST FORWARD	Eric Lindros (Canada)

1992 WORLD JUNIOR CHAMPIONSHIP

GERMANY, December 26, 1991–January 4, 1992

FINAL PLACINGS
GOLD MEDAL	Commonwealth of Independent States
SILVER MEDAL	Sweden
BRONZE MEDAL	United States
Fourth Place	Finland
Fifth Place	Czechoslovakia
Sixth Place	Canada
Seventh Place	Germany*
Eighth Place	Switzerland**

* promoted from 'B' pool in 1991
** relegated to 'B' pool for 1993

ALL-STAR TEAM
Goal	Mike Dunham (United States)
Defence	Scott Niedermayer (Canada)
	Janne Gronvall (Finland)
Forward	Alexei Kovalev (CIS)
	Michael Nylander (Sweden)
	Peter Ferraro (United States)

DIRECTORATE AWARDS
  BEST GOALIE   Mike Dunham (United States)
  BEST DEFENCEMAN   Darius Kasparaitis (CIS)
  BEST FORWARD   Michael Nylander (Sweden)

1993 WORLD JUNIOR CHAMPIONSHIP

SWEDEN, December 26, 1992–January 4, 1993

FINAL PLACINGS
  GOLD MEDAL   Canada
  SILVER MEDAL   Sweden
  BRONZE MEDAL   Czechoslovakia
  Fourth Place   United States
  Fifth Place   Finland
  Sixth Place   Russia
  Seventh Place   Germany
  Eighth place   Japan*
  * promoted from 'B' pool in 1992; relegated to 'B' pool for 1994

ALL-STAR TEAM
  Goal   Manny Legace (Canada)
  Defence   Brent Tully (Canada)
             Kenny Jonsson (Sweden)
  Forward   Paul Kariya (Canada)
             Markus Naslund (Sweden)
             Peter Forsberg (Sweden)

DIRECTORATE AWARDS
  BEST GOALIE   Manny Legace (Canada)
  BEST DEFENCEMAN   Janne Gronvall (Finland)
  BEST FORWARD   Peter Forsberg (Sweden)

1994 WORLD JUNIOR CHAMPIONSHIP

CZECH REPUBLIC, December 26, 1993–January 4, 1994

FINAL PLACINGS
  GOLD MEDAL   Canada
  SILVER MEDAL   Sweden
  BRONZE MEDAL   Russia

Fourth Place	Finland
Fifth Place	Czech Republic
Sixth Place	United States
Seventh Place	Germany
Eighth Place	Switzerland*

* promoted from 'B' pool in 1993; relegated to 'B' pool for 1995

ALL-STAR TEAM
Goal	Evgeny Riabchikov (Russia)
Defence	Kenny Jonsson (Sweden)
	Kimmo Timonen (Finland)
Forward	Niklas Sundstrom (Sweden)
	Valeri Bure (Russia)
	David Vyborny (Czech Republic)

DIRECTORATE AWARDS
BEST GOALIE	Jamie Storr (Canada)
BEST DEFENCEMAN	Kenny Jonsson (Sweden)
BEST FORWARD	Niklas Sundstrom (Sweden)

1995 WORLD JUNIOR CHAMPIONSHIP

CANADA, December 26, 1994–January 4, 1995

FINAL PLACINGS
GOLD MEDAL	Canada
SILVER MEDAL	Russia
BRONZE MEDAL	Sweden
Fourth Place	Finland
Fifth Place	United States
Sixth Place	Czech Republic
Seventh Place	Germany
Eighth Place	Ukraine*

* promoted from 'B' pool in 1994

Note: no team was relegated to 'B' pool from this year's tournament because in 1996 the 'A' pool expanded to ten teams and a new round-robin format

ALL-STAR TEAM
Goal	Igor Karpenko (Ukraine)
Defence	Bryan McCabe (Canada)
	Anders Eriksson (Sweden)

Forward   Jason Allison (Canada)
                 Eric Daze (Canada)
                 Marty Murray (Canada)

DIRECTORATE AWARDS
BEST GOALIE   Evgeny Tarasov (Russia)
BEST DEFENCEMAN   Bryan McCabe (Canada)
BEST FORWARD   Marty Murray (Canada)

1996 WORLD JUNIOR CHAMPIONSHIP

UNITED STATES, December 26, 1995–January 4, 1996

FINAL PLACINGS
GOLD MEDAL   Canada
SILVER MEDAL   Sweden
BRONZE MEDAL   Russia
Fourth Place   Czech Republic
Fifth Place   United States
Sixth Place   Finland
Seventh Place   Slovakia*
Eighth Place   Germany
Ninth Place   Switzerland*
Tenth Place   Ukraine**

* promoted from 'B' pool in 1995
** relegated to 'B' pool for 1997

ALL-STAR TEAM
Goal   Jose Theodore (Canada)
Defence   Nolan Baumgartner (Canada)
            Mattias Ohlund (Sweden)
Forward   Jarome Iginla (Canada)
            Johan Davidsson (Sweden)
            Alexei Morozov (Russia)

DIRECTORATE AWARDS
BEST GOALIE   Jose Theodore (Canada)
BEST DEFENCEMAN   Mattias Ohlund (Sweden)
BEST FORWARD   Jarome Iginla (Canada)

1997 WORLD JUNIOR CHAMPIONSHIP

SWITZERLAND, December 26, 1996–January 4, 1997

FINAL PLACINGS
GOLD MEDAL	Canada
SILVER MEDAL	United States
BRONZE MEDAL	Russia
Fourth Place	Czech Republic
Fifth Place	Finland
Sixth Place	Slovakia
Seventh Place	Switzerland
Eighth Place	Sweden
Ninth Place	Germany
Tenth Place	Poland*

* promoted from 'B' pool in 1996; relegated to 'B' pool for 1998

ALL-STAR TEAM
Goal	Brian Boucher (United States)
Defence	Chris Phillips (Canada)
	Mark Streit (Switzerland)
Forward	Christian Dube (Canada)
	Sergei Samsonov (Russia)
	Michael York (United States)

DIRECTORATE AWARDS
BEST GOALIE	Marc Denis (Canada)
BEST DEFENCEMAN	Joseph Corvo (United States)
BEST FORWARD	Alexei Morozov (Russia)

1998 WORLD JUNIOR CHAMPIONSHIP

FINLAND, December 25, 1997–January 3, 1998

FINAL PLACINGS
GOLD MEDAL	Finland
SILVER MEDAL	Russia
BRONZE MEDAL	Switzerland
Fourth Place	Czech Republic
Fifth Place	United States
Sixth Place	Sweden
Seventh Place	Kazakhstan*
Eighth Place	Canada

Ninth Place	Slovakia
Tenth Place	Germany**

* promoted from 'B' pool in 1997
** relegated to 'B' pool for 1999

ALL-STAR TEAM

Goal	David Aebischer (Switzerland)
Defence	Pierre Hedin (Sweden)
	Andrei Markov (Russia)
Forward	Olli Jokinen (Finland)
	Eero Somervuori (Finland)
	Maxim Balmochnykh (Russia)

DIRECTORATE AWARDS

BEST GOALIE	David Aebischer (Switzerland)
BEST DEFENCEMAN	Pavel Skrbek (Czech Republic)
BEST FORWARD	Olli Jokinen (Finland)

1999 WORLD JUNIOR CHAMPIONSHIP

CANADA, December 26, 1998–January 5, 1999

FINAL PLACINGS

GOLD MEDAL	Russia
SILVER MEDAL	Canada
BRONZE MEDAL	Slovakia
Fourth Place	Sweden
Fifth Place	Finland
Sixth Place	Kazakhstan
Seventh Place	Czech Republic
Eighth Place	United States
Ninth Place	Switzerland
Tenth Place	Belarus*

* promoted from 'B' pool in 1998; relegated to 'B' pool for 2000

ALL-STAR TEAM

Goal	Roberto Luongo (Canada)
Defence	Vitali Vishnevsky (Russia)
	Brian Campbell (Canada)
Forward	Daniel Tkachuk (Canada)
	Brian Gionta (United States)
	Maxim Balmochnykh (Russia)

DIRECTORATE AWARDS

BEST GOALIE	Roberto Luongo (Canada)
BEST DEFENCEMAN	Maxim Afinigenov (Russia)
BEST FORWARD	Vitali Vishnevski (Russia)

2000 WORLD JUNIOR CHAMPIONSHIP

SWEDEN, December 25, 1999–January 4, 2000

FINAL PLACINGS

GOLD MEDAL	Czech Republic
SILVER MEDAL	Russia
BRONZE MEDAL	Canada
Fourth Place	United States
Fifth Place	Sweden
Sixth Place	Switzerland
Seventh Place	Finland
Eighth Place	Kazakhstan
Ninth Place	Slovakia
Tenth Place	Ukraine*

* promoted from 'B' pool in 1999; demoted to 'B' pool for 2001

ALL-STAR TEAM

Goal	Rick DiPietro (United States)
Defence	Mathieu Biron (Canada)
	Alexander Rjasantsev (Russia)
Forward	Milan Kraft (Czech Republic)
	Alexei Tereschenko (Russia)
	Evgeny Muratov (Russia)

DIRECTORATE AWARDS

BEST GOALIE	Rick DiPietro (United States)
BEST DEFENCEMAN	Alexander Rjasantsev (Russia)
BEST FORWARD	Milan Kraft (Czech Republic)

2001 WORLD JUNIOR CHAMPIONSHIP

RUSSIA, December 26, 2000–January 5, 2001

FINAL PLACINGS

GOLD MEDAL	Czech Republic
SILVER MEDAL	Finland

BRONZE MEDAL	Canada
Fourth Place	Sweden
Fifth Place	United States
Sixth Place	Switzerland
Seventh Place	Russia
Eighth Place	Slovakia
Ninth Place	Belarus*
Tenth Place	Kazakhstan**

* promoted from 'B' pool in 2000
** demoted to 'B' pool for 2002

ALL-STAR TEAM

Goal	Ari Ahonen (Finland)
Defence	Rostislav Klesla (Czech Republic)
	Tuukka Mantyla (Finland)
Forward	Jason Spezza (Canada)
	Jani Rita (Finland)
	Pavel Brendl (Czech Republic)

DIRECTORATE AWARDS

BEST GOALIE	Tomas Duba (Czech Republic)
BEST DEFENCEMAN	Rostislav Klesla (Czech Republic)
BEST FORWARD	Pavel Brendl (Czech Republic)

2002 WORLD JUNIOR CHAMPIONSHIP

CZECH REPUBLIC, December 25, 2001–January 4, 2002

FINAL PLACINGS

GOLD MEDAL	Russia
SILVER MEDAL	Canada
BRONZE MEDAL	Finland
Fourth Place	Switzerland
Fifth Place	United States
Sixth Place	Sweden
Seventh Place	Czech Republic
Eighth Place	Slovakia
Ninth Place	Belarus
Tenth Place	France*

* promoted from 2001; demoted for 2003

ALL-STAR TEAM

Goal	Pascal Leclaire (Canada)
Defence	Jay Bouwmeester (Canada)
	Igor Knyazev (Russia)
Forward	Mike Cammalleri (Canada)
	Marek Svatos (Slovakia)
	Stanislav Chistov (Russia)

DIRECTORATE AWARDS

BEST GOALIE	Kari Lehtonen (Finland)
BEST DEFENCEMAN	Igor Knyazev (Russia)
BEST FORWARD	Mike Cammalleri (Canada)

2003 WORLD JUNIOR CHAMPIONSHIP

CANADA, December 26, 2002–January 5, 2003

FINAL PLACINGS

GOLD MEDAL	Russia
SILVER MEDAL	Canada
BRONZE MEDAL	Finland
Fourth Place	United States
Fifth Place	Slovakia
Sixth Place	Czech Republic
Seventh Place	Switzerland
Eighth Place	Sweden
Ninth Place	Germany*
Tenth Place	Belarus**

* promoted from 2002
** demoted for 2004

ALL-STAR TEAM

Goal	Marc-Andre Fleury (Canada)
Defence	Carlo Colaiacovo (Canada)
	Joni Pitkanen (Finland)
Forward	Scottie Upshall (Canada)
	Igor Grigorenko (Russia)
	Yuri Trubachev (Russia)

DIRECTORATE AWARDS

BEST GOALIE	Marc-Andre Fleury (Canada)
BEST DEFENCEMAN	Joni Pitkanen (Finland)
BEST FORWARD	Igor Grigorenko (Russia)

2004 WORLD JUNIOR CHAMPIONSHIP

FINLAND, December 26, 2003–January 6, 2004

FINAL PLACINGS

GOLD MEDAL	United States
SILVER MEDAL	Canada
BRONZE MEDAL	Finland
Fourth Place	Czech Republic
Fifth Place	Russia
Sixth Place	Slovakia
Seventh Place	Sweden
Eighth Place	Switzerland
Ninth Place	Austria*
Tenth Place	Ukraine**

* promoted from 2003
** demoted for 2005

ALL-STAR TEAM

Goal	Al Montoya (United States)
Defence	Dion Phaneuf (Canada)
	Sami Lepisto (Finland)
Forward	Jeff Carter (Canada)
	Valtteri Filppula (Finland)
	Zach Parise (United States)

DIRECTORATE AWARDS

BEST GOALIE	Al Montoya (United States)
BEST DEFENCEMAN	Sami Lepisto (Finland)
BEST FORWARD	Zach Parise (United States)

2005 WORLD JUNIOR CHAMPIONSHIP

UNITED STATES, December 25, 2004–January 4, 2005

FINAL PLACINGS

GOLD MEDAL	Canada
SILVER MEDAL	Russia
BRONZE MEDAL	Czech Republic
Fourth Place	United States
Fifth Place	Finland
Sixth Place	Sweden
Seventh Place	Slovakia

Eighth Place	Switzerland
Ninth Place	Germany*
Tenth Place	Belarus*

* promoted from 2004; demoted for 2006

ALL-STAR TEAM

Goal	Marek Schwarz (Czech Republic)
Defence	Dion Phaneuf (Canada)
	Gary Suter (United States)
Forward	Patrice Bergeron (Canada)
	Jeff Carter (Canada)
	Alexander Ovechkin (Russia)

DIRECTORATE AWARDS

BEST GOALIE   Marek Schwarz (Czech Republic)
BEST DEFENCEMAN Dion Phaneuf (Canada)
BEST FORWARD   Alexander Ovechkin (Russia)

2006 WORLD JUNIOR CHAMPIONSHIP

CANADA, December 26, 2005–January 5, 2006

FINAL PLACINGS

GOLD MEDAL	Canada
SILVER MEDAL	Russia
BRONZE MEDAL	Finland
Fourth Place	United States
Fifth Place	Sweden
Sixth Place	Czech Republic
Seventh Place	Switzerland
Eighth Place	Slovakia
Ninth Place	Latvia*
Tenth Place	Norway*

* promoted from 2005; demoted for 2007

ALL-STAR TEAM

Goal	Tuukka Rask (Finland)
Defence	Luc Bourdon (Canada)
	Jack Johnson (United States)
Forward	Steve Downie (Canada)
	Evgeni Malkin (Russia)
	Lauri Tukonen (Finland)

DIRECTORATE AWARDS

BEST GOALIE	Tuukka Rask (Finland)
BEST DEFENCEMAN	Marc Staal (Canada)
BEST FORWARD	Evgeni Malkin (Russia)

2007 WORLD JUNIOR CHAMPIONSHIP

SWEDEN, December 26, 2006–January 5, 2007

FINAL PLACINGS

GOLD MEDAL	Canada
SILVER MEDAL	Russia
BRONZE MEDAL	United States
Fourth Place	Sweden
Fifth Place	Czech Republic
Sixth Place	Finland
Seventh Place	Switzerland
Eighth Place	Slovakia
Ninth Place	Germany*
Tenth Place	Belarus*

* promoted from 2006; demoted for 2008

ALL-STAR TEAM

Goal	Carey Price (Canada)
Defence	Kristopher Letang (Canada)
	Erik Johnson (United States)
Forward	Jonathan Toews (Canada)
	Alexei Cherepanov (Russia)
	Patrick Kane (United States)

DIRECTORATE AWARDS

BEST GOALIE	Carey Price (Canada)
BEST DEFENCEMAN	Erik Johnson (United States)
BEST FORWARD	Alexei Cherepanov (Russia)
TOURNAMENT MVP	Carey Price (Canada)

2008 WORLD JUNIOR CHAMPIONSHIP

CZECH REPUBLIC, December 26, 2007–January 5, 2008

FINAL PLACINGS
GOLD MEDAL	Canada
SILVER MEDAL	Sweden
BRONZE MEDAL	Russia
Fourth Place	United States
Fifth Place	Czech Republic
Sixth Place	Finland
Seventh Place	Slovakia
Eighth Place	Kazakhstan*
Ninth Place	Switzerland†
Tenth Place	Denmark*†

* promoted from 2006; † demoted for 2009

ALL-STAR TEAM
Goal	Steve Mason (Canada)
Defence	Drew Doughty (Canada)
	Victor Hedman (Sweden)
Forward	Viktor Tikhonov (Russia)
	Patrik Berglund (Sweden)
	James van Riemsdyk (United States)

DIRECTORATE AWARDS
BEST GOALIE	Steve Mason (Canada)
BEST DEFENCEMAN	Drew Doughty (Canada)
BEST FORWARD	Viktor Tikhonov (Russia)
TOURNAMENT MVP	Steve Mason (Canada)

2009 WORLD JUNIOR CHAMPIONSHIP

CANADA, December 26, 2008–January 5, 2009

FINAL PLACINGS
GOLD MEDAL	Canada
SILVER MEDAL	Sweden
BRONZE MEDAL	Russia
Fourth Place	Slovakia
Fifth Place	United States
Sixth Place	Czech Republic
Seventh Place	Finland
Eighth Place	Latvia*

Ninth Place   Germany*†
Tenth Place   Kazakhstan†

* promoted from 2008; † demoted for 2010

ALL-STAR TEAM
Goal   Jaroslav Janus (SVK)
Defence   P.K. Subban (CAN), Erik Karlsson (SWE)
Forward   John Tavares (CAN), Cody Hodgson (CAN), Nikita Filatov (RUS)

DIRECTORATE AWARDS
BEST GOALIE   Jacob Markstrom (SWE)
BEST DEFENCEMAN   Erik Karlsson (SWE)
BEST FORWARD   John Tavares (CAN)
TOURNAMENT MVP   John Tavares (CAN)

2010 WORLD JUNIOR CHAMPIONSHIP

CANADA, December 26, 2009–January 5, 2010

FINAL PLACINGS
GOLD MEDAL   United States
SILVER MEDAL   Canada
BRONZE MEDAL   Sweden
Fourth Place   Switzerland
Fifth Place   Finland
Sixth Place   Russia
Seventh Place   Czech Republic
Eighth Place   Slovakia
Ninth Place   Latvia
Tenth Place   Austria

ALL-STAR TEAM
Goal   Benjamin Conx (SUI)
Defence   Alex Pietrangelo (CAN)
            John Carlson (USA)
Forward   Jordan Eberle (CAN)
            Derek Stepan (USA)
            Nino Niederreiter (SUI)

DIRECTORATE AWARDS
Best Goalie   Benjamin Conz (SUI)
Best Defenceman   Alex Pietrangelo (CAN)
Best Forward   Jordan Eberle (CAN)
Tournament MVP   Jordan Eberle (CAN)

2011 WORLD U20 (JUNIOR) CHAMPIONSHIP

BUFFALO/LEWISTON, UNITED STATES, December 26, 2010–January 5, 2011

FINAL PLACINGS

GOLD MEDAL	Russia
SILVER MEDAL	Canada
BRONZE MEDAL	United States
Fourth Place	Sweden
Fifth Place	Switzerland
Sixth Place	Finland
Seventh Place	Czech Republic
Eighth Place	Slovakia
Ninth Place	Norway
Tenth Place	Germany

All-Star Team

Goal	Jack Campbell (USA)
Defence	Ryan Ellis (CAN), Dmitri Orlov (RUS)
Forward	Yevgeni Kuznetsov (RUS), Brayden Schenn (CAN), Ryan Johansen (CAN)

Directorate Awards

Best Goalie	Jack Campbell (USA)
Best Defenceman	Ryan Ellis (CAN)
Best Forward	Brayden Schenn (CAN)
Tournament MVP	Brayden Schenn (CAN)

WORLD U18 CHAMPIONSHIPS, MEN, 1999–2011

1999 WORLD U18 CHAMPIONSHIP

FUSSEN/KAUFBEUREN, GERMANY, April 8–18, 1999

FINAL PLACINGS

GOLD MEDAL	Finland
SILVER MEDAL	Sweden
BRONZE MEDAL	Slovakia
Fourth Place	Switzerland
Fifth Place	Czech Republic
Sixth Place	Russia
Seventh Place	United States
Eighth Place	Ukraine
Ninth Place	Germany
Tenth Place	Norway

2000 WORLD U18 CHAMPIONSHIP

KLOTEN/WEINFELDEN, SWITZERLAND, April 14–24, 2000

FINAL PLACINGS

GOLD MEDAL	Finland
SILVER MEDAL	Russia
BRONZE MEDAL	Sweden
Fourth Place	Switzerland
Fifth Place	Slovakia
Sixth Place	Czech Republic
Seventh Place	Germany
Eighth Place	United States
Ninth Place	Ukraine
Tenth Place	Belarus

2001 WORLD U18 CHAMPIONSHIP

HEINOLA/HELSINKI/LAHTI, FINLAND, April 12–22, 2001

FINAL PLACINGS

GOLD MEDAL	Russia
SILVER MEDAL	Switzerland
BRONZE MEDAL	Finland

Fourth Place	Czech Republic
Fifth Place	Germany
Sixth Place	United States
Seventh Place	Sweden
Eighth Place	Slovakia
Ninth Place	Norway
Tenth Place	Ukraine

2002 WORLD U18 CHAMPIONSHIP

TRNAVA/PIESTANY, SLOVAKIA, April 11–21, 2002

FINAL PLACINGS

GOLD MEDAL	United States
SILVER MEDAL	Russia
BRONZE MEDAL	Czech Republic
Fourth Place	Finland
Fifth Place	Belarus
Sixth Place	Canada
Seventh Place	Switzerland
Eighth Place	Slovakia
Ninth Place	Sweden
Tenth Place	Germany
Eleventh Place	Norway
Twelfth Place	Ukraine

2003 WORLD U18 CHAMPIONSHIP

YAROSLAVL, RUSSIA, April 12–23 2003

FINAL PLACINGS

GOLD MEDAL	Canada
SILVER MEDAL	Slovakia
BRONZE MEDAL	Russia
Fourth Place	United States
Fifth Place	Sweden
Sixth Place	Czech Republic
Seventh Place	Finland
Eighth Place	Belarus
Ninth Place	Switzerland
Tenth Place	Kazakhstan

2004 WORLD U18 CHAMPIONSHIP

MINSK, BELARUS, April 8–18, 2004

FINAL PLACINGS

GOLD MEDAL	Russia
SILVER MEDAL	United States
BRONZE MEDAL	Czech Republic
Fourth Place	Canada
Fifth Place	Sweden
Sixth Place	Slovakia
Seventh Place	Finland
Eighth Place	Denmark
Ninth Place	Belarus
Tenth Place	Norway

2005 WORLD U18 CHAMPIONSHIP

CESKE BUDEJOVICE/PLZEN, CZECH REPUBLIC, April 14–24, 2005

FINAL PLACINGS

GOLD MEDAL	United States
SILVER MEDAL	Canada
BRONZE MEDAL	Sweden
Fourth Place	Czech Republic
Fifth Place	Russia
Sixth Place	Slovakia
Seventh Place	Finland
Eighth Place	Germany
Ninth Place	Switzerland
Tenth Place	Denmark

2006 WORLD U18 CHAMPIONSHIP

ANGELHOLM/HALMSTAD, SWEDEN, April 12–22, 2006

FINAL PLACINGS

GOLD MEDAL	United States
SILVER MEDAL	Finland
BRONZE MEDAL	Czech Republic
Fourth Place	Canada
Fifth Place	Russia
Sixth Place	Sweden
Seventh Place	Slovakia

Eighth Place   Germany
Ninth Place   Belarus
Tenth Place   Norway

2007 WORLD U18 CHAMPIONSHIP

TAMPERE/RAUMA, FINLAND, April 11–22, 2007

FINAL PLACINGS

GOLD MEDAL	Russia
SILVER MEDAL	United States
BRONZE MEDAL	Sweden
Fourth Place	Canada
Fifth Place	Slovakia
Sixth Place	Switzerland
Seventh Place	Finland
Eighth Place	Germany
Ninth Place	Czech Republic
Tenth Place	Latvia

2008 WORLD U18 CHAMPIONSHIP

KAZAN, RUSSIA, April 13–23, 2008

FINAL PLACINGS

GOLD MEDAL	Canada
SILVER MEDAL	Russia
BRONZE MEDAL	United States
Fourth Place	Sweden
Fifth Place	Germany
Sixth Place	Finland
Seventh Place	Slovakia
Eighth Place	Switzerland
Ninth Place	Belarus
Tenth Place	Denmark

2009 WORLD U18 CHAMPIONSHIP

FARGO/MOORHEAD, UNITED STATES, April 9–19, 2009

FINAL PLACINGS

GOLD MEDAL	United States
SILVER MEDAL	Russia
BRONZE MEDAL	Finland

Fourth Place	Canada
Fifth Place	Sweden
Sixth Place	Czech Republic
Seventh Place	Slovakia
Eighth Place	Switzerland
Ninth Place	Norway
Tenth Place	Germany

2010 WORLD U18 CHAMPIONSHIP

MINSK/BOBRUISK, BELARUS, April 13–23, 2010

FINAL PLACINGS

GOLD MEDAL	United States
SILVER MEDAL	Sweden
BRONZE MEDAL	Finland
Fourth Place	Russia
Fifth Place	Switzerland
Sixth Place	Czech Republic
Seventh Place	Canada
Eighth Place	Slovakia
Ninth Place	Latvia
Tenth Place	Belarus

2012 WORLD U18 CHAMPIONSHIP, MEN

CRIMMITSCHAU/DRESDEN, GERMANY, April 14–24, 2011

FINAL PLACINGS

GOLD MEDAL	United States
SILVER MEDAL	Sweden
BRONZE MEDAL	Russia
Fourth Place	Canada
Fifth Place	Finland
Sixth Place	Germany
Seventh Place	Switzerland
Eighth Place	Czech Republic
Ninth Place	Norway
Tenth Place	Slovakia

WORLD U18 CHAMPIONSHIPS, WOMEN, 2008–2011

2008 WORLD WOMEN'S U18 CHAMPIONSHIP

CALGARY, CANADA, January 7–12, 2008

FINAL PLACINGS

GOLD MEDAL	United States
SILVER MEDAL	Canada
BRONZE MEDAL	Czech Republic
Fourth Place	Sweden
Fifth Place	Germany
Sixth Place	Finland
Seventh Place	Switzerland
Eighth Place	Russia

2009 WORLD WOMEN'S U18 CHAMPIONSHIP

FUSSEN, GERMANY, January 1–10, 2009

FINAL PLACINGS

GOLD MEDAL	United States
SILVER MEDAL	Canada
BRONZE MEDAL	Sweden
Fourth Place	Czech Republic
Fifth Place	Finland
Sixth Place	Germany
Seventh Place	Russia
Eighth Place	Switzerland

2010 WORLD WOMEN'S U18 CHAMPIONSHIP

CHICAGO, UNITED STATES, March 27–April 3, 2010

FINAL PLACINGS

GOLD MEDAL	Canada
SILVER MEDAL	United States
BRONZE MEDAL	Sweden
Fourth Place	Germany
Fifth Place	Finland
Sixth Place	Japan
Seventh Place	Czech Republic
Eighth Place	Russia

2012 WORLD U18 CHAMPIONSHIP, WOMEN

STOCKHOLM, SWEDEN, January 1–8, 2011

FINAL PLACINGS

GOLD MEDAL	United States
SILVER MEDAL	Canada
BRONZE MEDAL	Finland
Fourth Place	Czech Republic
Fifth Place	Sweden
Sixth Place	Germany
Seventh Place	Switzerland
Eighth Place	Japan

PRO CLASSICS RESULTS

1972 SUMMIT SERIES

Canada/Moscow, September 2–28, 1972

	GP	W	L	T	GF	GA	P
Canada	8	4	3	1	31	32	9
Soviet Union	8	3	4	1	32	31	7

Results

Game 1	September 2	Montreal	Soviet Union 7/Canada 3
Game 2	September 4	Toronto	Canada 4/Soviet Union 1
Game 3	September 6	Winnipeg	Canada 4/Soviet Union 4
Game 4	September 8	Vancouver	Soviet Union 5/Canada 3
Exhibition	September 16	Stockholm	Canada 4/Swedish Nationals 1
Exhibition	September 17	Stockholm	Canada 4/Swedish Nationals 4
Game 5	September 22	Moscow	Soviet Union 5/Canada 4
Game 6	September 24	Moscow	Canada 3/Soviet Union 2
Game 7	September 26	Moscow	Canada 4/Soviet Union 3
Game 8	September 28	Moscow	Canada 6/Soviet Union 5

(Paul Henderson scores series winner at 19:26 of 3rd)

Exhibition	September 30	Prague	Canada 3/Czech Nationals 3

1976 CANADA CUP

Canada, September 2–15, 1976

Series MVP: Bobby Orr (Canada)

Team MVPs

Canada	Rogie Vachon
Czechoslovakia	Milan Novy
Soviet Union	Alexander Maltsev
Sweden	Borje Salming
United States	Robbie Ftorek
Finland	Matti Hagman

Final Standings (Round Robin)

	GP	W	L	T	GF	GA	P
Canada	5	4	1	0	22	6	8
Czechoslovakia	5	3	1	1	19	9	7
Soviet Union	5	2	2	1	23	14	5
Sweden	5	2	2	1	16	18	5
United States	5	1	3	1	14	21	3
Finland	5	1	4	0	16	42	2

Results

September 2	Ottawa	Canada 11/Finland 2
September 3	Toronto	Sweden 5/United States 2
	Montreal	Czechoslovakia 5/Soviet Union 3
September 5	Montreal	Canada 4/United States 2
	Montreal	Soviet Union 3/Sweden 3
	Toronto	Czechoslovakia 8/Finland 0
September 7	Toronto	Canada 4/Sweden 0
	Montreal	Soviet Union 11/Finland 3
	Philadelphia	Czechoslovakia 4/United States 4
September 9	Montreal	Czechoslovakia 1/Canada 0
	Winnipeg	Finland 8/Sweden 6
	Philadelphia	Soviet Union 5/United States 0
September 11	Toronto	Canada 3/Soviet Union 1
	Quebec City	Sweden 2/Czechoslovakia 1
	Montreal	United States 6/Finland 3

Finals (best two-of-three)

September 13	Toronto	Canada 6/Czechoslovakia 0
September 15	Montreal	Canada 5/Czechoslovakia 4
		(Sittler 11:33 OT)

1981 CANADA CUP

Canada, September 1–13, 1981

Tournament MVP: Vladislav Tretiak
Team Canada MVP: Mike Bossy

All-Star Team

Goal	Vladislav Tretiak (Soviet Union)
Defence	Alexei Kasatonov (Soviet Union)
	Arnold Kadlec (Czechoslovakia)

Forward	Gil Perreault (Canada)	
	Mike Bossy (Canada)	
	Sergei Shepelev (Soviet Union)	

Final Standings (Round Robin)

	GP	W	L	T	GF	GA	P
Canada	5	4	0	1	32	13	9
Soviet Union	5	3	1	1	20	13	7
Czechoslovakia	5	2	1	2	21	13	6
United States	5	2	2	1	17	19	5
Sweden	5	1	4	0	13	20	2
Finland	5	0	4	1	6	31	1

Results

September 1	Edmonton	Canada 9/Finland 0
	Edmonton	United States 3/Sweden 1
	Winnipeg	Czechoslovakia 1/Soviet Union 1
September 3	Edmonton	Canada 8/United States 3
	Edmonton	Czechoslovakia 7/Finland 1
	Winnipeg	Soviet Union 6/Sweden 3
September 5	Winnipeg	Canada 4/Czechoslovakia 4
	Winnipeg	Sweden 5/Finland 0
	Edmonton	Soviet Union 4/United States 1
September 7	Montreal	Canada 4/Sweden 3
	Winnipeg	Soviet Union 6/Finland 1
	Montreal	United States 6/Czechoslovakia 2
September 9	Montreal	Canada 7/Soviet Union 3
	Ottawa	Czechoslovakia 7/Sweden 1
	Montreal	Finland 4/United States 4

Semifinals

September 11	Montreal	Canada 4/United States 1
	Ottawa	Soviet Union 4/Czechoslovakia 1

Finals

September 13	Montreal	Soviet Union 8/Canada 1

1984 CANADA CUP

Canada, September 1–18, 1984
Tournament MVP: John Tonelli

All-Star Team
Goal	Vladimir Myshkin (Soviet Union)
Defence	Paul Coffey (Canada)
	Rod Langway (United States)
Forward	Wayne Gretzky (Canada)
	John Tonelli (Canada)
	Sergei Makarov (Soviet Union)

Final Standings (Round Robin)

	GP	W	L	T	GF	GA	P
Soviet Union	5	5	0	0	22	7	10
United States	5	3	1	1	21	13	7
Sweden	5	3	2	0	15	16	6
Canada	5	2	2	1	23	18	5
West Germany	5	0	4	1	13	29	1
Czechoslovakia	5	0	4	1	10	21	1

Results
September 1	Montreal	Canada 7/West Germany 2
	Halifax	United States 7/Sweden 1
September 2	Montreal	Soviet Union 3/Czechoslovakia 0
September 3	Montreal	Canada 4/United States 4
September 4	London	Czechoslovakia 4/West Germany 4
	Calgary	Soviet Union 3/Sweden 2
September 6	Vancouver	Sweden 4/Canada 2
	Edmonton	Soviet Union 8/West Germany 1
	Buffalo	United States 3/Czechoslovakia 2
September 8	Calgary	Canada 7/Czechoslovakia 2
	Calgary	Sweden 4/West Germany 2
	Edmonton	Soviet Union 2/United States 1
September 10	Edmonton	Soviet Union 6/Canada 3
	Vancouver	Sweden 4/Czechoslovakia 2
	Calgary	United States 6/West Germany 4

Semifinals
September 12	Edmonton	Sweden 9/United States 2
September 13	Calgary	Canada 3/Soviet Union 2 (Bossy 12:29 OT)

Finals (best two-of-three)

September 16	Calgary	Canada 5/Sweden 2
September 18	Edmonton	Canada 6/Sweden 5

1987 CANADA CUP

Canada, August 28–September 15, 1987

Tournament All-Star Team

Goal	Grant Fuhr (Canada)
Defence	Ray Bourque (Canada)
	Viacheslav Fetisov (Soviet Union)
Forward	Mario Lemieux (Canada)
	Wayne Gretzky (Canada)
	Vladimir Krutov (Soviet Union)

Final Standings (Round Robin)

	GP	W	L	T	GF	GA	P
Canada	5	3	0	2	19	13	8
Soviet Union	5	3	1	1	22	13	7
Sweden	5	3	2	0	17	14	6
Czechoslovakia	5	2	2	1	12	15	5
United States	5	2	3	0	13	14	4
Finland	5	0	5	0	9	23	0

Results

August 28	Calgary	Canada 4/Czechoslovakia 4
	Hartford	United States 4/Finland 1
August 29	Calgary	Sweden 5/Soviet Union 3
August 30	Hamilton	Canada 4/Finland 1
August 31	Regina	Soviet Union 4/Czechoslovakia 0
	Hamilton	United States 5/Sweden 2
September 2	Halifax	Soviet Union 7/Finland 4
	Hamilton	Canada 3/United States 2
	Regina	Sweden 4/Czechoslovakia 0
September 4	Hartford	Soviet Union 5/United States 1
	Sydney	Czechoslovakia 5/Finland 2
	Montreal	Canada 5/Sweden 3
September 6	Sydney	Sweden 3/Finland 1
	Sydney	Czechoslovakia 3/United States 1
	Hamilton	Canada 3/Soviet Union 3
September 8	Hamilton	Soviet Union 4/Sweden 2
	Montreal	Canada 5/Czechoslovakia 3

Finals (best two-of-three)

September 11	Montreal	Soviet Union 6/Canada 5 (Semak 5:33 OT)
September 13	Hamilton	Canada 6/Soviet Union 5 (Mario Lemieux 30:07 OT)
September 15	Hamilton	Canada 6/Soviet Union 5 (Lemieux scores winner at 18:34 of 3rd)

1991 CANADA CUP

Canada, August 31–September 16, 1991

Tournament All-Star Team

Goal	Bill Ranford (Canada)
Defence	Al MacInnis (Canada)
	Chris Chelios (United States)
Forward	Wayne Gretzky (Canada)
	Jeremy Roenick (United States)
	Mats Sundin (Sweden)

Final Standings (Round Robin)

	GP	W	L	T	GF	GA	P
Canada	5	3	0	2	21	11	8
United States	5	4	1	0	19	15	8
Finland	5	2	2	1	10	13	5
Sweden	5	2	3	0	13	17	4
Soviet Union	5	1	3	1	14	14	3
Czechoslovakia	5	1	4	0	11	18	2

Results

August 31	Toronto	Canada 2/Finland 2
	Saskatoon	Czechoslovakia 5/Soviet Union 2
	Pittsburgh	United States 6/Sweden 3
September 2	Hamilton	Canada 6/United States 3
	Montreal	Sweden 3/Soviet Union 2
	Saskatoon	Finland 1/Czechoslovakia 0
September 5	Toronto	Canada 4/Sweden 1
	Hamilton	Soviet Union 6/Finland 1
	Detroit	United States 4/Czechoslovakia 2
September 7	Montreal	Canada 6/Czechoslovakia 2
	Toronto	Finland 3/Sweden 1
	Chicago	United States 2/Soviet Union 1
September 9	Quebec City	Canada 3/Soviet Union 3
	Toronto	Sweden 5/Czechoslovakia 2
	Chicago	United States 4/Finland 3

Semifinals

September 11	Hamilton	United States 7/Finland 3
September 12	Toronto	Canada 4/Sweden 0

Finals (best two-of-three)

September 14	Montreal	Canada 4/United States 1
September 16	Hamilton	Canada 4/United States 2

WORLD CUP OF HOCKEY 1996

Canada/Europe/United States, August 30–September 14, 1996

FINAL STANDINGS (ROUND ROBIN)

North American Pool

	GP	W	L	T	GF	GA	P
United States	3	3	0	0	19	8	6
Canada	3	2	1	0	11	10	4
Russia	3	1	2	0	12	14	2
Slovakia	3	0	3	0	9	19	0

European Pool

	GP	W	L	T	GF	GA	P
Sweden	3	3	0	0	14	3	6
Finland	3	2	1	0	17	11	4
Germany	3	1	2	0	11	15	2
Czech Republic	3	0	3	0	4	17	0

Results

August 26	Stockholm	Sweden 6/Germany 1
August 27	Helsinki	Finland 7/Czech Republic 3
August 28	Helsinki	Finland 8/Germany 3
	Prague	Sweden 3/Czech Republic 0
	Vancouver	Canada 5/Russia 3
August 31	Philadelphia	United States 5/Canada 3
	Garmisch	Germany 7/Czech Republic 1
	Montreal	Russia 7/Slovakia 4
September 1	Ottawa	Canada 3/Slovakia 2
	Stockholm	Sweden 5/Finland 2
September 2	New York	United States 5/Russia 2
September 3	New York	United States 9/Slovakia 3

Quarter-finals

| September 5 | Montreal | Canada 4/Germany 1 |
| September 6 | Ottawa | Russia 5/Finland 0 |

Semifinals

| September 7 | Philadelphia | Canada 3/Sweden 2 (Fleury 39:47 OT) |
| September 8 | Ottawa | United States 5/Russia 2 |

Finals (best two-of-three)

September 10	Philadelphia	Canada 4/United States 3 (Yzerman 19:53 OT)
September 12	Montreal	United States 5/Canada 2
September 14	Montreal	United States 5/Canada 2

WORLD CUP OF HOCKEY 2004

August 30–September 14, 2004

Tournament MVP: Vincent Lecavalier (CAN)

All-Tournament Team

Goal	Martin Brodeur (CAN)
Defence	Adam Foote (CAN)
	Kimmo Timonen (FIN)
Forward	Vincent Lecavalier (CAN)
	Fredrik Modin (SWE)
	Saku Koivu (FIN)

PRELIMINARY ROUND STANDINGS

European Pool

	GP	W	L	T	GF	GA	P
Finland	3	2	0	1	11	4	5
Sweden	3	2	0	1	13	9	5
Czech Republic	3	1	2	0	10	10	2
Germany	3	0	3	0	4	15	0

August 30	Helsinki	Finland 4/Czech Republic 0
August 31	Stockholm	Sweden 5/Germany 2
September 1	Stockholm	Sweden 4/Czech Republic 3
September 2	Cologne	Finland 3/Germany 0
September 3	Prague	Czech Republic 7/Germany 2
September 4	Helsinki	Finland 4/Sweden 4 (5:00 OT)

North American Pool

	GP	W	L	T	GF	GA	P
Canada	3	3	0	0	10	3	6
Russia	3	2	1	0	9	6	4
USA	3	1	2	0	5	6	2
Slovakia	3	0	3	0	4	13	0

August 31	Montreal	Canada 2/USA 1
September 1	Montreal	Canada 5/Slovakia 1
September 2	St. Paul	Russia 3/USA 1
September 3	St. Paul	USA 3/Slovakia 1
September 4	Toronto	Canada 3/Russia 1
September 5	Toronto	Russia 5/Slovakia 2

Quarter-finals

September 6	Helsinki	Finland 2/Germany 1
September 7	Stockholm	Czech Republic 6/Sweden 1
September 7	St. Paul	USA 5/Russia 2
September 8	Toronto	Canada 5/Slovakia 1

Semifinals

September 11	St. Paul	Finland 2/USA 1
September 12	Toronto	Canada 4/Czech Republic 3 (Vincent Lecavalier 3:45 OT)

Finals

September 14	Toronto	Canada 3/Finland 2

WOMEN'S PRO HOCKEY LEAGUES, 1999–2012

1999–2000

NATIONAL WOMEN'S HOCKEY LEAGUE (NWHL) REGULAR-SEASON STANDINGS

Eastern Division

	GP	W	L	T	GF	GA	P
Sainte Julie Pantheres	35	20	8	7	109	68	47
Montreal Wingstar	35	18	7	10	116	62	46
Ottawa Raiders	35	9	20	6	61	109	24
Laval Le Mistral	35	7	23	5	78	177	19

Western Division

	GP	W	L	T	GF	GA	P
Beatrice Aeros	40	35	3	2	217	37	72
Brampton Thunder	40	29	5	6	208	64	64
Mississauga Chiefs	40	21	13	6	133	79	48
Clearnet Lightning	40	4	33	3	44	249	11
Scarborough Sting	40	3	34	3	49	170	9

CHAMPIONSHIP FINALS

March 18   Sainte Julie Pantheres 2/Beatrice Aeros 2
March 19   Beatrice Aeros 1/Sainte Julie Pantheres 0
Beatrice wins championship 3–1 in points

2000–01

NWHL REGULAR-SEASON STANDINGS

Eastern Division

	GP	W	L	T	GF	GA	P
Montreal Wingstar	40	30	6	4	163	63	64
Sainte Julie Pantheres	40	22	15	3	168	102	47
Ottawa Raiders	40	11	25	4	78	150	26
Laval Le Mistral	40	5	33	2	68	261	12

Western Division

	GP	W	L	T	GF	GA	P
Beatrice Aeros	40	35	2	3	222	46	73
Brampton Thunder	40	30	7	3	223	82	63
Mississauga Ice Bears	40	21	16	3	107	97	45
Toronto Sting	40	8	29	3	82	168	19

Clearnet Lightning	40	5	34	1	77	219	11
Vancouver Griffins	18	14	4	0	91	43	28

CHAMPIONSHIP FINALS
Beatrice Aeros 2/Sainte Julie Pantheres 2
Beatrice Aeros 8/Sainte Julie Pantheres 1
Beatrice wins championship 3–1 in points

2001–02

NWHL REGULAR-SEASON STANDINGS
Eastern Division

	GP	W	L	T	GF	GA	P
Ottawa Raiders	30	14	10	6	71	72	34
Montreal Wingstar	30	11	14	5	66	78	27
Le Cheyenne de la Metropol	30	11	15	4	73	85	26

Western Division

	GP	W	L	T	GF	GA	P
Beatrice Aeros	30	23	2	5	149	39	51
Mississauga Ice Bears	30	12	10	8	82	81	32
Brampton Thunder	30	8	14	8	73	97	24
Telus Lightning	30	4	18	8	59	120	16

Pacific Division

	GP	W	L	T	GF	GA	P
Vancouver Griffins	31	27	4	0	84	14	54

CHAMPIONSHIP FINALS
Beatrice Aeros 3/Brampton Thunder 2 (OT)

2002–03

NWHL REGULAR-SEASON STANDINGS
Eastern Division

	GP	W	L	T	OTL	GF	GA	P
Montreal Wingstar	36	18	15	3	0	83	81	39
Ottawa Raiders	36	13	20	1	2	96	122	29
Quebec Avalanche	36	10	20	5	1	87	120	26

Central Division

Beatrice Aeros	36	32	3	1	0	201	54	65
Brampton Thunder	36	27	9	0	0	152	71	54
Mississauga Ice Bears	36	19	13	3	1	122	111	42
Telus Lightning	36	0	34	1	1	54	236	2

Western Division

Calgary X-Treme	24	23	1	0	0	144	37	46
Vancouver Griffins	24	10	13	0	1	82	92	21
Edmonton Chimos	24	3	20	0	1	35	132	7

CHAMPIONSHIP FINALS

Calgary X-Treme 3/Beatrice Aeros 0

2003–04

NWHL REGULAR-SEASON STANDINGS

Eastern Division

	G	W	L	T	OTL	GF	GA	P
Montreal Axion	36	20	10	5	1	113	84	46
Ottawa Raiders	36	9	23	4	0	85	144	22
Quebec Avalanche	36	4	28	2	2	65	163	12

Central Division

Toronto Aeros	36	33	2	1	0	197	42	67
Brampton Thunder	36	28	6	2	0	190	72	58
Oakville Ice	36	17	17	2	0	118	99	36
Telus Lightning	36	8	28	0	0	66	224	16

Western Division

Calgary X-Treme	12	11	1	0	0	64	9	22
Edmonton Chimos	12	1	11	0	0	9	64	2

CHAMPIONSHIP FINALS

Calgary X-Treme 5/Brampton Thunder 4 (OT/SO)

2004–05

NWHL REGULAR-SEASON STANDINGS

Eastern Division

	G	W	L	T	OTL	GF	GA	P
Montreal Axion	36	24	9	2	1	140	85	51

Ottawa Raiders	36	14	19	2	1	101	128	31
Quebec Avalanche	36	5	25	4	2	53	132	16

Central Division

Brampton Thunder	36	30	3	2	1	165	70	63
Toronto Aeros	36	24	6	4	2	142	68	54
Oakville Ice	36	13	15	6	2	97	99	34
Telus Lightning	36	4	28	4	0	72	189	12

CHAMPIONSHIP FINALS

Toronto Aeros 5/Montreal Axion 4 (OT)

2005–06

NWHL REGULAR-SEASON STANDINGS

Eastern Division

	G	W	L	T	OTL	GF	GA	P
Ottawa Raiders	36	21	8	4	3	122	77	49
Montreal Axion	36	14	17	3	2	100	122	33
Quebec Avalanche	36	4	28	2	2	58	135	12

Central Division

Durham Lightning	36	23	6	5	2	107	74	53
Brampton Thunder	36	19	12	5	0	113	97	43
Oakville Ice	36	20	14	1	1	118	100	42
Toronto Aeros	36	13	17	4	2	114	127	32

CHAMPIONSHIP FINALS

April 15   Montreal Axion 1/Brampton Thunder 0

2006–07

NWHL REGULAR-SEASON STANDINGS

	G	W	L	T	OTL	GF	GA	P
Etobicoke Dolphins	20	15	1	2	2	87	66	64
Mississauga Aeros	21	15	5	0	1	107	51	31
Brampton Thunder	16	8	8	0	0	71	66	16
Oakville Ice	17	6	8	1	2	40	53	15
Montreal Axion	13	6	6	0	0	66	56	13
Quebec Avalanche	12	2	8	2	0	41	91	6
Ottawa Raiders	11	2	8	0	0	25	54	5

CHAMPIONSHIP FINALS
April 14   Brampton Thunder 4/Montreal Axion 0
* the NWHL was replaced by the CWHL in 2007

2007–08

CANADIAN WOMEN'S HOCKEY LEAGUE (CWHL) REGULAR-SEASON STANDINGS
Central Division

	GP	W	L	OT	GF	GA	P
Brampton Canadettes-Thunder	30	22	7	1	111	59	45
Mississauga Chiefs	30	21	8	1	115	61	43
Vaughan Flames	30	12	16	2	69	101	26
Burlington Barracudas	30	11	18	1	76	98	23

Eastern Division

	GP	W	L	OT	GF	GA	P
Montreal Stars	28	21	6	1	112	55	43
Ottawa Capital-Canucks	28	8	17	3	58	102	19
Quebec Phoenix	28	8	21	1	56	121	17

PLAYOFFS
February 23   Burlington 2/Ottawa 1
Burlington advanced

February 23   Mississauga 6/Vaughan 2
February 24   Mississauga 6/Vaughan 2

March 1   Mississauga 4/Montreal 3
March 2   Mississauga 1/Montreal 4
Mississauga won tie-breaker

March 1   Burlington 2/Brampton 5
March 2   Burlington 3/ Brampton 3
Brampton advanced

CHAMPIONSHIP FINALS
March 22   Mississauga Chiefs 3/Brampton Canadettes-Thunder 4 (OT)

2008–09*

CWHL REGULAR-SEASON STANDINGS

	GP	W	L	P
Montreal Stars	28	24	3	49
Brampton Thunder	26	19	6	39
Mississauga Chiefs	26	16	8	34
Burlington Barracudas	25	10	13	22
Vaughan Flames	25	4	19	10
Ottawa Senators	24	4	20	8

League Playoffs
(best-of-two plus sudden-death OT in case of tie)

| March 14 | Brampton 3/Mississauga 2 |
| March 15 | Mississauga 4/Brampton 1 |

OT tie-breaker: Brampton, Jayna Hefford
Brampton Thunder advance to Clarkson Cup finals

| March 14 | Montreal 6/Burlington 1 |
| March 15 | Burlington 3/Montreal 1 |

OT tie-breaker: Montreal, Noemie Marin
Montreal Stars advance to Clarkson Cup finals

WESTERN WOMEN'S HOCKEY LEAGUE (WWHL) REGULAR-SEASON STANDINGS

	GP	W	L	OTL	P
Calgary Oval X-Treme	23	20	2	1	42
Minnesota Whitecaps	22	18	3	1	38
Edmonton Chimos	24	14	10	0	28
Strathmore Rockies	23	6	16	1	13
B.C. Breakers	24	0	22	2	2

League Playoffs
Semifinals
| March 7 | Calgary 9/Strathmore 0 |
| March 7 | Minnesota 4/Edmonton 0 |

Finals
| March 8 | Minnesota 2/Calgary 0 |

Both finalists advance to Clarkson Cup finals

* In 2008, the National Women's Hockey League split into the Canadian Women's Hockey League and the Western Women's Hockey League.

CLARKSON CUP FINALS
Kingston, Ontario

Round Robin
March 19	Minnesota 4/Montreal 3
March 19	Brampton 4/Calgary 3

Semifinals
March 20	Montreal 4/Brampton 1
March 20	Minnesota 2/Calgary 1

Finals
March 21	Montreal 3/Minnesota 1

2009–10

CWHL REGULAR-SEASON STANDINGS

	GP	W	L	OTL	GF	GA	Pts
Montreal Stars*	30	23	5	2	122	70	48
Mississauga Chiefs*	30	21	8	1	94	60	43
Burlington Barracudas	30	19	8	3	94	80	41
Brampton Thunder	29	12	14	3	76	78	27
Vaughan Flames	29	9	19	1	77	111	19
Ottawa Senators	30	5	23	2	61	125	12

* advanced to Clarkson Cup as top two teams

Playoffs (winner advances to Clarkson Cup)
March 20	Brampton 4/Vaughan 1
March 20	Burlington 4/Ottawa 3 (OT)
March 21	Brampton 2/Burlington 1

WWHL REGULAR-SEASON STANDINGS

	GP	W	L	T	OTL	GF	GA	Pts
Minnesota Whitecaps*	12	10	2	0	0	44	24	20
Edmonton Chimos	18	7	7	0	4	40	48	18
Strathmore Rockies	18	7	10	0	1	43	55	15
Calgary Oval X-Treme	0	0	0	0	0	0	0	0
British Columbia Breakers		DID NOT PLAY						

* advanced to Clarkson Cup for finishing in first place

CLARKSON CUP FINALS
Richmond Hill, Ontario

Semifinals

March 27	Brampton 3/Montreal 2
March 27	Minnesota 3/Mississauga 1

Finals

March 28	Minnesota 4/Brampton 0

2010-11

CWHL REGULAR-SEASON STANDINGS

	GP	W	L	T	GF	GA	Pts
Montreal Stars	26	22	2	2	125	70	46
Brampton Thunder	26	19	6	1	111	69	39
Boston Blades	26	10	15	1	73	101	21
Toronto Aeros	26	8	13	5	83	98	21
Burlington Barracudas	26	6	18	2	54	108	14

Clarkson Cup Qualification

March 11	Toronto 4/Boston 2
March 11	Brampton 1/Montreal 2 (SO)
March 12	Toronto 3/Boston 1
March 12	Brampton 3/Montreal 4

Boston eliminated from Clarkson Cup competition

WWHL REGULAR-SEASON STANDINGS

	GP	W	L	T	OTL	GF	GA	Pts
Minnesota Whitecaps*	18	17	0	0	1	120	43	35
Edmonton Chimos	17	11	5	0	1	56	41	23
Manitoba Maple Leafs	12	1	11	0	0	31	80	2
Strathmore Rockies	11	0	10	0	1	21	64	1

* advanced to Clarkson Cup round-robin

CLARKSON CUP FINALS
Barrie, Ontario

Round-Robin Standings & Results

	GP	W	L	T	GF	GA	Pts
Montreal	3	3	0	0	14	6	6
Toronto	3	2	1	0	10	4	4
Brampton	3	1	2	0	13	12	2
Minnesota	3	0	3	0	3	18	0

March 24	Toronto 3/Brampton 2
March 24	Montreal 5/Minnesota 1
March 25	Toronto 6/Minnesota 0
March 25	Montreal 7/Brampton 4
March 26	Brampton 7/Minnesota 2
March 26	Montreal 2/Toronto 1

Finals

March 26	Montreal 5/Toronto 0

2011–12

CWHL Regular-Season Standings

	GP	W	L	OTL	GF	GA	Pts
Montreal	27	22	4	1	160	66	51*
Boston	27	20	7	0	107	61	46*
Brampton	27	18	7	2	102	80	40*
Toronto	27	9	13	5	75	105	26*
Alberta	15	5	10	0	38	66	20
Burlington	27	1	26	0	46	150	2

*qualified for Clarkson Cup weekend

CLARKSON CUP FINALS
Niagara Falls, Ontario

Round-Robin Standings & Results

	GP	W	L	OTL	GF	GA	Pts
Montreal	3	3	0	0	14	4	6
Brampton	3	2	1	0	7	6	4
Boston	3	1	1	1	11	10	3
Toronto	3	0	3	0	4	16	0

March 22	Montreal 7/Toronto 0
March 22	Brampton 3/Boston 2

March 23   Montreal 2/Brampton 0
March 23   Boston 5/Toronto 2
March 24   Brampton 4/Toronto 2
March 24   Montreal 5/Boston 4 (0:45 Caroline Ouellette OT)

Finals
March 25   Montreal 4/Brampton 2

HOCKEY POOL NOTES

HOCKEY POOL NOTES